D1603731

ABSTRACTS OF
PITTSYLVANIA COUNTY, VIRGINIA
WILLS, 1767-1820

Compiled by
Lela C. Adams
Bassett, Virginia

SOUTHERN HISTORICAL PRESS, INC.
c/o The Rev. Silas Emmett Lucas, Jr.
P.O. Box 738
Easley, South Carolina 29641-0738

ISBN 0-89308-581-2

PREFACE

Unless otherwise noted the persons in these wills were residents of what was then Pittsylvania County, Virginia.

The material in this book has been abstracted, as far as possible, as it appears in the records. Some of the hand writing is difficult to decipher and there are many mispelled words. The only changes made are for clarity.

In some wills surnames are given for legatees and these have been indexed under the name of the testator. An example of this is found in the will of AMBROSE PORTER where he makes bequests to his daughter ANNE and her five children.

Each will begins LWT (last will and testament), usually followed by the state of health of the testator and then the various bequests or instructions. As far as possible, only the pertinent data relating to relationships, locations and dates have been abstracted.

CONTENTS

Deeds & Wills Book 5, 1770-1780
Deeds & Wills Book 9, 1791-1794
Deeds & Wills Book 11, 1780-1820
Deeds & Wills Book 10, 1794-1796
Miscellaneous 1766-1770
Will Book I 1814-1820
Water features, cities and states

Page 367-368
22 September 1770
Pr: 29 November 1770

LWT PATRICK SHIELDS of Pittsylvania County being sick and low
in body but in perfect mind and memory.

To JEAN SHIELDS beloved wife, her full third of goods and chattels, moveable effects, also her living on the plantation where
we now live as long as she remains single and one roan mare.

To son THOMAS SHIELDS whole and sole right of the plantation and
a colt.

To son ROBERT SHIELDS a negro wench named Fillis & fifty pounds.

To my grandson PATRICK SHIELDS, son of SAMUEL SHIELDS, ten pounds

To son JOSEPH SHIELDS a heffer.

If there remains any estate it to be divided between THOMAS &
ROBERT SHIELDS.

At ROBERT SHIELDS decease the negro to be sold and his estate to
be equally divided between SAMUEL SHIELDS, JAMES SHIELDS, WILLIAM
SHIELDS, JOHN SHIELDS, JOSEPH SHIELDS and THOMAS SHIELDS.

Appoint JAMES, SAMUEL and JOHN SHIELDS as executors.

PATRICK (O) SHIELDS

Wit: JOSEPH CUNNINGHAM, THOMAS CUNNINGHAM

Presented by SAMUEL and JAMES SHIELDS with JOHN FULTON and JOHN
SMITH as their surety.

Page 369-371
30 January 1750
Pr: 29 August 1771

LWT MARY CLARK of the Parish of Nottoway in Amelia County being
very sick and weak in body but sound mind.

To grandchild REUBIN SHELTON 1 shilling

To son RALPH SHELTON 1 shilling

To son CRISPIN SHELTON 1 shilling

To son JOHN SHELTON 1 shilling

To son BENJAMIN SHELTON 1 shilling

To son JAMES SHELTON 1 shilling

To daughter ELIZABETH DAVIS the best of my wearing clothes.

To grandchild PATIENT CATEY BLACKEY 1 shilling

CLARK will cont'd:

To son DANIEL SHELTON negro Janey and her increase also all the rest of my estate.

Appoint son DANIEL SHELTON executor.

MARY (M) CLARK

Wit: none

Exhibited by DANIEL SHELTON with CRISPIN SHELTON his security.

Page 371-374
20 April 1771
Pr: 29 August 1771

LWT JOSHUA WORSHAM, SR. of Pittsylvania County weak in body but sound of mind and memory.

Lend to my dearly beloved wife MARY WORSHAM during her life negro man Francis, woman Phillis also the plantation and mill whereon I now live also 12 head of cattle, 1 good horse and saddle, beds and furniture. The horse and saddle to be hers forever. Also lend her stock and hogs during her abode.

To son JOHN WORSHAM or his male heir and in case of no heir to my son THOMAS WORSHAM one half of the land where I now live to be laid off at the lower end but not to be laid off till my son THOMAS shall come of age and not to hinder or molest MARY. If Mary does not think proper to cultivate the land the profits rising from same shall be for the rest of my children viz: DANIEL, ROBERT, JOSHUA, THOMAS, MARY, MICHEL, PATTY and PHEBE.

To son DANIEL WORSHAM half of a tract of land on that creek on the waters on Smith River it being the land I purchased from JOHN CHIPMAN.

To son ROBERT WORSHAM a tract of land on the south fork of Cherry Stone, 1 feather bed and furniture.

To son JOSHUA WORSHAM the other half of my land on Flat Creek on the waters of Smith River.

To son THOMAS WORSHAM the other half of the other half of my land whereon I now live and the Mill. Also that half already given unto my son JOHN WORSHAM should said JOHN die without an heir.

Give the remainder of my estate not given to be equally divided amongst my sons and daughters, that is to say: MARY, MICHEL, PATTY and PHEBE.

Appoint my dearly beloved wife MARY WORSHAM and son ROBERT WORSHAM executors.

JOSHUA WORSHAM

Wit: THOMAS DUNCAN, WILLIAM MELTON, GEORGE (X) SUTHERLAND

Presented by MARY WORSHAM and ROBERT WORSHAM with WILLIAM WYNNE and JOHN DIX as security.

Page 375-378
28 December 1769
Pr: 26 September 1771

LWT BENJAMIN TERRY, SR. of Pittsylvania County, Camden Parish
in perfect sense and memory.

Lend to my beloved wife ELIZABETH TERRY four negros: Abraham, Melinder and her children Baler and Lener, 6 cows and calves, all
hogs, 1 feather bed and furniture, 1 frying pan, 2 iron pots and
hooks and all the plantation working tools, 1 black mare Lazard,
her colt, sorrel plow mare, all during her natural life. At her
decease to be disposed of in the following manner: to son NATHAN-
IEL TERRY one survey of land being upper survey on Sandy Creek,
2 negros Jack and Gregory. To son BENJAMIN TERRY that tract of
land whereon I now live, that is the old and first tract containing 300 acres more or less, and negro Abraham. To son PETER TERRY
the survey of land on Mine Branch and negro boy Dave and girl,
Isbell and 1 rifle gun. To son JOSEPH TERRY, 3 negros Tommy ?,
Fanny and _____. To son ROBERT TERRY one survey of land that joins
PETER TERRY, 3 negros and a rifle gun.

Lend to my daughter ROZIA MURPHY 2 negros Harry and Phillis during her natural life, at her decease be equally divided between
her children she had by her former husband JAMES SCOTT and all
the children she has or shall have by her present husband RICHARD
MURPHY. If RICHARD MURPHY should not pay the children of JAMES
SCOTT what is or will be due them of their father's estate, for
which I am security for, it shall be paid them out of the sale
of the two negros.

Lend to my daughter LEVINIA KIND 2 negros Abbey and Ivey during
her natural life, then equally divided between her daughter GRACE
TERRY and her children that she has or may have by her husband
ELIJAH KING.

To daughter SARAH TERRY 3 negros, old Jenny, Pompy, and Willey
to her and her heirs.

To daughter ELIZABETH BUCKINGHAM 2 negros Bailer and Melinder,
not to be possessed until the death of my wife.

To daughter MARY TERRY 2 negros Cyner and Casshener, 1 side saddle, feather bed and furniture.

The rest of my estate to be sold and divided among all my children.

Appoint my wife ELIZABETH TERRY and sons NATHANIEL and BENJAMIN
TERRY as executors.

                          BENJAMIN (X) TERRY

Wit: THEOP. LACY, JOHN KING, WILLIAM KING

Presented by NATHANIEL TERRY and BENJAMIN TERRY with ISAAC READ
their security.

Page 379-381
27 April 1771
Pr: 26 November 1771 (cont'd next page)

3

LWT   JOHN KING being weak and in declining body but of perfect
mind.

To son MALACHI KING a negro boy Robbin on condition that he pay
the executors fifteen pounds in 12 months after my decease.

To my son ELIJAH KING half of that survey of land on the south
side of Sandy Creek, joins the tract where I now live, joins WIL-
LIAM CANNON, JACOB CAMPERTON, BENJAMIN TERRY on condition he pays
the executors five pounds ten shillings in 12 months.

To HUGH CHALLES the other half of the said survey of land above
mentioned.

ELIJAH KING is to have the lower part of the tract and HUGH CHAL-
LES the upper part.

To son MALACHI KING all the tract and plantation whereon I now
live agreeable to the line marked by my son WILLIAM KING and myself till my grandson JOHN KING, son of WILLIAM KING, shall become 21 years of age, then I give my grandson JOHN KING all the
said tract of land and plantation.

The remainder of my estate to be equally divided amongst the rest
of my children.

Appoint friend HUGH CHALLES my executor.

                              JOHN KING

Wit: ISHAM DALTON, JOHN STU....., WOODLIEF THOMAS, WILLIAM ASTIN

Proved by HUGH CHALLES with JOHN WIMBISH his security.

Page 381-382
3 April 1771
Pr: 26 March 1772

JOHN COUCH sick and weak.

Lend to MARY PETERSON all my personal estate of horses, cattle,
household furniture during her life or widowhood and after her
decease to her two children, MARY and UNIETY.

To my son GEORGE a dark bay horse not before given named Jocky.

Appoint WILLIAM TUNSTALL and MARY PETERSON executors.

                              JOHN (X) COUCH

Wit: ELIZABETH TUNSTALL, JOHN SAMUEL WALKER

Proved by WILLIAM TUNSTALL and MARY PETERSON with JOHN BLAGGE and
JOHN COX their security.

Page 383-385
20 May 1771
Pr: 24 September 1772
(cont'd next page)

JAMES BOULLING (BOLLING) well and in good health and sound memory.

I give to my children the estate at the death or marriage of my well beloved wife ELIZABETH BOLLING, to be divided as follows: JUDITH, JOHN, MARY, JAMES and ANN shall have one equal part and ANN and WILLIAM shall have 2 equal parts.

To my son WILLIAM BOLING (BOLLING) one tract of land in Pittsylvania County on Boling Creek.

Appoint my wife ELIZABETH BOLING and son JAMES BOLING, JR. as executors.

JAMES (X) BOLING

Wit: WILLIAM EDWARDS, SR., THOMAS EDWARDS, ISHAM EDWARDS

Proved by JAMES BOLING, JR. and ELIZABETH BOLING with THOMAS EDWARDS and JOHN REA their security.

Page 386-387
26 May 1772
Pr: 20 July 1772

JAMES WALDROPE (WALDROP)

To JEREMIAH WARD for five pounds ten pence half penny, paid in hand, one parcel of land on Fry Pan Creek.

To my wife SARAH WALDROP the remainder of my land during her lifetime or widowhood and at her decease to my son JAMES.

All my personal estate to my wife SARAH.

JAMES (X) WALDROP

Wit: SAMUEL BOLLING, EDWARD WADE, JOHN WALDROPE

SARAH WALDROP administratrix with SAMUEL BOLLING her security.

Page 387-389
19 November 1772
Pr: 25 February 1773

JOHN KERBY (KEARBY), weak and in a low condition but perfect mind and memory.

To my beloved son FRANCIS KEARBY 1 shilling

To son JOHN KEARBY 1 shilling

To son DAVID KEARBY 1 shilling

To son HENRY KEARBY 1 shilling

To son JOSIAH KEARBY 1 shilling

To daughter MARY HUBBARD 1 shilling

To son JESSE KEARBY 1 shilling

5

KEARBY will cont'd:

To daughter SUSANAH THOMSON 1 shilling

To my wife JOANNAH KERBY all the remainder of my estate.

Appoint dearly beloved wife JOANNAH as executrix.

JOHN (X) KERBY

Wit: WILLIAM DABNEY, JOHN DAVIS, PEYTON SMITH

Proved by JOANA KERBY with HENRY KERBY and PEYTON SMITH her security.

Page 390-393
26 August 1772
Pr: 25 March 1773

JAMES SIMS weak in body but of sound mind.

To my loving wife SARAH SIMS all my land and plantation whereon I now live with a survey of land joining same and likewise an entry on Middle Fork of the Mayo River during her life or widowhood and the use of a negro man Cose, all stock, household furniture and debts due me.

At the decease of my wife the executors shall sell all land and other property and divide among the children, everyone of them that is then found living. If any are deceased their heir shall inherit one equal share.

Appoint brothers MATHEW SIMS and JOHN SIMS executors.

JOHN SIMS

Wit: MATHEW (X) SIMS, SALLY (X) SIMS, JAMES (X) JOHNSON, ELIZABETH (X) PATTERSON, PHILIP DEATHERAGE

Proved by MATHEW SIMS and JOHN SIMS with PETER PERKINS and JOHN SALMON their security.

Page 394-395
10 March 1773
Pr: 27 May 1773

LWT GEORGE ROBERTS, SR. being sick and weak in body but perfect memory.

I desire that all my land be equally divided between four of my children viz: GEORGE ROBERTS, JR., DOROTHY CALDWELL, SARAH BLAIR and ALIE HAMLIN, and my bed and furniture to my daughter, DOROTHY CALDWELL.

To my daughter ALIE HAMLIN all the womens clothes now in my chest.

All the rest of my estate to be divided between the above children except for one shilling to all the rest of my children namely: MARY HAMILTON and JOHN ROBERTS.

6

ROBERTS will cont'd:

GEORGE (X) ROBERTS

Wit: GAB. RICHARDS, JOHN (X) CALDWELL, MARY (X) DURETT

Executors WILLIAM DURRETT and ALLEN CALDWELL with WILLIAM THOMAS security.

Page 396-399
18 June 1773
Pr: 22 July 1773

LWT AMBROSE PORTER being very sick in body but of perfect mind and memory.

To my daughter ANN 1 shilling

To my daughter ANN's five youngest children: JOHN, MILLEY, SUSAN-NA, AMBROSE and ARTHUR to each one a cow to be delivered to them as they come of age 9 or 10 years.

To my daughter MARY 150 acres with the plantation that she now lives on, on White Oak creek, likewise the 2 cows she now has, 1 feather bed and a side saddle.

To my two sons BENJAMIN and JOSEPH the remainder of my lands to be equally divided. BENJAMIN to have the first choice and to JO-SEPH one colt named Partner. If either or both sons die without issue, then their part or parts to go to my other children.

To my well beloved wife JEMIMA PORTER all the rest of my estate and the use of my plantation during her life or widowhood.

To my daughters JANE and SUSANNA at the death of my wife or her marriage, fifty pounds each out of the moveable estate.

Should there be anything over that, to be divided amongst my five youngest children: MARY, BENJAMIN, JANE, JOSEPH and SUSANNAH.

Appoint HENRY MC DANIEL and my son BENJAMIN PORTER executors.

AMBROSE PORTER

Wit: RICHARD TALIFAFERRO, PETER JAMES BAILEY, MARY (X) PROSIGH?

Codicil
25 June 1773

If negro wench Bett continues to breed, her increase to be divid-ed among my five youngest children as above mentioned.

JOHN DONELSON security for executors.

Page 400-402
2 October 1771?
Pr: 23 September 1773

LWT JOHN PAYNE being very sick and weak in body but in perfect memory.

7

PAYNE will cont'd:

Give to my son JOHN PAYNE 1 shilling and no more.

My land is to be equally divided between DANIEL PAYNE, MARK PAYNE and EDMOND PAYNE, my other three sons.

To my dear beloved wife HANNAH PAYNE, all the rest of my estate and to serve as executrix.

JOHN (X) PAYNE

Wit: DAVID HARRIS, JOSEPH (X) HARRIS, JOHN (X) HARRIS

Page 402-403
29 November 1772
Pr: 25 November 1773

LWT SAMUEL DAVIS being very weak in body but in perfect sense.

Lend all my estate to my dearly beloved wife SARAH DAVIS during her life, then to my five children: SARAH KEARBY, ELIZABETH KEAR-BY, JOHN DAVIS, WILMOTH DAVIS and SUSANNAH DAVIS equally divided.

Estate to be sold except wearing clothing and riding saddle to my son JOHN DAVIS.

Should my negro Fillis out live my wife, she is to have her maintenance out of the estate.

SAMUEL (X) DAVIS

Wit: PEYTON SMITH, JUDITH SMITH, JOHN LONG

Proved by JOHN DAVIS with JOHN KEARBY his security.

Page 402-403
20 July 1769
Pr: 24 February 1774

LWT JOHN WILDRICK BENDER being very sick and weak in body but perfect mind and memory.

To my dearly beloved wife MAGDALEN my only and sole heir of all my estate real and personal by her freely to be possessed until her death. At that time, to be divided as follows:

To my daughter MARY BENDER a tract of land on Stones Creek whereon I now live, 212 acres with all improvements for which she is to pay as follows:

To my grandson JOHN BENDER twenty five pounds; to my grandson, JACOB GOLDEN ten pounds and to his heirs a tract of land on Stone Creek above the place I gave my daughter MARY, containing 190-acres.

As to my stock, household goods and moveables, after the debts are paid shall be equally divided between the above named legatees.

BENDER will cont'd:

JOHN WILDRICK BENDER

Wit: ARCHELAUS HUGHES, HAMON CRITZ

Proved by HAMON CRITZ, executor, with ARCHELAUS HUGHES and JOHN PARR as his security.

Page 490-410
4 May 1774
Pr: 23 June 1774

LWT THOMAS DILLARD of perfect memory.

Lend to my son JAMES DILLARD during his lifetime negros: Witt, Tamer, Hanarn and their increase now in possession of the said JAMES and also Jefrey and Tamer, children of Sarah, after the death of JAMES DILLARD, then to THOMAS DILLARD, son of the said JAMES DILLARD, the last mentioned Tamer and her increase and the other negros lend said JAMES to be equally divided among the residue of the children of JAMES DILLARD.

The residue of my household furniture and stocks to be equally divided between my two sons, JAMES DILLARD and THOMAS DILLARD, JR.

Appoint my son THOMAS DILLARD, JR., brother of JAMES DILLARD, to be his Trustee.

Son JAMES DILLARD is to have the land on Stones Creek.

Whereas I have sold to JAMES MARTIN of Bedford County two tracts of land upon payment, a deed to be made to said Martin.

To my son THOMAS DILLARD, JR, the land and plantation whereon I now live and negros Will; Sarah and her children, Robin and Bess, Nan, Judey and her children, Sarah with the residue not before mentioned and appoint the said THOMAS DILLARD, JR. as executor.

THOMAS DILLARD

Wit: THOMAS VAUGHAN, JOHN DILLARD, ELIZABETH DILLARD

ROBERT WILLIAMS and JAMES CALLAWAY security for THOMAS DILLARD, JR executor.

Page 411
___ October 1771
Pr: 16 February 1774

LWT MATTHIAS EVERSON being very sick and weak in body, but of perfect memory.

To HAMON CRITZ, SR., my beloved friend my only and sole heir of all my estate, real and personal.

MATTHIAS (X) EVERSON

Wit: JACOB GOLDEN, PHILIP (X) SMITH, WILLIAM (X) WEBB, and HAMON

EVERSON will cont'd:

CRITZ, JR.

ARCHELAUS HUGHES security for executor.

Page 412-413
29 October 1774
Pr: 24 November 1774

LWT STEPHEN HEARD being very sick and weak but of perfect memory

All my personal estate to my well beloved wife MARY HEARD also
well beloved son JESSE HEARD also well beloved son STEPHEN HEARD,
to well beloved son GEORGE HEARD who I appoint as executor.

To well beloved daughter MARY HEARD the tract of land, 229 acres
more or less on Blackwater River.

To well beloved son JESSE HEARD the tract of land whereon I now
live, after the decease of my wife.

If God should call MARY HEARD without heirs, I Will said tract
of land bequeathed her to be sold and the funds divided between
my well beloved daughter ANN GILLIAM and well beloved daughter,
SUSANAH STANDEFER.

To wife MARY HEARD all my personal estate.

                              STEPHEN (X) HEARD

Wit: PETER GILLAM, ISAM (X) BELCHER, CHEDLE COCKERHAM, RICHARD
HUGHES, GEORGE HEARD

Executor JESSE HEARD with ISRAEL STANDEFER and WILLIAM TUNSTALL
security.

Page 413-414
23 September 1774
Pr: 25 March 1775

LWT MARK PAYNE

To my youngest brother STEPHEN PAYNE, 100 acres of land left me
by my father, JOHN PAYNE.

To GILBERT TURNER one horse and desire that he pay my funeral
charges.

Appoint my loving mother HANNAH PAYNE my executrix.

                              MARK (X) PAYNE

Wit: DAVID (X) PAYNE, EDMUND (X) PAYNE

Page 414-416
15 May 1772
Pr: 26 July 1775
(cont'd next page)

10

LWT THOMAS WEIR weak of body but sound and perfect memory.

Lend unto my beloved wife AGNES WEIR during her natural life one negro man Vall, 2 negro women Fanny and ----, the use of my plantation whereon I now live, 2 horses, tools, livestock, 1 copper still.

One negro man to be purchased of the funds in Major THOMAS MERRY-WEATHER's hands.

At the decease of my wife divided between my children WILLIAM, JOHN, BEZABEAL and MARGARET WEIR after the other legatees paid.

To my daughter ELIZABETH WEIR and heirs in the town of Dorchester, New England near Boston, the sum of fifty pounds, if daughter and no heirs found, to be divided between my sons JOHN, WILLIAM, BEZABEAL and daughter MARGARET.

To my son WILLIAM twenty pounds at the death of his mother, sell the horses and cattle if the money cannot be easily raised.

To my daughter MARGARET WEIR a negro girl Betty, 1 feather bed and furniture, 2 cows and calves, 1 horse, 2 ewes and rams, 1 sow and pigs, 1 flax wheel.

To my son JOHN WEIR one half of the tract of land whereon I now live and half of two entries joining, to be laid off at the lower end at the apple orchard should begin his part that my son BEZABEAL shall have the benefit of half of it for 10 years and 1 negro boy John, 1 bed and furniture and livestock.

To my son BEZABEAL the half of land, 2 entries at the upper end, negro Vall, a desk, furniture and livestock.

My 2 tracts of land on Cascade to be sold by PETER PERKINS and he to have 1/3 of the money and to pay the other 2/3 to my executors, to be made use of as follows: fifty pounds to my daughter ELIZABETH, balance divided between my sons WILLIAM, JOHN, BEZABEAL and my daughter MARGARET WEIR.

Appoint my wife AGNES WEIR as executrix.

                    THOMAS WEIR

Wit: THOMAS DUNCAN, THOMAS PISTOLL, WILLIAM (X) LAWSON

Continued:
I give to my grandson WEIR DICKERSON forty pounds to be paid when he come of age to be paid with a negro boy if any, raised from those left unto my wife, if not, paid in livestock or money out of the Carolina land.

Security for AGNES WEIR, PETER PERKINS and JOHN WILSON.

Page 416-418
28 January 1776
Pr: 23 May 1776

LWT JAMES HIX very sick and weak in body but of sound mind and perfect memory.

HIX will cont'd:

Just debts to be paid by selling stock as best determined by my executor and by the collection of a Bond on THOMAS CLAIBOURNE of Brunswick County in the hands of BENJAMIN HIX and to collect, also three pounds eight shillings due from GEORGE ELLIOTT of this county.

I lend unto my well beloved wife FRANCES HIX during her widowhood 4 working negros viz: Andrew, Hannah, Sarah and Peter, only that Peter be sold if required. Also to my wife possession of the lands and improvements where I now live during her widowhood, also my riding horse, 10 choice cows, 15 head of sheep, all of my working tools, all household furniture except 1 feather bed and furniture which I give to my wife and for her to dispose of as she thinks proper.

The land where I now live after the decease of my wife, I give to my son MILES HICKS (HIX) to be directed by the executor until he comes of age.

Son MILES when he comes of age shall pay to the child with which his mother FRANCES HIX is now pregnant, one hundred fifty pounds on the child coming of age, whether the child be a son or daughter. Should the child not live, the money to be divided amongst the other surviving children and their heirs: NANCY HIX, ELIZABETH HIX, PATSY HIX, FRANKY HIX, DOLLY HIX, the daughters of the said JAMES HIX.

Also to my son MILES HIX, a negro boy Abraham. Should MILES not live to enjoy the estate, the same boy to be sold and the money divided among my living children and the residue of my negros to wit: Andrew, Charlotte, Tazzy, Ben, Amea - I will to the first of my daughters that comes of age and divide the last mentioned negros into equal lots and the eldest daughter to have the first choice.

After the decease of my wife FRANCES, all things lent to her to be sold and the funds equally divided among all of my children.

Appoint my wife and my brother, BENJAMIN HIX of Brunswick County my executors.

JAMES HIX

Wit: JOHN SALMON, ELISHA HARBOUR, DAVID LANIER, THOMAS JAMISON

Security for the executors are JOHN SALMON, JAMES SHELTON, JESSE CHANDLER, DAVID LANIER.

Page 419
6 March 1776
Pr: 23 May 1776

LWT ROBERT MC CONWAY being sick and weak.

To my loving wife MARY during her natural life, the land and the plantation whereon she now lives, with the best bed and furniture I now possess and the remainder of the household furniture except 1 feather bed. After her decease, I give the same unto my son, JOHN MC CONWAY.

MC CONWAY will cont'd:

I give unto my daughter SARAH MC CONWAY 1 feather bed and furniture and also when she comes of age or marries, 1 horse of ten pounds value.

It is my desire that the cattle on the plantation be kept together until my son or daughter comes of age or marry, and the same be divided into three equal parts.

My son JOHN to give his sister SARAH 1 sow. Horses and sheep to be kept as above.

I give to my son JOHN all the rest of my estate real and personal.

Appoint my loving wife MARY MC CONWAY and my son JOHN MC CONWAY executors.

ROBERT (X) MC CONWAY

Wit: WILLIAM TUNSTALL, JOHN ACUFF, JAMES (X) ELKINS

JOHN BLAGGE and JOHN WELLS security for the executors.

Page 420
18 October 1775
Pr: 26 September 1776

LWT ARTHUR HOPKINS being very weak in body but of sound memory.

At the age of 21 years, my dear sons JAMES and SAMUEL HOPKINS to sell the tract of land where I now live and the money be equally divided between my four dear children: JAMES HOPKINS, SAMUEL HOPKINS, FRANCES HOPKINS and JEAN HOPKINS.

All my personal estate to the four children above mentioned.

Appoint JOHN SMITH and SAMUEL CALLAND as executors.

ARTHUR HOPKINS

Wit: PEYTON SMITH, DAVID WILLIS, MARY (X) BOLTON

SAMUEL CALLAND the surviving executor with WILLIAM TUNSTALL and GEORGE HAIRSTON and LEONARD TARRANT as his security.

Page 420-421
24 November 1775
Pr: 28 November 1776

LWT THOMAS WILLIAMSON of perfect mind and memory.

To my dearly beloved wife RACHEL, the plantation I now live on during her life and half of all my stock, half of all the household furniture and half of everything that I am worth.

To my son THOMAS WILLIAMSON, all my land I now possess after the death of my wife.

13

WILLIAMSON will cont'd:

My will and desire is that the other half of my estate shall be
equally divided amongst all of my children viz: ANNA SELF, SARAH
WILLIAMSON, THOMAS WILLIAMSON, JAMES WILLIAMSON, GEORGE HEATHLY
WILLIAMSON and ELIZABETH WILLIAMSON, and my wife now being with
child, should the child live, to have an equal part with the all
above mentioned.

My daughter HANNAH STONE's children I totally cut off with one
shilling each.

Appoint my loving wife RACHEL WILLIAMSON and CHARLES WILLIAMS as
executors.

                              THOMAS (X) WILLIAMSON

Wit: THOMAS OWEN, ANN WILLAMS

HENRY STONE and JOHN CHADWELL security for RACHEL WILLIAMSON.

Page 421-423
25 September 1776
Pr: 28 November 1776

LWT JOHN HUTCHINGS sick and weak of body but perfect memory.

The 225 acres of land that my father gave me joining Chamberlain
and the place whereon I now live, the appertenances, negro Leah,
household furniture, I lend unto my beloved wife, ANNE HUTCHINGS
to have the use of during her widowhood to raise my children. In
case she dies or marries, the land and appertenances are for the
benefit of my children until the youngest comes of age or marries
and then the land to be sold and the rest of the estate to be
eqaully divided amongst my four children: THOMAS, CHRISTOPHER,
ELIZABETH and JOHN and if the child my wife is now pregnant with
lives, to be made equal.

Furthermore, my will is that if my wife chooses not to continue
on this place, the executors to make a sale and purchase the land
where it may be most right for them.

Appoint my beloved wife ANNE, my brother THOMAS HUTCHINGS, and
CHARLES HUTCHINGS and beloved friend JOHN PARKS, JR. as my executors.

                              JOHN HUTCHINGS

Wit: JOHN RICHARD TALIAFERRO, JOSHUA WELCH, MOSES HUTCHINGS, and
AARON HUTCHINGS.

THOMAS DILLARD and BENJAMIN LANKFORD security for ANNE HUTCHINGS,
THOMAS HUTCHINGS and CHARLES HUTCHINGS.

Page 424
12 October 1776
Pr: 28 November 1776
(cont'd next page)

                              14

LWT JOSHUA LEAK very sick and weak but of sound mind.

To JEANY CROCKET 1/5 of my land, the whole of the stock and the household furniture and cash, after WILLIAM TRUMAN is paid for his trouble in taking me from Williamsburg.

The residue to be equally divided among my brothers JOHN, JOSEPH, JAMES and THOMAS LEAK.

WILLIAM PERMAN appointed executor.

                                    JOSHUA (X) LEAKE

Wit: MOSES WADE, WILLIAM SNEED, ROBERT SNEED

Page 425-428
1 December 1775
Pr: 28 November 1776

LWT JOHN SMITH weak in body but sound mind.

All of the estate, both real and personal, to be kept together except my two youngest negros, George and Jane, both of which and with a feather bed and furniture, a horse, 2 head of cattle to my daughter ELIZABETH SMITH to be delivered when she marries or comes to the age of 18 years.

Out of my crop of tobacco and corn now made, the sale of some livestock in the amount of twenty pounds to my daughter ANNAH CALLAWAY and her heirs, it being the balance of what I promised as her fortune.

Two hundred and fifty pounds to be raised out of the crops I give to my daughter ELIZABETH SMITH.

After the above is paid my two daughters mentioned, my son RALPH SMITH is to have the use of my negros Vall, Hampton and Anthony until a division of my estate and the remaining part to be kept together for one year. The profits from the said year to be applied toward raising three hundred pounds for my son SAMUEL SMITH.

At the expiration of the year, I give my son JOHN SMITH the use of my negros Joe, Rose and Jack until a division is made by my executors.

The remaining part of the estate to be kept together until the sum of three hundred pounds is raised as mentioned for my son SAMUEL SMITH to purchase a tract of land.

My wife is to have the use of negros Dick, Lucy, Doll and Phillis during her natural life also use of 1/5 part of the livestock and at her decease to be equally divided among my four sons: JOHN SMITH, RALPH SMITH, BOWKER SMITH and SAMUEL SMITH.

To my wife ELIZABETH SMITH during her lifetime or widowhood 1/3 part of the tract of land whereon I now live purchased from Col. PETER JEFFERSON including the dwelling house, at her decease to my son RALPH SMITH. Also to my said wife 1/4 part of the household furniture.

When the above mentioned sums are raised for my two daughters and

SMITH will cont'd:

for my son SAMUEL then all my negros, livestock not lent my wife, also negros lent to JOHN SMITH and RALPH SMITH to be equally divided among my four sons: RALPH, JOHN, BOWKER and SAMUEL SMITH.

I also give at the same time to my son RALPH SMITH, that tract whereon I now live, reserving the part lent to my wife.

Also to RALPH SMITH the land I purchased of JOHN COOK in Bedford County on both sides of Pocket Creek being 150 acres.

Also to RALPH SMITH the land I purchased of ROBERT ADDAMS, JR. on Stanton River in Bedford County on the west side of the Pocket Road.

Also to RALPH SMITH all the land I surveyed on the west side of Pocket Road lying on said rivers and branches of Pocket Creek.

All the land I hold on the east side of Pocket Road joining ROBERT ADAMS, JR. for which he has my bond and said ROBERT ADAMS, JR. make my son RALPH SMITH a deed to him for the land I purchased of him for which I have his Bond.

I give my son JOHN SMITH all the land I purchased from JEREMIAH WARD on both sides of Stanton River part of which lies in Bedford County and part in Pittsylvania County.

Also to my son JOHN SMITH a survey of 56 acres which joins the Bedford side, purchased of BENJAMIN HENSLEY and the certificates made in my name which Mr. JOHN TALBOT has to return to the Secretarys Office.

Also to my son JOHN SMITH the entry I purchased of JEREMIAH WARD joining the tract I purchased of WARD in Pittsylvania County.

To my son BOWKER SMITH all the land I hold on Pigg River containing 150 acres of WILLIAM ATKINSON and 150 acres opposite it where DAVID DILLON now lives on the Smith side of Pigg River.

Also 50 acres part of an entry purchased of WILLIAM ATKINSON and which entry is transferred from ATKINSON to RICHARD SHOCKLEY for which I have ATKINSON's bond on my paying one pistole toward the rights of the whole tract, which my executors are to pay SHOCKLEY.

I desire that the negros and other items purchased from JUDITH SMITH, which was part of the estate of BOWKER SMITH, deceased, to be kept together by the executors till the sums of money be raised by the work of them.

JUDITH SMITH to have the use of the negros and other items during her natural life, then to be equally divided amongst my deceased brother BOWKER SMITH's children viz: STEPHEN SMITH, BOWKER SMITH, GUY SMITH, WILLIAM SMITH, ACHILLIS SMITH, ELIZABETH SMITH and JUDITH SMITH. His will is in Bedford County.

I appoint my sons RALPH SMITH and JOHN SMITH and son-in-law Capt. WILLIAM CALLAWAY executors.

JOHN SMITH

Wit: STEPHEN SMITH, GUY SMITH, JUDITH SMITH, REYNOLDS ALLEN

16

SMITH will cont'd:

JAMES CALLAWAY and ROBERT ALEXANDER security for the executors.

Page 428-429
27 January 1777
Pr: 27 March 1777

LWT JEREMIAH STIMSON very sick and weak, but of full mind and memory.

To my son JEREMIAH STIMSON 121 acres including the plantation on which he now lives.

To my son ERASMUS STIMSON 122 acres where WILLIAM RIGHT once lived known as the Muster Field.

To my son LOYD STIMSON 123 acres including the plantation whereon I now live.

The land left my sons to be layed off by JOHN STAMPS.

As to my personal estate, I lend to my wife RACHEL STIMSON during her natural life. At the decease of my wife, this to be equally divided among all my children, male and female.

Appoint wife RACHEL and son JEREMIAH as executors.

                              JEREMIAH STIMSON

Wit: RICHARD ECHOLDS, JOHN STAMPS, DANIEL EVERETT, and JONATHAN MCEUZUK(?) MUSICK?

BENJAMIN THRASHER and JOHN WALLER are securities for executors.

Page 429-430
26 February 1776
Pr: 27 March 1777

LWT PHILIP LOCKE ELLIOTT sick and weak of body but of sound mind.

To my wife SARAH ELLIOTT, all the stock of cattle and hogs, a horse and mare and all the household goods and all the corn now in the house.

To my son THOMAS ELLIOTT my new country hatt and my yellow coat.

To my son JAMES ELLIOTT my gun, and shoemaking tools to my sons JAMES and THOMAS.

If my wife should marry, then the estate to be divided among my five children: JOSHUA, RUTH, ANN, JESSE and SIMON.

                              PHILLIP LOCK ELLIOTT

Wit: BENJAMIN (X) WILLIAMS, GEORGE ROSS

Page 430-431
11 August 1776 (cont'd next page)

17

Pr: 22 January 1777

LWT JAMES KING weak in body, but perfect and sound memory.

Appoint WILLIAM COLLINS, MICHAEL GILBERT and JOHN HURT my executors.

Lend to my loving wife SUSANAH KING my land during her natural life and after her decease, I give my land to be equally divided between three children MARY WEST and NANCY KING in case the child my wife is with should die, then my two daughters to hold land.

All my hogs to be sold and my horse and if necessary, the cattle.

JAMES KING

Wit: JOHN MINTER, SR., WILLIAM HUMPHRIES, HANNAH HUMPHRIES

Executor WILLIAM CHICK with securities JOHN GEORGE and JAMES BREWER.

Page 431-433
9 September 1776
Pr: 22 January 1778

LWT HENRY LANSFORD well in health and good and sound memory.

To my eldest sons, ISHAM and HENRY LANSFORD, one parcel of land in the county of Pittsylvania on Cascade Creek containing 270 ac. to be divided equally.

To my son ISHAM a negro boy Bob.

To my son HENRY a negro girl Nan.

To my son ELIJAH a negro boy Allet.

I will that my son ELIJAH and his negro Allet be under the care of my two sons ISHAM and HENRY until he shall be of age. Should ELIJAH die without issue, then the negro to his two brothers.

To my daughter CATE LANSFORD 1 mare, cow and calf.

To my daughter SUSANNAH LANSFORD 1 mare, cow and calf.

To my grandson JOSIAH LANSFORD ten pounds at the age of 21 years.

I lend unto my beloved wife CATHERINE LANSFORD the land and plantation, all stock, household goods during her lifetime and a negro Jude. At her decease all to be sold and each child to have an equal share.

Appoint my wife CATHERINE and my son ISHAM to be executors.

HENRY (X) LANSFORD

Wit: WILLIAM EDWARDS, GEORGE JONES, HUMPHREY SCOGGINS(?)

GEORGE YOUNG security for executors.

Page 434
2 October 1776
Pr: 22 May 1777

LWT FORTUNE DODSON weak in body but sound in mind.

To my loving wife MARGARET DODSON all my estate personal and real during her natural life. At her decease all my land to my son DAVID DODSON.

To my three daughters LIDDIE DODSON, SARAH DODSON, and DEBORAH DODSON all my moveable estate to be equally divided.

Appoint JESSE DODSON and ELISHA DODSON, JR. as my executors.

FORTUNE (X) DODSON

Wit: DANIEL GARDNER, WILLIAM (X) INGRUM, ELIZABETH (X) INGRUM

GEORGE DODSON and JOHN CREEL security for JESSE DODSON.

Page 435-436
3 September 1776
Pr: 22 May 1777

LWT NATHANIEL AYRES of Halifax County, at my decease all my moveables and land to be sold for money and disposed of amongst my children:

To my eldest son THOMAS AYRES forty pounds in lieu of all my lands that he may inherit none of my lands (O).

To my son MOSES AYRES forty pounds, which I am indebted to him.

To my well beloved wife RHODY AYRES one third part of all the rest of my estate. Over and above her third I dispose of as follows: to PATIENCE JONES my grand daughter, five pounds.

To MARY AYRES, daughter of MOSES AYRES, ten pounds.

To my son REGIMABEK(?) BAKER AYRES, twenty five pounds.

The rest of my estate to be divided in ten equal parts and given to: MOSES AYRES 2 parts; son DANIEL AYRES 2 parts; and the six parts remaining equally divided between my daughter YANOKE PAYNE, son REGIMALIAH BAKER AYRES, THOMAS AYRES my eldest sons.

Appoint my sons THOMAS and MOSES AYRES executors to make my son DANIEL AYRES a deed to 86 1/2 acre tract on Double Creek, that joins Spurlock and divide from the rest of my land.

NATHANIEL AYRES

Wit: JOHN JAMES, JR., WILLIAM LYNCH, CHARLES BARNETT

DAVID TERRY and WILLIAM LYNCH security for executors.

Page 436-437
12 April 1776
Pr: 22 May 1777 (cont'd next page)

19

LWT GIDEON MARR sick and weak but of sound mind and memory.

I empower my son-in-law CONSTANT PERKINS, to recover my bond a-
gainst HENRY BILL and when recovered make JOHN MARR a title to
that part of the said bond agreeable to my bargain with him.

To my daughter AGGATHA PERKINS one half of the residue of the sd
bond.

To my son JOHN MARR five shillings.

To my son RICHARD MARR the same.

To my faithful servant MARY FURSTON five pounds and her freedom
at the decease of my wife.

My wife SARAH MARR should not be deprived of her land or negros
during her lifetime.

Lend unto my wife SARAH MARR the remainder of my claim against
HENRY BILL and all other parts of my estate. At her decease, to
such of her children or grand children as she shall think fit.
In case she fails to dispose of the estate, then to my daughter
AGGATHA PERKINS.

Appoint my wife SARAH MARR and CONSTANT PERKINS executors.

G. MARR

Wit: NICHOLAS PERKINS, ROBERT CROCKETT, RUSEL (X) WATS

Void that part relative to MARY FURSTON, she has since proved un-
faithful and rebellious. 2 September 1776.

Wit: ROBERT CROCKETT, THOMAS HARDEMAN

NICHOLAS PERKINS security for executors.

Page 438
6 June 1776
Pr: 26 March 1778

LWT JOHN HALL in a good state of health.

Lend unto my beloved wife all my land and estate, real and personal, during her life or widowhood, then the land to be equally
divided between my two sons, MATHEW HALL and JAMES HALL.

I give to my daughter MARY HALL 1 cow and her increase that we
brought from Amelia County, 1 feather bed and furniture.

The other part of my estate to be equally divided between my 3
youngest children: MATHEW HALL, JAMES HALL and PRISCILLER HALL.

Appoint my friends CHARLES BURTON and FRANCIS ROSE executors.

JOHN HALL

Wit: CHARLES BURTON, JAMES BURTON, PETER WILSON

ROBERT WILLIAMS security for executor CHARLES BURTON.

Page 439-440

LWT   JOHN YATES sick and weak but of perfect memory.

Unto my beloved wife ELIZABETH YATES during her lifetime my estate real and personal, and after her decease, the land and negros to be divided as follows:

To my eldest son JOHN YATES a part of the land whereon I now live
lines on Hughes Creek and Dan River and a negro man Bob.

To my son GEORGE YATES another part of the land whereon I now
live, likewise a part of a survey last made adjoining where I now
dwell up to THOMAS WATT's line and a negro Lain and all my smith
tools.

To my son ELIJAH YATES all the remaining part of the tract where
I now live and a negro boy Peter and a girl Judith.

I give unto my daughter HANNAH SHELTON wife of WILLIAM SHELTON,
two negros Cate and her daughter Chole.

To my daughter ANN GIBSON, negro Easther also the remainder of
a tract of land where she now dwells being 100 acres.

To my daughter MARTHA WATTS 100 acres where she now dwells.

My stock of horses, cattle, hogs, sheep, household furniture and
negro Little Cate to be divided among my children at the discretion of my wife at or before her decease.

Appoint my wife and WILLIAM SHELTON as executors.

                                    JOHN YATES

Wit: GEORGE ROSS, JAMES ELLIOTT, THOMAS (X) WRIGHT

JOHN WILSON security for executor.

Page 440-441
3 December 1777
Pr: 20 May 1778

LWT   WILLIAM BARKER sick and weak but of sound memory.

My land to be divided between my two sons. To my eldest son STEP-
HEN BARKER that part on Fall Creek.

To my youngest son MOSES BARKER the land on the west side.

The remainder of the moveable estate my wife to have the use of.
At her decease, to be sold for money and divided between my three
daughters, KEZIAH, MARY and TABITHIA.

Appoint my loving friends ROBERT WALTERS and THOMAS WYNNE executors.

                                    WILLIAM (X) BARKER

Wit: JOHN JONES, ELIAS BARKER, SUSANNAH (X) BARKER

21

BARKER will cont'd:

ROBERT WYNNE security for executors.

Page 442
19 December 1777
Pr: 28 May 1778

LWT PATTY WORSHAM weak of body but sound mind.

I give my bed and furniture to my brother DANIEL WORSHAM and fifteen pounds.

The balance of my estate to be equally divided between my sister
PHEBE WORSHAM and my sister MICHAEL's two children LUCY and ELIZ-
ABETH.

Appoint my brother DANIEL WORSHAM executor.

                              PATTY (X) WORSHAM

Wit: THOMAS DUNCAN, THOMAS WILKINSON, JAMES HENRY ROBERSON

GEORGE SUTHERLAND security for executor.

Page 443
17 May 1774
Pr: 25 September 1777

LWT SARAH RIDDLE in perfect health and sound memory.

I lend unto WILLIAM RAGSDALE all my wordly goods until his son
THOMAS RAGSDALE shall come of age, then to him.

Appoint WILLIAM RAGSDALE executor.

                              SARAH (X) RIDDLE

Wit: THOMAS HUTCHINGS, CATHERINE HUTCHINGS

JOSEPH FINNEY security for executor.

Page 443-444
21 March 1776
Pr: 22 October 1777

LWT HENRY CLAY in good health and perfect memory.

To my three brothers, THOMAS, MATHEW and GREEN CLAY, 1,000 acres
in Pittsylvania County on Cascade Creek to be equally divided.

To my sister PRISCILLA CLAY the land I now live on, 400 acres,
more or less.

To my sister MARTHA CLAY 300 acres on the waters of Sandy River
where the Church now stands.

To my three brothers and two sisters, THOMAS CLAY, MATHEW CLAY,
GREEN CLAY, PRISCILLA CLAY and MARTHA CLAY, all my other estate
to be equally divided.

CLAY will cont'd:

Appoint my brothers THOMAS and MATHEW CLAY and friend, CHARLES BURTON executors.

HENRY CLAY

Wit: CHARLES BURTON, JOHN GWYNE, EDMUND GWYNE

GREEN CLAY and CHARLES BURTON security for THOMAS CLAY, executor.

Page 444-445
8 October 1777
Pr: 26 November 1778

LWT WILLIAM WYNNE being very weak in body but perfect memory.

To my grandson WILLIAM WYNNE the son of daughter MARY WYNNE, a tract of land on the waters of Sandy Creek, 295 acres, the land whereon I now live allowing my wife FRANCES WYNNE, the liberty of the said land during her lifetime.

Also to my grandson a negro boy Dick, feather bed and furniture, stock and kitchen furniture, after the decease of my wife.

The residue of my estate consisting of several negros to be as equally divided among all of my children namely: WILLIAM WYNNE, THOMAS WYNNE, JOHN WYNNE, ROBERT WYNNE, MARGARET HENDRICK, ELIZABETH ECHOLS, MARY WYNNE and MARTHA DIXON.

Appoint my sons WILLIAM and THOMAS WYNNE as executors.

WILLIAM WYNNE

Wit: WILLIAM COLLIER, CHARLES COLLIER, STEPHEN VATETO(?), PHEBEE (X) WORSHAM, MARY (X) COLLIE

ROBERT PAYNE security for executors.

Page 446
11 November 1778
Pr: 28 January 1779

LWT ROBERT DALTON, SR. weak in health but sound memory.

Lend unto my beloved wife MARY DALTON all real and personal property during her natural life or widowhood.

To my son SOLOMAN DALTON after the decease of my wife, my land on his paying his sister NANCY ten pounds at the time of her marriage or being of age.

After the decease of my wife, my personal estate to be equally divided between my son SOLOMAN DALTON and my daughter NANCY DALTON.

Appoint as executors, JOHN DALTON and BENJAMIN TARRANT.

ROBERT (X) DALTON

23

DALTON will cont'd:

Wit: JAMES LIDDLE, JAMES MITCHELL

JAMES MITCHELL and DANIEL WITCHER security for executors.

Page 447-448
20 November 1778
Pr: 25 February 1779

LWT THOMAS HARDY sick and weak in body but of perfect mind and memory.

To my daughter ELIZABETH one shilling.

To my daughter MARY, 200 acres on the south side of Banister River that joins ZACHARIAH WALLER.

To my eldest son JOHN one shilling.

To my son THOMAS one shilling.

To my daughter SARAH during her widowhood 100 acres on the south side of Double Creek with the plantation she is now possessed of at her death to fall to her daughter SUSANAH.

To my daughter ANN 200 acres more or less on the south side of Double Creek at the lower end of SARAH's land also at my decease my riding horse and saddle, bed and furniture that I now lye in.

To THOMAS HARDY, the son of WILLIAM HARDY, deceased, 100 acres on Cherry Stone Creek with my plantation and 400 acres on north side of Double Creek, should he die without issue, all the lands and premises to my son THOMAS HARDY.

Appoint THOMAS HARDY, JR. and JOHN BAILEY executors.

                                        THOMAS HARDY

Wit: JOHN ALLEN, FREDERICK RAGSDALE, JAMES (X) ALLEN

RICHARD GWYNE security for THOMAS HARDY, JR.

Codicil:
12 December 1778

THOMAS HARDY, SR.

200 acres on the north side of Banister and a small piece not 100 acres on the north side of Banister and a small piece not 100 ac. on the north side of Banister that joins HENRY HALL I give to my son THOMAS HARDY for raising and maintaining the son of WILLIAM HARDY, deceased.

Page 449-450
11 October 1778
Pr: 18 May 1779

LWT BENJAMIN HARRISON of sound mind and memory.

HARRISON will cont'd:

To daughter DIANER MASTIN five shillings.

To daughter SARAH THERMAN five shillings.

To daughter LUCY BRYANT five shillings.

To my wife SARAH HARRISON during her widowhood the residue of my
estate and in case my wife should marry or die, the estate equally divided between my son WILLIAM HARRISON and my daughters FRAN-
CES RICHARDSON, NELLY HUNT, MOLLEY HARRISON, POLLY HARRISON, BET-
SY HARRISON and SUKEY HARRISON.

Appoint my wife SARAH HARRISON and my son WILLIAM HARRISON as my
executors.

                    BENJAMIN HARRISON

Wit: CHARLES KENNON, THOMAS BUCK, BENJAMIN JAMES

CHARLES HARRISON and WILLIAM DURRETT security for WILLIAM HARRIS-
ON, executor.

Page 450-451
1 August 1779
Pr: 21 September 1779

LWT AYRES HODNETT very sick but of sound memory.

The land I sold to JEREMIAH WHITE I now make him a right if he
pays the money remaining to our bargain.

To my son BENJAMIN HODNETT one shilling.

The balance of my land to be equally divided between my 3 sons:
JOHN HODNETT, JAMES HODNETT and DANIEL HODNETT, and if my wife
should conceive and bring forth a son in nine months after my
death he is to receive an equal part, if a daughter, then treated
as the other daughters. All of my tools to the sons.

Remaining negros, stock, furniture to be equally divided between
the children after the decease of my wife.

Appoint FLOYD TANNER and BENJAMIN TERRY executors.

                    AYRES (X) HODNETT

Wit: FLOYD TANNER, BENJAMIN TERRY, GEORGE HARDY

SYLVANUS STOKES security for BENJAMIN TERRY.

Page 451-452
13 July 1779
Pr: 21 September 1779

LWT ABRAHAM GOAD

To my daughter SARAH GOAD one shilling.

GOAD will cont'd:

To my daughter HANNAH BURDET one shilling.

To my daughter ELIZABETH COLLIER one shilling.

To my daughter JUDITH HOLLAY one shilling.

To my son WILLIAM GOAD one shilling.

To my daughter RUTH DILLARD one shilling.

To my son ABRAHAM GOAD the cow I lent him, and half my land on Frying Pan Creek.

To my son ROBERT GOAD one half of my land and all the remaining part of my personal estate. Should either of these die without issue, then to his brother.

Appoint son ROBERT GOAD executor.

ABRAHAM (X) GOAD

Wit: GEORGE PHILLIPS, WILLIAM GOAD, SR., JOHN GOAD, SR.

GEORGE PHILLPS and BENJAMIN TARRANT security for executor.

Page 452-453
3 August 1779
Pr: 21 December 1779

LWT JAMES SHIELDS in perfect health, mind and memory.

To my beloved wife ELIZABETH SHIELDS one third of my estate.

To my son PATRICK, one third of real and personal estate.

To my daughter MOLLY, one third part.

My son PATRICK SHIELDS to have above his share, sufficient to pay for his learning through several degrees of college.

Appoint my wife as executor.

As my wife is with child, should it survive, it is to have an equal share with the others.

JAMES SHIELDS

Wit: JOHN SMITH, SAMUEL SHIELDS, JOSHUA CANTRILL

SAMUEL SHIELDS and JOSHUA CANTRILL security for executor.

Page 495-496
25 February 1779
Pr: 21 March 1780

LWT CHRISTOPHER MARR very sick but of perfect memory.

To my grandson, JOSEPH MARR, my horse and saddle, bed and furni-

26

MARR will cont'd:

ture, and my land whereon I now live, 112 acres.

To my daughter ABBIGAIL MARR my cattle, hogs, sheep, household goods, and all my estate in and out of doors.

Appoint my friend CHARLES BURTON executor.

CHRISTOPHER (X) MARR

Wit: MARY BURTON, JOHN (X) PREWETT, MARY (X) PAYN, JOHN (X) PAYN

GEORGE SUTHERLAND security for the executor.

Deeds & Wills Book 9
1791-1794

Page 14-16
6 November 1785
Pr: 6 May 1791

LWT ROBERT PAYNE in perfect health, mind and memory.

Lend unto my loving wife the following negros: Buck, Dick, Bett, Pheby, Nan and Archer during her life or widowhood with the use of the plantation whereon I now live, on the south side of Dan River. After her decease to descend to my son CHARLES PAYNE and the said negros to be equally divided amongst all my children who are then surviving. I also lend to my wife all my stock.

It is my desire that the tract of land purchased of EDWARD SPARKS be sold to pay my debts.

Give to my son ROBERT PAYNE a negro boy Joe if he lives, if not the value.

To my son JOHN PAYNE the upper half of my land in Goochland County to be equally divided with a negro boy Tom if he gets possession, if not the value, a horse and saddle to the value of twenty five pounds.

To my son ROBERT PAYNE the lower half of my land in Goochland County with a negro boy James, horse and saddle to the value of twenty five pounds.

To my daughter BETSY SANDERS two negros Annaka and Frank which she now has in her possession.

To my daughter KITURAH PAYNE at her marriage, besides the negro Betty left her by her grandfather, a negro Pompy, a horse value of twenty pounds and her saddle.

To my daughter ANN HARRISON, exclusive of the negro girl Milly left her by her grandfather, a negro girl Agga, a horse or twenty five pounds.

To my daughter SUSANNA two negro girls Hannah and Juda if they live or the value of same, horse and saddle to the value of twenty five pounds.

27

PAYNE will cont'd:

To daughter AGNES, two negros Jane and Watt if they live or their value, horse and saddle value of twenty five pounds.

To my daughter MARY WOODSON two negros Lucy and Ben, horse and saddle.

Appoint MRS. WILLIAM HARRISON, her son ROBERT HARRISON, my son ROBERT PAYNE and my wife ANNE PAYNE, as executors.

ROBERT PAYNE

Wit: ROBERT BURTON, THOMAS FARN(?), EDMUND BURTON

N. B.
Since writing this will I have purchased 131 acres from ROBERT BURTON, the upper end where his land joins mine, which I give to my son CHARLES PAYNE.

Wit: THOMAS FARN, SAMUEL HARRIS, WILLIAM B. BURTON

THOMAS FEARN security for ROBERT PAYNE and ANNE PAYNE.

Page 16-17
4 March 1791
Pr: 16 May 1791

LWT CHARLES RIGNEY in perfect health and good memory.

Lend unto my wife MARY RIGNEY during her life my whole estate, personal and real. My wife is to give to my son JESSE RIGNEY the whole estate at her decease.

After my debts are paid, the executor is to make a deed to WILLIAM GRIFFITH and HENRY NEWTON for the land where they now live.

Appoint my son JESSE RIGNEY and wife MARY RIGNEY executors.

CHARLES (X) RIGNEY

Wit: JONATHAN (X) RIGNEY, DELILAH (X) NEWTON

JAMES TAYLOR security for executors.

Page 23-25
30 March 1791
Pr: 20 June 1791

LWT JOHN PRESTAGE infirm and weak in body but sound in mind and memory.

To my son JOHN PRESTAGE all my smith tools now in his possession and one shilling.

To my grandson LARKIN PRESTAGE all the tract of land where I now live.

To my grand-daughters LETTY and NANCY PRESTAGE all my stock and household furniture excepting my white mare, 1 cow and calf and

PRESTAGE will cont'd:

the bed SARAH D. P. lies on, which I give to SARAH D. P. (DUPEE).

To my grand daughter NANCY PRESTAGE all my wife's wearing apparel.

Appoint JOHN WILSON and DAVID TERRY executors.

JOHN PRESTAGE

Wit: WILLIAM WALTERS, SILVANG GARDNER, SARAH D. P., JR.

Codicil:
24 March 1791

Whereas SARAH DUPEE and her family has laboured and done service for me, I give unto her and her heirs 50 acres that joins BENJAMIN HARDY. Desire that SARAH and her children shall not be interrupted on the place I now live till 25 December 1791, and that she shall have the crops made this year.

JOHN (X) PRESTAGE

Wit: WILLIAM WALTER, P. WADE , SARAH (X) DUPEE, and SUSANNAH (X) DUPEE

WILLIAM WALTERS and THOMAS WILLIAMS security for executors.

Page 28-30
11 November 1782
Pr: 18 July 1791

LWT JOHN BENNETT very sick and weak in body but perfect mind and memory.

To my beloved wife ELISABETH all the estate, real and personal, during her life.

To my son JOHN, 70 acres, joins ALEXANDER LEE.

To my son JESSE, 100 acres with my plantation after the decease of my wife.

To my son WILLIAM, half the appraised value of negro Peter.

The other half of the appraised price of Peter is to be equally divided between my four children: JOHN BENNETT, ELISABETH BENNETT, JESSE BENNETT and RUTH BENNETT.

My son WILLIAM is to possess the said Peter after paying the above mentioned children their part.

All the rest of my effects to be equally divided between my nine children: WILLIAM BENNETT, THOMAS BENNETT, JOHN BENNETT, JESSE BENNETT, SARAH LEE, WINIFRED MC DANIEL, MILLY WATSON, ELISABETH BENNETT and ANN BENNETT.

Appoint sons WILLIAM and THOMAS BENNETT executors.

JOHN (X) BENNETT

29

BENNETT will cont'd:

Wit: GEORGE DODSON, ROTHERICK MC DANIEL

JOHN WILSON and WILLIAM MADDING security for WILLIAM BENNETT, the eldest son, executor.

Court
20 February 1797
Will further approved.

Page 37-39
16 January 1791
Pr: 18 July 1791

LWT WILLIAM REYNOLDS in perfect health, sense and memory.

To my loving wife MARTHA REYNOLDS the plantation with improvements where I now live, together with one moeity of whole tract being 104 acres on the same side of the road with my plantation during her life.

To my beloved son JOSEPH REYNOLDS at the decease of my wife, 54 acres of said land and plantation.

The other 50 acres and plantation on Gease Branch where my beloved son RICHARD COLE REYNOLDS now lives, to him and his heirs.

To my wife, two feather beds and furniture, the pewter, 2 chests, spining wheels, rest of the household furniture, my riding horse, her saddle, 2 cows, 1 heafer, 9 head of hogs to be hers during her lifetime. At her decease, to be sold and divided among my children: SALLY, TIFFEY, BETTY, THOMAS, JOHAN, JESSEY, WILLIAM, JAMES, ALICE, THOMAS, LUCY, JOSEPH, RICHARD COLE REYNOLDS and ANNA DAVIS.

Appoint my wife and ROBERT WALTER, JR. executors.

                                WILLIAM (X) REYNOLDS

Wit: THOMAS CISSELL, SAMUEL CONSTABLE

JOHN WILSON and WILLIAM LYNCH security for executors.

Page 69-70
29 December 1790
Pr: 15 August 1791

LWT JOHN BARROTT very sick and weak of body but sound mind and perfect memory.

To my beloved wife ELIZABETH BARROTT, all my estate real and personal, except one shilling which I give my son JOHN BARROTT.

At the decease of my wife, she may give the estate to whom she pleases.

                                JOHN BARROTT

BARROTT will cont'd:

Wit: MATHEW MC GLASSON, THOMAS BARROTT, UBEBOTH (X) MC GLASSON

THOMAS TUNSTALL and THOMAS BARROTT security for ELIZABETH BARROT.

Page 83-84
30 July 1791
Pr: 17 October 1791

LWT JOHN WRIGHT of sound mind and memory.

To my beloved son JOHN, negro Lucy and cow and calf.

To my beloved son THOMAS, the land and plantation whereon I now
live, containing 182 acres and a negro Stephen.

To my beloved daughter SUSANNA KERBY, negro Doll.

To my beloved daughter ELIZABETH KERBY, negro boy Daniel.

The balance to be divided between the 3 children: THOMAS WRIGHT,
SUSANNA KERBY and ELIZABETH KERBY.

                          JOHN (X) WRIGHT

Wit: CHARLES CADER, MARY (X) MEACHUM

WILLIAM PRICE and MARK CHELTON security for THOMAS WRIGHT.

Page 119-120
6 November 1791
Pr: 21 November 1791

LWT THOMAS MUSTAIN - weak in body.

To my beloved wife MARY MUSTAIN, a sufficient maintenance suit-
able to her surcomstance, free and undesturbed during her life
or widowhood.

To my son JESSE, 200 acres to be taken off the upper end of the
tract where I now live.

The rest of this tract to be sold.

To daughters, REBECKAH and MOLLY, twenty shillings each from the
sale of the above land.

To daughters MARY ANN and SALLY, ten pounds each.

To son AVERY MUSTAIN and daughters ANNA BUCKNER, MILLEY KEESE,
TABETH BRUCE, WINNEY LEWIS and SILUDEY SHELTON one equal part of
the money from the sale of the land.

To THOMAS MUSTAIN, son of JESSE MUSTAIN and his wife JENNEY, has
promised to live with me and my wife during our lives for which
I give and bequeath unto the said THOMAS MUSTAIN a tract of land
on both sides of Nixes(?) Creek, 170 acres.

The balance of my moveable property to be divided among my last

31

MUSTAIN will cont'd:

six named children.

Appoint son JESSE MUSTAIN and JOEL SHELTON executors.

                    THOMAS (X) MUSTAIN

Wit: FRANCIS (X) IVY, NATHANIEL FARIS, GRIFFITH DICKINSON

VINCENT SHELTON and CHARLES LEWIS, JR. security for executors.

Page 257-258
13 September 1792 (as written)
Pr: 16 July 1792

LWT WILLIAM DURRETT being sick and weak.

I lend everything to my wife MOLLEY DURRETT as long as she is a
widow, then at her decease the land to be equally divided between
my three sons: FRANCIS DURRETT, WIAT DURRETT and TANDY DURRETT.
If any should die before of age, then to the survivors.

The rest of my estate to be divided amongst my children: LEAH
HARRIS, CATY DURRETT, RODAY DURRETT, FRANCIS DURRETT, POLLY DUR-
RETT, WIAT DURRETT, TANDY DURRETT, ELIZABETH DURRETT and MOLLEY
DURRETT.

To GABRIEL RICHARDS, to whom I sold 50 acres 13 years ago last
May, and have never made a deed, I give and bequeath this 50 ac.
to him.

Appoint DURRETT RICHARDS, ASA THOMAS and my wife MOLLEY DURRETT
executors.

                    WILLIAM DURRETT

Wit: NOEL WADDELL, JR., ALLEN WADDELL, CHARLES WADDELL

WILLIAM THOMAS and NOEL WADDELL, JR. security for MOLLEY DURRETT
and DURRETT RICHARDS.

Page 258-259
31 March 1792
Pr: 16 July 1792

LWT THOMAS PRICE being very sick and weak.

To EASTER ROBINSON five shillings.

To REESE PRICE five shillings.

To MARTHA CREWS five shillings.

To JOHN PRICE five shillings.

To THOMAS PRICE five shillings.

To DAVID PRICE five shillings.

PRICE will cont'd:

To ISAAC PRICE five shillings.

To ELIZABETH BUKIS PRICE 1 beast, saddle, feather bed and furniture, cow and calf, two English pounds, and 20 shillings cash,
the beast at ten pounds value, one gound(?) at forty shillings
and the other at thirty shillings price.

Lend unto my wife MARY PRICE all my whole and sole estate land,
negros, stock and furniture during her natural life or widowhood
to raise her children on. Should my wife remarry the executor to
take the estate and divide it among my last wife's children.

Appoint my wife MARY PRICE and son JOHN PRICE as executors.

THOMAS PRICE

Wit: ABRAM PARRISH, GODFREY (X) BURNETT, JOHN TURTLE

Presented secondly 17 March 1800 by the executrix MARY PRICE with
securities RICHARD JOHNSON, JOSHUA SAFFOLD, WILLIAM SHELTON, and
TARLTON PRICE.

Page 342-343
8 October 1786
Pr: 21 January 1793

LWT THOMAS CORBIN in perfect health and memory.

To my beloved wife ELIZABETH CORBIN the tract of land whereon I
now dwell and the personal estate during her lifetime.

After the decease of my wife my land is to be equally divided between my daughters LUCY and SUSANNAH.

My daughter LUCY is to have the plantation that lies across the
road and SUSANNAH to have my dwelling plantation.

The personal estate, after my wifes decease, to be equally divided between my two daughters above mentioned.

To my son AMEGI(?) five shillings.

To my son RAWLEY five shillings with these payments made after
the decease of my wife.

Appoint my wife ELIZABETH CORBIN executrix.

THOMAS (X) CORBIN

Wit: JOHN HAMMOND, SR., SABRA (X) HAMMOND

Page 464
23 June 1793
Pr: 16 December 1793

LWT JOHN HUBBARD being very sick but of sound mind and memory.

HUBBARD will cont'd:

To my beloved wife KEZZIA HUBBARD the plantation whereon I now
live with 200 acres of land, also my grist mill and all of the
estate real and personal for 15 years.

I appoint my son ISAM HUBBARD to have the management of my estate
and to be paid out of the estate for his trouble. After the 15
years my whole and sole estate to be equally divided between my
living children and my wife, except for the land.

To my son JOHN HUBBARD, after 15 years, the plantation where I
now live, his mother keeping possession during her lifetime to
the 100 acres I lent her.

To my son ISAM HUBBARD, after the 15 years, my mill and land she
stands on with 100 acres on the north side of my survey.

To my son SAMUEL HUBBARD, 200 acres laid off Polecat Creek of the
Banister River.

To my son HEZEKIAH HUBBARD, the remaining part of my land patent
of SAMUEL EMMERSON.

To my grandson JOHN LEAGUE, the plantation his father made at the
head of the creek I live on with 100 acres of land.

To my son DAVIS HUBBARD, the remaining part of my land lying on
the north side of where I now live, 350 acres.

To my son JOHN HUBBARD's children, five shillings.

Appoint my wife KEZZIA HUBBARD and my son ISHAM HUBBARD as executors.

                              JOHN HUBBARD

Wit: ABRAM PARRISH, JOHN HODGES, WILLIAM LEANY

Page 468
27 September 1793
Pr: 21 October 1793 and 16 December 1793

Nuncupative Will spoken by him and committed to writing the 30th.
JOHN PANNILL in a low state of health in the presence of: THOMAS
TUNSTALL, DANIEL SAYRE and MILLY TUNSTALL.

He desires his affectionate wife NANCY PANNILL to have what part
of his estate as the Law directs and that she may build a dwelling house.

Executors to make a sale of the balance of the timber after wife
NANCY PANNILL has had the timber fit for her dwelling.

He had a trunk containing his money which he desires DAVID PAN-
NILL, WILLIAM WIMBISH and SEBERT CRUTCHER to open and count.

Appoints DAVID PANNILL and WILLIAM WIMBISH as executors.

He requested DAVID PANNILL to become a member of his family and
devote his time to settling the accounts and business of the es-

PANNILL will cont'd:

tate and be reimbursed for such.

He also recommended SEBERT CRUTCHER - as a fit person to assist DAVID PANNILL.

Wit: THOMAS TUNSTALL, MILLEY TUNSTALL, DAVID SAYRE

Court 20 January 1794

DAVID PANNILL and WILLIAM WIMBISH executors with WILLIAM MORTON, SAMUEL PANNILL, CRISPIN SHELTON, VINCENT SHELTON, BEVERLY SHELTON, CHARLES LEWIS, JOSEPH TERRY, RICHARD BAYNE as security for DAVID PANNILL.

Security for WILLIAM WIMBISH are RICHARD JOHNSON, JAMES JOHNSON, JOHN WIMBISH, CRISPIN SHELTON, ELIJAH KING and RICHARD BAYNE.

Page 493-494
3 October 1793
Pr: 17 December 1793

LWT JOHN CRADDOCK being very sick and weak but of sound mind and memory.

Lend to my beloved wife MARY CRADDOCK 150 acres of land part of the tract whereon I now live to include the dwelling house and 5 negros, 3 grown and 2 small, being her choice of all the negros. To be possessed by her during her life or widowhood for herself and her children.

To my youngest son NATHANIEL CRADDOCK 300 acres of land to include the 150 acres devised to his mother and 150 acres adjoining.

To my son JOHN CRADDOCK 100 acres at the upper end of this tract whereon he now lives.

To my son RICHARD CRADDOCK 100 acres lying on one edge of my land and being an improvement on the fork of Panther Branch.

The rest of my land to be equally divided among my children viz: ELIZABETH COLLINS, PRISCILLA CRADDOCK, JUDITH CRADDOCK, SARAH CRADDOCK, MARY CRADDOCK and FRANKEY CRADDOCK.

The balance of my estate of whatever source to be equally divided among the above children and my son WILLIAM CRADDOCK.

Appoint my friend JAMES HURT and son RICHARD CRADDOCK as executors.

JOHN CRADDOCK

Wit: NATHANIEL LUCK, WILLIAM RICE, JOHN JENKINS

20 January 1794

WILLIAM CRADDOCK, ISHAM JOHNSON, RICHARD BROWN, CHARLES A. BARDET, WILLIAM LEWIS, ISAAC GREGORY, EDWARD BOUDLES(?), THOMAS LINTHICUM, THOMAS B. JONES, CHARLES LEWIS, JR. and BEVERLY SHELTON

CRADDOCK will cont'd:

security for RICHARD CRADDOCK.

Page 494
10 August 1793
Pr: 20 January 1794

LWT CURTIS PARROT being in my present sense and memory.

To my wife ANN PARROTT my whole estate during her life or widowhood. After her decease or marriage, the estate to be sold and
equally divided amongst my children except my land whereon I now
live and that I give unto my son JOHN PARROTT and to my grandson
TYRE PARROTT.

I give to my son JOHN PARROTT the land from the lower end up the
river to the mouth of the spring branch.

I leave the land that is in Louisa County to be sold and equally
divided amongst all my children.

Should my grandson TYRE die before of age, then to my son JOHN
PARROTT.

CURTIS PARROTT

Wit: BENJAMIN (X) CANNY(?), JR., JESSE BOE(?), WILLIAM NEIGHBORS

Page 497
9 March 1789
Pr: 20 January 1794

LWT RICHARD KESSEE being in proper health and sound mind.

To my beloved wife ANN KESSEE all my estate, real and personal,
during her life or widowhood. At her decease the estate to be
equally divided amongst all my children to wit: MARY GRAY, JOHN
KESSEE, CHARLES KESSEE, JEREMIAH KESSEE, JESSE KESSEE, ANN KESSEE

Appoint my sons CHARLES and JEREMIAH KESSEE as executors.

RICHARD KESSEE

Wit: NATHANIEL HICKS, JINNAH HICKS

Codicil:

Should any child die prior to my or my wifes decease, their heirs
to have no part.

JACOB BERGER and FREDERICK SHELTON security for JESSE KESSEE.

Page 509-510
1 February 1793
Pr: 17 February 1794

LWT MOURNING WALDEN very sick and weak but of sound mind.

36

WALDEN will cont'd:

I lend to my dearly beloved Mother all my household furniture and stock during her life and at her death I give to my sister MILLEY WARD 1 feather bed and furniture and the balance of my household furniture except one large chest, one small hare trunk, half a dozen chairs, one table which I give to my brother CHARLES WALDEN at the death of my Mother.

To my brother CHARLES WALDEN the balance of my father's estate which is coming to me.

To my sister MILLEY WARD a negro boy Jolly during her life and at her decease Jolly and the furniture above given to her first born daughter ANNEY WARD.

To my brother RICHARD WALDEN negro Betty which was willed him by my father at my decease.

To my sister CANDACE BABER a negro girl Sarah which my father willed her at my decease.

Appoint my brother CHARLES WALDEN and WILLIAM WARD executors.

MOURNING WALDEN

Wit: EDWARD BYBEE, NATHAN THURMAN

ROBERT A. WARD security for executor.

Page 524
29 October 1787
Pr: 17 February 1794

LWT CRISPIN SHELTON being low and weak of body but of sound mind.

To my son ABRAHAM SHELTON negros: Primus, Page, Old Lucy, Tenor and Dicey and their increase.

To my son GABRIEL SHELTON negros: Sam, Patrick, Old Phillis, and Young Phillis and their increase and one feather bed.

To my son LEWIS SHELTON negros: Nern(?), Moses, Jane and Sarah and a bay horse Brandy and one feather bed.

To my son BEVERLEY SHELTON negros: James, Cancer, Fanney, Bide, a bay colt, cow and stear, 4 head sheep, feather bed.

To my son SPENCER SHELTON negros: Charles, Hampton, Young Pat and Young Lucy.

To my son ARMISTEAD SHELTON negros: Squire, Lewis, Sally, Anne and a feather bed.

To my son VINCENT SHELTON negros: Essex, West, Betty, Rhoda and Edey, my watch, sorrel mare, 2 cows and calves, 6 head sheep also my large book Beckat.

To my grandson CRISPIN SHELTON son of ABRAHAM SHELTON, a negro named Davy.

I lend to my daughter ELIZABETH HURT during her lifetime negros:

37

SHELTON will cont'd:

Amey, Agge, Aaron and Isaac and a feather bed. At her decease the above to be equally divided amongst her children.

To my daughter JANE TODD during her life negros: Joe, Randolph, Patt and Priscilla and a feather bed, to her children at her decease.

To my daughter SUSANNA DICKERSON during her life negros: Will, Stephen, Rachel and Delpha, at her decease to her children.

Should any of the above daughters or their husbands embezzle or waste or cause to suffer the negros, my executors are to take possession and hire them out and the funds kept for the children of the said daughters.

To my daughter SUSANNA DICKERSON my large bay mare, cow and calf and 3 ewes.

To my beloved wife LETTICE SHELTON, during her life or widowhood, 400 acres of land, the upper part of the tract I lie on to include the houses and plantation where I now live.

At her decease, the 400 acres, house and plantation to go to my son VINCENT SHELTON.

Also to VINCENT SHELTON, all the residue of the tract whereon I now live, the lower part.

Also to Vincent, all my tract of land on both sides of Whitethorn Creek, also my late survey adjoining the tract on Whitethorn.

Lend unto my wife LETTICE SHELTON these negros: Gloucester, Gruff and Sue, all the stock, furniture and plantation tools.

At her decease, distribute amongst all my children as follows:

To my son ABRAHAM SHELTON, the negro Gruff

To my son GABRIEL SHELTON, the mulatto Gloucester

To my son VINCENT SHELTON, the negro Sue

The remainder of my stock of horses, cattle, et al, to be equally divided among all of my children.

My still and wagon to be sold to discharge my debts.

I appoint my sons ABRAHAM, BEVERLEY and VINCENT SHELTON as executors.

CRISPIN SHELTON

Wit: LEONARD SHELTON, EDMUND TAYLOR, DANIEL SHELTON, THOMAS TUNSTALL, JR.

DAVID PANNILL, JOHN SHELTON, CRISPIN SHELTON, WILLIAM TODD, SPENCER SHELTON, ARMISTEAD SHELTON, GRIFFITH DICKERSON, security for BEVERLEY SHELTON and VINCENT SHELTON.

Page 114-115
10 December 1777
Pr: 16 May 1780

LWT WILLIAM WILLIAMS being in a weak and low condition but of perfect mind and memory.

To my beloved son LEWIS WILLIAMS, one eighth part of my land and ten pounds cash.

To my loving daughter SUSANNAH WILLIAMS, twenty pounds cash.

To my beloved wife LUCY WILLIAMS, the use of the remainder of my estate both real and personal until my son THOMAS TERRY WILLIAMS shall arrive at the age of 21 years. Should he die before that time then to be divided equally between my wife and seven sons: JOSEPH TERRY WILLIAMS, JOHN WILLIAMS, JAMES MASTIN WILLIAMS, THOMAS TERRY WILLIAMS, DAVID CHAMPNESS WILLIAMS, WILLIAM MASTIN WILLIAMS, and DOCTOR CRAFORD WILLIAMS.

I appoint my wife and DAVID TERRY and JOSEPH TERRY WILLIAMS as executors.

                    WILLIAM (X) WILLIAMS

Wit: DAVID GIVEN, DAVID TERRY, CHAMPNESS TERRY

DAVID TERRY security for LUCY WILLIAMS and JOSEPH TERRY WILLIAMS.

Page 115-116
30 March 1780
Pr: 18 April 1780

LWT BENJAMIN CLEMENT sick in body but of sound and perfect memory.
Lend to my wife SUSANNA CLEMENT one third part of my moveable estate.

To my granddaughter SUSANNA CLEMENT, daughter of BENJAMIN CLEMENT one of my best beds and furniture and five pounds when she comes of proper age to receive it.

To the heirs at law of my daughter JERIAH GILBERT, deceased, one shilling.

To the heirs at law of my daughter RACHEL ABSTON, deceased, one shilling.

To the heirs at law of my daughter ELIZABETH BUTTERWORTH, deceased, one shilling.

To my son JOHN CLEMENT the tract where he now lives, 50 acres, more or less, that I purchased of JOHN GIVAN(?) on Frying Pan Ck. (Creek)

Lend unto my wife SUSANNA CLEMENT the use of the land where I now live with all surveys and one third part of the profits of the mill during her widowhood. Said wife not to sell, lease or let

CLEMENT will cont'd:

the land or the mill. At her decease or marriage, the land and the mill to be sold and all my legesees excepted moveables to be sold, negros and all than can be collected after the land sale be divided in ten equal parts. One part between JAMES GILBERT and RACHEL GILBERT children of JERIAH GILBERT, deceased. One part between JOHN ABSTON, FRANCES ABSTON, SUSANA ABSTON and RACHEL AB- STON children of RACHEL ABSTON, deceased. One part to ISAAC BUT- TERWORTH, STEPHEN BUTTERWORTH, JANE BUTTERWORTH and SUSANA BUT- TERWORTH children of ELIZABETH BUTTERWORTH, deceased.

The above children to be paid when they come of age.

The other seven parts to be equally divided amongst my children: STEPHEN CLEMENT, ISAAC CLEMENT, BENJAMIN CLEMENT, ADAM CLEMENT, JOHN CLEMENT, SUSANNA EVANS and one part to MARTHA CLEMENT widow of JAMES CLEMENT and her children.

Appoint sons ISAAC and ADAM CLEMENT executors.

BENJAMIN CLEMENT

Wit: JOHN BOBBITT, BENJAMIN (X) FOSTER, THOMAS (X) ROBERSON, WIL- LIAM (X) CASH, RUTH (X) CASH

JOHN WILSON and WILLIAM TODD security for BENJAMIN CLEMENT.

20 June 1780
JOHN WILSON and ABRAHAM SHELTON security for ADAM CLEMENT

Page 116-117
29 April 1779
Pr: 20 June 1780

LWT EDWARD HUBBARD sick and weak but of good and sound memory.

To my sons, NATHANIEL HUBBARD and JOHN HUBBARD my tract of land whereon I now live, equally divided with John to have the plan- tation.

To my daughter TABITHIA a feather bed and furniture.

To my son REUBEN HUBBARD a dun colored horse when he comes of age.

To my son EDWARD HUBBARD a sorrel mare and if the mare has a colt that to my son JOSEPH HUBBARD.

To my wife the remaining part of the estate during her life or widowhood, then to be equally divided between the children.

My survey of land on the branches of St--stone(?), joining JOSEPH COLLINS and WILLIAM CHICK be sold.

EDWARD (X) HUBBARD

Wit: BENJAMIN LANKFORD, BENJAMIN WEST, WILLIAM COLLINS

JOHN GEORGE and WILLIAM COLLINS security for ELIZABETH HUBBARD.

Page 117-118 (cont'd next page)

40

13 June 1780
Pr: 18 July 1780

LWT MORRIS HAMBLET of sound mind and memory.

To my son WILLIAM HAMBLET one shilling

To my son JAMES HAMBLET a smooth bore gun

To my son ABNER HAMBLET a chest

To my son THOMAS HAMBLET all my land and a middle sized pot

To my daughter FILLITHAUMY(?) HAMBLET a bed, frying pan and one small iron pot.

To my daughter RACHEL HAMBLET a bed, side saddle and largest iron pot.

To my daughter DARCUS HAMBLET a bed, one dish, one plate and one spoon, 1 box iron and heter.

To my daughter HANNAH HAMBLET a bed, one dish, one plate and one spoon, and a spice mortar.

My desire is for my children to stay together and the livestock and tools to be for the use of the plantation and the children until they are raised, then equally divided between my four sons.

Appoint AMBROS BEAFORD and daughter RACHEL HAMBLET as executors.

                    MORRIS (X) HAMBLET

Wit: W. PACE, NEWSOM PACE, SUSANNAH (X) PACE

GABRIEL SHELTON and NEWSOM PACE security for AMBROS BEAFORD and RACHEL HAMBLET.

Page 118-119
13 May 1780
Pr: 15 August 1780

LWT WILLIAM GRIFFETH sick and weak but of perfect mind and memory.

The plantation whereon I now live with all the stock, except one horse colt, I deliver into the hands of WILLIAM PERSISE till the year 1784 upon half stocke according to a contract by me with him the said WILLIAM PERSIZE.

At the end of that time I lend to my beloved wife RACHEL GRIFFETH the increase of my stock with the plantation whereon I now live with all household goods and furniture during her life. At her decease to my son JONATHAN GRIFFETH, 100 acres, part of the tract where I now live with the plantation whereon he now lives being the upper part. The remainder to my son WILLIAM GRIFFETH.

To my sons JONATHAN and WILLIAM one entry of land on Southertons Branch to be equally divided.

The increase of my cattle, after the decease of my wife, to be

41

GRIFFETH will cont'd:

equally divided between the following or their heirs: MARGET PAR-
SONS, ANNE PARSONS, MARY RIGNY, SUSANNER ADKINSON, SARRAH GRIF-
FETH, WILLIAM GRIFFETH and JONATHAN GRIFFETH.

To my son WILLIAM GRIFFETH all my stock of horses, sheep, hogs,
with the household and moveables after the death of my wife.

WILLIAM GRIFF<u>ITH</u>

Wit: SETH (X) COLWELL, JOSEPH (X) PARSONS, WILLIAM PROSSESE, REU-
BIN PAYNE

SAMUEL PARSONS and CHARLES RIGNEY security for RACHEL GRIFF<u>ITH.</u>

Page 119-120
3 December 1774
Pr: 17 October 1780

LWT JOHN MADING, SR. very sick and weak, but of perfect mind and
memory.

I desire that money to be raised out of the moveable estate to
pay my debts and raise my part of the money to clear the land.

To my son WILLIAM MADING the land he now lives on.

To WILLIAM PETTEY as much of my land as lies in his enclosure,
quantity unknown.

To my son ROBERT MADING the upper half of my tract when he comes
of age and my saddle.

To my well beloved wife MARY MADING to have quite (quit?) possession of the lower end of the land and the plantation during
her lifetime and then to my son CHAMPNESS MADING.

Appoint my wife and GEORGE DODSON as executors.

JOHN (X) MADING

Wit: WILLIAM <u>PETTY</u>, THOMAS (X) MADING, ROBERT (X) MADING

ELISHA DODSON security for executors.

Page 120-121
19 December 1780
Pr: 16 January 1781

LWT J. ROBERT ROLLSTONE (RALSTON?) in low state of health but
a fullness of reason.

To loving wife JEAN RALSTON one third of all my estate, real and
personal.

The land to be sold at auction to be made of what remains (except
the pewter that was hers before our marriage, her bed and furniture) and to be equally divided amongst my children.

42

ROLLSTONE (RALSTON) will cont'd:

Appoint JOHN SHIELDS and HENRY BURNETT as executors.

                              ROBERT RALSTON

Wit: THOMAS CUNNINGHAM, THOMAS GRESHAM, GILBERT BURNETT

THOMAS CUNNINGHAM and GILBERT BURNETT security.

Page 121-122
26 March 1781
Pr: 15 May 1781

LWT THOMAS ROGERS of Guilford County, North Carolina, weak of
body but in perfect mind and memory.

To my loving wife SARAH ROGERS, her mare, saddle, bed and furniture.

All the remaining effects to be sold and equally divided between
MARTHY ROGERS, MARY ROGERS and ROBERT ROGERS, and the child my
wife SARAH is now pregnant with.

To my wife SARAH ROGERS, two cows.

Appoint THOMAS BLACK and GEORGE ROGERS executors.

                              THOMAS (X) ROGERS

Wit: ROBERT ROGERS, MARY (X) ROGERS, MARY (X) BLACK

LODOWICK TUGGLE security for executors.

Page 122-123
4 November 1780
Pr: 15 May 1780

LWT JOHN PAYNE very sick and weak but in perfect mind and memory.

To my son WILLIAM, SAMUEL, JOSAH (JOSIAH?), RHODA and MARY PAYNE
one shilling.

To my son CHARLES PAYNE the land I now live on.

The land I sold ZACHARAH BOOTS he shall have a right to. The land
I intended to live on where the new cabin is built, I lease to
my son REUBEN PAYNE.

To my son JOHN PAYNE two cows and calves when he marries.

I lend to my loving wife all my moveable estate during her widowhood. She is not to dispose of anything at her own will. At her
marriage or decease, the estate to be sold and the money equally
divided between JOHN PAYNE and CHARLES PAYNE and the children of
my last marriage.

Appoint WILLIAM DURRETT and JOHN PAYNE executors.

N. B. (cont'd next page)

43

PAYNE will cont'd:

I have a piece of land in Wilkes County, North Carolina which is to be sold and divided as above.

JOHN (X) PAYNE

Wit: MOSES AYERS, CHARLES PAYNE, GABRIEL RICHARDS

Will exhibited by WILLIAM DURRETT and ELIZABETH PAYNE, widow, objects to receiving any benefits or dower from the said Will.

MOSES AYRES and GABRIEL RICHARDS security for WILLIAM DURRETT.

Page 123-124
14 October 1772
Pr: 15 May 1781

LWT THOMAS SMITH weak in body.

To my loving wife SARAH and my youngest son THOMAS be executor and executrix.

I lend to my wife SARAH a negro woman Finn, a black horse called Jack and a saddle, a feather ed and furniture, and half of the rest of my household furniture, half of my stock. Also to my wife the third of the land and plantation whereon I now dwell for her use during her life and no longer.

To my son, the youngest son, THOMAS SMITH, the tract where I now live containing 400 acres. I also give to him the other half of my stock, two horses, two mares. Also to him 400 acres on Camp Branch. Also the other half of my household furniture and negros Bob and Dinah.

To my grandson THOMAS SMITH, son of JOHN SMITH, 100 acres on the north side of Sandy River.

After the decease of my wife, the part of the stock she possessed to be equally divided amongst all my six children: JOHN, JANE, EDWARD, SARAH, MARTHA and THOMAS SMITH, and their heirs.

I also give to my son THOMAS SMITH, a negro woman named Finn after the decease of my wife.

THOMAS SMITH

Wit: JOHN FULTON, WILLIAM ORR, JOHN WILSON

JOHN WILSON and THOMAS BOAZ security for executors.

Page 124-125
1 February 1778
Pr: 15 May 1778

LWT WILLIAM COLLINS being of perfect health and memory.

To my beloved THOMAS COLLINS my plantation whereon I now live after the decease of my wife with the land of Ballinger's line to the glade line to the black pond. He is to also have the young

COLLINS will cont'd:

mare called his and his feather bed, two heifers, two sheep also
the gun called his.

To my daughter FANEY, all the land lying between my son THOMAS
and the land I gave to JESSEY HODGES. Also a mare, two head of
sheep and her saddle.

I give to my daughter ELISABETH HODGES about 100 acres being part
of the old survey on Camp Branch running a straight line to JAMES
KING, joining the land I formerly gave her.

The residue of my estate during the life of my wife, ...my manor
house and plantation and after her decease to be divided between
my beloved son and daughters.

Appoint beloved son JESSEY HODGES and my wife executors.

                         WILLIAM COLLINS

Wit: THOMAS DILLARD, JOEL (X) HURT, JOHN COLLINS

THOMAS DILLARD and JOHN COLLINS security for executor.

Page 125-126
6 January 1781
Pr: 15 May 1781

LWT DRURY OLIVER in perfect mind and memory but in a low state
of -health.

To my beloved wife MARY OLIVER all my personal estate during her
life or widowhood.

To my son THOMAS OLIVER my manner (manor) plantation with the 200
acres bounded by MITCHELL and ROBERTS. Also to my son THOMAS, a
negro named Peter.

To my son JOHN OLIVER, 292 acres which was surveyed by RICHARD
YATES and a negro named Bobb.

To my son WILLIAM OLIVER, a negro named Sarah.

It is my desire after the decease of my wife, the personal estate
in her possession be equally divided between my surviving gails
(girls?) or daughters.

It is my desire that my sons be bound to some trade as soon as
they are capable of learning.

Appoint my friends THOMAS BLACK, HENRY CONWAY and JAMES ROBERTS
as my executors.

                         DRURY OLIVER

Wit: JAMES ROBERTS, DAVID RAY, MARY RAY

19 June 1781
STEPHEN COLEMAN and RICHARD BROWN security for THOMAS BLACK and
HENRY CONWAY.

                              45

Page 126-127
16 March 1780
Pr: 17 July 1781

LWT FRANCIS LUCK being sick and weak in body but in perfect mind,
sense and memory.

Lend to my beloved wife SARAH LUCK all my estate both real and
personal during her natural life or widowhood. At her decease or
marriage, my estate to be sold and the money divided equally between my children to wit: JOHN LUCK, NATHANIEL LUCK, RICHARD HUB-
BARD LUCK, JOYCE, RHODA, BETTY, SARAH, ANN DEADMAN and CATEY EV-
ANS LUCK, with my grand daughter MARY LUCK who is to have equal
share with my children.

Should any of my sons die before coming of age 18 years, their
part to be equally divided amongst my daughters.

Should my grand daughter MARY LUCK die without issue, her part
to fall to my son RICHARD HUBBARD LUCK.

Appoint my wife SARAH LUCK and my son JOHN LUCK executors.

                              FRANCIS LUCK

Wit: NATHANIEL HENDRICK, JOEL HURT, WILL LANDON

ARMISTEAD DUDLEY and CORNELIUS MC HANEY security.
WILLIAM PEMBERTON and BENJAMIN GORNEY security for JOHN LUCK.

Page 127-128
21 September 1780
Pr: 21 August 1781

LWT GEORGE MORGAN being in perfect health and memory.

Give my whole estate be it whatsoever, unto my sister SARAH MOR-
GAN and her heirs.

Appoint MESHACK TURNER and WILLIAM TODD executors.

                              GEORGE MORGAN

Wit: MESHACK TURNER, ABEDNEGO TURNER, DANIEL TURNER

HAYNES MORGAN security for executors.

Page 128
17 March 1781
Pr: 20 November 1781

LWT SARAH BRISCOE being very sick and weak but of sound mind and
memory.

To my beloved mother MARY STONE the use of my two negros George
and Charity during her natural life.

At the decease of my Mother, I give to my brother JOHN BRISCOE
the two negros, also to my brother one gold (ring?).

BRISCOE will cont'd:

To my beloved brother HARRISON MUSGROVE one gold ring.

I give and bequeath the remainder of my estate to my mother MARY STONE and appoint her my executrix.

SARAH BRISCOE

Wit: EDWARD WARREN, PHILIP JENKINS

Page 128-129
4 March 1780
Pr: 20 November 1781

LWT AMBROS BUFORD being in proper health and in my proper sense.

To my dear and beloved wife MARY, all my personal estate to be disposed of as she thinks best for the good of my children while she remains a widow. At her marriage the personal estate to be sold at public vandue (vendue) and the money to be divided in the following manner:

To be equally divided between my wife MARY and my daughter ELISA-BETH and my daughter LUCY.

I do will to my son JOHN all my estate real, viz: the plantation I now live on with all appertenances.

Appoint my wife and JOHN WALLER as executors.

AMBROS BUFORD

Wit: THOMAS WOODS, TAVINOR BIRD BUFORD

JOHN WALLER security for executrix MARY BUFORD.

Page 129-130
18 December 1781
Pr: 15 October 1782

LWT JONATHAN WELDON being sick and weak of body but of perfect sense and memory.

I lend unto my wife MARY WELDON the plantation whereon I now live and the stock of all kind and one bed and furniture during her lifetime.

To my son JONATHAN WELDON, 100 acres at the upper end of my land.

To my son ISACK WELDON, 100 acres joining Jonathan's.

To my son WILLIAM DALE WELDON, 50 acres where I now live, after the decease of my wife, and ten pounds cash.

To my daughter SUSANAH WELDON, one feather bed and furniture.

To my four youngest daughters: ELIZABETH WELDON, SARAH WELDON, MARY WELDON and LIDA WELDON, all my moveable estate that my wife is possessed of at her death with the exception of the ten pounds

47

WELDON will cont'd:

that is to be paid to my son WILLIAM DALE WELDON.

Appoint my wife, with MOSES HANKS and JOHN WALLER executors.

JONATHAN (X) WELDON

Wit: JOHN CREEL, JAMES ADAMS, JOHN (X) POND, FORTAN DODSON

JOHN POND and JAMES ADAMS security for MARY WELDON.

Page 130-131
3 July 1781
Pr: 18 June 1782

LWT MOSES JOHNSON being very sick but of perfect mind and memory

To my son ARTHER JOHNSON one half of my land.

To my son OBEDIAH JOHNSON the other half with the plantation I now live on.

MOSES (X) JOHNSON

Wit: THOMAS BOAZ, HENRY RAWLINGS, CONSTANTINE CLARKSON

Page 131
6 October 1780
Pr: 15 October 1782

LWT SHADRACK FARRAR, a Sholgger (Soldier?) being in health but of perfect mind and memory.

To my brother SETH FARRAR 200 acres and my plantation.

To my Mother, her lifetime support on the plantation.

To my brother RENARD FARRAR a bay horse.

To my sister ELISABETH FARRAR one cow and calf.

To my sister PESELAY FARRAR one cow and calf.

To my Mother one gray mare.

My brother RENARD FARRAR my sole executor.

SHADRACK FARRAR

Wit: JAMES YOUNG, RENARD (X) FARRAR, ANTY (X) YOUNG

JAMES YOUNG security for the executor.

Page 131-133
7 September 1778
Pr: 17 December 1782

LWT EDMUND HODGES being through the abundant mercy and goodness

48

HODGES will cont'd:

of God, well of body and of sound and perfect understanding.

Lend to my loving wife NEPHANY during her life or widowhood my whole estate.

I give to my five sons: JOHN HODGES, THOMAS HODGES, MOSES HODGES, DAVID HODGES and JESSE HODGES, 800 acres of land to be divided amongst them so that my son Thomas to have his land where I now dwell and my son David to have his land taking the place where SAMUEL MOSELEY did settle. If it please God to take me before I clear out the survey adjoining the Pattern land the money to be paid out of my estate for the clearing.

To my sons MOSES and DAVID HODGES, a feather bed and furniture each.

Also to my three sons JOHN, MOSES and DAVID HODGES, a cow and a calf each.

I give my moveable estate to be equally divided between my sons and daughters after the decease of my wife.

Should any child die without an heir, then their part to go to the others.

Appoint my sons JOHN, THOMAS, MOSES, DAVID and JESSE HODGES to be executors.

                    EDMOND (X) HODGES

Wit: NOTON DICKINSON, JOSEPH AKIN, JOHN BUCKLEY

Codicil:

I hereby revoke that part for my daughter SUSANNAH SLAYTON as she is now deceased. I bequeath that part to be equally divided among her six children:
JAMES SLAYTON, RACHEL SLAYTON, PATTSEY SLAYTON, JOHN SLAYTON, EDMUND SLAYTON and ARTHER PORTER SLAYTON.

  11 February 1782

                    EDMUND (X) HODGES

Wit: JOSEPH AKIN, WILLIAM BISWELL, ROBERT HOPPER

NOTON DICKINSON, SAMUEL EMMERSON, ABRAHAM SHELTON and EPAPHRODITUS WHITE as security for JOHN HODGES and THOMAS HODGES.

Page 133-134
12 August 1779
Pr: 21 October 1783

LWT   THOMAS DODSON in good health and perfect and sound memory as common.

To my grandson THOMAS DODSON, son of JOSEPH DODSON, deceased, the sum of one shilling sterling.

49

DODSON will cont'd:

To my son THOMAS DODSON, my whip saw.

To my son GEORGE DODSON, a negro girl Levina.

To my son WILLIAM DODSON, after the death of my wife, the plantation and tract of land whereon I now live.

To my daughter SARAH NEVIL, one shilling.

To my daughter ELIZABETH BENNETT, one shilling.

To ELSE DODSON, one shilling.

To my daughter RHODY CREAL, one shilling.

To my loving wife ELLENOR DODSON all my moveable estate except my still and whip saw, such as horses, cattle, hogs, sheep, all my household and kitchen furniture provided she will give up her Join and what I had with her and if not as much to be sold as will pay her and she have the remainder. Likewise I lend to her the negro woman Vilet during her natural life and afterwards to my son JESSE DODSON.

Also to my son JESSE DODSON my still, it to be valued and he is to pay his brothers and sisters their equal share.

I give to the use of the seperate and regular Baptist to meet in the worship service of the Lord the meeting house near JOHN CREEL mill with the 3 acres of land.

Appoint loving wife ELENOR DODSON and my son GEORGE DODSON executors.

THOMAS DODSON

Wit: DANIEL GARDNER, HEATH GARDNER, SILVANY GARDNER, NATHANIEL GARDNER

RICHARD BROWN and WILLIAM HERRING security for the executors.

Page 135-136
19 May 1783
Pr: 18 November 1783

LWT ROBERT ADAMS much indisposed and weak in body but enjoying my usual reason and memory.

To my son ABSOLOM ADAMS, 100 acres, that is to say all my land lying on the north side of Banister River.

To my son THOMAS ADAMS, my part of a wagon and geers which is now in the possession of my son Absolom.

To my son ELIJAH ADAMS, all my land lying on the south side of the river, it being the land whereon I now live, reserving to my wife MOURNING ADAMS, her lifetime in said land. Also to my son Elijah, a sorrel mare, one feather bed and furniture.

To daughter MILLEY ADAMS, a feather bed and furniture.

50

ADAMS will cont'd:

To my daughter SUCKEY, a feather bed and furniture.

To my grand daughter MOLLY MEAD, 2 cows and calves, 2 ewes and lambs, 6 head of hogs when she comes of age out of my estate.

To my youngest daughter MOLLY ADAMS, a negro boy Peter, feather bed and furniture.

Lend to my well beloved wife MOURNING ADAMS, all my estate not yet mentioned during her life. At her decease the remainder, after paying to MOLLY MEAD her legacy, be equally divided among my three children: ELIJAH, MILLY and SUCKEY. If either of my last mentioned children die without heir, their part to be equally divided between the survivors.

Should the negro left to my daughter MOLLEY ADAMS die before she comes of age, then she is to have an equal part with ELIJAH, MILLEY and SUCKEY. Should she die without an heir, then her part descend to the estate and be equally divided among the three children mentioned, that is to say ELIJAH, MILLEY and SUCKEY ADAMS.

Appoint GEORGE PROSIZE and BURREL VADEN executors.

                    ROBERT (X) ADAMS

Wit: JOHN PARKS, ROBERT WOODING, JOHN SHORT

NATHAN ADAMS and THOMAS HARDY security for MOURNING ADAMS and GEORGE PROSIZE.

Page 136-137
2 January 1784
Pr: 15 March 1784

LWT WILLIAM ATKINS being weak of body but of sound mind and memory.

To my daughter ELISABETH SHOCKLEY one shilling.

To my daughter LIDDY WITCHER one shilling.

To my daughter AGNESS POLLEY one shilling.

To my daughter NANCY WITCHER one shilling.

To my daughter SARAH PARSON one shilling.

To my son OWEN ATKINS a negro girl Milley.

To my son JESSE ATKINS a negro named Hannah, a negro boy named James, a negro Eady, one gray horse, all the household furniture and beds and all the moveable utensils with half of my stock of cattle, hogs and sheep, also all the land on the north side of the creek that my mill is on, with the plantation and buildings.

To my son WILLIAM ATKINS, all the land on the south side of the creek that the mill is on which I possess with my mill and the balance that is not willed to JESSE, also a negro girl Ginney, half of my stock, also a steel plate whipsaw.

ATKINS will cont'd:

WILLIAM (X) ATKINS

Wit: NOTON DICKINSON, ISAAC MARTIN, JOSEPH STANDLEY

THOMAS HODGES and NOTON DICKINSON security for JESSE ATKINS.

Page 137-138
28 October 1783
Pr: 17 February 1784

LWT JOHN DIX being in perfect mind and memory.

To my son LARKIN DIX, one negro Peter.

To my son WILLIAM DIX, all my land that I now possess whereon I now live, together with the Ferrie, not to interrupt nor disturb my beloved wife in any way during her natural life.

Also to my son WILLIAM DIX, a negro Daniel.

To SUSANNA TURNER, two negros, Winney and Baechus.

To SALLY WILKERSON, two negros, Frank and Milley.

To MARTHA PAYNE, two negros, Sall and Rose, and their increase.

To MATILDA FRANCES DIX, two negros, Rachel and Peter.

To HENRIETTA DIX, two negros, Amey and Jane.

To my daughter SUSANNA TURNER, a tract of land in Caswell County, North Carolina, containing 600 acres, the land I purchased from JOHN CHARGILL.

To LARKIN DIX, all of my wearing apparel.

My desire is that my still be sold.

The remainder of my estate of what kind or ever - negros, stock and all other property (clock and boat to be considered as free-hold), I lend unto my wife KERUNHAPPUCK DIX for and during her natural life and at her decease to be equally divided between my daughters:

SUSANNA TURNER, wife of BERRYMAN TURNER; MARTHA PAYNE, wife of WILLIAM PAYNE; SALLY WILKERSON, wife of WILLIAM WILKERSON; MAR-TILDA FRANCES DIX, HENRIETTA DIX.

The entry of land near the seven mile springs in this County I desire to be transferred to my wife and sold by her and the money to be divided amongst my five daughters above mentioned.

Appoint my beloved wife KERENHAPPUCH DIX executrix, and WILLIAM DIX, BERRYMAN TURNER, WILLIAM WILKERSON, executors.

JOHN DIX

Wit: WILLIAM HARRISON, JAMES BURTON

DIX will cont'd:

WILLIAM HARRISON and JOSEPH MORTON security for executors.

Page 139-140
8 December 1783
Pr: 19 April 1784

LWT HENRY TERRY being sick in body but of perfect memory.

Lend unto my beloved wife MARGET TERRY the plantation whereon I
now live with all the stock of every kind, household and kitchen
furniture, and after her death to my son THOMAS TERRY.

To my son BARTON TERRY all the land above the little branch below
his fence.

To my son CHARLES TERRY all my land above the water.

I have given my son HENRY TERRY twenty odd pounds which is all
I alot for him.

I have given my daughter SARAH MC LAUGHLOR and PATIENCE DICKEN-
SON at their marriages, all I alot them.

Appoint BARTON TERRY and THOMAS TERRY my executors.

                          HENRY (X) TERRY

Wit: DAVID TERRY, THOMAS TERRY, DAVID (X) DODSON

DAVID TERRY and RAWLEY WHITE security.

Page 140-141
26 March 1784
Pr: 20 July 1784

LWT RICHARD BROWN being sick in body but sound in mind.

Lend to my dear and well beloved wife SARAH BROWN my whole estate
real and personal during her life or widowhood, and at the end
of that period my will is that all the land I am possessed of,
to be sold and the money arising be equally divided amongst all
my children to wit: MORAH FARGUSON, RICHARD BROWN, SALLY FITZGER-
OLD, JOHN BROWN and NANCY WILLIAMS.

Should any of these die, their part to go to their children.

Appoint STEPHEN COLEMAN and STEPHEN TERRY executors.

                          RICHARD BROWN

Wit: WILL TODD, LEA. (X) BRADLEY, JOHN WIMBISH

ABRAHAM SHELTON, WILLIAM DIX, RICHARD BROWN and JOHN BROWN are
security for STEPHEN COLEMAN.

Page 141-142 (cont'd next page)

24 January 1784
Pr: 10 July 1784

LWT JOSEPH FORTUNE being sick and weak, but being of sound mind and memory.

To my loving wife MARY FORTUNE during her widowhood or life, an equal part of my estate with my children, to wit: ELIZABETH and SARAH. But as my wife is with child, should the child survive to receive an equal part with the rest.

It is my desire that as long as my wife remains a widow to keep the estate in her possession.

The 250 acres in the state of South Carolina that I purchased of LEONARD NOBLES and adjoining that of JAMES HARGROVE, should my executors think it best, sell this and purchase other land for the benefit of the estate. But if my wife think proper, she may go and live upon said land.

A stud horse called Whyne now in the possession of SPENCER REYNOLDS but half mine, should remain with Reynolds until a sale can be made but if Reynolds should want to purchase same, to pay my estate and deduct the expense for upkeep.

Appoint loving wife and SPENCER REYNOLDS executors.

JOSEPH (X) FORTUNE

Wit: GEORGE REYNOLDS, RICHARD REYNOLDS, PHEBE (X) FARRER, WILL. TUNSTALL

JACOB REIGER and DAVID HARRIS security.

Page 142
6 June 1784
Pr: 18 October 1784

LWT JOSEPH BURTON being weak and low in health but of perfect judgement and sound memory.

To my loving wife ANN BURTON, 100 acres whereon is my dwelling plantation during her life and then it is to belong to my son, LEVI BURTON.

To my eldest son WILLIAM BURTON 100 acres next to the cross roads

To my son JOSEPH BURTON the remainder of my tract of land, 100 acres more or less.

Should any of the brothers die before they inherit their land or have an heir, then their part to be divided among the surviving brothers.

To my daughter ANN BURTON a black mare called Silver, a bed and furniture.

After my debts are paid, then my personal estate, taking out one bed which I give to my loving wife ANN BURTON during her natural life, to be equally divided amongst my five children.

54

BURTON will cont'd:

JOSEPH BURTON

Wit: JO. CONN, IGNATIUS WILSON, ROBERT (X) WALKER.

JOSEPH CONN and IGNATIUS WILSON security for ANN BURTON.

Page 143-144
17 June 1782
Pr: 15 November 1784

LWT JOHN SMITH being in sound mind and memory.

To my son DRURY SMITH, the land I bought of JOSEPH MORTON lying on both sides of Crocket Creek, also the land I bought of ADAM STULTS.

To my son THOMAS SMITH, my mill and still with the old survey I bought of JOHN WILSON being 150 acres being on both sides of Sandy River also part of a tract that I and JAMES FULTON was connected in, clearing out in Office.

To my son JOHN SMITH, 400 acres lying on both sides of the Rackon Branch.

To my son JOSEPH SMITH, all the land on the south side of Sandy River, it being part of a tract I bought of DRURY STITH, also 150 acres that joins PATRICK STILTS old place.

To my son EDWARD WASHINGTON SMITH, the plantation whereon I now live, the whole of the plantation being two tracts of land.

To my daughter ANNA SMITH, a negro man Cuffe.

To my daughter ELISABETH SMITH, a negro boy Abe.

To my daughter SARAH SMITH, a negro boy Sam, also 100 acres purchased of JOSEPH CUNNINGHAM on the south side of Sandy River.

To my daughter GINNA SMITH, part of a tract on Rackcoon Branch being part of the same willed to my son JOHN SMITH, but at the upper end.

I give to my daughter GINNA SMITH a tract on the ridge between Puddin Creek and the waters that run into Banister above Capt. JOHN PIGG's.

To my daughter MARTHA SMITH, a tract of land lying on the Pole Bridge Branch, also another tract joining the same and with JOHN MULLER's and JAMES FULTON.

I give and bequeath to my beloved wife a negro man Will during her natural life also a negro man Crow, a negro woman Dyna.

I request my wife to dispose of the livestock amongst her children as equal as possible after all my debts are paid.

Appoint THOMAS BOAZE, JOHN WILSON and MARTHA SMITH as my executors.

(cont'd next page)

SMITH will cont'd:

JOHN SMITH

Wit: JOHN FULTON, THOMAS SMITH, JAMES FULTON

JOHN STOCKTON and THOMAS SMITH security for JOHN WILSON and MAR-
THA SMITH.

Page 144
30 April 1784
Pr: 20 June 1785

LWT MOSES SWENEY am normal at this time in proper health and my
right mind and sense.

To my son JAMES SEMORE SWENEY my land, only his Mother is to have
her third till her decease. With her consent the land should be
sold and she to have her third of the price.

To my wife ANNE SWENEY all my personal estate after all debts are
paid and appoint her my executrix.

At the decease of my wife, all the moveable property to be divided between all my children and JOSIAH MAPPLES.

MOSES SWENEY

Wit: THOMAS LACKEY, CHARLES RIGNEY, JESSE RIGNEY

Page 145
6 October 1784
Pr: 21 February 1785

LWT DAVIS HOLDER weak and sick of body but in perfect sense and
memory.

Appoint loving wife SUSANNA HOLDER and my son DANIEL HOLDER executors.

To my son WILLIAM HOLDER one shilling

To my son JOHN HOLDER one shilling

To my son BENJAMIN HOLDER one shilling

To my son DAVIS HOLDER one shilling

To my son DANIEL HOLDER one shilling

To my daughter HANNAH one shilling

To my daughter ELIZABETH one shilling

To my beloved wife SUSANNA HOLDER during her life the rest of my
estate both real and personal and after her decease the land and
plantation to my son DANIEL HOLDER, and the moveable estate to
my daughter ELIZABETH and my grand daughter LEVINA HOLDER SPRAD-
LING, to be equally divided between them.

HOLDER will cont'd:

DAVIS HOLDER

Wit: MARK HARDIN, WILLIAM WRIGHT

WILLIAM WRIGHT and MARK HARDIN security for executors.

Page 145-147
10 October 1782
Pr: 21 February 1785

LWT JOHN PIGG sick in body but of good and sound memory.

Lend unto my beloved wife ANNE PIGG all my real and personal estate during her life or widowhood except half the Mill which I
lend unto my son HEZEKIAH PIGG during her life, each to attend
with their hands to keep the Mill in good repair.

To my son HEZEKIAH PIGG two negros Joe and Ned, two guns and one
rifle and one smooth bore, my set of silver buckles, shoe, nee
(knee) and stock.

To my daughter KEZIAH HUBBARD two negros Simon and Rose to her
and her heirs, also the land I hold on the north side of Barskin
Creek.

To my daughter EADY OWEN two negros Luce and Nell to her and her
heirs, also the land on the south side of Barskin Creek, except
a piece I give to my son HEZEKIAH PIGG, agreeable to a contract
between us for a piece against the Mill.

To my grandson FIELD ROBERTSON a negro Jack, should he die without an heir to return to my estate.

To my daughter ELIZABETH ROBERTSON two negros Fisher and Ned and
(to) her heirs.

To JESEY ROBERTSON, after the death of my wife, my watch.

After the decease of my wife, all the rest of the estate to be
equally divided amongst all my children.

Appoint ANNE PIGG and HEZEKIAH PIGG executors.

JOHN PIGG

Wit: WILLIAM SHORT, SR., JAMES (X) ALLEN, WILLIAM SHORT

JESSE ROBINSON and WILLIAM OWEN security for executors.

Page 147-148
2 July 1784
Pr: 21 November 1785

LWT HEZEKIAH PIGG weak in body but sound of mind and of perfect
memory.

Lend to my well beloved wife ELISABETH the plantation with 400

57

PIGG will cont'd:

acres adjoining the same whereon I now live, during her widowhood and also negros Jane, Sarah, Big Bett, Little Bett, a black mare and bay colt, a pacing bay horse, all stock and all furniture.

To my eldest son HEZEKIAH PIGG, a horse called the long bay and a new saddle, to dispose of as he pleases.

When he comes of age negro Morrice and his equal part of the land I possess and a bed and furniture.

To my son JOHN PIGG when he comes of age, horse and saddle, bed and furniture, and a negro named Joe and his equal part of the land.

To my daughter ANN PIGG a good horse and saddle, a bed and furniture, and a negro girl Patt.

To my son CLEMMENT PIGG a horse and saddle, a bed and furniture, a negro Abraham, and his equal part of the land.

Should any of the legacies given die before given to the children, then they are to be made equal with the others.

I desire that Easther and Ruth be sold also a gelding and a covering horse also my store goods.

At the death of my wife, all remaining estate to be equally divided among all my children.

Appoint my wife, NICLAS PICK and SILVENAS STOK executors.

HEZEKIAH PIGG

Wit: JOHN BAILEY, WILLIAM PIGG, CATRON TUNBRIDG

WILLIAM PIGG and JOHN CHATTING security for ELIZABETH PIGG.

Page 148-149
4 DEcember 1785
Pr: 19 December 1785

LWT JOSEPH TERRY being of sound and disposing memory and in good health of body.

To my son DAVID TERRY, a negro woman Kate and her issue, which are in his possession, also Sarah and her issue.

Lend to my son THOMAS TERRY negro Peter and Lucy and her issue, also a mulato boy Harry to him during his lifetime then to his heirs.

Lend to my son JOSEPH TERRY a negro man he has in his possession also a negro boy Jack and a girl Grace, during his lifetime then to his heirs.

To my daughter ANNA BARKSDALE a negro woman Zilpha, a mulato girl Anna to her and her heirs. Also a mulatto woman Sarah Martain for the term of 6 years then she is to go free, should she have any

58

TERRY will cont'd:

children they are to belong to my daughter ANNA BARKSDALE and to
her heirs.

Lend to my daughter LUCY WILLIAMS a negro boy Abram during her
natural life, then to her youngest son, DOCTOR CRAWFORD WILLIAMS.

To my grandson THOMAS TERRY, son of DAVID TERRY, a negro girl
Fillis.

To my daughter ELIZABETH OLIVER, twenty shillings.

To my son CHAMPNESS TERRY's heirs, twenty shillings.

I leave 230 acres on the branches of Jermins fork and a negro boy
George to be sold.

Balance of my estate to be equally divided among my three sons:
DAVID TERRY, THOMAS TERRY and JOSEPH TERRY and two daughters: AN-
NA BARKSDALE and LUCY WILLIAMS.

Appoint BEVERLEY BARKSDALE, THOMAS TERRY and DAVID TERRY, executors.

JOSEPH TERRY

Wit: CHARLES TERRY, JOHN TERRY, SAMUEL SLOAN

WILLIAM RYBURN and ISHAM FARMER security for BEVERLEY BARKSDALE.

Page 150-151
12 January 1785
Pr: 19 December 1785

LWT JOSIAS PAYNE being in perfect health, mind and memory.

To my son WILLIAM PAYNE the negros he now has in his possession
and the tract of land whereon he now lives in Fluvanna County,
being 400 acres with the following negros: Long Tom, Squire and
Pat.

I confirm the gift I made to my son JOSIAS PAYNE of 700 acres in
Goochland County on the waters of Beaverdam Creek with the following negros: London, Ned and Rice.

I confirm the gift made to my son GEORGE PAYNE of 200 acres on
Lickinghole Creek also 200 acres on Three Chopt(?) Road with the
following negros: Will, Rose and Jude, and fifty pounds cash in
lieu of a negro.

I confirm the gift to my son JOHN PAYNE of 200 acres on Little
Bird Creek also 400 acres on the fork of the James River and the
following negros: Peter, Ned and Bob.

I confirm the gift made to WILLIAM HEALE who married my daughter
SUSANNA of 365 acres on the waters of Little Bird Creek, with the
following negros: Phillis and her children and Tiller.

To my son ROBERT PAYNE 800 acres on Lickinghole Creek being the

59

PAYNE will cont'd:

plantation and land whereon I formerly lived, and also the negros formerly given him with the following negros: Joe, Nan, Lucy and James, also my still, household furniture and plantation tools.

To my daughter AGNES MICHEL the negros she received at her marriage and the following negros: Jane, Moll and her child Hanah.

I give to my daughter ANNA HARRISON the negros in her possession plus the following: Tom, Harah and his wife and Bon their son.

I give to my grand daughter ANNE, the daughter of my son ROBERT, a negro girl Milley.

To my grand daughter KITURAH, daughter of my son ROBERT, a negro girl Betty.

The rest of the estate to be sold and after debts are paid the money to be equally divided among all my children.

Appoint my sons WILLIAM and ROBERT PAYNE and my son-in-law WILLIAM HARRISON executors.

JOSIAS PAYNE

Wit: JAMES SANDERS, CHARLES DIXON, SA. HOPSON

Will further proved on 18 July 1786 with WILLIAM HARRISON as executor.
WILLIAM OWEN his security.

Page 151-152
7 February 1786
Pr: 19 June 1786

LWT JOHN THOMSON being in perfect strength of memory and mind.

I give my bay mare called Faney to MRS. MILLICENT FARGUSON, SR.

I appoint my friend ROBERT FARGUSON, SR. sole executor.

JOHN THOMSON

Wit: none

WILLIAM TODD security for executor.

Page 152-153
16 June 1784
Pr: 17 April 1786

LWT REDMAN FALLING being weak in body but of sound memory.

To my wife SUSANNAH FALLON, my black horse, a side saddle and a bridle, bed and furniture, and all the pewter I had with her, 2 wheels and cards, 2 cows and calves, one chest, one pale, and one pigon, one tin can.

FALLING (FALLON) will cont'd:

To my son EDMOND FALLON all my land on that side of the creek--
where he now lives.

To my grandson REDMOND FALLON, son of EDMOND FALLON, all my land
and plantation this side of the creek, and the tools.

To my grandson EDMOND FALLON, son of EDMOND FALLON, my bay mare
and he is to pay my daughter HANNAH WHITWORTH, forty shillings.

To my two grand daughters, daughters of EDMOND FALLON, all of my
part of the pewter.

To my daughter ESTER LITTLE, forty shillings in the hands of Edmond Fallon and the box iron.

To my daughter HANNAH WHITWORTH, forty shillings from Edmond Fallon and my big iron pot.

Appoint my wife SUSANNAH FALLON executrix.

I make my loving JAMES MC DONALD overseer of this my will to take
care and see that the same is performed to the true intent and
meaning.

                         REDMOND FALLING

Wit: WILLIAM COLEMAN, GEO. HO. GUIN, DAVID LAY

Page 153-155
6 September 1785
Pr: 20 March 1786

LWT JOHN OWEN in perfect mind and sound memory.

I give to ADAM LEGRAND, SR. of Halifax County the land and plantation where my eldest son WILLIAM OWEN lives, as he had sold the
land to said Legrand of 100 acres more or less.

I give my eldest son WILLIAM OWEN five shillings.

To my daughter LUCY LEGRAND one feather bed and furniture, 2 cows
and calves.

To my daughter AGNES OWEN a bed and furniture and a mare that
came of JAMES FARLEY, 2 cows and calves.

To my youngest son OBEDIAH OWEN, a horse, a saddle and bridle,
a suit of clothes when he becomes 18 years of age, a bed and furniture, two cows and calves at 20 years of age or when he marries.

I give my two sons JOHN OWEN and DAVID OWEN twenty five pounds
each to be paid out of a bond of ABRAM LEGRAND.

My horse Carles, and my still to be sold to pay my debts.

To my beloved wife ELIZABETH OWEN my plantation, horses and the
land that lies above Rock Branch, bed and furniture, negros Sue,
Harry and Fluet, and all stock as long as she remains a widow.

OWEN will con'd:

At her decease my lands on the Dan River to be sold also the land purchased of JOHN PARRIS and THOMAS WILLIAMSON.

I desire that the first money collected be used to buy four young negros.

A boy to my son OBEDIAH OWEN, a girl to my daughter LUCY LEGRAND, a girl to daughter AGNES OWEN and a girl to son OBEDIAH OWEN.

To my sons DAVID OWEN and JOHN OWEN thirty pounds each.

My executor to purchase a womans saddle for my daughter AGNES OW-EN.

The balance to be equally divided amongst my youngest children: JOHN OWEN, DAVID OWEN, OBEDIAH OWEN, LUCY LEGRAND and AGNES OWEN.

Should OBEDIAH OWEN or AGNES OWEN die without an heir, their part to go to the other named children.

Appoint my sons JOHN OWEN, DAVID OWEN and friend GEORGE ADAMS as executors.

                              JOHN OWEN

Wit: SIMON ADAMS, PETER WILSON, JOHN NICHOLS

GEORGE ADAMS and PETER WILSON security for DAVID OWEN.

15 June 1820:

DAVID OWEN the executor has departed this life as well as the widow, ELIZABETH OWEN. GEORGE ADAMS another executor with PETER WILSON and RICHARD JOHNSON entered into bond.

Page 155-156
2 May 1782
Pr: 19 June 1786

LWT JOHN HALL being sick in body but of sound mind and memory.

I give unto my wife JEAN HALL during her widowhood all my horses, cows and household furnishings, and all the farm equipment.

At her decease to be equally divided among all my children after her third.

Lkewise my wife to have the 275 acre tract, whereon I now live during her widowhood.

At the decease of my wife the land is to be equally divided between my two sons, JOSEPH and JOHN.

The entry I bought of ZACHERIAH WALLER to my son GEORGE.

I appoint THOMAS WATERS and THOMAS HILL executors.

HALL will cont'd:

JOHN (X) HALL

Wit: GEORGE (O) ROBERTS, THOMAS HILL, JONATHAN HILL

JONATHAN HILL, JOSEPH HALL and SOLOMON HEAL security for THOMAS
HILL.

Page 156-157
6 September 1786
Pr: 15 January 1787

LWT THOMAS JONES being very sick and weak of body but of perfect
mind and memory.

To my beloved wife MARY, a negro girl Mary to dispose of as she
thinks proper.

All my land to be divided between my beloved son THOMAS and my
son EMANUAL and my daughter MARY and their heirs.

The land to be divided when my son Thomas comes to the age of 21
years. Should my sons and daughter not be able to agree on the
division, the land to be sold with my son Emanuel to choose his
guardian to act for him.

It is my desire that my daughter ANN IVISON DAWSON should have
an equal part of my parcelling estate if her husband, JONATHAN
BROOKS DAWSON replaces the money that he has of mine. The said
money to be returned with interest by the first day of December.
Should he not return the money, my daughter Ann Ivison Dawson,
should have no more of my estate.

Appoint my wife MARY and my son THOMAS and FLAUED TANNER as executors.

THOMAS JONES

Wit: JOHN HAMMOND, ARCHER (X) KATES, CHARLES KEATES

ABRAHAM SHELTON security for MARY JONES and THOMAS B. JONES.

Page 158
12 April 1787
Pr: 16 September 1787

LWT ROBERT CULLOM being weak in body but in perfect noledg and
sense.

I leave my well beloved wife ELISABETH CULLOM and JOHN HARVE as
executors.

I give 100 acres of land to SAMUEL HARVE.

I give 116 acres of land, horses, cattle, sheep, and all household furniture and other possessions to my wife ELISABETH during
her lifetime and then to be equally divided between her children:

63

CULLOM (COLLOM) will cont'd:

SAMUEL HARVE, SARAH HARVE, LENDER HARVE and ELLENDER HARVE.

ROBERT (X) COLLOM

Wit: MATHEW SPARKS, SAMUEL SPARKS, THOMAS SPARKS

Page 159-160
22 December 1783
Pr: 21 February 1785

LWT RICHARD PARSONS being old and weak in body but enjoying my usual reason and memory.

To my well beloved daughter HANNAH MADKIFF and her husband JOSEPH MADKIFF, one shilling.

To my well beloved daughter AGNES MADKIFF and her husband JOHN MADKIFF, one shilling.

To my well beloved son GEORGE PARSONS one shilling.

To my well beloved son JOSEPH PARSONS one shilling.

To my well beloved son JOHN PARSONS one shilling.

To my well beloved son SAMUEL PARSONS the land where he now lives a dividing line to be made by Samuel and my son WILLIAM.

To my well beloved son WILLIAM PARSONS the land whereon he now lives to be divided as above.

The above land is under a mortgage for which Samuel is liable, should he not pay this, the land to be sold and the mortgage paid.

To my well beloved daughter LYDIA YATES and her husband STEPHEN YATES, all my blacksmith tools.

My wife and I are now living with my daughter Lydia and her husband Stephen Yates, and they are treating us with the greatest kindness, it is my desire that they have the remainder of my estate at the decease of myself and my wife.

Appoint my sons JOSEPH and WILLIAM PARSONS executors.

RICHARD (X) PARSONS

Wit: JOHN PARKS, SAMUEL PARKS, RICHARD JOHNSON

Page 160-161
7 October 1780
Pr: 19 September 1785

LWT THOMAS HENDREN being in good health both of body and mind, but about to enter into the Countrys service as a soldier and knowing the uncertainty of life, make this will.

I appoint JOSHUA STONE executor.

HENDREN will cont'd:

I give unto my friend JOSHUA STONE all my goods and chattels, debts and legacys which I am now or hereafter possessed.

THOMAS (X) HENDREN

Wit: JOHN STONE, WILLIAM L. GEFFREYS, DOLLY STONE

Page 161-162
23 September 1787
Pr: 18 February 1788

LWT JOHN FULTON being very weak in body but of sound judgement.

To my son JAMES FULTON land on the north side of the road beginning at THOMAS SMITH's corner.

To my daughter MARGRET twenty pounds and the bed and furniture in her possession.

To my daughter ANN five shillings.

I desire the land whereon I now live to be sold by my executors.

To my daughters ELISABETH and MARTHA twenty pounds each and a bed and furniture.

The rest of my estate, real and personal, to be divided between my six children: JANE SHIELDS, JAMES FULTON, CATHERINE ROBISON, ELISABETH FULTON, MARTHA FULTON and MARGRET BARR.

I appoint JAMES SHELTON and WILLIAM SHIELDS executors.

JOHN FULTON

Wit: ROBERT DEVIN, JAMES ROBISON

JOSEPH MORTON security for executors.

Page 162-163
6 December 1787
Pr: 21 July 1788

LWT WILLIAM NEALE (NEALEY/NELY) being very sick and weak but of perfect mind and memory.

To my beloved daughter MARY REYNOLDS a mare.

To my beloved grandson WILLIAM REYNOLDS all my lands and my tenaments.

To my beloved grandson JOSEPH REYNOLDS all and every other part of my estate.

Appoint JOSEPH REYNOLDS and WILLIAM REYNOLDS executors.

WILLIAM NELY

NEALE (NEALEY-NELY) will cont'd:

Wit: GEORGE SMITH, MICAJAH HUGHS

HUGH REYNOLDS security for executors.

Page 163-164
25 June 1788
Pr: 21 July 1788

LWT LUCY WILLIAMS being in a weak and low condition but of perfect mind and memory.

To my beloved son DAVID CHAMPNES WILLIAMS a negro girl Lettie.

To my six sons: JOSEPH TERRY WILLIAMS, JOHN WILLIAMS, JAMES MAS-
TIN WILLIAMS, THOMAS TERRY WILLIAMS, WILLIAM MASTIN WILLIAMS and
DOCTOR CRAWFORD WILLIAMS the remainder of my estate to be equal-
ly divided between them.

Appoint JAMES MASTIN WILLIAMS and THOMAS TERRY WILLIAMS executors.

                         LUCY WILLIAMS

Wit: JOHN FITZGERALD, DAVID TERRY, JOHN TERRY

JOSEPH TERRY WILLIAMS and THOMAS WILLIAMS security for JAMES M.
WILLIAMS.

Page 164-165
4 September 1787
Pr: 15 September 1788

LWT ARCHIBALD JOHNSTON being weak in body but of sound mind and
memory.

I lend to my dearly beloved wife the land and plantation whereon
I now live with all the money I have in the house at this time
after my debts are paid.

To my daughter SILLER MARTIN a proportionable part with the rest
of my children of my estate.

To my son JAMES JOHNSTON a proportionable part.

To my daughter SALLY the same as above.

To my son WILLIAM JOHNSTON the same as above.

To my son OBEDIAH JOHNSTON the same as above.

To my son SAMUEL JOHNSTON the same as above.

To my daughter MARY JOHNSTON the same as above.

To my daughter ELISABETH JOHNSTON the same as above.

Appoint JOSEPH TERRY and WILLIAM RYBORN executors.

JOHNSTON will cont'd:

ARCHIBALD JOHNSTON

Wit: ABEDNEGO TURNER, T. D. HOLT

ISHAM TURNER security for JOSEPH TERRY.

Page 166-167
30 December 1786
Pr: 21 January 1788

LWT THOMAS VAUGHAN, SR., planter, being in perfect health and
memory.

To my well beloved wife, SARAH VAUGHAN, that is I lend her all
my moveable estate, household goods, during her life or widowhood
and at her decease to be equally divided among my children.

To my son THOMAS VAUGHAN a negro Esther, should she die before
he receives her, to be replaced with negro boy Cob.

I give a negro girl Philice to my children. The negro girl to go
to which child can pay her value to the others. The names of my
sons and daughters are as follows:

THOMAS VAUGHAN, MARY FARRIS, SARAH WILCOX, ELISABETH DAVIS, USLEY
STOTT, JERUSHA FARRIS, RUTH DILLARD and NATHANIEL VAUGHAN.

NATHANIEL VAUGHAN's part is to go to THOMAS VAUGHAN and my grandson JOHN THOMAS VAUGHAN after his decease.

Should Esther live, then Cob to be disposed of in the same manner
as Philice.

To my grandson JOHN THOMAS VAUGHAN a feather bed and furniture.

To son NATHANIEL VAUGHAN a bed and furniture, at his decease to
THOMAS.

The balance of my estate to be divided between my children.

To my daughters ELISABETH DAVIS and JERUSHA FARRIS, forty pounds
each.

To my son WILLIAM VAUGHAN the land whereon he now lives.

The balance of the land to be sold and the money divided between
my grandson JOHN THOMAS VAUGHAN, MARY FARRIS, SARAH WILCOX, ELI-
SABETH DAVIS, USLEY STOTT, JERUSHA FARRIS, RUTH DILLARD and NA-
THANIEL VAUGHAN.

To my son JOHN VAUGHAN five pounds, which he has.

Appoint my son THOMAS VAUGHAN and my wife SARAH VAUGHAN executors.

THOMAS (X) VAUGHAN, SR.

Wit: DANIEL JENKINS, FRANCIS IRBY, JEAN (X) IRBY

JOHN BUCKLEY and EDWARD NUNNELLEE security for THOMAS VAUGHAN.

Page 168
10 October 1789
Pr: 19 April 1790

LWT NEHEMIAH MATHIS, his land to the two boys.

To LUKE 100 acres.

To THOMAS 100 acres.

190 acres left for sale to pay debts.

NEHEMIAH MATHIS

Wit: BETSY MATHIS, JESSE PEEK

Page 168-169
30 August 1787
Pr: 19 May 1788

LWT THOMAS TUNSTALL being infirm in health but of sound mind and memory.

To my daughter REBECCA and her heirs, a negro girl Delphia.

I desire the land whereon I now dwell to be sold, also a tract in Halifax County on Terrible Creek which Mr. JOHN PHILPS is to make title for and after paying my son EDMUND one hundred pounds and my son JOHN seventy five pounds, to make them equal with my son WILLIAM and my daughter REBECCA to whom I have given a negro each.

The balance to be divided among my children:
EDMUND, WILLIAM, JOHN and REBECCA with my slaves and other estate.

Appoint Col. JOHN MARKHAM and my son THOMAS as executors.

T. TUNSTALL

WILLIAM TODD and JOSHUA STONE security for JOHN MARKHAM.

Page 169-173

28 April 1788
Pr: 19 May 1788

LWT JEREMIAH WHITE in a low state of health but of perfect mind and memory.

To my beloved wife JANE WHITE use of my manor plantation during her natural life and enable her to bring up and educate our younger children. Also lend the following negros: Peter, Creecy, Antony, Tom, Phillis, Lucy and Chole.

My wife is also to have the use of all the slavess and personal estate which I shall give in this Will to such of my children that is underage or unmarried at my death. To be given them when

68

WHITE will cont'd:

they come of age or marry.

I give my two sons WILLIAM and JEREMIAH the tract of land on the
south side of Sandy Creek which I purchased of AYRS HODNETT with
another tract containing 325 acres, which I purchased from HUGH
CHARLES being a moiety of land which is to be equally divided between me and the orphans of Mr. CONWAY's for which I obtained a
certificate dated 6 March 1780. What I mean to say is that WILL-
IAM and JEREMIAH each to have one moiety of my part.

Should JEREMIAH die before he comes of age or marries, his part
to go to my son JOHN.

To my son JOHN WHITE, a tract on a fork of Sandy Creek. Should
JOHN die before coming of age or marries, the land to go to my
sons JEREMIAH and WILLIAM.

To my son HAMILTON, all that land that lies between Sweeting Fork
and Col. ROBERT WILLIAMS. Should he die before coming of age or
marries, his part to go to my son ROBERT.

To my son ROBERT my manor plantation, and the remainder of the
land on the north side of the creek that I live on.

I except ten acres with the Mill to be equally divided between
JOHN, HAMILTON and ROBERT.

To my wife, the use of the Mill during her lifetime, but also the
children to have use of the Mill.

To my son-in-law BRAXTON MABRY the negros he has in his possession, 200 acres of land on Horsepen Creek, joining JOSHUA CHAF-
ING in Charlotte County, part of a tract of 400 acres.

I give to WILLIAM CLARK the remainder of the said tract.

The part that would belong to my daughter MARY HARDAWAY, I give
to my grandson PETER HARDAWAY viz:
Pegg and what children she has except a girl Ussey that I lent
to my grandson Peter Hardaway which I desire to go into the residue of my estate to be equally divided among all my children.

To my son-in-law WILLIAM CLARK two negros Adkin and Hall with the
stock and furniture in his possession.

To my son WILLAM WHITE two negros Bob and Stephen and the household goods in his possession.

To my son-in-law JAMES HINTON two negros Isaack and Betty, part
of a tract of land whereon he now lives which I purchased of MARK
HARDEN near Banister River.

To my daughter NANCY WHITE the other part of the tract and also
a tract purchased of WILLAM HOLDER being 87 acres, it being the
plantation where Holder did live. Should Nancy die underage or
unmarried, to my son-in-law JAMES HINTON.

To my son JEREMIAH WHITE, two negros David and York with equal
part of the household goods and stock equal with my other children.

69

WHITE will cont'd:

To my son JOHN WHITE a negro boy George, horse, saddle, bridle, twenty five pounds in cash and household goods.

To my son HAMILTON WHITE a negro boy Len, horse, bridle, saddle, twenty five pounds, and household goods.

To my daughter NANCY WHITE a negro girl Eve and a boy Luis, horse and saddle, bridle, twenty five pounds, an equal share of household goods and stock.

To my son ROBERT negros Winney and Adkin, hors, an equal share of household goods and stock.

It is my desire that John and Hamilton to have one more negro each.

The remainder of my estate not given to be divided amongst all my children at the decease of my wife.

Appoint my wife, sons WILLIAM, JEREMIAH, JOHN and HAMILTON and ROBERT WHITE, WILLAM CLARK and JAMES HINTON executors.

JEREMIAH WHITE

Wit: GEORGE WRIGHT, MICAJAH (X) DODSON, TABITHA (X) DODSON, WILLIAM STRATTON

WILLIAM TODD, JOHN WILSON, JOSHUA STONE and JAMES GALLAWAY security for WILLIAM WHITE, WILLIAM CLARK and JAMES HINTON.

Page 173-174
27 September 1787
Pr: 21 January 1788

LWT JAMES BUCKLEY being sick and weak of body but of perfect and sound memory.

To my well beloved wife MARY and my son JAMES BUCKLEY and JESSE BUCKLEY my whole estate of moveables and land.

That is to say, are to give that they make three equals and be it in consideratioin to my son JOHN BUCKLEY if he will make over the deed of HARRIS' land to my estate. Then I give unto him the place whereon he now lives.

JAMES BUCKLEY

Wit: WILLIAM HENDERSON, JAMES HENDERSON

JOSHUA STONE security for the widow MARY BUCKLEY.

Page 174-175
15 October 1788
Pr: 16 March 1788

LWT JOHN ASHWORTH being weak in body but of perfect and sound

70

ASHWORTH will cont'd:

mind, memory and reason.

To my beloved wife JEAN ASHWORTH, the use of my moveable estate, land and plantation, a negro woman Sarah during her natural life.

To my son NATHANIEL MOORFIELD alias ASHWORTH, a negro boy Woodard but to pay his Mother a fee of five pounds per year as long as she lives.

To my daughter DORCUS TALIAFERRO a negro woman Sarah.

To my son JOHN ASHWORTH alias MOORFIELD six pounds.

At the decease of my wife, the land and moveable estate be sold, then John is to be paid, and this will make him equal with his brother Nathan.

The balance of the monies to be equally divided between my three children: NATHAN MOORFIELD alias ASHFORD, DORCUS TALIAFERRO and JOHN MOORFIELD alias ASHFORD. (N. B. Ashford shown in place of an Ashworth)

Appoint my wife JEAN ASHWORTH executrix.

JOHN ASHWORTH

Wit: SILVANUS STOKES, EDWARD GIVAN, JOHN COUSINS

JOHN MAY and WILLIAM ASTIN security for JEAN ASHWORTH and NATHAN ASHWORTH.

Page 176
4 October 1788
Pr: 19 February 1789

Nuncupative will of JOSEPH STANLEY.

Proved by oath of NATHANIEL ATKINS and JOEL ATKINS before Justice WILLIAM SHORT.

The said JOSEPH STANLEY left his son JOSEPH STANLEY the upper half of his land, livestock and working tools.

To his son ISAAC STANLEY the lower part of his land and his live-stock.

ISAAC STANLEY appointed executor with GEORGE ROBINSON his secur-ity.

Page 176-177
15 December 1789
Pr: 16 August 1790

LWT ORLANDO SMITH being sick and weak in body but in my proper sense.

Lend unto my beloved wife MARTHA SMITH during her life time or

71

SMITH will cont'd:

widowhood the land, plantatioin whereon I now live, with the Mill
being 240 acres to bring up my children in a Christian like manner.

My daughters as long as they remain single to remain a member of
my family.

At the decease of my wife the 240 acres lent to my wife, to go
to my son AMBROSE JOSHUA SMITH.

To my two eldest sons, JESSE SMITH and ORLANDO SMITH, 656 acres
on Sandy Creek to be equally divided.

The land to be valued and an equal proportion to my seven daughters: ELIZABETH, CASSANDER, MARTHA, NAOMY, RHODA, ELENDER and
MARY.

To my son WHITFIELD SMITH, 200 acres I purchased of MARK SHELTON.

Appoint my wife and sons JESSE and ORLANDO SMITH executors.

                              ORLANDO SMITH

Wit: MARK (X) SHELTON, CHARLES CARTER, ROSS J.(?) GIPSON

CHARLES CARTER, ABSALOM ADAMS and GEORGE WRIGHT security for JES-
SE SMITH and MARTHA SMITH.

Page 177-178
26 April 1790
Pr: 16 August 1790

LWT   THOMAS RAMSBE (RAMSEY) being in a low state of health but
of sound memory.

I lend to my beloved wife all the lands whereon I now live with
all the stock, furniture and tools during her natural life time
or widowhood.

At her decease the land to be equally divided amongst my seven
children: CHARITY ADKINSON, THOMAS RAMSEY, SUSANNAH COOK, LEVINA,
ANNY, BETSEY and SALLY.

To my six sons named: GEORGE RAMSBE, WOODSAY RAMSBE, ISAAC RAMS-
BE, JOHN RAMSBE, NOTEN RAMSBE and WILLIAM NEWMAN RAMSBE, a tract
of land in Franklin County on Chestnut Creek joining JOHN WOODS,
being 328 acres.

The land to be divided by Capt. Woods and EDWARD RICHARDS at my
death.

To my son GEORGE a cow and yearling.

To my daughter VINAH a heffer and yearling.

To my daughter ANNY a heffer and calf.

My wife may sell my guns. At her decease the personal estate to
be equally divided among my thirteen children.

RAMSEY (RAMSBE) will cont'd:

THOMAS (T R) RAMSBE

Wit: JOHN REES, WILLIAM WITCHER, JR., MOLLEY WITCHER

THOMAS DYER and HENRY ATKINS security for GEORGE RAMSEY and WOOD-SEY RAMSEY.

Page 178-180
15 January 1789
Pr: 18 May 1789

LWT ARTHUR KEESEE being weak yet of sound and perfect memory and understanding.

Lend to my dear and loving wife TABITHA this house and furniture, the land and tenaments and four negros: Lucy, Moll, Jack and Joe and stock during her life or widowhood, to raise and school my five children that are now with her viz: JESSE STOBALL KEESEE, JEREMIAH KEESEE, PHEBE KEESEE, BENJAMIN KEESEE and GEORGE KEESEE.

At the decease of my wife, the aforementioned to be sold and then equally divided among these five children.

To my daughter BETTY BURTON one shilling.

To my son JOHN KEESEE one shilling.

I desire my plantation on Potters Creek, 267 acres, to be sold to discharge my debts.

Appoint my wife and my two brothers, JEREMIAH KEESEE and JESSE KEESEE executors.

ARTHUR (X) KEESEE

Wit: JAMES (X) DOWNING, GEORGE MARLOW, BRYAN W. NOWLIN, PEYTON NOWLIN.

GEORGE ADAMS security for SAMUEL CALLAND, administrator.

Page 180-182
24 February 1790
Pr: 17 May 1790

LWT CONSTANT PERKINS being very low and weak in body but in perfect mind.

To my beloved wife AGATHA PERKINS the following negros: Leu, Patt and her child Tilda, Bett and her three children, Harry, Rachel and James, to her and her heirs forever, also my household goods and stock except for a mare, colt and a stallion. She is to have the use of the plantation on Dan River whereon I now live during her lifetime.

At her decease to my brother NICHOLAS PERKINS son CONSTANT PER-KINS.

PERKINS will cont'd:

To my brother NICHOLAS PERKINS, my negros: Doll, Arch, Isham, Dinah, Sarah, Velora, Sucke, Silva, Roda, Elijah and Flora.

To my well beloved nephew NICHOLAS PERKINS, son of CHARLES PERKINS, all my lands on the Western Waters that are in partnership with JOHN MARR, NICHOLAS PERKINS & CO. and in particular the 640 acres purchased of WILLIAM ARMSTRONG in Cumberland and the sorrel horse he now has.

It is my desire that my negro man Jacob be set free.

The land I bought of WILLIAM BARKER to be sold to pay my debts.

To GEORGE PERKINS 400 acres being the tract where Old Poor now lives.

I give to RICHARD MARR the land I bought of WILLIAM NORTON and the survey joining it and my half of the land bought of ARMSTRONG the other half being in partnership with the Store.

I give to WILLIAM ATKINS 300 acres on Burchfield's Fork.

Appoint my wife and my brother NICHOLAS PERKINS executors.

CONSTANT PERKINS

Wit: JOS. AKIN, OBEDIAH TUCKER, PETER PERKINS, PETER (X) FERGUS.

Memorandom:

To be annexed to my last will and testament: I appoint my brother JOHN MARR whole and sole manager of all my concerns in my partnership with Galaways and give him one half of my part of that estate. And one fourth of the said estate to my brother-in-law JOSEPH SCALES. The other fourth I give to my brother PETER PERKINS' daughter ELIZABETH PERKINS.

JOSEPH SCALES and SAMUEL LEWIS security for the executors.

Page 182-183
27 June 1788
Pr: 20 July 1789

LWT ABRAHAM SHELTON being in perfect health, sound of mind, and sense and memory.

To my beloved wife CHLOE during her lifetime all that tract of land whereon I now live on Buck Branch with all my plantation utensils, one half my household effects, hogs, half the cattle, three horses, negros: Big Ned, Nat, Lydia and Lilly.

To my daughter LETTIE a negro girl Hannah, a feather bed and furniture.

To my daughter ANN a negro girl Lucy, a feather bed and furniture.

To my daughter JANE a negro girl Siller, a feather bed and furniture.

SHELTON will cont'd:

To my son ABRAHAM, a negro boy Warwick, a feather bed and furniture.

The residue of my estate, both real and personal, to be equally divided between my sons: CRISPEN, WILLIAM, TAVENOR, FREDERICK, MEACON and ROBERTSON.

After the decease of my wife, the residue of my estate to be divided between my children: CRISPIN, WILLIAM, TAVENOR, FREDERICK, MEACON, ROBERTSON and ABRAHAM, and my daughters, LETTICE, ANNE and JANE.

Appoint sons CRISPIN and WILLIAM as executors.

ABRAHAM SHELTON

GABRIEL SHELTON, WILLIAM TODD, ARMISTEAD SHELTON, VINCENT SHELTON, THOMAS TUNSTALL, GRIFFETH DICKINSON, BEVERLY SHELTON, and SPENCER SHELTON as security for the executors.

Page 183-184
27 January 1790
Pr: 17 May 1790

LWT JAMES DIX, SR.

To my son JAMES DIX, my land and negros Lewis and Paul, and two beds and furniture.

To my son THOMAS DIX, negros John and Dixon, and a bed and furniture.

To my son JOHN DIX, negros Jacob and Jane.

To my son TANDY DIX, twelve shillings, and no more unless he will come in and pay his debts and then his brothers and sisters are to make up one hundred pounds out of their share.

All my moveable estate, not before given, be divided between the following children: JAMES, JOHN, WILLIAM and THOMAS DIX.

To WILLIAM DIX, ELIZABETH GATEWOOD, SARAH WILLIAMS, and MARY WILSON, negros: Baccas, Sam, Sarah, Suf, Delsa, Chloe, Roger and Milla. There is to be no division till next Christmas.

Appoint JAMES DIX, ROBERT PAYNE and DUDLEY GATEWOOD executors.

JAMES DIX

Wit: BENJAMIN LANKFORD, WILLIAM DIX, THOMAS FEARN, JOHN PAYNE.

Page 185-186
10 February 1790
Pr: 19 July 1790

LWT RICHARD WALDEN in perfect health.

WALDEN will cont'd:

To my well beloved wife CANDACE, the house and plantation where I now live during her widowhood and negros: Cupit, Lucy and Hannah, beds and furniture. Also cattle.

To my son CHARLES WALDEN, the land where I now live and negro: Cupit; a desk, bed and furniture and a mare.

To my son JOHN, the lower tract of land where he formerly fived and negro Robin.

To my son RICHARD, land in Campbell County on Stanton River, a table and negro Burnett.

My cross cut saw and carpenter tools to sons RICHARD and CHARLES.

To my daughter LUCY HUDSON, negros Judah and Jenny.

To my daughter MARY WHITWORTH, negro Winney and a bed and furniture.

To my daughter MILLEY, negro Dinah and her daughter Dinah, a bed and furniture, chest, table, chairs and a trunk.

To my daughter MOURNING WALDEN, a negro Betty and her daughter Sarah, a bed and furniture, chest, chairs, table and a trunk.

To my daughter FANNY BOBITT, a negro Hannah, a bed and furniture, and at her mothers death, her equal part.

My son RICHARD's negro to be given up at years end after my death. Also JOHN WALDEN, LUCY HUDSON and MARY WHITWORTH's.

Should either of my daughters MILLEY or MOURNING die without issue, the negro Betty to return to my son RICHARD, and her daughter Sarah to go to CANDICE BARBER.

If my daugher MILLEY die without issue, negro Dinah to go to LUCY HUDSON and negro Dinah, Jr. to my grand daughter MILLEY WHITWORTH.

To my daughters MILLEY and MOURNING, 6 head of cattle each.

To my daughter ELIZABETH BALLARD, a cow and a calf.

To my wife CANDACE, my wagon, horses and gears and at her decease the horses to be divided between my three sons: JOHN, RICHARD and CHARLES.

Appoint my sons RICHARD and CHARLES WALDEN executors.

RICHARD (X) WALDEN

Wit: RALPH SMITH, BOWKER SMITH

WILLIAM WARD and BOWKER SMITH security for executors.

Page 187
5 May 1789
Pr: 19 July 1790 (cont'd next page)

LWT JOSHUA WELSH being sick but of perfect understanding and memory.

To my beloved wife JAMINIA (WELCH) my land whereon I now live
during her lifetime and at her decease to be equally divided between all my children.

The residue of my whole estate to be divided between my children.

Appoint wife executrix of my estate.

JOSHUA WELSH

Wit: JAMES HUTCHINGS, JOHN MIERS, LISHE (X) NUCKLES

JAMES HUTCHINGS security for <u>JAMIMA</u> <u>WELSH</u>.

Page 188-189
28 March 1788
Pr: 17 May 1790

LWT WILLIAM CHICK being in a declining state of health.

To my two sons HARDIN and ANDERSON CHICK the tract of land whereon I now live.

To my beloved wife SUSANNAH during her natrual life or widowhood
my negro James, one third of household goods and livestock. At
her decease to my sons HARDIN and ANDERSON.

There are debts due me and when collected to be equally divided
between my sons: WILLIAM, RICHARD, HARDIN and ANDERSON.

To my grandson DUDLEY CHICK, forty shillings to school him, to
be paid by my son HAR<u>DEN</u> CHICK.

Appoint my wife and sons WILLIAM and HARDEN CHICK executors.

WILLIAM CHICK

Wit: BEN LANKFORD, JOHN WEST

SUSANNAH CHICK came into Court and claims her third. Susannah
Chick and ANDERSON CHICK are security for HARDEN CHICK.

Page 190
7 February 1797
Pr: 20 February 1797

LWT JOHN GRANT being sick and weak but in perfect mind and memory.

It is my desire that my land whereon I now live be sold in order
to pay my debts and the balance of the money to my beloved wife
ANNE during her lifetime.

At the decease of my wife, my estate to be sold and the monies
divided amongst my five children: JAMES GRANT, SARAH GRANT, WIL-
LIAM GRANT, ELIZABETH GRANT and MARY GRANT.

GRANT will cont'd:

Appoint my wife ANNE GRANT executrix and JOSHUA STONE executor.

JOHN GRANT

Wit: ZAS. LEWIS, FRANCIS IRBY, JENCEY IRBY

DAVID HUNT security for JOSHUA STONE.

Page 191-192
28 July 1790
Pr: 16 January 1797

LWT   THOMAS HAMPTON in health and sound and perfect understanding.

I give to my dear and loving wife, for the term of her life, one third of the tract of land whereon I now live, with all the furniture and livestock and negros, on the condition she does not marry. After her decease to be distributed in the following manner:

To my son HENRY HAMPTON a tract of land in North Carolina, Surry County, where he now lives, being 646 acres.

I give to my son JAMES HAMPTON a negro boy Bob and half the tract of land whereon I now live to be divided between him and my son JOHN HAMPTON being 195 acres.

To my son JAMES HAMPTON my riding horse, a mare, a gun and one fifth of all my stock.

To my son PRESTON HAMPTON 100 acres of land whereon he now lives to him and his heirs or any one he chooses except his wife ELIZABETH HAMPTON, also a gun and one fifth part of my stock.

To my son JOHN HAMPTON a negro Dick, my still, a feather bed, a horse, all the household lumber and a negro woman Sue, which is to be equally divided between him and his brother JAMES, 1/5 part of my stock, also one more feather bed.

The residue of the beds and furniture not given left to my wife to dispose of.

To my son-in-law and daughter, JAMES and MARGARET F. COLQUET, 100 acres whereon they now live, a negro Hannah to my daughter Margaret. Should Hannah breed and have children, the first to go to Margaret and the second to NANCY's oldest son THOMAS H. YOUNG. The third child to JAMES HAMPTON's second son JOHN HAMPTON. The fourth living child to go to HENRY HAMPTON's oldest son THOMAS HAMPTON and heirs for want of such to his next eldest brother if want of heirs to the third daughter HANNAH HAMPTON.

At the decease of MARGARET the negro Hannah and her increase not given to her sister NANCY YOUNG.

To my daughter NANCY YOUNG a negro boy Daniel and after her death to THOMAS HAMPTON YOUNG.

Also to MARGARET one roan mare and her colt to NANCY YOUNG.

78

HAMPTON will cont'd:

Appoint my wife SARAH HAMPTON and my sons PRESTON and JOHN HAMP-
TON executors.

                    THOMAS HAMPTON

Wit: JESSE BARNES, NICHOLAS SCALES, THOMAS PERKINS

GEORGE HANKINS, WILLIAM M. NANI---, SAMUEL MC GUFFORD security
for executors.

Page 193
25 January 1793
Pr: 19 June 1797

LWT NATHANIEL HENDRICK in perfect health, sound mind and memory.

To my beloved wife PRISCILLA HENDRICK during her life all my estate both real and personal.

After her decease I give unto my daughter MARY CRADOCK a negro
fellow Stephen.

To my son EZEKIEL HENDRICK, after the decease of his mother, a
negro wench Phaney, a negro girl Rachel, all the upper part of
my land from the Mill Stone Branch up Buffalo Creek.

To my daughter SARAH DEWS(?) a negro girl Betty and an equal part
of the land not given away.

And the other part of my land to my daughter MARY CRADDOCK after
the death of her mother. Also to have the plantation I now live
on, a bed and furniture, other furniture, stock and also a leather trunk.

To my son EZEKIEL, after the death of my wife, a desk, bed and
furniture and stock.

To my daughter SARAH DEWS a cubbard, chest, bed and furniture and
other furniture, and stock.

Appoint my wife executrix.

                    NATHANIEL HENDRICK

Wit: BEN LANKFORD, KITTY (X) LANKFORD, HAMILTON LANKFORD, STEPHEN
LANKFORD.

CORNELIUS MC HANEY and EZEKIEL HENDRICK security for executrix.

Page 194-195
15 July 1797
Pr: 21 August 1797

LWT DAVID OWEN being very sick and weak of body but in perfect
memory.

To my well beloved wife PEGGY OWEN the land and plantation whereon I live being 258 acres during her life or widowhood.

OWEN will cont'd:

At her decease, to be divided between my son, JOHN OWEN and my daughter, PEGGY OWEN equally, also a negro man Ben and a woman Amilia, two mares and cattle.

To my son DAVID OWEN, a tract purchased of WILLIAM OWEN on Banister River and a horse.

I desire my negros George and Sook to be sold with the rest of my personal estate except the beds, furniture, 7 head of sheep, all stock of hogs, which goes to my wife during her life time.

After my debts are paid, the balance of any money to be divided between my three children: DAVID, JOHN and PEGGY, as they come of age.

Also two thirds of the money arising from the sale of the land on Dan River, whereon my Mother now lives, to be for the three children.

To my brother OBEDIAH OWEN, one half of the land joining where my Mother lives.

Appoint SAMUEL FRENCH and GEORGE ADAMS executors.

                              DAVID (X) OWEN

Wit: DAVID RICE, JOHN (X) NELSON

WILLIAM WARE and SAMUEL MC GUFFORD security for executors.

Page 195-196
2 October 1797
Pr: 16 October 1797

LWT THOMAS CUNNINGHAM weak in body but of perfect and sound understanding.

To my daughter JENNY CUNNINGHAM a mare, saddle and bed.

To my daughter ELEANOR CUNNINGHAM a cow and calf and bed.

To my children: ISABEL CUNNINGHAM, JOSEPH CUNNINGHAM, WILLIAM CUNNINGHAM, ELIZABETH CUNNINGHAM and PEGGY BURNET and MARTHY GRESHAM one dollar each.

To my son EPHRAIM CUNNINGHAM after all my debts are paid whole of my real estate being the tract of land I now live on also the remainder of my personal estate.

EPHRAIM is to look after my youngest son THOMAS CUNNINGHAM who is incapacitated.

Appoint my son EPHRAIM and GILBERT BURNETT executors.

                              THOMAS CUNNINGHAM

Wit: JOHN SHIELDS, ROBERT MACK, JOHN PAIN, JOHN JEFFERYS.

JOHN SHIELDS and LEBAN GRESHAM security for executors.

Page 196
25 May 1796
Pr: 16 October 1797

LWT HENRY HARDIN, being sick and weak but of perfect mind and memory.

To my grandson JIMMY HARDIN, son of ARAILLAH WRIGHT the land and plantation whereon I now live being 232 acres.

I lend to my wife JUDITH HARDIN half of all my moveable estate during her lifetime.

At her decease to my grandson JIMMY HARDIN, the son of AVARILLAH WRIGHT.

As to my children: MARY TALIFERO, MARK HARDIN, WILLIAM HARDIN, ELIZABETH WILSON, JUDITH BURGESS, MARTIN HARDIN, HENRY HARDIN, AVARILLAH WRIGHT and SARAH BUCKHALTER, I give each of them two shillings and six pence.

To my grandson HENRY HARDIN, son of WILLIAM HARDIN, my survey on the waters of New River.

Appoint my wife JUDITH HARDIN executrix with my son MARTIN HARDIN and JIMMY HARDIN executors.

HENRY HARDIN

Wit: CHARLES CARTER, JOHN WRIGHT, WILLIAM BURGESS

CHARLES CARTER security for MARTIN HARDIN.

Page 196-197
18 May 1797
Pr: 16 October 1797

LWT STEPHEN TERRY being sick and weak but of sound mind and disposing memory.

To my dear and well beloved wife SARAH TERRY, three negros: Ben, Will and Hannah, the mansion house and plantation lying on Banister River below the cart way, also the tract I purchased of ARCHIBALD CAMPBELL, two horses, all the stock, furniture and the plantation tools for and during her natural life.

After the decease of my wife, to go to my son NATHANIEL TERRY, the house and plantation.

And to my son JAMES TERRY the land I purchased of ARCHIBALD CAMPBELL with negros Will and Hannah, a horse and saddle, bed and furniture.

The remainder of what I have given to my wife, after her decease, to be equally divided between my daughters: RHODA TERRY, ELIZABETH FUQUA TERRY and ANNE TERRY.

To my son WILLIAM TERRY all that part of my land on north side of Banister River, a negro Charles, a horse, saddle, a bed and furniture and my chest.

TERRY will cont'd:

To my daughter RHODA TERRY a negro girl Charity, my sorrel horse, a bed and furniture, a cow and calf.

To my son JOHN TERRY all that part of my land above the cart way, a negro Bob, a horse, saddle, bed and furniture.

To my son NATHANIEL TERRY a negro boy Reubin, horse, saddle, bed and furniture.

To my daughter ELIZABETH FUQUA TERRY a negro boy Ned, horse, saddle, bed and furniture.

To my daughter ANNE TERRY a negro girl Jude, horse and saddle, bed and furniture.

Appoint my wife guardian for all my children.

Appoint my wife and STEPHEN COLEMAN executors.

STEPHEN (X) TERRY

Wit: JOHN JENKINS, JOSHUA STONE, JR.

JOSEPH TERRY and JOSHUA STONE security for SARAH TERRY.

Page 198
7 August 1797
Pr: 16 October 1797

LWT THOMAS GRESHAM being in my ordinary sense tho weak in body.

To my son LABAN GRESHAM the tract of land where I now live.

To my daughter SALLY a feather bed, cow and calf.

To the rest of my children one dollar each.

The balance of my estate is for my wife to dispose of at her own pleasure.

My son LABAN is to afford his Mother a decent, comfortable maintainence during her natural lifetime.

THOMAS (X) GRESHAM

Wit: JOHN MARK, JR., GILBERT BURNETT, JOHN SHIELDS, SAMUEL STRONG and THOMAS GARRETT.

Page 198
26 September 1797
Pr: 15 January 1798

LWT BASIL HAWKER being at present sick and very weak but still remaining in a proper mind and memory.

I lend to my beloved wife 85 acres of land whereon I now live, the livestock, and furniture during her natural life. I lend her

HAWKER will cont'd:

all my worldly estate.

At her decease, I give and bequeath to my son REUBIN HAWKER all the estate.

Appoint my wife MARY HAWKER and ZACHARIAH BEELL(?) executors.

BASIL HAWKER

Wit: LOYD SAMPSON(?), JONAS EARP, ELIZABETH BEELL(?)

JACKSON WALTERS and GEORGE COOK security for executors.

Page 199
4 January 1798
Pr: 16 April 1798

LWT JAMES CONWAY being sick and weak of body but of sound mind.

To my brother CHRISTOPHER CONWAY, negro Kize and her girl child Peg, also all the debts owed me.

I desire that he pay all my debts out of that money. Also all of cloath(?) I give unto him.

I give DANIEL SLAYDEN my saddle and to his daughter ANNA SLAYDEN my mare and bridle.

I appoint my brother CHRISTOPHER CONWAY and ROBERT WALLERS executors.

JAMES CONWAY

Wit: R. WALLERS, WILLIAM (X) SLAYDEN, S. SLAYDEN, JOHN SLAYDEN

THOMAS B. JONES and WILLIAM SHELTON security for the executor.

Page 199-200
30 October 1797
Pr: 16 April 1798

LWT WILLIAM BURGESS being sick and very weak of body but of perfect mind and memory.

To my dearly and well beloved wife JANE BURGESS, 50 acre tract in my plantation adjoining my present dwelling house during her natrual life.

To my beloved son PENDLETON, a mare colt, chesnut sorrel which he is not to sell until he becomes 21 years of age.

To my beloved son HARRISON a horse at age 21.

My lands to my four sons: JOHN, WILLIAM, HARRISON and PENDLETON, to be equallydivided after my youngest child is of age, that is to each 50 acres and likewise other property divided amongst my daughters that are now unmarried.

BURGESS will cont'd:

Appoint friend WILLIAM BECK executor.

It is my desire that my son JOHN come and live on the plantation until my family is raised and of age.

WILLIAM (X) BURGESS

Wit: STEPHEN WATKINS, WILLIAM CUNNINGHAM, FREDERICK UHLS

JOHN BURGESS and STEPHEN WATKINS security for JANE BURGESS.

Page 200-201
21 April 1798
Pr: 18 June 1798

LWT SILVANUS STOKES being weak in body but sound of mind, memory and reason.

To my son ALLEN STOKES all my land on the south side of White Oak Creek, also a negro man Cyrus with the stock and household furniture he has in his possession.

To my son SILVANUS STOKES all my land on the south side of White Oak Creek from the mouth of Camp Branch to the mouth of ALLEN STOKES spring branch, a negro man Bradock, also items he has in his possession.

To my sons ALLEN STOKES and SILVANUS STOKES, all my land between the north and middle fork of White Oak Creek.

To my son JOEL ALLEN STOKES all the land and plantation whereon I now live, a negro Peter and Celis and other items he already received.
It is my desire that JOEL STOKES return from Kentucky and settle this land and take care of his Mother during her lifetime and at her decease have the full enjoyment of the whole.

To my daughter SUSANAH MAY fifty pounds.

To my daughter ELIZABETH ALLEN NEAL fifty pounds.

To my daughter SALLY WALKER DUPUY fifty pounds.

To my wife SARAH STOKES the use of my plantation and all that is on it during her lifetime or widowhood, with the following negros: Cate, Bob, Tom, Jack, Abram, Martin, Lucy, Nancy, Cloe, Lucey, Fanney, Anraca, Dinah, Juno, Hannah and Diley.

All my estate not heretofore given to my three above named daughters, be and remain in the possession of them.

The balance that remains after the decease of my wife, be equally divided among all my sons and daughters.

Appoint my sons ALLEN STOKES and SILVANUS STOKES executors.

SILVANUS STOKES

Wit: CHRISTOPHER ROBERTSON, JOSEPH ROGERS, JAMES SAYERS, JEDUTHUN

84

STOKES will cont'd:

CARTER.

WILLIAM BEAVERS, JAMES SAYERS and WILLIAM ASTIN security for the executors.

Page 202-203
17 November 1790
Pr: 18 April 1791

LWT THOMAS EDWARDS sick and weak in body but of sound memory.

To my son EDMUND EDWARDS five shillings.

To JAMES EDWARDS the land whereon he now lives, 150 acres more or less.

To JOHN EDWARDS five shillings.

To THOMAS EDWARDS fifty pounds in property.

To NATHAN EDWARDS fifty pounds in property.

To WILLIAM EDWARDS fifty pounds in property, and a bay mare.

To my daughter MARTHA SAMS, a negro girl Jane now in her possession.

To my daughter ELIZABETH LANSFORD five shillings.

To my daughter HANNAH SCROGGINS a negro girl Easter in her possession.

To my daughter MARY BRITTAIN a negro girl Hannah in her possession.

I lend the residue of my estate to my beloved wife LUCY EDWARDS during her natural life or widowhood.

At her death all the negros with a debt due me from JOHN MARR, (being the land I sold him on Smith River where he now lives), to be equally divided between my six sons and ELIZABETH LANSFORD my daughter and the balance of my estate to be divided between my other three daughters, above named.

Appoint my wife and son JAMES EDWARDS and HENRY LANSFORD, executors.

THOMAS EDWARDS

Wit: CLEMENT NANCE, MARY (X) NANCE, ANN (X) DURHAM, ISHAM LANSFORD, THOMAS HARRIS.

SILVANUS STOKES and JOEL CLARK security for executors.

Page 203
10 November 1789
Pr: 6 July 1790

85

LWT JOHN MARRICK being very sick and weak of body but of perfect mind and memory.

To my well beloved son WILLIAM MARRICK, the choice of my three tracts of land.

To my well beloved son HENRY MARRICK the second choice.

The third tract with my personal property to be sold and the money to be equally divided between my five daughters: ELIZABETH, ELLENDER, IMMALIA, RACHEL and SUSANNAH, except my wearing clothes and a bay mare which I give to my son WILLIAM.

Appoint my sons HENRY and WILLIAM MARRICK executors.

                                    JOHN MARRICK

Wit: THOS. JENKINS, WILLIAM (X) WATSON, JOHN VANJEW(?)

At a Court for Chester County, South Carolina was ordered to be recorded.
6 July 1790

At a Court for Pittsylvania County, Virginia on 21 March 1791, the will of JOHN MARRICK presented with GEORGE DAVIS and HEZEKIAH SMITH security for the executors.

Page 204-205
22 September 1797
Pr: 17 September 1798

LWT STEPHEN COLEMAN being sick and weak in body but sound of mind and disposing memory.

To my son DANIEL COLEMAN the land where he is now settled.

To my beloved wife SARAH COLEMAN during her natural life, my land and plantation and the mansion house where I now live with fifteen negros: Hercules, Bransley, Sam, Dick, Sal, Winney, Cloe, Clary, Lucy, Silvey, Janney, Jonney, Liddey, Nat and Leviney, all household furniture, stock, my still except what I shall hereafter name. After her decease the same be divided in the manner and form following:

To my son STEPHEN COLEMAN my land and plantation whereon I now live.

The remaining part I lent my wife divided among my eight children and the heirs of my daughter ANNEY TOWNES, deceased, allowing my daughter ELIZABETH MC DANIEL one ninth part.

To son STEPHEN COLEMAN one ninth part.

To daughter PATSY TURNER one ninth part.

To my son DANIEL COLEMAN one ninth part.

To my daughter LUCY PRICE one ninth part.

To my daughter JUDITH TURNER one ninth part.

COLEMAN will cont'd:

To my daughter POLLY COLEMAN one ninth part.

To my son STEPHEN COLEMAN one ninth part.

To the heirs of my daughter ANNY TOWNERS one ninth part.

To my son THOMPSON COLEMAN all my interest in the state of Kentucky.

To my son STEPHEN COLEMAN two negros: Tom and Ambrose, a bay colt and a bed and furniture.

Appoint my wife and son DANIEL COLEMAN executors.

STEPHEN COLEMAN

Wit: ISHAM FARMER, JAMES WELCH, HENRY STEPHENS.

STOKLEY TURNER, WILLIAM PRICE, WILLIAM GLASCOCK, ISHAM FARMER(?) security for the executors.

Page 205-206
5 May 1798
Pr: 21 January 1799

LWT OBEDIAH ECHOLS being sound of mind and memory.

I direct my executor to purchase a valuable negro man with part of the money due me from THOMAS B. MC ROBERT payable the 25th of December 1799 and lay out one hundred twenty five pounds to purchase a tract of land that my wife LUCY A. ECHOLS may choose.

I lend unto my wife the land the negro above mentioned, three horses, bed and furniture, half my livestock, plantation tools, my ox cart and twenty six pounds due me from my son JAMES ECHOLS. This during her lifetime.

At the death of my wife, what I have lent her to be divided between my three children: PHILLIP J. ECHOLS, SAMUEL B. ECHOLS and POLLY C. ECHOLS.

If MRS. ELIZABETH JACKSON, the mother of my wife, should depart this life before my death, the negros I should be entitled to under the Will of Mr. CLAYBORN LAWSON be disposed of as follows: To HENRY A. JONES and EDWARD D. JONES, sons of my said wife, negros Sophia and Brandon.

I lend to my wife during her lifetime the rest of my negros, then to my three children: PHILLIP J. ECHOLS, SAMUEL B. ECHOLS and POLLY C. ECHOLS.

To my son OBEDIAH ECHOLS a mare.

To my daughter BETSY ECHOLS a bed and furniture and one fourth part of the cattle.

To my daughter NANCY ECHOLS a bed and furniture, a horse, saddle and bridle worth eighty pounds, to be purchased of the hire of my negros which are in Georgia.

ECHOLS will cont'd:

To my son ELIJAH ECHOLS a gun and one fourth part of my cattle.

To my son BENJAMIN ECHOLS five shillings, he has already received his part.

The following negros: Archer, Phillis, Mary, Lester, Tabby, Silvia, Critey and Minor which I gave my five children: JAMES ECHOLS, OBEDIAH ECHOLS, NANCY ECHOLS, ELIJAH ECHOLS and BETSY ECHOLS by Deed of Gift to be hired out until Elijah becomes of age.

The residue of my estate to be sold.

Appoint my wife, brother JOSEPH ECHOLS, MATHEW BATES and EDMUND FITZGERALD executors.

OBEDIAH ECHOLS

Wit: THO. H. WOODING, THO.B. MC ROBERT.

MATHEW BATES and EDMUND FITZGERALD refuse to take the executorship and on the motion of WILLIAM RANEY who has intermarried with the widow of said Obediah Echols, with MARTIN FARMER and PEYTON FARMER his security entered into Bond.

Page 207
(No date)
Pr: 21 January 1799

LWT MOSES HURT sick in body but in perfect memory.

To my beloved wife ELIZABETH HURT all that I possess during her lifetime or widowhood.

To my son WEST DANDRIDGE HURT a negro named Daniel and one shilling.

To my beloved son GARLAND HURT a negro named Aaron.

To my beloved son MOSES HURT a negro boy Isaac alias Peet.

To my beloved son ABSALOM HURT a negro girl Agnes.

I desire that my land, four feather beds, a negro named Amey, furniture, and stock to be sold and equally divided between my four daughters: ANN SHELTON, JANE HENDRICK, SALLY L. HURT and RODEY S. HURT.

Appoint GARLAND HURT, MOSES HURT and BENJAMIN SHELTON executors.

MOSES HURT

Wit: EDMUND TAYLOR, WILLIAM BOULDING, JANE ALEXANDER.

Page 208
6 May 1786
Pr: 18 February 1799

LWT AMBROSE NELSON being of sound mind and memory.

NELSON will cont'd:

To my son BAZEL NELSON two shillings six pence.

To my daughter BARSHABA RICKETS two shillings six pence.

To my son JAMES NELSON the land and plantation whereon I now live with all my stock, all household furniture, after paying my son WILLIAM NELSON fifteen pounds.

I appoint BAZEL NELSON and WILLIAM RICKETS executors.

AMBRUS NELSON

Wit: SILLV. STOKES, WARE STOKES, ALLEN STOKES.

ALLEN STOKES and JOSEPH RICHARDS security for the executors.

Page 208-209
27 February 1798
Pr: 15 April 1799

LWT BENJAMIN BURNETT in perfect health.

I give to my wife FRANCES BURNETT during her lifetime or widow-hood, all my estate both real and personal.

At the death of my wife, my estate as follows:

To my three sons EDWARD, JEREMIAH and THOMAS, a tract adjoining this, equally divided.

To my son JOHN, the land where I now live, all of this side of Right's branch.

The other piece of land on Sailers Creek to be sold, my debtss to be paid out of this and the balance to be equally divided between my two daughters SALLY and POLLY.

I give my son THOMAS his choice of a horse.

To my two sons and two daughters SALLY and POLLY, JEREMIAH and THOMAS my stock.

To my daughter ELZY a bed.

To my daughter POLLY a bed.

To my daughter SALLY a bed.

The judgement I have against DUNN to be divided between all my children only JOHN and JEREMIAH I give five pounds more than the rest.

I give my son GODSSEY one shilling.

I give my son BURNETT BURNETT one shilling.

To my son BENJAMIN one shilling.

Appoint my wife and my son JOHN BURNETT executors.

BURNETT will cont'd:

BENJAMIN BURNETT

Wit: ABRAHAM (X) MARTIN, JOHN (X) MARTIN.

Page 209-210
14 February 1799
Pr: 15 April 1799

LWT JOHN GILES being sick in body but of sound mind.

To my beloved wife JANE I gill all my estate real and personal during her lifetime.

At her decease all my land whereon I now live except 100 acres which I sold my son JOHN and was paid, to my son WILLIAM GILES. The lines to John's land were marked off by JOHN HUTCHINSON and WILLIAM GILES and fully described to WALTER LAMB. Also to my son WILLIAM, a mare, bed, and a negro girl Amey.

To my son EPHRAM GILES a negro girl Nancy, a bed and sixty pounds.

To my son GEORGE GILES a negro girl Tell on his paying my sons JOHN and JAMES twenty pounds each.

To my four daughters: ELIZABETH RIDDLE, PATSEY SHORT, SUSANNAH RIDDLE and REBECCA VARDEN(?) a negro woman Lucy to be of equal benefit, but I do not desire her to be sold out of the family.

What is left after the death of my wife, to be equally divided between my four daughters.

I want my grandson PHILO GILES, son of my daughter PATSEY SHORT, to be given a good education, board and kept in decent clothing until manhood.

Appoint my sons JOHN and WILLIAM as executors.

JOHN (X) GILES

Wit: WALTER LAMB, CATY LAMB, EDWARD CARTER.

WALTER LAMB and ABRAHAM PARRISH security for the executors.

Page 210-211
19 December 1798
Pr: 17 June 1799

LWT JAMES GEORGE being very sick and weak in body but of perfect mind and memory.

To my beloved daughter MARY HENDERSON 350 acres which joins BARBER's, PARKER's and THURMAN's lines on Ceder branch. At the decease of my wife, I give to said MARY HENDERSON a negro girl Rose.

To my beloved son JAMES JORDON GEORGE 300 acres land on the Wolf branch.

To my beloved daughter FRANCES HASKINS 300 acres.

GEORGE will cont'd:

To my beloved son HUGH GEORGE the plantation on Camp branch also a negro man Holiday at the decease of my wife.

To my beloved wife ELIZABETH GEORGE during her lifetime the place whereon we now live with the balance of land joining. After her decease I give the land and premises to my son HUGH.

I also lend to my wife my livestock, horses and five slaves: Goliah, Holiday, Luce, Rose and Annekey. At her decease Goliah, Luc and Annekey to my daughter FRANCES HASKINS and JAMES J. GEORGE.

At my wife's decease the personal property to be divided among my four children.

JAMES GEORGE

Wit: NATHAN THURMAN, SR., NATHAN THURMAN, JR., JOSEPH (X) BYBEE.

NATHAN THURMAN, SR. & JR. security for ELIZABETH GEORGE and HUGH GEORGE.

Page 211-212
8 April 1789
Pr: 17 June 1799

LWT WILLIAM TOLER in perfect health, mind and memory.

To my son JOSEPH TOLER, the negros: Daniel, Stephen, Hannah, Nan, Dick and Sarah, a bed, the whole of my stock.

I desire that my son JOSEPH pay to my daughter FRANCIS DIX twenty five pounds and to my daughter LUCY BOWLS twenty five pounds to be paid to wit: five pounds a year for five years.

JOSEPH is to pay my son JAMES(?) TOLER's widow and his five children as follows: to the widow nine pounds, to his daughter NANCY nine pounds when she becomes 18, to his daughter MOLLY, also nine pounds at age 18, and nine pounds to each of his sons: BARNABAS, JOHN and CORNELIUS when they arrive at 21 years.

Appoint Col. JAMES CALLAWAY and my son JOSEPH TOLER executors.

WILLIAM (X) TOLER

Wit: THOS. LEFTWICH, JOSEPH ROBINSON, WILLIAM TOWLER, JR.

THOMAS LEFTWICH security for JOSEPH TOLER.

Page 212-214
8 March 1789
Pr: 17 June 1799

LWT FLOYD TANNER in reasonable health and sound memory and perfectly in my senses.

Should my dear and well beloved wife SALLY TANNER bring forth a child within nine months of my death either a son or daughter, all my estate be equally divided between my wife and her child.

TANNER will cont'd:

Should my wife not have a child, I give her the following negros:
Will, Borwon, Jacob, Jesse, Burwel, Peter, Salle, Siller, Silpah
and Lydia plus one thousand dollars cash which is due me from
STEPHEN NEAL, JR., all my stock, household furniture to my wife
and her heirs forever.

To my nephew FLOYD TANNER, son of my brother THOMAS TANNER, all
my tract of land which I purchased of MARTIN FARMER being 55 ac.
more or less, four negros: Charity, Millia, Cyrus and Agnes and
one thousand dollars which is due from STEPHEN NEAL, JR.

My crop of tobacco to be sold to pay my just debts, and should
there be a surplus, this is to be used to educate my nephew FLOYD
TANNER.

Appoint my wife and brother THOMAS TANNER executors.

                              FLOYD TANNER

DAVID MOTLEY, SILVANUS STOKES, SAMUEL MOTLEY and JOHN ADAMS, JR.
for the executors.

(No witnesses shown).

Page 214-215
13 April 1799
Pr: 17 June 1799

LWT JAMES BLEAKLEY, SR. being in a low state of health but of
sound mind and disposing memory.

To my beloved wife REBECCA BLEAKLEY one third part of all my estate during her lifetime.

To my son JOHN BLEAKLEY twenty shillings over and above what he
has received.

To my daughter LUCY MORTON twenty shillings.

To my daughter MARY LOGAN twenty shillings.

To my son JAMES BLEAKLEY twenty shillings.

To my son CHARLES BLEAKLEY twenty one pounds being the price of
a horse I give him, but when paid I made use of the money and also give him twenty shillings.

To my daughter REBECCA WARD twenty pounds.

To my grandson GEORGE WARD ten pounds to school him.

To my son THOMAS BLEAKLEY 100 acres to be taken off the tract I
now live on on Big Strawberry Creek.

To my son BENJAMIN BLEAKLEY a bed and furniture, two thirds part
of all my land not before given.

After the death of my wife, her part of the land is to be included in the gift to Benjamin.

BLEAKLEY will cont'd:

If there is any left after the above gifts, to be equally divided
between all my children.

Appoint my beloved son JAMES BLEAKLEY and my friend ROBERT DEVIN
executors.

                                      JAMES (X) BLEAKLEY

Wit: ROBERT FINLEY, PH. THOMAS, WILLIAM DEVIN, SR., and WILLIAM
DEVIN, JR.

JOHN SMITH and JOSEPH DEVIN security for the executors.

Page 215
8 April 1798
Pr: 17 September 1798

LWT ROBERT FERGUSON in a very low state of health of body but
of sound mind and memory.

To my well beloved wife MILICENT FERGUSON the land and plantation
whereon I now live during her natural life.

At her decease the land to be sold and the money to be divided
equally between my grandsons: WILLIAM GREGORY, TUNSTALL GREGORY,
JOHN GREGORY and ISAAC GREGORY, sons of ISAAC GREGORY, and DONALD
MC NEAL FERGUSON, son of my daughter ELIZABETH GREGORY.

To my wife MILICENT FERGUSON all the rest of my estate to be disposed of as she judges necessary.

Appoint WALTER LAMB and JOHN GREGORY executors.

                                      ROBERT (X) FERGUSON

Wit: JOHN JENKINS, JESSE ROLLEN, NATHANIEL TUNSTALL.

WILLIAM SMITH and EDMUND TUNSTALL security for the executors.

Page 216
19 June 1798
Pr: 17 June 1799

LWT THOMAS MORTAN (MARTIN) being sick and weak but of perfect
mind and memory.

To my wife LUCY (LUCEY) MORTON five pounds.

To my children bound out to LEONARD DOVE that is: MILLY MARTON,
STYTH MARTON, WINNEY MORTON, LEANNER MARTON and JOHN MARTON. I
desire that Milley, Winney and Leanner should be bound out until
18 years of age and that Styth and John to be bound out till 21
years of age.

LEONARD DOVE to have my estate to raise my children until they
come of age, then the children to have the estate.

Dove is to collect what is owed me and to pay my just debts.

MORTAN (MARTON) (MARTAN) will cont'd:

Wit: ELISHA (X) CUNDIFF, JOHN TRASHER

THOMAS SAMPSON and WILLIAM SAUNDERS security for LEONARD DOVE.

Page 216-218
4 June 1790
Pr: 20 June 1791

LWT WILLIAM DAVIS far advanced in life though of perfect mind and memory.

To my son JOHN DAVIS three head of cattle.

To my son BENJAMIN DAVIS 150 acres including my mansion house and plantation which begins on the south side of Great Cherrystone Creek and my negro man James.

To my son JOSEPH DAVIS 150 acres joining his brother Benjamin's lines, to include Booth's cabin.

To my son THOMAS DAVIS the remaining part of my tract except one acre on the south side which joins ROBERT WOODING and JOHN PARKS.

I lend to my daughter NANCY RICKET a negro girl Dafney, should Nancy have no heirs to her husband WILLIAM RICKET.

To my daughter PEGGY DAVIS a negro girl Queen, a boy Abraham, and my stock of geese.

To my son-in-law WILLIAM CORBIN a negro boy Harry, a feather bed in consideration of due him from me on my brothers account.

To my son-in-law THOMAS MAIDE(?) the money he owes me on a bond.

To my sons JOSEPH and THOMAS DAVIS my grist mill with one acre of land and that part of my land contigeous thereto.

The remainder of my estate both real and personal to my three youngest children: JOSEPH DAVIS, THOMAS DAVIS and LUCY DAVIS.

My son BENJAMIN shall rebuild my mill and in consideration he is to keep possession of the mill and my working slaves for three years and the end of that period of time to have the mill in good repair and return the slaves to my children as my will directs.

My daughters to have the use of my little room as long as they remain single.

To my son-in-law GEORGE MIRES nothing more of my estate than already given.

To my son-in-law DANIEL BRADLEY nothing more than already given.

My executors to sell what is necessary of my crops to pay DANIEL BRADLEY what is owed by me for my brothers estate deducting seven pounds for a feather bed in his possession.

Appoint my son BENJAMIN DAVIS executor.

DAVIS will cont'd:

WILLIAM (X) DAVIS

Wit: THOS. H. WOODING, WILLIAM MIERS, JACOB MIERS, GEORGE MIERS, JR.

Page 218-219
2 May 1798
Pr: 16 September 1799

LWT WILLIAM HERRING being in perfect health, sense and memory.

To my well beloved wife MARY, three negros: Phill, Hanner and Sarah, a bed and furniture.

To ODORICK FARMER, a negro boy Moses in his possession.

To my son LANGFORD HERRING, five shillings plus what I have given him.

To my daughter IRMIN FARMER, the negro man Adden in her possession.

To my son ARMSTEAD HERRING, negros Kyer and Peg, 200 acres whereon he now lives.

To my son JOHN HERRING, 229 acres joining ARMSTEAD, forty pounds cash, and the negro girl Alie he has.

To my son WILLIAM HERRING, 225 acres on the lower end of where I live, two negros Ritter and Joe.

To my daughter POLLEY WEST HERRING, twonegros Winney and Orange.

To my son WASHINGTON HERRING, 225 acres which is the upper part of my tract, two negros Dave and Pat.

My stock I desire to be equally divided between my four children: JOHN, WILLIAM, POLLY WEST and WASHINGTON.

The negros not given are to remain with the rest of my estate for the support and schooling of my youngest children. When WASHINGTON becomes of age, these negros to be equally divided between my daughter IRMIN and my daughter POLLEY WEST and my sons ARMISTEAD, JOHN, WILLIAM and WASHINGTON which I give them.

Appoint my friend BEVERLEY BARKSDALE and my son JOHN executors.

WILLIAM HERRING

Wit: GIDEON RAGLAND, HENRY FORD, JARREL FORD, MICAJAH CREEL.

GIDEON RAGLAND, HENRY FORD and THOMAS CHELTON security for BEVERLEY BARKSDALE.

Page 219-220
2 May 1795
Pr: 16 September 1799

LWT LAZARUS DODSON being weak and infirm but of perfect mind and memory.

To my well beloved wife ALIE (ALICE?) DODSON a negro woman called Young Lucy and a negro Marjory, the use of my house and plantation, as much of my household furniture as she desires during her lifetime.

To my son GEORGE DODSON my land and plantation after the death of his Mother.

To my daughter MARGARET DODSON a bed and furniture, a flax wheel, mare and saddle which is called hers.

I give the remainder of my personal estate equally, between my seven children: ELISHA DODSON, GEORGE DODSON, ELISABETH INGRAM, RACHEL MADING, RHODA DODSON, TABITHIA DODSON and MARGARET DODSON.

Appoint my son GEORGE DODSON executor.

LAZARUS (X) DODSON

Wit: GEORGE DODSON, ROBERT (X) MADING, LARKIN INGRAM.

GEORGE DODSON, ROBERT CLOPTON and ROBERT MADDING security for the executor.

Page 220-221
7 December 1797
Pr: 15 July 1799

LWT HUGH KELLY being sick and weak of body but in perfect memory and sound judgement.

To my grand daughter ELIZABETH KELLY a bed and furniture, iron pot, two hooks, dutch oven and a walnut chest.

To my grand daughter VESHE(?) KELLY a bed and furniture, and a chest.

To my grandson PATRICK KELLY twenty pounds.

To my four grand daughters NISHE(?) KELLY, ELIZABETH KELLY, MARY KELLY and LEAH KELLY, twenty pounds each to be raised from the sale of my negro boy Moses.

I leave the residue of my estate to my five grandchildren above mentioned.

Appoint my son HUGH KELLY and CUTBERT HUDSON my executors.

HUGH (X) KELLY

Wit: ARMSTEAD HERRING, MARTIN (X) HARDIN, BOLIN (X) KERBY.

Page 221-222
19 January 1797
Pr: 21 October 1799

LWT JAMES RICHARDSON, SR. being sick in body but of perfect mind

96

RICHARDSON, SR. will cont'd:

and memory.

I give my negro woman Moll her freedom at the expiration of ten years after my death and her children when they reach 25 years of age.

To my loving wife MARY RICHARDSON the use of all my estate during her widowhood upon her paying my son BENJAMIN and the child she is now pregnant with such amount that would make them equal with my four oldest children: WILLIAM, JAMES, LUCY and HENRY who have received money from the VAIDINGS and MORRIS estates.

Should my wife marry to have one third part of my estate during her natural life then to my children.

At her marriage two thirds of the personal estate be sold and the same rented out and the money divided between my children.

At the death of my wife, all lands and personal property to be sold and the money be divided equally between all my children.

I desire that my children be schooled and when my executors think proper my sons to be bound out to some trade.

Appoint my brother WILLIAM RICHARDSON and JOSEPH DODSON executors.

                                        JAMES RICHARDSON

Wit: DANIEL S. FARLEY, THOMAS (X) FERBISH, JESSE RICHARDSON, ELI-JAH HENDRICK.

GARDNER MAYS, THOMAS SHELTON and BENNETT SHELTON security for JO-SEPH DODSON.

Notation on this side states:................. (This will is void by reason of a will of the said JAMES RICHARDSON subsequent .... being proved and recorded on page 225", signed WILL. TUNSTALL)

Page 222-224
13 January 1799
Pr: 21 October 1799

LWT SAMUEL HARRIS being sound of mind.

Request the minister to deliver a solemn discourse from 2nd Timothy chapter 4 verses 7 and 8.

My lands including the plantation lately occupied by my son SAMUEL and at present by my son BENJAMIN with all the lands and the houses I possess to be divided into three parts. This to my sons: NATHANIEL, BENJAMIN and SAMUEL.

Five of my negros: Hannibal, Pompey, Old Bob, Jenny and York are to be set free if they choose.

All my personal estate and that I have lent to my children is to be considered as loans, except the increase of a negro lent my daughter MARY BUCKLEY.

HARRIS will cont'd:

To MARY twenty dollars worth of clothing .

The balance to be divided in five parts to my son NATHANIEL, son BENJAMIN, daughter ELIZABETH PERKINS, one part to my Executor for my son SAMUEL, to daughter MARY BUCKLEY as long as she is in need.

Appoint my sons NATHANIEL and BENJAMIN executors.

SAMUEL HARRIS

Wit: GEORGE SUTHERLAND, JR., ALLEN STOKES, THOMAS PISTOLE, SR., JAMES MC DONALD.

WILLIAM WILKINSON, ABIA CHEATHAM, WILLIAM PAYNE, GEORGE SUTHERLAND, JR. security for executor.

Page 224-225
10 May 1790
Pr: 19 November 1799

LWT THOMAS ELLIOT being of sound mind and memory.

To my loving wife ELIZABETH ELLIOT a horse, hunting saddle and bridle, a cow and calf, 4 head of sheep, a sow and ten head of hogs, all the household furniture.

My wife is to have the use of my plantation during her widowhood.

To my son JAMES ELLIOT one pound five shillings.

To my son SIMON ELLIOT all my land, should he die without issue, then to my brother JAMES ELLIOT's sons THOMAS and WILLIAM.

To my brother JAMES ELLIOT my great coat, a blue waistcoat, pair of leather britches.

The residue of my personal estate to be sold with the money to be kept by my executor until my son SIMON comes of age.

I will my son SIMON ELLIOT fifteen pounds to be kept for him.

Appoint WILLIAM SUMMERS, CHRISTOPHER and ALLEN STOKES executors.

THOMAS ELLIOT

Wit: BENJAMIN (X) WILLIAMS, ANN (X) WILLIAMS.

ALLEN STOKES refused to take executorship. ELIZABETH the widow and relict married JOSHUA GRAY, failed to give security. On the motion of MOSES HUTCHINGS and JAMES SAYARS to serve as executors with Allen Stokes their security.

Page 225-226
21 September 1797
Pr: 16 December 1799

LWT JAMES RICHARDSON, SR. being sick in body but of perfect mind and memory.

RICHARDSON will cont'd:

I give my negro woman Milly her freedom at the beginning of the year 1807 and her children to have their freedom when they reach 25 years of age.

To my loving wife MARY RICHARDSON the use of my land and planta- tion during her widowhood with all my personal estate. Should she marry, she is to have the use of one third of my estate during her lifetime.

At her decease to revert to my children: WILLIAM, JAMES, LUCY, HENRY, BENJAMIN and ROBERT.

The land I purchased of ROBERT SCOTT and JACOB GOLDSTON be rented during my wife's lifetime, but not planted in corn every year and as much money paid my four eldest children from Vaiden's Morris' estate make my two youngest children equal.

The two thirds be divided among all my children should my wife marry.

At the death of my wife, the land be valued and divided between my sons: WILLIAM, JAMES, HENRY, BENJAMIN and ROBERT and the per- sonal estate sold to pay LUCY, my daughter, to make her equal.

I desire my children to have schooling and be bound out to learn a trade.

Appoint my brother WILLIAM RICHARDSON, and JOSEPH DODSON as exe- cutors.

                              JAMES RICHARDSON

Wit: PETER (X) SMITH, THOMAS (X) FURBISH.

HENRY COOK and WILLIAM RICHARDSON security for JOSEPH DODSON.

Page 226-227
15 October 1799
Pr: 16 December 1799

LWT GEORGE THOMAS being sick in body but of perfect mind and of memory.

To my brother JOHN THOMAS a piece of land joining CHARLES LEWIS and SAMUEL HOPSON.

All the rest of my land to be divided between my brothers: ASA THOMAS and PEYTON THOMAS and they are to have the rest of my es- tate.

Appoint ASA and PEYTON THOMAS my executors.

                              GEORGE (X) THOMAS

Wit: DANIEL S. FARLEY, JOHN (X) BROCK, SARAH THOMAS, PHILIP COCKS

Page 227-228
26 February 1800
Pr: 21 April 1800 (cont'd next page)

LWT WILLIAM DIX being in perfect mind and memory.

To my daughter PHEBY BOOKER HILL wife of ISAAC HILL my land on
the south side of Hanses Creek provided my son-in-law claims no
more of the property in the Deed of Gift made to his wife. Should
he, then the land to my two youngest sons: JOHN M. DIX and KEREN-
HAPPUCH DIX.

To my son JOHN M. DIX that part of the land on the north side of
Hanses Creek including the mill and ferry landings.

To my daughter KERENHAPPUCH DIX the balance of my river tract of
land also my land on Sandy River.

Lend to my wife my personal estate also lend her the land I have
given to my two youngest children. The children are to be schooled in a decent and genteel manner.

The land purchased of HUMPHREY HENDRICK and my land in Cumberland
to be sold.

Appoint my wife, ISAAC HILL, LARKIN DIX, DUDLEY GATEWOOD and SIM-
ON ADAMS executors.

                              WILLIAM (X) DIX

Wit: SIMON ADAMS, WILLIAM WRIGHT, WILLIAM PAYNE, JOHN GILFOY.

17 May 1802, THOMAS BARNETT with BENJAMIN HARRIS his security,
becomes administrator.

Page 228
7 April 1800
Pr: 16 June 1800

LWT JOHN COX in perfect memory and reasonable health.

To my daughter UNITY NELSON, the land whereon she and JOSHUA NEL-
SON now live during her life, not to be sold by her husband.

Should she outlive her husband, she may dispose of the property,
but should she die first, then to my children.

To my daughter PRUDENCE COX the land whereon I now live.

To my daughter CHARITY COX the land whereon ISRAEL CURRY now resides.

The rest of my estate to my daughters PRUDENCE and CHARITY.

                              JOHN (X) COX

Wit: GILBERT BURNETT, JOHN (X) JEFFRES

GILBERT BURNETT and LABAN GRESHAM security for JAMES COX.

Page 229-230
2 April 1800
Pr: 21 July 1800
(cont'd next page)

LWT WILLIAM BUTCHER, SR. being in perfect mind and memory.

Lend to my beloved wife JANE BUTCHER the land whereon I now live, all my stock, furniture during her natural life or widowhood except what is given to my young children:

To my son GEORGE a horse, saddle, and bridle of equal value to his older brothers that is of age: JAMES, JOHN, WILLIAM BUTCHER.

My son ISAAC to have the same.

To my daughter LIDDA BUTCHER a bed and furniture a cow and calf, when she comes of age or marries.

To my daughter ELIZABETH BUTCHER the same.

To my daughter POLLY BUTCHER the same.

To daughters CASSEY MURPHEY and PHEBE DAVIS - they have received their part.

To my youngest son BENJAMIN my dwelling house, 150 acres at the decease of my wife.

Two bonds are due from me to WILLIAM HOPWOOD, to be paid.

After the death of my wife, the personal property to be divided between all my children.

Appoint my wife JANE BUTCHER and son JOHN BUTCHER executors.

                                        WILLIAM BUTCHER

Wit: WILLIAM CLARK, WILLIAM WILLIAMS, JOHN NEAL, SAMUEL GOODMAN.

JAMES BUTCHER and JAMES MURPHY security for the executors.

Page 230-231
31 August 1800
Pr: 15 December 1800

Nuncupative will of JOHN MADDING.....

We, MARY MADDING and MARGARET DODSON certify that JOHN MADDING on his death bed stated that he did not want the will he had formerly lodged in the possession of GEORGE DODSON proved. That he desired that his youngest son SCARLET MADDING have 150 acres including the house they lived in, and that his wife SARAH MADDING should have her living.

The balance of his land divided among his other five sons: LARKIN MADDING, THOMAS MADDING, JOHN MADDING, JOEL MADDING and ABSALOM MADDING.

Desires his daughter NANCY DODSON to have a cow, and his other property divided among his daughters.

ROBERT MADDING and JONAS WALLER security for LARKIN MADDING.

Page 231-232 (cont'd next page)

21 November 1800
Pr: 16 February 1801

LWT LEONARD WILLIAMS being in a low state of health but of sound mind.

To my beloved brother BENNETT WILLIAMS my land on Dix branch in Warren County, North Carolina, 107 acres it being the tract left me by my father FRANCIS WILLIAMS, a negro Jim, the money owed me by JAMES BURGESS, twenty six pounds, JOHN GUNN twenty five pounds both of Warren. Also that part of the estate left me by my father in the possession of my mother MARGET WILLIAMS.

Appoint my brother BENNETT WILLIAMS and my uncle PERMINAS WILL-IAMS executors.

LEONARD WILLIAMS

Wit: JAMES WILLIAMS, THOMAS WORTHAM, ROWLAND THORNTON.

THOMAS WORTHAM, DRURY PULLIAM and HALCOTT TOWNES security for the executor.

Page 232-233
2 March 1795
Pr: 16 February 1801

LWT WILLIAM WILLIAMS being in a low state of health but in my perfect senses.

To my beloved wife CONSTANT WILLIAMS my land where I live, the stock and household furniture.

At her decease to be divided as follows:

To my son WILLIAM WILLIAMS one shilling.

To my son RICHARD WILLIAMS one shilling.

To my son LEVY WILLIAMS one shilling.

To my son GEORGE WILLIAMS one shilling.

To my son STEVEN WILLIAMS one shilling.

To my daughter ELISABETH SPURLIN one shilling.

To my daughter ANN SEBASTAN one shilling.

To my daughter SARAH ROE one shilling.

The above mentioned estate I give to my daughter ALSE WILLIAMS, JUDITH WILLIAMS, CONSTANT WILLIAMS and my step-daughter ANN BAL-LENGER equally divided.

WILLIAM (X) WILLIAMS

Wit: NATHAN (X) FRIZZEL, WILLIAM (X) ELIOT, CHARLES BLAKLEY.

Page 233-234
26 September 1800 (cont'd next page)

Pr: 20 April 1801

LWT WILLIAM GLASCOCK being sick and weak of body but of sound
mind.

Apoint my beloved wife ELIZABETH GLASCOCK and brother-in-law JO-
SEPH SANFORD of Halifax County executors.

To my beloved wife one third part of my estate both real and personal during her natural life.

To my daughter CHLOE GLASCOCK my part of a tract on Polecat Creek
in Halifax County being 500 acres to be divided between me and
my brother GEORGE GLASCOCK.

I give my beloved friend JOHN JENKINS, minister of the gospel,
50 acres on Squirrel Creek, joining STEPHEN NEAL, SR., with the
dwelling house for his lifetime and no longer.

To my three sons: THOMAS, JOHN and HIRAM GLASCOCK, all the lands
not given and when those given return to the estate, to be theirs.

My personal estate divided between: THOMAS, JOHN, HIRAM and CHLOE
GLASCOCK.

                                        WILLIAM GLASCOCK

Wit: GEORGE GLASCOCK, SUSANNA SANDFORD, JOSHUA (X) BAYS.

JAMES LYNN, EDMUND TUNSTALL, JOEL CLARK, GEORGE BOYD and BEVERLY
WHITE security for the executors.

Page 234
4 April 1800
Pr: 15 June 1801

LWT SAMUEL HOPSON

To my loving wife ELIZABETH all the land I possess and half of
my negros and half of the rest of my personal property, to her
forever to dispose of as she thinks proper.

The balance of my estate to my daughter MILDRED.

                                        SAMUEL HOPSON

Wit: SAMUEL DABNEY, JOHN LEWIS

ROBERT LEWIS and JOHN LEWIS security for ELIZABETH HOPSON.

Page 235
23 December 1795
Pr: 20 July 1801

LWT JOHN FITZPATRICK

To my son JOHN FITZPATRICK my tract of land in Charlotte County
on Cub Creek being 475 acres more or less.

To my son WILLIAM FITZPATRICK my tract of land in Campbell County

FITZPATRICK will cont'd:

on Molley Creek, being 700 acres more or less and a negro fellow
Pompey.

To my son DAVID FITZPATRICK the tract of land where I now live
being 700 acres more or less, and after the death of his mother,
the negro boys George and James, a feather bed and furniture, a
desk, bookcase. The negro boy when he arrives at age 21.

My tract of land in Campbell County called the Buzzard Mountain,
276 acres to be sold and the monies divided amongst all my children.

Tomy beloved wife BAHATHALUND FITZPATRICK the tract of land where
I now live and all the personal estate thereon during her natural
life, except such as previously willed and at her decease to be
equally divided among all my children or their heirs.

Appoint sons JOHN and EDMUND FITZPATRICK executors.

                                        JOHN (X) FITZPATRICK

Wit: NAT. LUCK, JOSEPH (X) PEMBERTON, CORNELIUS MC LANEY(?), JOHN
PEMBERTON.

DAVID PANNILL and CORNELIUS MC HANEY security for executors.

Page 236
15 April 1801
Pr: 21 September 1801

LWT JOHN THOMAS being in a low state of health but of sound mind
and memory.

All my worldly estate to be sold and the monies divided between
JOHN THOMAS, son of PHILLIP THOMAS, WILLIAM THOMAS, son of NATHAN-
IEL THOMAS, deceased, NATHANIEL P. THOMAS, son of NATHANIEL THOM-
AS, deceased.

Appoint DURRETT RICHARD and ASA THOMAS executors.

                                        JOHN THOMAS

Wit:JOHN ROGERS, SHADRACK TAYLOR, WILLIAM FUQUA

THOMAS FEARN, CLEMENT MC DANIEL, BENJAMIN HARRIS and JOSEPH JOHNS
security for executors.

Page 237-238
11 January 1800
Pr: 24 September 1801

LWT JACOB CHANEY very sick and weak but in perfect mind and memory.

To my well beloved wife SARAH CHANEY my land and plantation where
I now live, my household furniture, stock of all kinds, except
that which is called MARY's and SARAH's, during her natural life-

CHANEY will cont'd:

time.

I have heretofore given to my son JAMES CHANEY, deceased, all I intended him and his heirs, and want it to remain with his heirs.

I hve already given all I intended to my son EZEKIEL CHANEY.

I have heretofore given my son ISAAH CHANEY now deceased, all I intended.

I have heretofore given to my son JACOB CHANEY all I intended.

Same to my son JOSEPH CHANEY.

Same to my son ABRAHAM CHANEY.

Same to my son NATHAN CHANEY.

Same to my son JOHN CHANEY.

Same to my son MOSES CHANEY.

To my son CHARLES CHANEY my land and plantatioin, 175 acres more or less, after the death of his mother.

I have given all I intended to my daughter ELIZABETH DAVIS.

After the death of my wife, what is left is to be divided between daughters MARY CHANEY and SARAH CHANEY.

To HEATH GARDNER a small tract of land now in his possession, 10 acres on the south side of Birches Creek.

Appoint JOSEPH and CHARLES CHANEY executors.

                                   JACOB (X) CHANEY

Wit: GEORGE DODSON, DAVID DODSON, THOMAS MIDKIFF, THOMAS GREEN.

Page 239
25 April 1801
Pr: 16 November 1801

LWT PETER WILSON being sick and weak but of sound mind and dis-posing memory.

I desire the perishable part of my estate and negro Sary to be sold immediately.

To my wife SARAH WILSON my estate both real and personal during her natural life to raise and maintain my children and to educate them.

Should either of my children marry before the decease of my wife, let them have one or two negros as she thinks fit, a bed and fur-niture and some stock.

At the death of my wife, to my children: ELLIS WILSON, JOHN WIL-SON, GILES WILSON, NANCY WILSON, PETER WILSON, BETSY WILSON, WIL-

105

WILSON will cont'd:

LIAM WILSON and MEAD WILSON, all the negros, stock, and furniture. Also the land to be sold and money divided among the within named children then surviving.

Appoint beloved wife and friend GEORGE ADAMS executors.

PETER WILSON

Wit: JOHN WILSON, ELISABETH (X) ASTIN, MILLEY (X) GWIN, SAMUEL BATES, WILLIAM BATES.

JOHN WILSON, JEREMIAH WHITE and DAVID RICE security for executors

Page 240
(No date shown)
(No date shown)

LWT SAMUEL PRUETT being weak of body but of sound mind and perfect memory.

To my son PHILIP PRUETT five shillings, besides what he has already received.

To my son ZACHARIAH PRUETT 100 acres whereon he now lives.

To my daughter RUTH COOK, five shillings plus what she already has.

To my son SAMUEL PRUETT 100 acres that he sold.

To my daughter ELIZABETH BUTT a cow and calf.

To my son BENJAMIN PRUETT a gray horse.

To my daughter POLLY HAWKES a heffer besides what she has already received.

Lend to my daughter SALLY PRUETT during her natural life or as long as she is single, the land where the orchard is, to ATKERSON's line, to the old field.

Also to SALLY a mare and colt, cows, furniture and hogs.

To my son JOSEPH PRUETT 192 acres whereon I now live, a cow and calf.

To my daughter SALLY, all the household furniture, the balance of my cattle to be equally divided between my daughters: RUTH COOK, ELIZABETH BUTT, POLLEY HOCKKER, SALLY PRUETT.

SAMUEL PRUETT

Wit: GEORGE SPRATL(?), WILLIAM STAMPS, POLLEY STAMPS.

Page 241
5 June 1797
Pr: 18 January 1802
(cont'd next page)

LWT ELIZABETH OLIVER being in good health and sound mind.

To my son WILLIAM OLIVER a negro man Peter.

To my grandson JOHN OLIVER, son of DREWREY OLIVER, a negro man named Bob.

To my grandson WILLIAM OLIVER, son of DREWREY OLIVER, the negro boys Will and Sam.

To my grand daughter MARYAN OLIVER, a negro woman Sarah, should she die without issue, then to my son WILLIAM.

Appoint friends WILLIAM OLIVER and EDWARD NUNNELEE executors.

ELIZABETH (X) OLIVER

Wit: WILLIAM CROSS, DRURY OLIVER, MARY (X) CROSS.

Page 242
22 October 1794
Pr: 19 April 1802

LWT JOHN WATSON being in perfect health and mind.

To my beloved son WILLIAM WATSON my dwelling plantation and all the land thereto belonging, the moveable estate also and to be my executor.

To my son THOMAS WATSON, son JOHN WATSON and daughter, GRISELL FARTHING, daughter CEZIAH HUGHS, daughter APHILEDA TOWNSON, one shilling each.

JOHN WATSON

Wit: JOHN HAMMOND, SR., JOSIAH FARGUSON, ELISHA BURTON.

Page 243-244
25 November 1800
Pr: 19 April 1802

LWT WILLIAM DEVIN being in good health and sound and disposing mind.

To my children: JAMES DEVIN, MARY BEGGAR, WILLIAM DEVIN, JR., ROBERT DEVIN and JOSEPH DEVIN, twenty shillings each.

To my daughter SARAH DEVIN, the house in which I now live and the land joining, a negro boy Alleck, a mare, cattle, bed, half the household furniture, a sow and pigs, and provisions of every kind for the support of those free persons I may leave in my family for one year. Should Sarah die without issue she may dispose of only half the property, the other half to my surviving children.

To the children of my daughter MARGARET REYNOLDS, twenty pounds under the direction of their father JOSEPH REYNOLDS.

All remaining property real and personal to be sold and after my debts are paid, divided between: WILLIAM DEVIN, JR., MARY BIGAR, ROBERT DEVIN, the children of MARGARET REYNOLDS, deceased, SARAH

107

DEVIN will cont'd:

DEVIN and JOSEPH DEVIN.

Appoint my beloved sons ROBERT and JOSEPH DEVIN executors.

WILLIAM DEVIN

Wit: JOSEPH MORTON, JAMES EDWARDS

ROBERT FENLAW, JOSEPH MORTON, JOHN HODGES, ABRAHAM PARRISH, JESSE HODGES and EDWARD NUNNELLEE security for executors.

Page 244
25 May 1801
Pr: 21 June 1802

LWT MARK SHELTON being very weak in body but sound and perfect mind.

Lend to my wife RACHEL SHELTON all my estate real and personal during her natural life. At her decease my land and plantation to be equally divided between my two youngest sons: HENRY SHELTON and SPENCER SHELTON. At the same time all my personal estate be divided among my nine children:

JOHN SHELTON, NANCY DAVIDSON, SPENCER SHELTON, RACHEL DAVIDSON, FRANKY WRITE, WILLIAM SHELTON, CHARLES SHELTON, HENRY SHELTON and GEORGE SHELTON.

Appoint sons JOHN and GEORGE executors.

MARK SHELTON

Wit: CUTHBERT HUSON, WILLIS HOPWOOD, LUCY HUDSON.

Page 245
28 October 1801
Pr: 20 September 1802

LWT NATHAN ADAMS, SR. being of sound mind and sickly constitution.

Wife ANN ADAMS to sell any part of my personal estate to pay my just debts.

To my son JOHN ADAMS the land whereon he now lives, 50 acres.

To my son JOEL ADAMS 50 acres to be layed off the upper end of my tract.

Lend to my wife during her natural life the balance of the tract at her death to my son NATHAN ADAMS.

To my children: WILLIAM ADAMS, SARAH BEGLES, BETTY PROSISE, REBECCAH MABRY whatever they had at their marriage and no more.

To my daughter POLLEY ADAMS a bed and furniture.

The residue of my estate to my wife ANN to dispose of as pleases

ADAMS SR. will cont'd:

Appoint my wife ANN ADAMS executrix.

NATHAN (X) ADAMS, SR.

Wit: THOMAS H. WOODING, JOHN ADAMS, JAMES (X) SANDS

Page 246-249
2 July 1797
Pr: 20 December 1802

LWT JOHN WIMBISH being of perfect and sound mind.

On the 15th of February 1796, I gave my daughter POLLY, the following negros: Bob, Brunswick, Peter and Lavena, a gift recorded
in Pittsylvania Court, I confirm her title to Peter and Lavinda
and she has conveyed back to me Bob and Brunswick, in lieu of I
give her a mulatto lad Ben, a negro boy Stephen, a wench Jinny
and a male child Jerry, bed and furniture, cattle, money for a
folding walnut table, 8 windsor chairs.

Lend to my wife MARY WIMBISH during her natural life half of the
tract whereon I now live containing 670 acres including the town
of Peytonsburg, reserving the rents of the Ordinary and the use
of the store and lumber houses for the use of my son JOHN, but
to be entitled to half the rents and the following slaves: Sall,
Aggy, Rhoda, Anthony, Yellow Cyrus, Jimmy and Jesse but not to
have possession of it until 1 January 1801.

Also lend to her one third of my household furniture, horses and
cattle, pigs, and sheep.

My mill to be kept in good repair.

My library of books to be sold.

My negros, except those given and those needed by my wife, to be
rented out as well as the plantation to help pay my debts to DOB-
SON, DLTERA(?) & WALKER and to NANCY PANNILL.

The following tracts to be sold: one of 250 acres in Charlotte,
Prince Edward and Lunenburg Counties joining WILLIAM BOLLING and
others, another tract in Henry County joining JOSEPH SCALES being
85 acres; one of 400 acres in Pittsylvania County on Little Bearskin Creek.

The store to be continued under the firm of JOHN WIMBISH & SON
until 1801.

To my son JOHN WIMBISH the tract whereon I now live, 670 acres
after the death of his mother, also part of the tract known as
the Mill tract.

To my son WILLIAM a tract of 215 acres that joins STEPHEN NEAL,
BENJAMIN BRAWNER and a tract on Elkhorn Creek containing 464 ac.
and a tract of 300 acres joining ROBERT DEVIN.

To my son SAMUEL the following tracts: one being 723 acres with
my mill, one in Halifax County of 70 acres. It is my will that
Samuel be put to the study of Law. I give the preference to my

WIMBISH will cont'd:

friend RICHARD N. VENABLE of Prince Edward County if he would be
kind enough to take him, then send him to Richmond for further
study.

After the decease of my wife, the balance of my estate to be divided between my sons: JOHN, WILLIAM and SAMUEL.

I have already given all I intended to my daughter NANCY PANNILL
at her marriage.

Appoint friend JOHN WIMBISH of Halifax, my sons JOHN and WILLIAM
WIMBISH executors.

                                        JOHN WIMBISH

Wit: JAMES RYBURN, JACOB ANDERSON, ROBERT TOMPKINS

JOHN WHITE, JESSE LEFTWICH, STOCKLEY TURNER, JAMES F. JOHNSON,
JAMES JOHNSON, and JEREMIAH WHITE security for the executors.

Page 249-251
22 November 1802
Pr: 20 December 1802

LWT JOHN KEATTS being of sound mind and disposing memory.

Lend to my beloved wife MARY KEATTS during her lifetime, these
negros: Essea, Lucy, Dick, Cindy, Cerus and Old Lucy, my land and
plantation whereon I now live.

To my son RICHARD negros Jimmey, and little girl Bethey.

To my son JAMES GOWER my negro Terrar.

To my daughter PATSY SHELTON negro Phillis.

To my son JOHN half of the tract where I now live also a negro
Winney.

To my daughter TABBY ARCHER, negro girl Rachel, bed and furniture

To my son HENRY the other half of my land whereon I now live, a
negro Nancy, and a colt.

To my son PARSKILL a negro Selah and at the death of my wife negros Cindy and Cirus.

At the decease of my wife the following is to be given:

To my son JOHN a cow and calf, furniture.

To daughter TABBY ARCHER a cow and calf and horse and saddle.

To son HENRY a cow and calf and furniture.

To son PARSKILL a horse and saddle, cow and calf, and furniture.

Appoint my trusty and beloved sons RICHARD, JAMES GOWER and JOHN
executors.

KEATTS will cont'd:

JOHN KEATTS

Wit: ARMISTEAD SHELTON, FRED. SHELTON, STEPHEN SHELTON, ABRAHAM
SHELTON.

YOUNG SHELTON, EMANUEL JONES, VACHEL CLEMENT and CHARLES KEATTS
security for the executors.

Page 251-252
23 November 1802
Pr: 17 January 1803

LWT JACOB REIGER being very sick of body but of sound mind and
memory.

To my daughter SALLY GARNER one feather bed and furniture.

To my daughter ELIZABETH REIGER $100.00 in cash, a bed and furni-
ture.

To my daughter NANCY REIGER $100.00, a bed and furniture.

To my daughter MARY REIGER $100.00, a bed and furniture.

To my son JOHN REIGER twenty pounds for his education.

To my son GEORGE REIGER the same as above.

I desire my estate to be sold, the above legacies paid and the
balance divided equally between all my children: RICHARD REIGER,
JACOB REIGER, GEORGE REIGER, ROSIAN CARTER, SARY GARNER, ELIZA-
BETH REIGER, NANCY REIGER and MARY REIGER.

To my son JACOB I give $50.00 cash.

Appoint friends GEORGE REYNOLDS and JOHN CARTER executors.

JACOB REIGER

Wit: DAVID LANIER, EDWARD NUNNELEE, MATHEW WELLS

DAVID RICE, EDWARD NUNNELEE, and ABRAHAM PARRISH security for the
executors.

Page 252-253
12 December 1802
Pr: 17 January 1803

LWT PLEASANT HARDWICK very sick and weak but of perfect mind and
memory.

Appoint my dearly beloved wife MESKEY (MICKEY) HARDWICK executrix and WILLIAM SPILLEA executor.

To my dearly beloved wife all my estate during her natural life.

Reserving unto my negro boy Fountain for his good services, the
privilege of being set free when he becomes 31 years of age (he

111

HARDWICK will cont'd:

is now 10 years of age.)

PLEASANT HARDWICK

Wit: L. B. ALLEN, JOHN WALLACE, JAMES WATTS, CHARLES SIMONES of
Burke County, Georgia where the said PLEASANT HARDWICK   signed
this will.

JOHN SUTHERLIN, WILLIAM SUTHERLIN and QUINN MARTIN security for
MICKY HARDWICK.

Page 253-254
7 December 1802
Pr: 21 February 1803

LWT NAOMI BLANKS of sound mind and memory.

To my sons JOHN BLANKS and JOSEPH BLANKS all my household and the
kitchen furniture, a cow and yearling, and one hog.

Ten pounds to my son JOSEPH BLANKS.

Three pounds fourteen shillings and three pence on THOMAS HAM.

Three pounds fourteen shillings and three pence on VACHEL CLEM-
ENTS.

I desire the above money and property to be divided between JOHN
and JOSEPH.

Appoint JOSEPH BLANKS executor.

NAOMI (X) BLANKS

Wit: THOMAS ANDERSON, GABRIEL BROOKS, JOSHUA ADAMS.

Page 254-255
21 April 1803
Pr: 20 June 1803

LWT GABRIEL SHELTON being in a low state of health but of sound
mind and memory.

To my son WIATT SHELTON part of the tract whereon I now live next
to Panter Creek, and five pounds cash.

To my son GREGORY SHELTON one part of my land joining that of his
brother Wiatt's.

To my son GABRIEL SHELTON all that part of my land on the south
side of Whitethorn Creek also the profits arising out of Black-
house land which I purchased under the Exterstt(?) Law.

To my son BEVERLY SHELTON the residue of my land, saving to my
wife MARY SHELTON her lifetime on the land with the mansion house
and orchards and mill.

To my wife MARY a bed and furniture, lend her a horse, kitchen

112

SHELTON will cont'd:

furniture, cows and ewes.

To my daughter ELIZABETH my negro girl Delpha.

To my daughter CATHERINE PAYNE fifty pounds cash.

To my daughter ANNE TAYLOR fifty pounds.

To my sons BEVERLY and GABRIEL a bed and furniture.

I desire that the remaining negros and furniture not given, be sold and the money used for the above bequests.

I appoint sons LEMUEL, GREGORY, GABRIEL and BEVERLY executors. (N. B. Earlier he stated four sons: WYATT, GREGORY, GABRIEL and BEVERLY.)

                                        GABRIEL SHELTON

Wit: ARMSTEAD SHELTON, WEST D. HURT, ABSALOM E. HURT.

The executors refused to take administration of the estate and MARY the widow relinquished her right of administration and was taken on by ARMSTEAD SHELTON with JOSHUA STONE, DANIEL COLEMAN, JOHN WHITE and STOKLEY TURNER his securities.

Page 256
7 August 1798
Pr: 20 June 1803

LWT JOHN STONE being weak in body but of sound and perfect memory.

Lend to my beloved wife JEAN STONE, that part of my plantation whereon I now live called young orchard, to have use of my bay mare called Bounce, household goods, a cow and calf, during her lifetime.

To my son JOHN STONE one shilling if demanded.

To my daughter ELIZABETH BALDWIN one shilling if demanded.

To my daughter ESILPHA SCOTT one shilling if demanded.

To my daughter SARAH QUEN one shilling if demanded.

To my daughter KEZIAH SPARKS all my lands and all my other estate after the death of my wife.

To my grand daughter JEAN SPARKS a mare colt and the first colt she has is for my grand daughter ELENEAR SPARKS.

Appoint my wife and friend MATHEW SPARKS executors.

                                        JOHN (X) STONE

Wit: THOMAS DUNCAN, JOSIAH GWIN, THOMAS GWIN.

ADAM SUTHERLIN and THOMAS SUTHERLIN security for MATHEW SPARKS.

Page 257
25 July 1798
Pr: 20 June 1803

LWT WILLIAM INMAN being weak and sickly in body but in perfect mind and memory.

To my beloved wife SUSANNAH INMAN my whole estate during her life time.

At her decease, the personal estate to be equally divided amongst my five children: HENRY INMAN, NANCY INMAN, EDMUND INMAN, SHADRACK INMAN, JESSE INMAN and their heirs.

My land to be sold and the money divided amongst all my children: WILLIAM INMAN, POLLY MORRIS, SARAH MORGIN, LYDIA BOAZ, and the five children above mentioned.

Appoint DANIEL BOAZ and WILLIAM INMAN executors.

WILLIAM (X) INMAN

Wit: JAMES FULTON, SHADRACK BOAZ, EDMUND BOAZ.

ROBERT BULLINGTON, EDMUND BOAZ and JOHN TURMAN, SR. security for executors.

Page 257-258
2 May 1803
Pr: 20 June 1803

LWT JACOB THOMAS being weak in body but sound of mind and memory

My wife HANNAH THOMAS shall possess negros: Rachel, Thomas, Miller and Moses during her lifetime, at her decease or marriage, to be equally divided between my two sons: MADDISON and JACOB.

Should my sons die without issue then the negros to return to the Thomas estate to the two sons of NATHANIEL THOMAS, WILLIAM THOMAS and NATHANIEL P. THOMAS.

The balance of my estate be equally divided between my two sons: MADDISON THOMAS and JACOB THOMAS.

Appoint JOHN FARLEY and ASA THOMAS executors.

JACOB THOMAS

Wit: ASA THOMAS, CHARLES THOMAS, PEYN. THOMAS.

JOHN GREGORY, GEORGE SUTHERLIN and JOHN WALTERS security for executors.

Page 259
5 April 1803
Pr: 18 July 1803

LWT HALCOTT TOWNES.

TOWNES will cont'd:

To my beloved wife POLLY TOWNES all the negros that come by her and $500.00.

To my four sons: GEORGE, ROBERT, EDWARD and STEPHEN, all the rest and residue of my estate.

The estate to be rented out till they come of age.

Appoint my friend Maj. DANIEL COLEMAN, son of STEPHEN COLEMAN, executor. To be their guardian.

HALCOTT TOWNES

Wit: JAMES COLQUHOUN, DANIEL COLEMAN, JR., GIDEON MITCHELL, WILLIAM LINN.

DANIEL COLEMAN will not take the executorship, certificate granted to ROBERT PAYNE with JAMES COLQUHOUN, THOMAS STEWART, HICKMAN SPILLER his security.

Page 260
10 May 180_
Pr: 19 September 1803

LWT JAMES SMITH being of sound and perfect memory.

Lend to my dearly beloved wife ELIZABETH SMITH one third of the land whereon I now live, the plantation, household goods, a horse and stock of cattle.

I lend to GENEY SANFORD one acre of land and the house and spring where she now lives.

I lend to my daughter NANCY GUNNEL the house and plantation where she lives for five years.

To my son and daughters: JAMES SMITH, SARAH BROOKS and NANCY GUNNEL five shillings each as I have given them all I was able to afford.

To my grandson ALLEN SMITH a mare and a gun.

To my son JOSEPH SMITH the whole tract of land whereon I now live with all improvements, tools and a mare.

My wheelright tools to be sold to pay my just debts.

JAMES SMITH

Wit: ZACHARIAH (X) PRUIT, GEORGE SPRATLEN, WILLIAM BURGESS.

JOHN WALTERS and ASA THOMAS security for JOSEPH SMITH.

Page 260-261
25 June 1803
Pr: 19 September 1803

LWT CHESLEY KING weak of body but of sound and perfect under-

115

KING will cont'd:

standing.

To my dear and loving mother GRACE KING 43 acres of land on Sandy Creek and the tenaments thereon, my bay mare, 2 colts, hogs, a note on SHOWDER CRAFFORD for $12.00, the money in the hands of SAMUEL MOTLEY to her.

Appoint SAMUEL MOTLEY executor.

                                        CHESLEY (X) KING

Wit: DAVID TERRY, FORTUNE DODSON, WILLIAM RUSSELL, SAMUEL GREY.

DANIEL MOTLEY and HENRY GLASS security for executor.

Page 261-264
28 May 18__
Pr: 21 November 1803

LWT DAVID PANNILL being in perfect health both of body and mind.

I desire my store of goods at Chalk Level and at Sandy River to be sold off.

Also desire my one half interest in WILLIAM WIMBISH & CO., one third interest in GRATSY & PANNILL, one third interest in JESSE LEFTWICH & CO. to be sold.

When all of the above is sold and debts collected from the store to be divided as follows:

One third to my loving wife BETHENIA PANNILL and the other two thirds be reserved for the child or children my wife is now pregnant with.

To my brother GEORGE PANNILL my sword given by my Uncle DAVID PAN_-NILL to my brother JOHN PANNILL, deceased, and purchased by me at his sale, given with a serious belief and request that it never will be drawn in favor of a Jacobine or rebellious party.

To my wife BETHENIA PANNILL all stock, household furniture, plantation tools, my riding chair harness, and horses. Also the use of my land on Whitethorn and Chalk Level and to be excluded from the other lands.

My wife to make title to her right in land on Arrart River in Patrick County deeded her by JOHN MARR over to my heirs.

My negros to be divided between my wife and my heirs.

My executor to have sole guardianship of my child or children til of age or marry, if they should be girls, to be under the guardianship of my wife, but if a male child then at age of 10 years be under the guardianship of my executor. My children are to be raised decently, genteally and be liberally educated. If a son, to be acquainted with agriculture and practical labour.

Should I have no heir, the property devised my child to my brothers: SAMUEL PANNILL, GEORGE PANNILL, my sister ELIZABETH DAVIS,

PANNILL will cont'd:

SARAH BN. PANNILL, FANNY PANNILL, NANCY PANNILL and POLLY PANNILL equally.

Appoint my brother SAMUEL PANNILL executor. Should he die before, then my brother MORTON PANNILL in his stead.

                                        DAVID PANNILL

Wit: WILLIAM SHELTON, ZACH. LEWIS, JAMES LINN.

Page 264
(no date)
Pr: 19 December 1803

LWT SYLVESTER GARNER (GARNOR) being in perfect mind and memory.

To my grand daughter NANCY HUTCHISON, the daughter of ELENOR RIDDEL, a negro girl Rachel.

The balance of my estate to my only daughter ELENOR RIDDEL now the wife of ZACHARIAH RIDDEL, three negros: Hercules, Harry and Letty, during her lifetime, then to all of her children equally.

                                        SYLVESTOR (X) GARNOR

Wit: WILLIAM NELSON, JAMES SOYEARS, JAMES NELTON, ZACHARIAH RIDDEL.

Page 265-266
1 January 1803
Pr: 20 February 1804

LWT CHLOE SHELTON being weak in body though of sound mind and memory.

To my beloved sons: CRISPIN SHELTON, WILLIAM SHELTON, TAVENOR SHELTON and FREDERICK SHELTON, one dollar each.

To my beloved daughter LETTICE WHITE during her natural life the following negros: Hannah and her three children Ned, Joe and Lucinda, at her decease to her children. These are in her possession.

To my beloved daughter JANE STONE during her natural life a negro girl Siller, woman Liddia, a bed and furniture, saddle at her decease to her children.

To my beloved son ABRAHAM SHELTON negros Sam and Ambross, a mare and colt, bed and furniture on the condition that he make no improper use of the property. To be under the direction of sons: CRISPIN and ROBERTSON SHELTON.

To my beloved son ROBERTSON SHELTON negros Ned and Lilly and her two children Scott and Matilda, bed and furniture, all my household furniture, stock, tools, tobacco, corn, etc.

Appoint my son ROBERTSON SHELTON executor.

117

SHELTON will cont'd:

                                        CHLOE (X) SHELTON

Wit: WILLIAM SHELTON, JOEL SHELTON, JOHN SHELTON.

CRISPIN SHELTON, TAVENOR SHELTON, ABRAHAM SHELTON, JOHN STONE,
WILLIAM BARNES and STOOKLEY TURNER security for executor.

Page 266-267
5 January 1804
Pr: 20 February 1804

LWT SUSANNAH SANDFORD in a low state of health but of sound mind
and memory.

I do order my burying place to be beside my mother KEREN SANDFORD
on my brother JOSEPH SANDFORD's land at the place called Millers
Church and the Rev'ds JOHN BROWN, JAMES TOMPKINS, JAMES HART and
JOHN ADKENSON or any of them to preach my funeral. I desire my
grave and my mother's be walled in with rocks and to be painted
white edged with black to be paid out of my estate.

My estate to be divided as follows: to my brother JOSEPH SANDFORD
my negros Winney, William, and George on his paying SUSAN SAND-
FORD, daughter of my brother JAMES SANDFORD, one hundred pounds
in 1805 and put to interest till she comes of age or marries.

To SUSAN MEDLOCK my niece negros Lucy and Fanny, should she die
without issue to my sister ELIZA GLASCOCK and her children.

I give KEREN YANCEY my niece fifty seven pounds in the hands of
ROBERT HARVEY for the hire of Fanny, Winney and Lucey and George,
to purchase a negro for KEREN YANCEY.

To my niece SUSAN YANCEY a negro girl Winney, daughter of Fanney.

To THOMAS GLASCOCK my riding horse Lampliter.

To my niece CHLOE GLASCOCK negros Ester and child David and Patty
daughter of Fanny and my compass, bed and quilt.

To my sister ELIZA GLASCOCK my feather bed, furniture and all my
household furniture.

Should my brother JOSEPH SANDFORD die without issue then to my
sister ELIZA GLASCOCK.

                                        SUSAN. SANDFORD

Wit: RAWLEY WHITE, CHAMPNESS TERRY, GEORGE GLASCOCK.

ELIZABETH GLASCOCK executrix.

Page 268-269
2 December 1803
Pr: 18 June 1804

LWT CURTIS KEATTS of sound mind and memory.

                    118

KEATTS will cont'd:

To my grandson RICHARD KEATTS, son of my deceased son JOHN KEATTS one shilling.

To my grandson JAMES GOWER KEATTS, son of my deceased son JOHN KEATTS one shilling.

To my grandson JOHN KEATTS, son of my deceased son JOHN KEATTS, one shilling.

To my grandson HENRY KEATTS, son of my deceased son JOHN KEATTS, one shilling.

To my grand daughter MARTHA SHELTON, daughter of my deceased son JOHN KEATTS, one shilling.

To my grand daughter TABITHA, daughter of my deceased son JOHN KEATTS, one shilling.

To my grandson PARSKILL KEATTS, son of my deceased son JOHN, the tract of land where I now live on the waters of Straitstone Creek 246 acres, a negro Primus.

To my grandsons and grand daughters, children of my deceased son JAMES KEATTS, one shilling each.

To my son WILLIAM KEATTS negros Arthur and John.

To my son CHARLES KEATTS negros Bower and Ceaser.

To my sons WILLIAM and CHARLES, and my daughter MARTHA, all of my library of books.

Residue of my estate not before given to be sold, and the money equally divided between my three daughters: MARTHA, MARY and TA-BITHA.

Appoint sons CHARLES and WILLIAM KEATTS executors.

CURTIS (X) KEATTS

Wit: JOHN HUNT, BENJAMIN WALLER

ROBERTSON SHELTON, BENJAMIN GOSNEY, JOHN LEWIS and WILLIAM LEWIS security for executors.

Page 269-270
26 November 1801
Pr: 18 June 1804

LWT JOHN SHELTON in tolerable good health and sound mind and of disposing memory.

To my son ABRAHAM SHELTON all my tract of land whereon I now live.

To my daughter JANE LEWIS one dollar.

To my grand daughter FRANCIS SHELTON, wife of TUNSTALL SHELTON, fifty cents.

SHELTON will cont'd:

To my daughter MARY POORE $50.00.

I lend to my children hereinafter named and their heirs my negros to be equally divided: WILLIAM SHELTON, JOEL SHELTON, CLAIBORNE SHELTON, ABRAHAM SHELTON, FRANCIS SHELTON, MARTHA TUCKER, CHARLOTTE SHELTON, NANCY WHITE, LUCY HUNT and LETTICE SHELTON.

My stock and still and all tools and furniture be sold and the money divided between: WILLIAM SHELTON, JOEL SHELTON, CLAIBORNE SHELTON, ABRAM SHELTON, FRANCIS SHELTON, MARTHA TUCKER, CHARLOTTE SHELTON, NANCY WHITE, LUCY HURT and LETTICE SHELTON.

Appoint sons ABRAHAM and JOEL SHELTON and friend VINCENT SHELTON as executors.

JOHN SHELTON

Wit: WILLIAM SHELTON, LEWIS SHELTON, HENRY R. SHELTON.

WEST D. HURT, CLAIBORNE SHELTON, LEROY SHELTON, ABRAHAM SHELTON (son of GABRIEL), RICHARD SHELTON, BEVERLEY SHELTON, VINCENT SHELTON, JAMES LINN and JOHN ADAMS, JR. security for the executors.

Page 271
17 January 1803
Pr: 18 June 1804

LWT GEORGE SUTHERLIN weak in body but in perfect sense and memory.

To my son JOHN SUTHERLIN negros Will and Sampson.

To my son GEORGE SUTHERLIN negros Cuff and Price, and furniture.

To my son HENRY SUTHERLIN negros Sam, Isaac and Janey.

Tomy son WILLIAM SUTHERLIN negros Ake and Darcos.

To my son ADAMS SUTHERLIN negros Jack and Frank, also 100 acres of land joining his land on Sandy Creek.

To my son JAMES SUTHERLIN negros Archa and Yardo, furniture, all my land on Dan River, Sandy River and Sandy Creek excepting the 100 acres for Adams.

To my daughter MILLIN GWIN negros James and Phillis with my land on Sandy River bought of JOHN STONE, JR.

To - daughter ELESEBATH MICKELBORROUGH my negros Squar and Sabra.

To - daughter NANCY MC DANIEL negro Sharlot and her child and $50.00.

To - daughter SALLY SMITH negros Mamnuel and Sarah.

Residue of property to be sold and equally divided amongst all my children.

Appoint trusty sons THOMAS SUTHERLIN and ADAMS SUTHERLIN ex's.

120

SUTHERLIN will cont'd:

GEORGE (X) SUTHERLIN

Wit: THOMAS DUNCAN, MATHEW (X) SPARKS, BROOKS (X) SPARKS.

JOHN SUTHERLIN, ROBERT MICKLEBERRY, WILLIAM SMITH and JOHN GWIN
security for executors.

Page 272
6 August 1803
Pr: 17 September 1804

LWT NEHEMIAH TRAHERN being weak in body but of sound mind and
memory.

To my daughter MARY ANN, a negro woman Cas.

To my son JAMES a negro boy named George.

To my son JOHN, a negro named Phillis.

To my daughter ELIZABETH HESTER a negro Hannah.

To my son SAMUEL, negro Stepney.

To my daughter SERENA a negro Bob.

To my son WESLEY, a negro called Gilbert.

To my daughter MILLEY a negro girl Little Lucy.

To my son WILLIAM a negro girl Mary.

I desire my daughter POLLEY to have as much money as to make her
equal with the value of the negros given the others.

I gave my daughter HESTER a negro earlier.

To my beloved wife AMELIA, during her natural life, the tract of
land whereon I now live with all the stock, furniture and negros:
Harry, Watt, Lucy, Cloe and Jenny. At her decease the negros to
be divided between my children above named.

I desire the children under age remain with their mother until
of lawful age.

Appoint my son JAMES and SAMUEL HESTER executors.

NEHEMIAH TRAHERN

Wit: THOMAS SPARKS, JAMES CHAPPELL

JAMES TRAHERN not a resident of this state and SAMUEL HESTER a
resident of Mecklenburg County, refused to serve as executors.
JAMES PATTERSON and SAMUEL TRAHERN with WILLIAM WARE and JEDU-
THURE CARTER their security as executors.

Page 273
Pr: 15 October 1804 (no other date)

121

LWT RICHARD REYNOLDS in perfect memory and state of mind.

To my beloved wife NANCY REYNOLDS to have and enjoy my personal estate during her lifetime. At her decease all my estate, real and personal, to be equally divided among my beloved children having JOHN BENNETT, JESSE REYNOLDS and my wife executors.

RICHARD (X) REYNOLDS

Wit: WILLIAM WRIGHT, FRANCIS EPPERSON.

WILLIAM WRIGHT, and FRANCIS EPPERSON security for JOHN BENNETT.

Page 274-275
15 December 1795
Pr: 15 April 1805

LWT WILLIAM DAVIS of sound mind and memory.

I lend unto my loving sister LUCY DAVIS, during her life, 100 acs whereon I now live, being part of a patent to JOHN GRAVEN dated 25 March 1762, being 384 acres more or less.

To my niece ANN MURPHY, daughter of my brother JOHN DAVIS, deceased, 100 acres after the death of my sister LUCY DAVIS.

To the heirs of my late brother JOHN DAVIS, deceased, the rest of the tract of 384 acres less the 100 acres, excepting four acs.

Four acres to the heirs of my deceased brother GEORGE DAVIS.

Lend to my sister LUCY DAVIS, 100 acres joining the other granted me, 360 acres total.

To my sister LUCY DAVIS all my personal property.

To JAMES DAVIS, son of JOHN DAVIS, five pounds.

To the heirs of GEORGE DAVIS, deceased, all the tract of land.. granted me..360 acres, but Lucy Davis to have free use of the 100 acres during her lifetime.

Appoint my sister LUCY DAVIS and nephew WILLIAM DAVIS, son of my deceased brother GEORGE DAVIS, executors.

WILLIAM DAVIS

Wit: WILLIAM BURTON, JAMES (X) SCOOT, WILLIAM (X) SCOOT, THOMAS (X) SCOOT, LEVI (X) BURTON.

SHADRACK BOAZ and JOHN MURPHY security for LUCY DAVIS.

Page 275-276
3 September 1804
Pr: 17 June 1805

LWT BENJAMIN HARRIS sound in mind but in a low state of health.

To be buried in a Christian life manner on the third day after my decease or sooner should I be offensive in the house.

HARRIS will cont'd:

I appoint my worthy friend CHRISTOPHER CONWAY to sell as much of
my land joining WILLIAM HARRIS, CARTER MICKELBOROUGH and HENRY
MICKELBOROUGH as to pay my debts and to first pay my good friend
Dr. JAMES D. PATTEN.

The remaining part as follows: my wife to have possession of the
plantation, negros, stock and household goods, during her natural
life and to give or lend to the children as they leave her, what
she can spare. Should she marry, my plantation and negros to be
rented out for the benefit of my children. I desire they be well
schooled. Negro Sall not to be rented out.

To my son ACHILLES HARRIS what may remain of my land. All my negros, all other property except the negros lent to my wife to be
equally divided in four parts. One fourth part to each: my daughter POLLY, my daughter LUCY KEMP, my son ACHILLES, my daughter
BETSEY --- HARRIS.

The negros lent my wife to be equally divided between my three
daughters.

((No signature or wit-
                                          ness)

In Court WILLIAM BEAVERS and ALEXANDER BROWN made oath that the
handwriting was that of BENJAMIN HARRIS. CHRISTOPHER CONWAY executor refused to serve and the widow LUCY HARRIS with DANIEL SUL-
LIVAN and WILLIAM WILKINSON and ABIA CHEATHEM their security.

Page 276-277
24 January 1805
Pr: 17 June 1805

LWT OBEDIAH ECHOLS being weak in body but of sound and disposing
memory.

To my brother DAVID ECHOLS all my part of my father's tract of
land he purchased of JOHN HUBBARD and his wife KEZIAH, my part
on the north side of Bearskin Creek, being 33 1/3 acres that the
said David purchased of me for ten pounds, the residue of which
I bequeath him for the trouble he has had with me from the 12th
of August to the 23rd of January 1805.

The money due me from the rent of my land adjoining DANIEL MAR-
SHAL and SAMUEL HUBBARD to be equally divided among my brothers:
DAVID ECHOLS, MOSES ECHOLS and JOSEPH ECHOLS.

All of my lands, excepting the above to David, be sold and the
money divided between my brothers and sisters DAVID ECHOLS, MOSES
ECHOLS, JOSEPH ECHOLS, MARY STREET, TABITHA LACEY, RHODA ECHOLS.

Appoint my brother David executor.

                                    OBEDIAH (X) ECHOLS

Wit: GEORGE GILES, BENJAMIN RIDDLE, JOSEPH HUTCHERSON

GEORGE GILES and BENJAMIN RIDDLE security for executor.

Page 277-278
23 August 1799
Pr: 17 June 1805

LWT JOSEPH HUGHES being infirm and weak in body but sound mind and memory.

I lend to my beloved wife PHEBY my land and plantation whereon I now live, stock, household furniture during her lfe.

After the death of my wife, the lands I lent to my daughter MARY WHITE for her lifetime after her death to my grandson REASON B. WHITE, should he die without issue, then the land to WILLIAM H. WHITE.

After the decease of my wife, my grandson WILLIAM H. WHITE is to have all my personal property.

To my daughter SUSANNAH SHAW, five shillings.

Appoint REASON B. WHITE executor.

JOSEPH HUGHES

Wit: JOHN WILSON, BENJAMIN TREDWELL, JOHN WILSON, JAMES NELSON, ROBERT WRIGHT.

Proved by the oath of ROBERT WRIGHT and the affirmation of JOHN WILSON. RICHARD B. WRIGHT security for executor.

Page 278
24 March 1796
Pr: 16 September 1805

LWT SIMON ROWLAND in perfect health of body and mind.

To my beloved wife ELISABETH ROWLAND my whole of my estate during her lifetime.

At her decease, I give the residue to my son NATHAN ROWLAND.

Appoint wife and son NATHAN ROWLAND executors.

SIMON (X) ROWLAND

Wit: THOMAS VAUGHAN, MOLLY TURNER VAUGHAN, WILL TODD, EDMD. TUN-STALL.

Page 279-280
30 March 1802
Pr: 19 October 1805

LWT CHARLES LEWIS in tolerable good health and sound mind.

To my son CHARLES a negro Sam, furniture.

To my son ZACHARIAH, a negro Essex, furniture, a negro Delpha.

To my son EDWARD, a negro woman Phillis, bed and furniture.

LEWIS will cont'd:

I lend to my son JAMES LEWIS during his life, negros Dinah and Ransdom, at his decease to his children.

I lend to my son JOHN during his lfie negros Ben and Frankey, at his decease to his children.

To my son WILLIAM, negros Roger, Anna, Polly and Jinney, two beds and all my tract whereon I now live, 300 acres more or less, except one acre to remain for the graveyard, also the plantation, all furniture and stock.

To my daughter MARY KEATTS a negro James, a bed.

Lend to my daughter LUCREASY CLEMENT negro Lucy, after her decease, to her children.

Son WILLIAM is to pay all my just debts and is to be executor.

                                        CHARLES LEWIS

Wit: VINCENT SHELTON, WILLIAM SHELTON, HENRY B. SHELTON.

Page 280-281
26 February 1800
Pr: 21 October 1805

LWT WILLIAM TUCKER in perfect health and memory.

To my wife SUSANNA TUCKER all that I possess during her lifetime.

To JILLICA HAYNES the bed myself and her mother lays upon.

To my son ROBERT TUCKER $1.00

To my daughter MARY ELDEN $1.00

To my daughter MILLEY WILLIAMS negro Delphia, and livestock.

To JOHN WILLIAMS, son of MILLEY WILLIAMS, negro Siller.

To my son DANIEL TUCKER, all the land that remains after his mothers death, negro Fountain, all my stock and half the furniture.

To my daughter SUSANNAH TUCKER the negro Fountain after the decease of Daniel, also lend to her negro Isam, bed and half the furniture.

To my grand daughter ELIZABETH TUCKER, the negro Sam, after her mother SUSANNAH's marriage or death.

Appoint Col. WILLIAM CLARK, ARMSTEAD SHELTON and THOS. PAYNE executors.

                                        WILLIAM TUCKER

Wit: THOMAS B. JONES, WILLIAM BARNES, GABRIEL SHELTON, STEPHEN SHELTON, GRIFFITH DICKENSON.

(cont'd next page)

TUCKER will cont'd:

N. B.
I have this date, 4 August 1802, given my beloved son DANIEL TUCK-
ER, my negro boy David.

Page 281-282
11 February 1797
Pr: 15 July 1805

LWT WILLIAM WALLER sick and weak in body but of perfect mind
and memory.

To my beloved wife JANE WALLER all my estate during her widowhood
and should she marry, I lend her negros Frank and Peter during
her lifetime.

My estate to be divided between my six children: MARY, DANIEL,
CHRISTOPHER, JAMES, TABITHA and SARAH. Should my wife be pregnant
then that child be equal with the others.

The negros lent my wife to return to my estate and be divided between my children.

Appoint DANIEL GUNN, HAMPTON WALLER and JOHN MORGAN executors.

                              WILLIAM WALLER

Wit: WILLIAM WHITE, STETH HARDY, SARAH BOOKER GUNN, RICHARD BEN-
NANT.

JANE WALLER executor.

Page 283
29 January 1801
Pr: 21 October 1805

LWT CHARLES WILLIAMS sick and weak in body but of sound mind.

To my beloved wife SALLY WILLIAMS all the land and premises where
I now live with a tract of land joining given me by JOHN WILSON.
Also negros: Dick, Young Dick, Old Sarah, Young Sarah, Sam, Jacob, Pheby, Gabriel, Milley, George, Judy, Peter and Peggy, all
my stock, furniture...except such I shall hereafter give to my
daughter NANCY WILLIAMS.

After the death of my wife all personal estate to be divided between my four children.

To my son PETER WILLIAMS negros: Cambridge, Beck and Esther, a
horse and saddle, furniture.

To my son CHARLES WILLIAMS negros: Ted, Young Holly, Bell, horse
and saddle, furniture and all the land willed to my wife after
her death.

To my daughter SUSANNAH CROUCH, wife of JOHN CROUCH, negros: Holly and Joe, furniture, a horse and saddle.

                              126

WILLIAMS will cont'd:

To my daughter NANCY WILLIAMS negros: Jenny, Sam and Diley, horse and saddle, and furniture.

To my grand daughter POLLEY WILLIAMS CROUCH, a negro girl Beck.

Appoint my wife SALLY WILLIAMS and son CHARLES WILLIAMS and with GEORGE ADAMS executors.

CHARLES WILLIAMS

Wit: WILLIAM WARE, WILLIAM RUSSELL, LEVE (X) STONE

WILLIAM WARE and WILLIAM HARRISON security for executors.

Page 284-285
28 September 1805
Pr: 16 December 1805

LWT THOMAS FARN (FEARN) being sick and weak but sound and disposing memory.

To my wife MARY FEARN one third of my estate during her natural life or widowhood.

The remaining two thirds to be equally possessed by my five sons: JOHN, THOMAS, ROBERT, GEORGE and RICHARD FEARN as tenants in common to divide as they think proper.

At the marriage or decease of my wife, her third to the above 5 sons.

I loan to my daughter SEANAH LEE PAYNE negros: William (or Buck), James, Diley and three of her children viz: Fanny, Milley and Joe during her life then to her heirs.

Lend to my wife MARY FEARN during her natural life negros: Charles, Pompey, Agga and the three children of Charles by Pallan viz: Mary, Isaac and Sam. At her marriage or death to my children: JOHN, THOMAS, ROBERT, GEORGE and RICHARD FEARN and my daughter POLLY FEARN and the heirs of my daughter LEANAH LEE PAYNE.

To my daughter POLLY FEARN negros: Patty and her two children, Milley, John, Jim, Wynney and her child Nance.

The remaining slaves: Pallace, Daniel, Sall, Sylva, Will, Joe, Peter, Nell, Hannah, Tom, Nat, Peter and Jim who are the children of Deley be divided between my sons: JOHN, THOMAS, GEORGE and RICHARD.

The remaining part of my personal estate to be sold and the proceeds divided amongst my children: JOHN, THOMAS, GEORGE, RICHARD and POLLY FEARN one seventh part the heirs of my daughter LEANAH LEE PAYNE.

Appoint my wife and my son JOHN FEARN and friend DUDLEY GATEWOOD and JAMES D. PATTON executors.

THOMAS FEARN

Wit: W. CLARKE, DUDLEY GATEWOOD, JAMES D. PATTON, JOSEPH (X) FER-

FEARN will cont'd:

GUSON. DUDLEY GATEWOOD refuses to act as executor, JOHN FEARN the other executor is dead, on the motion of MARY FEARN and JAMES D. PATTON, with WILLIAM BEAVERS, WILLIAM ASTIN, JAMES SOYARS, WILLIAM CLARK and THOMAS STUART security for them.

Page 286-289
30 August 1805
Pr: 16 December 1805

LWT PRESTON GILBERT weak and sick but in perfect memory.

Lend to my beloved wife JEMIAH GILBERT negros: Lewis, Ben, Dina, Rachel, girl Rachel, Jack, Ceasar. I give to her forever a negro girl Polley. I lend my wife all lands and houses located on Stanton River and my mill branch, use of the livestock and household furniture, except that which I hereafter will bequeath. My wife to have the use of all the slaves until my legatees come of age.

To my beloved daughter MARY EDDS negros Tom and Jack at the decease of my wife and furniture and stock.

To my beloved son JOHN GILBERT a tract of land on Stanton River including my mill, negro boy Bob, furniture and livestock all of which he now has in his possession.

To my beloved daughter LEVENA HODGES a negro boy Micajah and girl Jenny, furniture, horse, cow and calf.

To my beloved son GEORGE GILBERT all the residue of my land, negro Charles, a horse, cow and calf, and furniture.

To my beloved daughter BETSEY PRESTON SCRUGGS a negro named Ceasar, and a girl Easter, a mare, furniture and a cow and calf.

To my daughter CATHARINE GILBERT negros Billey and Alee, furniture and a horse.

To my daughter NANCY GILBERT negros Jesse and Fanney, furniture, cow and calf, a horse.

To my beloved daughter LOCKEY GILBERT negros Guye and Pheby, cow and calf, a horse, and furniture.

Should any of my children die without issue, their bequeaths to be returned to the estate.

At the death of my wife, the residue of my estate be equally divided between all my children.

Appoint my wife JEMIAH GILBERT and son JOHN GILBERT and GEORGE GILBERT executors.

                                          PRESTON GILBERT

Wit: THOMAS COCK, DAVID HAMRICK, JOHN LEAGUE.

THOMAS COCK, GEORGE GILBERT and DRURY SCRUGGS security for JOHN GILBERT.

Page 289-290
9 February 1805
Pr: 20 January 1806

LWT ABRAHAM CAMPBELL weak in body but sound mind and memory.

To my son RICHARD CAMPBELL the old plantation whereon I now live
and the land on the east side of the road that leads to the Courthouse.

The residue of my land and personal estate to be sold and the
money equally divided between my daughters; AGGA ADAMS, MILLY
KERBY, ANNA THOMAS, FRANKY WATSON, BETSY CAMPBELL, SALLY RICHARDS,
LUCY WORSHAM and MOLLY WORSHAM.

Appoint my son-in-laws NATHAN ADAMS and FRANCIS WORSHAM executors.

                              ABRAHAM (X) CAMPBELL

Wit; JEDUTHAN CARTER, WILLIAM WELCH, RICHARD ELLIOT, JOHN LONG.

JOHN ADAMS (son of NATHAN ADAMS, deceased) security for executors
NATHAN ADAMS and FRANCIS WORSHAM.

Page 290-291
24 July 1805
Pr: 20 January 1806

LWT SAMUEL SLATE being weak in body.

My beloved wife MARY SLATE to possess and enjoy the plantation
whereon I now live during her natural life.

To my son JOHN SLATE 100 acres, to take in the plantation where
he formerly lived, the land and no more as he has already received his part.

To my son SAMUEL SLATE thirty three pounds cash.

To my son WILLIAM SLATE five shillings with what he has already
received.

To my son ABRUM SLATE the land whereon he now lives being 100 ac.

To my son ISUM SLATE 106 acres, after the death of my wife to him
the part alloted to her for taking care of his mother.

To my five daughters SARY, ANNE, LUCY and PNEBY(?) the sixty acs.
where my son WILLIAM formerly lived.

The residue of my estate to be sold and the money divided between
my wife and five daughters.

                              SAMUEL SLATE

Wit: ABRUM (X) CHANEY, JAMES (X) MADCAFF, JOHN DUN

RAWLEY WHITE and ISHAM SLATE security for GARDNER MAYES executor.

Page 291-292 (cont'd next page)

15 August 1803
Pr: 21 April 1806

LWT RICHARD THURMAN being in perfect mind and memory.

To my daughter EDDY BRUES a tract of land on Panter Branch.

To my daughter ELISABETH THURMAN and to my daughter POLLEY THURMAN, 50 acres to be equally divided.

To my daughter RACHEL BUEER(?) land on Timbard fork to JOHN EDDES line.

To my son LABAN THURMAN the balance of my land, negro Bob, and all livestock.

To my daughter AGNES BARNET twenty shillings.

To my daughter SUSANNAH MULLINS twenty shillings.

To my daughter ANNA DOSS twenty shillings.

To my son WILLIAM THURMAN twenty shillings.

To my daughter RHODA BOW twenty shillings.

To my daughter FRANCES ABSTON twenty shillings.

To my daughter SALLY DOSS twenty shillings.

Appoint my son LABAN THURMAN and NATHANIEL BOW and THOMAS BRUES (BRUCE?) executors.

RICHARD THURMAN

Wit: ELISHE BARBER, FRANCIS (X) DOSS, LABAN FARMER.

EDMUND TUNSTALL, JAMES BRUCE, JOSEPH MAYES security for executors

Page 292-294
16 May 1806
Pr: 16 June 1806

LWT GEORGE HERNDON weak in health but of perfect mind and memory.

To my dearly beloved wife SARAH HERNDON during her natural life that tract of land called Strawberry being composed of three surveys.

The executors to collect money owed me and pay all my outstanding debts and the money left over to be used to purchase shares of stock in the Bank of Virginia. The dividends to be used by my beloved wife for her support.

At the death of my wife, my estate to be used for funding and endowing a Charity School in Pittsylvania County and for the support of a teacher for the same, for the education of the poor people of this County.

A committee to be appointed for this purpose.

130

HERNDON will cont'd:

To my well beloved wife SARAH HERNDON my negro woman Mary, all
the household goods and livestock.

Appoint PEYTON GRAVES and WILLIAM WITCHER, JR. executors.

                              GEORGE HERNDON

Wit: J. COLQUHOLEN(?), DANIEL C. EDWARDS, JOHN (X) HAMMOCK, WIL-
LIAM SMITH

WILLIAM SWANSON, JR. and DANIEL C. EDWARDS security for executors.

Page 295
20 October 1804
Pr: 16 June 1806

LWT ALLAS JOHNSON

To my grandson SAMUEL LOGAIN, after my debts are paid, the residue of my estate.

Appoint JOSHUA STONE executor.

                              ALLAS (X) JOHNSON

Wit: COLEMAN STONE

WILLIAM TUNSTALL security for the executor.

Page 295-296
12 April 1805
Pr: 21 July 1806

LWT NATHANIEL THACKER weak in body but sound of mind.

To my wife CASSE, the plantation and 150 acres adjoining, four
negros: Frank, Jude, Sam and Moses, all the livestock, furniture
and tools during her lifetime.

At her decease to be divided between my two daughters MOLLY AD-
KINS and LAVINA MALICOAH(?).

My personal property to be sold and the money divided between my
six children: BETSY, PETER, JOEL, ISAAC, MOLLEY and LAVINA also
all debts due me collected and the money divided among the children.

Appoint sons PETER THACKER and JOEL THACKER executors.

                              NATHANIEL (X) THACKER

Wit: JOS. HUBBARD, ELISHA BURTON, ROBERT (X) NASH

JAMES HART, ELISHA BURTON and JOSEPH HUBBARD security for the executors.

Page 296-297 (cont'd next page)

131

13 October 1804
Pr: 20 August 1806

EDWARD LONG, SR. in a low state of health but of sound and disposing memory.

To my beloved wife JANE LONG all and every part of my estate during her lifetime.

After the decease of my wife, the land and all other property to be sold and the money divided equally between my son EDWARD LONG, my grandson EDWARD LONG (son of THOMAS LONG), my grandson EDWARD LONG (son of WILL LONG), my grandson EDWARD LONG (son of JAMES LONG), my grandson EDWARD MAPLES (son of WILLIAM MAPLES), also my grand daughter JANE LONG (daughter of THOMAS LONG), my grand daughter JANE LONG (daughter of WILLIAM LONG), my grand daughter JANE LONG (daughter of JAMES LONG), my grand daughter JANE LONG (daughter of ISAAC LONG), my grand daughter JANE HERNDON (daughter of REUBEN HERNDON), my grand daughter JANE GRIGGS (daughter of JOHN GRIGGS). Should any of the above die without issue, their part to the rest.

To my daughter ELIZABETH LONG, over and above what she has been given, a cow and calf, and all kitchen furniture.

I further give to each of my children ten shillings over/above what they have received.

Appoint beloved friends ROBERT DEVIN and PHILIP THOMAS executors.

EDWARD (X) LONG

Wit: ROBERT DEVIN, ISHAM HARDEY, DAVID FREZZELL, JAMES GRIGGS.

Page 298-299
15 August 1805
Pr: 20 October 1806

LWT WILLIAM MITCHELL, blacksmith, being in perfect health.

I relinquish and forgive my brother JAMES MITCHELL whatever sum he owes me both bonds and open account and further give him 100 acres of land which joins JACOB BURGER, LEONARD CLASS, CHRISTIAN TURKE and CHRISTIAN CREAMER.

To my brothers son HENRY MITCHELL a bed and furniture.

To my dearly beloved wife HELEN MITCHELL the use of my estate, real and personal, during her life.

After my decease I desire that PETER CLARK and his family to continue to live on my plantation and transact all business for my wife and care for her.

After the decease of my beloved wife, in consideration for all the favors and service done by PETER CLARK the remainder of my estate, real and personal, I bequeath to PETER CLARK.

Appoint my friends Maj. JOHN SMITH and PETER CLARK my executors.

WILLIAM MITCHELL

MITCHELL will cont'd:

Wit: SAMUEL CALLAND, WILLIAM CALLAND, HENRY J. CALLAWAY.

PEYTON GRAVES security for executor PETER CLARK.

Page 299-300
8 November 1804
Pr: 15 December 1806

LWT JOSEPH MOTLEY being weak in body but of sound mind.

To my beloved wife ELIZABETH MOTLEY one hundred pounds also lend her during her natural life the land and plantation where I now live and negros: Primor, Will, Mat, Hannah and children, livestock, furniture and a London still.

The remainder of my estate to be divided into eleven parts to: my grand daughter PATSEY MOTLEY (daughter of DAVID MOTLEY), son DANIEL MOTLEY, son SAMUEL MOTLEY, son JOHN MOTLEY, and to MARTHA STEWART's four children one part, daughter OBEDIENCE MOREHEAD one part, to daughter PRUDENCE STONE one part, to daughter SALLY ANDERSON one part, to my daughter AMEY CARTER, lend her one part during her lifetime then to her children; to my daughter DELILAH TERRY one part, to my grandson JOSEPH MOTLEY TANNER, should he die without issue to his two brothers JOEL TANNER and ASA TANNER.

At the death of my wife what has been lent to her to be divided to the legatees above named in the same manner.

                                        JOSEPH MOTLEY

Wit: JOHN R. HALL, RHODA (X) OLIVER, WILLIAM HALL.

DANIEL MOTLEY, WILLIAM IRBY (Dr.), WILLIAM HALL, JAMES M. WILLIAMS, DOCTOR C. WILLIAMS security for CHRISTOPHER TERRY.

Page 300-302
3 December 1806
Pr: 16 February 1807

LWT JOHN WILSON, SR. being infirm and sick of body but of sound mind and memory.

Lend to my wife during her lifetime the land and plantation where I now live excepting the parts some of my children has the priviledge of settling on, three negros: Will, Tom and Fanny, horse, furniture and livestock.

To my daughter RACHEL PAYNE, exclusive of what was given her at her marriage, five shillings, but if she lives longer than her husband, she is to have an equal part of my personal estate deducting fifty two pounds.

To my son HENRY WILSON a bed, livestock, and furniture plus $100 to be deducted when a division of my property takes place.

HENRY to have the privilege of settling on my land adjoining REASON B. WHITE without rent.

WILSON will cont'd:

My son THOMAS WILSON to have the place whereon he now lives. He is to transact all my business in the state of North Carolina.

To my son MARK WILSON, a mare and when he comes of age, a bed and furniture, livestock and some tools, he may also settle on a part of my land.

When my son ASA WILSON comes of age, he is to have a bed and furniture, livestock and may settle on my lands.

To my son WILLIAM WILSON, a mare, and when he comes of age, the same as the rest.

My crop of tobacco and other property not mentioned be sold and the money divided between my eleven children: JAMES, JOHN, HENRY, MARTIN, THOMAS, LEAH, HARDIN, ARTIMESIA, ASA, MARK and WILLIAM.

At the death of my wife, all property lent her to be sold and divided equally between my eleven children, deducting JAMES WILSON, forty pounds; JOHN WILSON, JR., forty six pounds; MARTIN WILSON, forty six pounds; LEAH STAMPS, forty four pounds; HARDIN WILSON, thirty nine pounds; and ARTIMISEA RAGLAND, thirty three pounds.

Appoint JAMES WILSON, JOHN WILSON, JR. and HENRY WILSON executors.

JOHN WILSON

Wit: ROYAL (X) KING, PEYTON KING, ABNER LYNCH, SHADRACK (X) MATHERLEY.

THOMAS H. WOODING and JAMES SOYARS security for executors.

Page 302-303
1 November 1806
Pr: 16 February 1807

LWT HENRY FOARD weak in body but have my common reason, mind and understanding.

To my oldest son JOHN FOARD, the tract of land where he now lives coming to the dividing between him and ELISHA FOARD.

To my son JARRALD FOARD the tract on Prestridges branch bounded by STOKELY TURNER, GIDEON and WILLIAM THOMSON.

To my son ELISHA FOARD the tract between JOHN FORD and JARRALD FORD, the place where I now live and my negro Alen.

To my well beloved wife FRANCES FOARD my negros: Will, Betty and Luse during her lifetime and at her death then to my daughters: ELISABETH ASHER, FATHY(?) SHELTON and POLLY HALEY.

To my daughter SARAH MURPHY the negro Edy in her possession.

My son JOHN FOARD to pay my son WILLIAM FOARD $50.00 and son JARRALD FOARD pay my son THOMAS FOARD $50.00; my son ELISHA FOARD to pay my son THOMAS FOARD $50.00.

The plantation where we now live to my wife during her lifetime

FOARD will cont'd:

and at her decease, to ELISHA FOARD.

To my son JARRALD FOARD my negro boy Charles.

The residue of household furniture, after the death of my wife,
to be equally divided between: ELIZABETH ASHER, FATHY(?) SHELTON,
SARAH MURPHY and POLLY HALEY. The stock to be divided between my
sons.

ELISHA FOARD to take care of his mother.

BEVERLY BARKSDALE, WILLIAM THOMSON, JOHN SHELTON and WASHINGTON
THOMSON appointed as executors.

HENRY (X) FOARD

Wit: GIDEON RAGLAND, SR., GIDEON RAGLAND, JR., WILLIAM RAGLAND.

THOMAS SHELTON, GIDEON RAGLAND and JAMES MURPHY security for WIL-
LIAM THOMSON.

Page 304-305
12 September 1805
Pr: 16 March 1807

LWT   CRISPIN SHELTON

To my son CHARLES IRBY my negro Stewart.

To my son ABRAHAM COWPER my negro Billey.

To my son MEACON ASHLEY my negro West.

To my daughter CHLOE ROBERTSON during her natural life, negro
Jenney, at my daughters death, to her children.

To my daughter MARTHA IRBY during her lifetime a negro Stella and
then to her children.

I lend to my beloved wife SUSANNA during her natural life my negros: Gruss, Major, Patrick, Phillis, Lucy, Lidda, Pattey, Agge
and Castille, two beds and furniture.

At the death of my wife, to be equally divided among all my said
children: CHARLES IRBY, ABRAHAM COWPER, MEACON ASHLEY, CHLOE ROB-
ERTSON and MARTHA IRBY.

The residue of my estate to be sold to pay my just debts, if this
is not sufficient, sell my 518 acre tract where I now live, but
should there be sufficient without selling the land, the land is
to be sold and other land purchased and my wife is to live on the
land.

At the death of my wife to be divided between my three sons: AB-
RAHAM COWPER, CHARLES IRBY and MEACON ASHLEY.

Appoint my wife and sons CHARLES IRBY and ABRAHAM COWPER executors.
CRISPIN SHELTON

SHELTON will cont'd:

Wit: VINCENT SHELTON, SUSANNA R. SHELTON, HENRY R. SHELTON.

JOHN IRBY, JOHN STONE, JR. and JEREMIAH WHITE security for SUSAN-
NA SHELTON, CHARLES I. SHELTON and ABRAHAM C. SHELTON.

Page 305-306
2 February 1801
Pr: 15 June 1807

LWT JOHN DUNN, SR. being weak in body but of perfect mind and
memory.

To my son JOHN five shillings.

To my son WILLIAM five shillings.

To my daughter SARY five shillings.

To my daughter ELIZABETH's heirs five shillings.

To my daughter MARY five shillings.

To my daughter CATHERINE five shillings.

To my daughter LUCRESY five shillings.

I lend to my beloved wife LUCY DUNN my whole estate during her
natural life.

To my sons THOMAS and JAMES DUNN I leave all my whole estate.

Appoint my wife executrix.

                              JOHN (X) DUNN

Wit: LUCY DUNN, NATHANIEL POPEJOY, EDWARD ADKINS, JOHN ADKINS.

Page 306-307
28 May 1806
Pr: 20 July 1807

LWT DAVID J. PATRICK of sound mind and memory.

I request my executor sell to HARVEY WYLAND land I purchased of
THOMAS BLACK in Campbell County. Also to purchase the tract where
on SARAH LUCK now lives when sold under the Will of FRANCIS LUCK,
deceased.

No division of my estate to be made before five years after my
death. I wish my estate divided between my wife SARAH and children as the law directs.

My executors to be guardians of my children and have the management of my estate and to raise and educate them as well and gen-
teely as the income will allow.

That my male children be bred to that of business. Also I wish
my children to remain with their mother until ten years of age

PATRICK will cont'd: at least.

Appoint my friends SAMUEL PANNILL and JEREMIAH PANNILL executors.

DAVID J. PATRICK

Wit: CLACK STONE, NATHL. CRADDOCK, BOOKER SHELTON.

Page 307-308
13 May 1803
Pr: 20 May 1807

LWT CHRISTOPHER HUTCHINGS being of sound mind and memory.

To my loving wife ELIZABETH during her natural life all my estate
both real and personal except that part of land I shall herein
will to my son MOSES HUTCHINGS.

As I have fully provided for my son JOHN HUTCHINGS, deceased, I
leave nothing to his heirs.

To my son THOMAS HUTCHINGS my tract of land on Cedarlick Creek
in Tn which I purchased of MARTIN HARDIN.

I lend to my son-in-law BRYANT W. NOWLING and my daughter MILLEY
NOWLING a negro Easter and at their death to my grandson, LEMUEL
HUTCHINGS, son of JAMES HUTCHINGS.

To my daughter ANN DILLARD a negro named Prudence, should ANN die
before the division of my estate, then the negro is to go to my
son JAMES HUTCHINGS.

To my daughter JEMIMA WELCH negros June and Sally, bed and furniture and a cow and calf.

I have fully provided for my son CHARLES HUTCHINGS and he is to
receive no more.

To my son MOSES HUTCHINGS the tract of land where he now lives
and a survey of 120 acres adjoining, negros Jack and Harvey.

To my son JAMES HUTCHINGS at the death of his mother, all my land
whereon I now live, with six negros: Lewis, Bell, Charity, Abraham, Ben and June a daughter of Bells, my stock of cattle and the
horses, furniture and tools.

I have provided for my son AARON HUTCHINGS and he is to receive
no more.

Appoint my sons MOSES and JAMES executors.

CHRISTOPHER (X) HUTCHINGS

Wit: WILLIAM WALTON, JAMES SOYARS, WILLIAM SOYARS, DAVID RICHARDS
and JESSE WALTON.

THOMAS H. WOODING, JESSE LEFTWICH, and JAMES SOYARS security for
MOSES HUTCHINGS.

Page 308-309
7 May 1807
Pr: 19 October 1807 (cont'd next page)

137

LWT NATHAN CURRY in perfect mind and memory.

After the payment of my just debts the balance to remain in the hands of my beloved wife NANCY CURRY for the purpose of schooling and raising my children. At the marriage or death of my wife a division of my estate to be made to my children.

Appoint my wife executrix.

NATHAN CURRY

Wit: THOMAS GARRETT, THOMAS HARRIS, WILLIAM (X) HINES

THOMAS HARRIS and WILLIAM HINES security for the executrix.

Page 309-310
1 November 1807
Pr: 21 December 1807

LWT JAMES NELSON weak in body but perfect memory.

To my loving wife SARAH NELSON one wagon and four mares, two from COOK, one of YEAMAN and of JOHN BRYANT, the household furniture.

To my son WILLIAM NELSON a mare.

I have previously given my married children all I intended and bequeath them one shilling each.

I lend to my wife the mare Bonney and at her decease to ELIZABETH NELSON, LYDDA NELSON, JOHN NELSON and MARTHA SEWEL.

I give my wife $80.00.

The balance of my estate to my single children.

JAMES (X) NELSON

Wit: GEORGE SPRATTIN, THOMAS BROWN, HENRY (X) PELL, GEORGE (X) DODSON.

HENRY PELL and GEORGE SPRATTIN security for JOSEPH FLIPPIN.

Page 310
10 August 1808 (as written)
Pr: 21 December 1807

LWT HENRY BOHANNON of sound mind and memory.

To my daughter MARY five shillinigs for her to freely enjoy forever.

To my son HENRY five shillings.

To my daughter NANCY five shillings.

To my son JOHN five shillings.

To my son ELLICK five shillings.

138

BOHANNON will cont'd:

To my son JOSEPH five shillings.

To my son NATHANIEL five shillings.

To my son AMBROSE five shillings.

I lend to my beloved wife NANCY BOHANNON during her natural life all my estate real and personal for the benefit of raising my children that I had by her.

At her death what remains be sold and divided between: LUOWELL BOHANNON, REBECKAH BOHANNON, DOLLEY BOHANNON, BERTON BOHANNON, THOMAS BOHANNON, PEGGY BOHANNON, YANCEY BOHANNON and RITTA BOHAN-NON. To be equal except that BERTON is to receive 5 pounds more.

HENRY (X) BOHANNON

Wit: DEVERINX HIGHTOWER, WILLIAM ROCE, JOHN BAYNESS, THOMAS SHAN-FIELD, ARCHER WALTER, WILLIAM WILES.

Page 310-312
11 December 1807
Pr: 18 January 1808

LWT THOMAS HARPER being in sound mind and memory.

I lend to my beloved wife ANN HARPER during her natural life or as long as she remains my chaste widow, all my estate except for the land on Sandy Creek joining HENRY HALL and JOHN MAY.

To my daughter SALLY HALL, wife of HENRY HALL, $1.00, should my daughter survive her husband then my son GEORGE HARPER is to pay her $10.00 for twenty years.

To my son NICHOLAS HARPER $1.00, should he survive his present wife NANCY, at the decease of my wife a negro Lysh to him.

To my son JACOB HARPER $1.00, and the mare he has in his posses-sion.

To my daughter ANNA HARPER, all my land on the west side of West Branch of Sandy Creek not to be conveyed as long as her mother lives, also at the death of my wife, a negro girl Rachel. Should ANNA die without issue, then to my son GEORGE HARPER.

To my son GEORGE HARPER at the expiration of my wifes chaste wid-owhood, all my estate both real and personal.

Appoint my wife ANN HARPER my executrix and friend WILLIAM WALTON and son GEORGE HARPER executors.

THOMAS HARPER

Wit: ALLEN STOKES, SR., JESSE WALTON, JR., CHRISTOPHER ROBERTSON, Sr., RANDOLPH SMITH, SAMUEL THOMPSON.

Page 312-313
28 April 1808 (cont'd next page)

Pr: 20 June 1808

LWT JOHN PARSONS, SR. being sick and weak but in perfect mind and memory.

To my beloved wife SARAH PARSONS lend her the use of my plantation and personal estate during her lifetime.

At her decease the personal property to be divided between my two sons and two daughters viz: ELI PARSONS, FREDERICK PARSONS, LEVINEY PARSONS and SALLY PARSONS.

To my son ELI the colt he now has.

My four children above mentioned to have my tract of land, 237 acres, where I now live.

My son GABRIEL PARSONS has had his full share.

My son JESSE PARSONS has had his full share as well as my son WILLIAM PARSONS.

My daughter LYDIA MIDKIFF has had her share.

My son RICHARD has had his share.

My son JOHN PARSONS has had his share.

Appoint WILLIAM ATKINSON my executor.

                                        JOHN (X) PARSONS, SR.

Wit: MARTIN WAGONER, COONROD (X) TRAIN

Page 313-314
1 June 1808
Pr: 18 July 1808

LWT THOMAS SHELTON being very sick and weak but of perfect mind.

I lend to my well beloved wife JANE SHELTON my land and plantation where I now live, livestock during her natural life.

To BETSEY SHELTON daughter of my nephew CHARLES SHELTON, deceased a feather bed.

I give all the cows as was lent to my children when they went to housekeeping, except my daughter LUCY SLAYDEN which I want to be kept in the power of my executors.

After the death of my wife, my estate to be sold and equally divided between my seven children: WILLIAM SHELTON, THOMAS SHELTON, BURNETT SHELTON, JAMES SHELTON, NANCY SLAYDON, SALLEY JOHNSON and LUCY SLAYDON.

Appoint my sons WILLIAM and THOMAS SHELTON executors.

                                        THOMAS (X) SHELTON

Wit: GEORGE DODSON, MARGARET DODSON, JOHN SHELTON, NOAH SHELTON, WILLIAM RAGLAND, JONATHAN GARDNER.

SHELTON will cont'd:

CREED TANNER, THOMAS SHELTON, JR., CHARLES COLLEY security for WILLIAM SHELTON.

Page 314-316
8 December 1806
Pr: 18 July 1808

LWT WILLIAM WITCHER, SR. being weak of body but sound memory.

To my son JOHN WITCHER, JR. my negro Sarah and her children Sinda, Ceala, and Anna in addition to what he has received.

To my son WILLIAM WITCHER, JR. my negro Tamer and her child Betsey and Peyton in addition to what he has received.

I lend to my son DANIEL WITCHER, JR. my negros Stephen and Anderson during his life, at his decease to his heirs.

I give to my son EPHRAIM WITCHER, JR. my negros: Bob, Abraham, Lunt, Phillis, Sucok and Will, also all the land I own in Pittsylvania County on Pigg River where I now live joining JOHN SMITH, JOHN WITCHER, JR., DANIEL C. EDWARDS and WILLIAM SWANSON, JR.

To my son JAMES WITCHER, JR. negros Hannah and Sellar and a set of smith tools.

To my son CALEB WITCHER one hundred pounds to discharge a judgement against him by JOHN SMITH and also to discharge his bond to GEORGE HERNDON. I lend Caleb during his lifetime my negro girl Bethsheba and at his decease to his eldest child THELLADA, should she die without issue, then to her brothers and sisters.

I lend to my daughter ELIZABETH RAZOR negros Edmond and Rose, at her decease to her heirs.

I give to my daughter RACHEL MORRISON a tract of land whereon WILLIAM MORRISON (her husband) now lives on Pigg River of 100 ac. more or less.

What money is left to be divided between my sons: JOHN WITCHER, JR., WILLIAM WITCHER, JR., DANIEL WITCHER, JR., EPHRAIM WITCHER, JR. and JAMES WITCHER, JR.

After my decease all my stock, furniture and crops to be sold and the money be divided between my sons: JOHN WITCHER, JR., WILLIAM WITCHER, JR., DANIEL WITCHER, JR., EPHRAIM WITCHER, JR. and JAMES WITCHER, JR.

Appoint my sons WILLIAM and JOHN executors.

                                        WILLIAM WITCHER

Wit: JOSEPH HATCHER, PEYTON GRAVES

PEYTON GRAVES, EPHRAIM WITCHER, WILLIAM WALKER and WILLIAM SWANSON, JR. security for the executors.

Page 317 (cont'd next page)

27 February 1807
Pr: 19 September 1808

LWT JOHN DAVIS of sound mind and memory.

Tomy beloved wife FRANCES DAVIS all my real and personal estate during her widowhood.

I desire my two sons live on the land until it is divided.

To my son WILLIAM DAVIS 100 acres where he lives.

To my son JOHN DAVIS 100 acres where he lives.

To my son FREDERICK DAVIS 100 acres the place whereon I now live.

My personal estate divided between my five daughters: CATREEN, ROSEAN, EFFY, SALLY and LUCY.

Appoint my sons WILLIAM and JOHN DAVIS executors.

                                        JOHN DAVIS

Wit: JOHN BOBBETT, HENRY ADKINSON, ROB. PANNILL, JOHN M_____

Widow FRANCES DAVIS executrix.

Page 318-320
1 July 1808
Pr: 17 October 1808

LWT HENRY MECKELBOROUGH sick and weak but perfect mind and memory.

To my daughter FRANCES CHEATHAM negro Hannah.

To my daughter ELIZABETH HARPER twenty five pounds.

To my son ROBERT a negro Randolph.

To my daughter LURAH KERBY a bed and furniture and negro Peter.

To my daughter MARAH SUTHERLIN negro Edmond.

To my son CARTER negro Joseph.

To my daughter JANE MECKELBURROUGH negro Aylee, and a colt.

To my son ALDIN negro Abrum.

To my daughter PATSEY LUMKIN negro Tom.

To my son JAMES negro Wiley.

My daughter SARAH KERBY to have but one half a childs part of the residue of my estate.

My grandchildren LUCY DAVIS, ELIZABETH CORNWELL and LARKIN CHEATHAM should have one childs part of my personal estate.

Residue to my children: ELIZABETH, the heirs of my son ROBERT,

MECKELBOROUGH will cont'd:

CARTER, POLLEY, JANE, PATSEY, ALDIN and JAMES.

Appoint my wife and son Carter executors.

HENRY MECKELBOROUGH

Wit: ROBERT (X) GLASGO, FRANCIS (X) WORSHAM, ELIZABETH (X) CAMP-
BELL.

WILLIAM YANCEY and CHARLES PISTOLE security for executor.

Page 320-321
3 September 1808
Pr: 19 December 1808

LWT JAMES STRANGE being of sound mind and memory.

I lend to my beloved wife SUSANNAH the plantation where I live,
negro Stephey, livestock for her use during her lifetime.

At the death of my wife, my estate divided between all my children: SMITH STRANGE, JOHN STRANGE, JESSE STRANGE, ELIZABETH SUMATE,
FRANCES STRANGE and MARY STRANGE.

As I have already given my married children some things, I think
it proper to give my other three children the following property:
to JESSE STRANGE a cow and calf; to FRANCES T. STRANGE and MARY
STRANGE each seven pounds of feathers, also to FRANCES a bed, cow
and calf, same to MARY. These last two daughters to remain with
their mother during their single life.

I desire my negro Dick and other stock to be sold and the money
divided between all my children.

JAMES STRANGE

Wit: TAPLY AKIN, SMITH STRANGE, JESSE STRANGE.

THOMAS CURRY and RICHARD JOHNSON security for the executors.

Page 322-323
28 December 1808
Pr: 20 February 1809

LWT JOHN WALLER being sick and weak but of perfect mind and memory.

To my beloved wife REBECAH WALLER, the right and title to that
tract on Dan River in Rockingham County with the negros on the
place during her lifetime, it being property that came by her.
At her decease to be disposed of as further directed.

To my daughter PHEBE BOLTON one hundred pounds, and negro Hannah.

To my son JOEL WALLER five shillings with what I have given him.

To MAJOR PRICE former husband of my daughter SARAH PRICE, decd.,
five shillings.

WALLER will cont'd:

To my son OBD. WALLER five shillings with what he has received.

To my daughter LIDDA WHITE five shillings with what she already has received.

To my son JOHN WALLER the tract called the Creek tract except the part layed off for my son JOEL WALLER if he should come back.

To my son PLEASANT WALLER the tract where I live.

To my sons JOHN and PLEASANT and my daughter LIDDA WHITE, to have use of the property until her children come of age.

To my son JOHN negros Harry, Simon, Phillis and her two children Jezbel and Peter, a mare, a horse on the Rockingham property.

To PLEASANT negros Abram, Daniel, Kear and her children Mary and Terry, and 3 horses.

To my daughter LIDDA WHITE negros Adam, Kupit, Sill and children Pott, Ben, Alphred and a horse.

Appoint WILLIAM STAMPS and WILLIAM WALKER executors.

                                        JOHN (X) WALLER

Wit: GEORGE DODSON, SR., WILLIAM WALKER, WILLIAM (X) COLLEY

JACKSON WALTER, RAWLEY WHITE, WILLIAM DODSON, JOHN PESTOLE, NOEL WADDELL, THOMAS SHELTON, STOOKLEY TURNER, WILLIAM WILLIAMS, WILLIAM YANCEY and DOCTOR C. WILLIAMS security for the executors.

Page 324
4 May 1804
Pr: 20 February 1809

LWT THOMAS SMITH being in my proper sense.

Appoint GEORGE ADAMS and JOSEPH MORTON executors.

To my loving wife FRANCES SMITH all my negros during her lifetime for her to dispose of as she sees cause. To have all my personal property.

To MARTHA JONES a tract on Sandy Creek of 400 acres.

At the decease of my wife the rest of my land be equally divided between: SMITH FULLON and WILLIAM SMITH, son of JOHN SMITH, deceased.

                                        THOMAS SMITH

Wit: JOSEPH SMITH, NANCY DRAIN, JOHN STILL, WILLIAM STILL, JONATHAN ELLIOTT

THOMAS S. JONES ecxecutor.

Page 325 (cont'd next page)

29 July 1808
Pr: 15 May 1809

LWT GEORGE SMITH in perfect health.

To my daughter BEHEATHERLAND LAURENCE thirty pounds.

To my _____ LUCY WATSON fifteen pounds.

To my dutiful son JABEZ SMITH my plantation, lands and tenaments
and my slaves: Symie, Ruben, Stephen, Dick, Easter, Vilotte, Jude
and Nancy, all the livestock and furniture.

Appoint son JABEZ and friend JAMES HOPKINS executors.

                                        GEORGE SMITH

Wit: GEORGE K. SMITH, JOSEPH REYNOLDS, JAMES HOPKINS, HARTWELL
ALLEN.

HARTWELL ALLEN and HENRY G. CALLOWAY security for executors.

Page 327
10 February 1809
Pr: 18 May 1809

LWT THOMAS DAVIS weak in body but of sound mind.

I lend to my wife ANNE, my whole estate during her lifetime, at
her decease to my daughter NANCY after she pays my son JOHN DAV-
IS's son THOMAS five pounds and my daughter ELIZABETH's daughter
NANCY five pounds.

                                        THOMAS (X) DAVIS

Wit: BENJ. STONE, CORNELIES MC HANEY, JOHN TURNER

P. S.
Provided there is more than one child named JOHN DAVIS he is to
receive five pounds.

HENRY ARNOLD executor.

Page 327-329
4 June 1809
Pr: 7 July 1809

LWT PHILIP MEASE

To my beloved wife CATY that part of the plantation where I now
live during her natural life, a horse, furniture and cattle and
other personal property. At her decease to my son ABRAHAM MEASE.

To my son PHILIP MEASE the land where he lives, he is to pay fifty pounds to my three daughters: CATY HENDRICK, ANA MEASE & SALLY
MEASE.

To my son JOHN MEASE a tract of 180 acres purchased of CHARLES
GREEN, my large bible in the Dutch language.

                        145

MEASE will cont'd:

To my son ABRAHAM, after the death of my wife, the balance of my tract where I now live after paying fifty pounds to my daughters: CATY HEADRICK, CHRISTINA MEASE and SALLY MEASE. Also other personal property.

To my daughter CHRISTINA MEASE a bed, cow and calf, and a spinning wheel.

To my daughter SALLY MEASE a bed, cow and calf, and a spinning wheel.

The residue of my estate to be sold to pay my just debts.

PHILIP MEASE is to pay an annual rent to my wife during her natural life.

Appoint my wife CATY MEASE and Capt. PEYTON GRAVES executors.

PHILIP (X) MEASE

Wit: CHARLES W. BIRD, JOSEPH HATCHETT, DAVID VANCE, DANIEL C. EDWARDS.

PEYTON GRAVES, DAVID VANCE, WILLIAM SWANSON, JR., security for CATY MEASE.

Page 329-330
3 August 1807
Pr: 19 December 1808

LWT   AMBROSE CORBIN

To my wife JINCEY CORBIN during her lfetime the tract of land we now live 226 acres, negro Dinah, beds, and livestock.

At the decease of my wife I give my son DAVID CORBIN the above mentioned tract and negro, all tools, bed and furniture.

To my son RANDOLPH CORBIN a cow and calf and a bed.

To my daughter MOLLY CORBIN a cow and calf and a bed.

To my daughter SALLY CORBIN a cow and calf and a bed.

To my daughter BETSY CORBIN a cow and calf and a bed.

After the death of my wife the rest of my personal property to be sold and my executors pay my daughters; SALLY, MOLLY and BETSY five pounds each. The balance to be divided between all my children.

Appoint DAVID CORBIN executor.

AMBROS CORBIN

Wit: ROBERT LEFTWICH, JOHN SANDERS, ARTHER CRAWFORD.

JAMES GARLAND security for the executor.

Page 331
__ June 1809
Pr: 21 August 1809

LWT JAMES FARMER being very sick and weak.

To my sons REUTON FARMER and JOHN FARMER the tract and plantation where I now live after the decease of my wife.

To my grand daughters SELINA, ROSEY and SALLY POSEY, children of my daughter JINCEY POSEY, a negro girl Rachel.

To my daughters ALCEY FARMER and BETSY FARMER a negro boy Anderson when they reach 12 years of age.

I desire my estate be kept together till my children come of age.

JAMES (X) FARMER

Wit: HARRISON (X) BURNS, JUDA (X) BURNS, TAMSON (X) ARNOLD.

ELIZABETH FARMER relinquishes her right of administration to HUBBARD FARMER, with WILLIAM ECHOLS and VACHEL CLEMENTS as his security.

Page 332-333
7 March 1808
Pr: 18 September 1809

LWT DANIEL SHELTON being weak in body.

To my beloved daughter SUSANNA SHELTON twenty five pounds during her life, then to her children.

To the children of my beloved daughter CLARY SHELTON, twenty five pounds.

I lend to my beloved daughter MILLEY TAYLOR twenty five pounds during her life, then to her children.

I lend to my daughter ANN BAILEY twenty five pounds during her life, then to her children.

I lend to my daughter SALLY PAIN five pounds during her life then to her children.

I lend to my daughter POLLY SHELTON twenty five pounds, then to her children.

To my grand daughter JANE ASQUA SHELTON a negro girl Edith, also a feather bed and furniture, and a large trunk. Should she die without an heir, then to my chidlren.

I lend to my beloved wife LETTICE, negros: Bob, Ester, Lucy, Randolph, Isaac, Chloe, Matildy, Moses and Little Bob, all my livestock, my still and all my furniture. At her decease to be divided among my sons: YOUNG, LEROY, DANIEL, TUNSTALL and to WILLES' children: LEROY, GETER, POLLY, MOUNTEGUE, MERRIT, MACCA, LEFAS, ELIZABETH and WILLES. These children to have 1/5 part, which I give them instead of to WILLES.

I desire my sons to divide the negros between them and keep them

147

SHELTON will cont'd:

in the family.

I desire my sons to let my two old negros Bob and Easter to stay
with whom they please as it is contrary to laws of my country to
free them.

Appoint my sons YOUNG and TUNSTALL executors.

DANIEL SHELTON

Wit: JOHN STONE, JR., ABRAHAM SHELTON, BERRY LEWIS.

THOMAS RAGSDALE, HENRY R. SHELTON, HENRY C. KEATTS, JOHN LEWIS
and THOMPSON ROBERTSON security for executors.

Page 333-334
24 July 1809
Pr: 18 September 1809

LWT HENRY G. CALLAWAY being weak in body.

My beloved wife HANNAH CALLAWAY to have the use of my estate, except what is hereafter devised, during her widowhood or natural
life.

At her death the whole to be equally divided among my children:
JOHN M. CALLAWAY and MATILDA CALLAWAY.

In my grandfather's Will, he has devised certain property to my
Mother during her life and at her death to my brother DAVID CALL-
AWAY, my sister PEGGY CALLAWAY and myself. After the decease of
my Father and Mother, I give my part to my deceased brother WIL-
LIAM's children.

Appoint my friends RALPH SMITH, WILLIAM STEPTOE and WILLIAM CAL-
LAWAY, JR. as executors.

They are to assist in building my wife a house and WILLIAM STEP-
TOE is to act as guardian for my children.

HENRY G. CALLAWAY

Wit: HARTWELL ALLEN, WILLIAM CALLAWAY, JOHN CALLAWAY.

WILLIAM CALLAWAY, SR. and JOHN SMITH security for executors.

Page 334-336
5 February 1806
Pr: 18 December 1809

LWT MATHEW TANNER being affected in body but of sound mind.

My beloved wife LUCY TANNER to have possession of one third of
the land where I now live during her lifetime and negros Jude and
Cate, a third of my livestock, household furniture and tools.

To my son JOSEAH TANNER a negro Isbell and to his son MATHEW a
negro Guy now in their possession.

148

TANNER will cont'd:

To my son MATHEW TANNER five shillings.

To my son CREED TANNER all the land where I now live, at the decease of my wife. I give him negros Abra, Jinney, Cate and Mingo also my copper still, and a mare.

To my son THOMAS TANNER sixty pounds.

To my daughter MARTHA ANDERSON after the death of my wife, negro Peter.

To my daughter BETSEY CALDWELL after the death of my wife, negros Robert and Viney.

To my daughter POLLY CALDWELL after my death negro Amay and after my wifes death, negros Jude and Ben.

To my grandson BIRD LEWIS TANNER a negro Joe.

To my grand daughter BETSEY RAINS WALTERS a cow and calf.

The residue not given to be sold to pay my debts and the balance to my son THOMAS TANNER.

Appoint my wife LUCY and my son CREED executors.

MATHEW TANNER

Wit: THOMAS TANNER, MARY (X) TANNER, SAL___ GARDNER.

JOHN WILSON, JAMES WILSON, HENRY WILSON, DANIEL MOTLEY and JOEL WILLIS security for executors.

Page 336-337
25 January 1810
Pr: 19 February 1810

LWT LUCY (LUSCEY) DAVIS of sound mind.

To ELIZABETH STORDE a negro named Cloey.

To THOMAS MURPHY and WILLIAM DAVIS, the rest of my property and appoint them executors.

LUSCEY DAVIS

Wit: SUSANNER (X) PATTEN, PATSEY (X) CASEY, THOMAS CASEY, JOHN LEWIS, JACOB NORTEN.

Page 337-340
27 April 1810
Pr: 21 May 1810

LWT HARMON COOK, SR. being weak in body but of sound mind.

I made ample provisions for my wife before our marriage, jointure in Pittsylvania County records, and desire she hold the same during her life.

149

COOK will cont'd:

To my son JOHN COOK land on Turkey Cock Creek, land on Sandy River, fifteen pounds, land on Wetsleave joining MOSES HUBBARD, JACOB ARON and Widow MITCHELL.

To my son HARMON COOK, JR. the use only of a parcel of land on Pigg River. Whenever his children desire to settle, my executors to allot them a portion of said tract, but can not be sold during the lifetime of their father. At his death divided between all his children.

The land deeded my wife, after her death, to be considered as included in this bequeath to the children of HARMON COOK, JR. Also all the personal property lent to her.

Lend to my son-in-law ABRAHAM ROARER, SR. land on Pigg River to include land on Potters Creek except where JOHN SEVER lives who is entitled to live there during his and his wifes lifetime. The land, after his decease, to be divided among his children by his present wife (except son JOHN who has received 200 acres.)

Lend to my daughter CATHERINE WRIGHT negros Randolph and Suckey and at her death to PAUL RAZOR and my daughter MARY RAZOR. To CATHERINE fifty pounds.

Lend to my daughter MARY RAZOR negros Fanny and George, at her decease to her children, also fifty pounds.

I have given ABRAHAM COOK what I intended, give him five pounds.

My executors to sell my other lands five years after my death and the money divided between the children of HARMON COOK, JR. and ABRAHAM ROARER, SR. by his present wife.

To my son HARMON my wearing apparel.

My daughter NANCY ROARER to keep the store she has.

Many years ago I deposited with JOSHUA STONE County Surveyor, Treasury Land Warrants for several thousand acres, executors to sell these and divide the money between HARMON COOK and ABRAHAM ROARER.

My executors to sell the rest of the personal estate to pay my legacies and debts, what is left over to the children of HARMON COOK, JR. and ABRAHAM ROARER, SR. by his present wife.

Should I die before the suit with JOHN STOCKTON's (deceased) representatives is settled my executors to push it with utmost vigor.

Appoint friends ROBERT DEVIN and JAMES HOPKINS executors.

HARMON COOK

Wit: JOHN HOFFMAN, JOHN (X) DANGERFIELD, ALEXANDER JEFFERSON, SAMUEL A. JEFFERSON, JOHN LOVELL.

ROBERT ADAMS, JAMES ADAMS, RAWLEY WHITE, WILLIAM PARRISH, MATHEW PARRISH, WILLIAM CLARK, THOMAS H. WOODING, HARTWELL ALLEN and SAMUEL CALLANDS security for the executors.

Page 341-342
29 January 1801
Pr: 16 April 1810

LWT STEPHEN NEAL, SR. considering the advanced state of my age.

To my son WILLIAM NEAL besides what I have given him, one cow.

To my son SAMUEL NEAL four negros: Phillis, Bristol, Nancy and Sherry.

To my son SIMON NEAL negros: Milly and her children, Sarah and Doll.

To my daughter SARAH TERRY negros: Lewis, Amey and Lydia, now in her and her husband JOHN's possession.

To my son JOHN NEAL negros: Saul and Johnson and a bay colt.

To my daughter JOANNA NEAL negros: Philip and Isbel, horse, saddle and bridle, bed and furniture.

To my son STEPHEN NEAL negros: Frank and Clarburn, horse and saddle.

To my daughter MARY NEAL negros: Robbin, Jinney and Rachel, bed and furniture.

To my son JOEL NEAL negros: George, Sherry the elder, Jack, Peter, Len, Branch, two Peggys, Cinna and Patty together with all my other property with the condition that he pays my wife ANNA NEAL $100.00 every year.

Appoint son JOEL NEAL and DOCTOR JAMES LINN executors.

                              STEPHEN (X) NEAL, SR.

Wit: WILLIAM LOGAN, VACHEL CLEMENT, OBEDIAH (X) ___AN

Page 342-343
4 March 1809
Pr: 18 June 1810

LWT RICHARD FARTHING of sound mind and memory.

To my son LANDY FARTHING 50 acres, it being part of the tract whereon I now live.

To my son JOHN FARTHING 30 acres of land.

To my son WILLIAM FARTHING 30 acres including the tract where he now lives and the use of the spring in common with his brother RICHARD FARTHING.

To my son ABNER FARTHING 30 acres where he now lives.

To my son SOLOMAN FARTHING 30 acres where he now lives.

To my son DUDLEY FARTHING a bed and furniture.

I give nothing more to my daughters MISHAEL NICOLDS and REBECCA

FARTHING will cont'd:

PARSONS than they have received.

To my son RICHARD FARTHING the remainder of my estate both real
and personal subject to the maintenance of his mother GRISELL
FARTHING during her lifetime.

Appoint RICHARD FARTHING and friend THOMAS H. WOODING executors.

                                        RICHARD FARTHING

Wit: DANIEL BRADLEY, ZACHARIAH RIDDLE, SUSANA WOODING.

Page 344-346
11 December 1806
Pr: 16 July 1810

LWT BRYAN WARD NOWLIN being in perfect health.

My crop, my stock and if necessary three acres where the Mill is
located to be sold to pay my just debts and the residue for my
son SHERAD when he comes of age which will be November 13, 1810.
My estate to be kept together till Sherad comes of age.

To my beloved wife MILDRED NOWLIN a negro named Luna and also the
negro Esther which she received from her father, along with her
increase: Isaac, Mary, Juno, Lucrecia and Ben, and at her death
to go to the will of her father CHRISTOPHER HUTCHINGS, also a bed
and furniture, chest and items she brought with her.

I lend to my wife 115 acres including house and household furniture and some livestock. At her decease to be sold and the money
divided equally between my children.

I lend to my daughter ELIZABETH DEVIN a negro girl Hannah and at
her death, to her children.

I have formerly given my son BRYAN WARD NOWLIN as much as I intended but as a token of love, give him five pounds.

I desire my negros: Pat, her daughter Esther and children Peter
and Liza, Phillis and her five children Candace, Wheeler, Brancer,
Milley, Carter and Davie be divided between my eleven children:
PEYTON NOWLIN, LUCY BENNETT, SUCKY DEVIN, JAMES NOWLIN, DAVID NOW-
LIN, MARY MAHAN, RICHARD WADE NOWLIN, CATY BARGER, SAMUEL NOWLIN,
ANNE NOWLIN and SHERAD NOWLIN.

I desire my father to be kindly treated and continue to have his
house and be supported as usual.

After the marriage or death of my wife the residue of my estate
to be sold and the money divided between my eleven children.

Appoint sons JAMES, DAVID and SAMUEL NOWLIN executors.

                                        BRYAN WARD NOWLIN

Wit: ISHAM HARDY, LEWIS ATKINSON, GEORGE BERGER, JOHN (X) KEESEE

Page 347-348 (cont'd next page)

28 June 1810
Pr: 20 August 1810

LWT THOMAS BARNETT being weak in body but of sound and disposing
memory.

To my wife FRANCES BARNETT during her life the two houses and lot
in Danville, Virginia and furniture except otherwise given.

To my son JOSEPH BARNETT 1234 acres on Rutledge Creek in consideration of his allowing me to sell negros Lee and Sam for my benefit.

To my daughter SALLY BARNETT 546 acres on the branches of the Dan
River, negros Dolly and Isaac.

To my daughter FRANCES BARNETT 211 acres on Rutledge Creek and
negros Milley and Bill.

To my son JOSEPH, a bed and furniture, a burow (burro?) and colt.

To my daughter SALLY bed and furniture, one burow, horse and saddle.

To my daughter FRANCES the same.

I give my wife FRANCES the rest of my slaves: Davy, Cyrus, Sarah,
Patience, Lidia, Keziah and Adam to dispose of as she may see fit
and I desire my remaining stock, my carriage, and a wagon remain
with my wife.

My one third part of the tole bridge across the Dan River near
Danville to be sold also two lots in Danville to be sold.

Appoint beloved wife FRANCES BARNETT executrix and son JOSEPH executor.

                                        THOMAS BARNETT

Wit: JAMES D. PATTON, THOMAS STEWART, JAMES GATEWOOD, ALEX. A.
CAMPBELL.

20 April 1818:
DANIEL SULLIVAN appointed executor with GEORGE T. LANDAREN, CAR-
TER MICKLEBOROUGH and THOMAS SUTHERLIN security.

Page 348-350
2 April 1810
Pr: 17 September 1810

LWT THOMAS MADDING being very sick and weak of body but of perfect mind and memory.

I lend my well beloved wife RACHEL MADDING my negro Letty, house
and 150 acres, furniture, livestock, horse and saddle during her
natural life. I desire the rest of my negros remain with my wife
untill all my children shall be of age.

The rest of my estate to my nine children: ELISHA MADDING, RAL-
EIGH MADDING, ROBERT MADDING, ALBERT MADDING, THOMAS MADDING, AL-
ES MC LAUGHLIN, POLLY MADDING, WILMOUTH MADDING and ELIZABETH

MADDING will cont'd:

MADDING. Also that part lent my wife be equally divided at her death.

Appoint son ELISHA executor.

THOMAS (X) MADDING

Wit: GEORGE DODSON, MARGARET DODSON.

ELISHA MADDING refuses to be executor, widow RACHEL MADDING relinquishes her right to RAWLEY MADDING, who with GEORGE DODSON and THOMAS SHELTON his security entered into bond.

Page 351
6 September 1805
Pr: 17 September 1810

LWT BENJAMIN LANKFORD being very sick and weak but sound mind.

To my son BENJAMIN LANKFORD all the tract of land whereon I now live being 500 acres more or less.

The remaining part of my estate to be equally divided between my sons BENJAMIN LANKFORD, STEPHEN LANKFORD and my daughters MARY TODD, ANNE MADISON, SARAH BROWN, KITTY TURNER and HENRETTA LANKFORD.

Appoint JOHN TURNER and my son STEPHEN LANKFORD executors.

BEN. LANKFORD

(No witnesses)

It appears to the Court that the Will is in the handwriting of the said LANKFORD.

RICHARD JOHNSON, EDWARD DOUGLASS, STEPHEN C. MC DANIEL, HENRY ARNOLD and JOHN FARRIS security for JOHN TURNER.

Page 351-353
8 April 180
Pr: 15 October 1810

LWT JAMES MC DONALD being weak in body but of sound mind.

Lend to my beloved wife MARY MC DONALD all my land where I now live and negro Rose, furniture and livestock.

To my daughter NANCEY DOUTAN wife of JAMES DOUTAN one dollar with all else she has received.

To my son RANDOLPH MC DONALD one dollar with what else he has received.

To my daughter SUSANAH MC DONALD the upper end of my land on Sandy Creek of 30 acres more or less.

To my daughter PEGGEY WHETWORTH wife of ABRAHAM WHETWORTH one

MC DONALD will cont'd:

dollar with what else she has received.

To my son ABSALOM MC DONALD the same.

To my son ABNER MC DONALD the same.

To my son ABSEL MC DONALD the same.

To my son DANIEL MC DONALD the same.

To my daughter ZERIAH MC DONALD negro Lucy and after the decease of my wife, half the land where I now live, half my livestock, and furniture.

After the decease of my wife the negro Rose to my daughters ZER-IAH and ZEPORA MC DONALD.

To my daughter ZERISHA BURTON wife of THOMAS BURTON one dollar and what she has already received.

To my daughter ZEPORA MC DONALD negro Darcus and after the decease of my wife, half the land before mentioned, stock and furniture also negro Kese.

To my daughter ZELLA TAYLOR wife of JOHN TAYLOR one dollar and what she has received.

To my son CLEMENT MC DONALD the lower end of the tract whereon I now live after the death of my wife, and negro Mary.

Appoint sons RANDOLPH and ABSALOM MC DONALD executors.

JAMES MC DONALD

Wit: GEORGE ADAMS, JOHN MATNEY, JOHN ADAMS, REDMUND FALLEN, MARK WILSON.

REDMON FALLEN, BENJAMIN WATKINS and GEORGE SUTHERLIN security for RANDOLPH MC DONALD.

Page 353-354
28 September 1810
Pr: 19 November 1810

LWT JOHN SNODDY very sick and weak of body but sound mind.

To my daughter BETSEY SNODDY negro Cloey, horse, bed and furniture, quilt, shawl, counterpin and a large pot.

To my son ROBERT SNODDY negro Samuel to be left in the care of my son THOMAS SNODDY until ROBERT and Samuel come of age.

THOMAS SNODDY must give ROBERT two years schooling.

Should ROBERT die without issue, the negro Samuel to my daughter POLLEY SNODDY.

The balance of my estate be sold and the money equally divided between my children: WILLIAM SNODDY, THOMAS SNODDY, SALLEY HAWKES,

SNODDY will cont'd:

FRANCES JONES, JINNEY HAWKES, ANNEY CLARK and POLLEY SNODDY.

There is one acre laid off for the use of the Meeting House which I except.

Appoint MATHEW FITZGERALD executor.

JOHN SNODDY

Wit: WILLIAM SIMPSON, ELIZABETH SNODDY, ELIJAH COOK.

PHILIP HAWKER and WILLIAM SNODDY security for executor.

Page 354
9 February 1810
Pr: 17 December 1810

LWT JOHN OWEN being very sick and weak but of sound mind.

To my beloved wife MARY OWEN all my estate both real and personal to enjoy during her natural life.

To my son DAVID OWEN the land and plantation where I now reside after the death of my wife.

To my daughter ELIZABETH HOLDER and SUSANNAH WOOD, my granddaughter MILLEY OWEN and SALLY OWEN all the rest of my estate.

JOHN (X) OWEN

Wit: JOSHUA STONE, JR., THOMAS JAMES, ELIZ. PATHER.

JOSHUA STONE, JR. and WILLIAM ECHOLS security for MARY OWEN.

Page 355
4 August 1809
Pr: 21 January 1811

LWT JAMES HENDERSON being weak of body but of sound mind and of memory.

Whereas some doubts may arise respecting the negro slave Dinah which was the property of my wife MARY HENDERSON, formerly MARY BUCKLEY, and in order to remove such doubts, I relinquish any and all claim I may have to my wife MARY.

I lend to my wife MARY HENDERSON during her natural life my land and negros, stock and furniture.

To ANNE MOORE daughter of WILLIAM MOORE, deceased, $50.00 to be paid after the decease of my wife.

After the death of my wife the balance of my estate to be equally divided between my two sons WILLIAM HENDERSON and JAMES HENDERSON.

Appoint WILLIAM SMITH and JESSE BUCKLEY my executors.

JAMES (X) HENDERSON

156

HENDERSON will cont'd:

Wit: JOHN GREGORY, THOMAS GREGORY, ISAAC (X) GREGORY.

JAMES HENDERSON, JESSE BUCKLEY and JAMES HART security for WIL-
LIAM SMITH.

Page 356
26 January 1811
Pr: 18 February 1811

THOMAS PISTOLE, SR. being very sick in body but of sound mind.

To my wife HANNAH my estate real and personal during her lifetime
including negro Jord.

To my son JAMES thirty pounds with what he has already received.

I have given my other children all I desired for them.

After the decease of my wife the land to my son JOHN and all the
other personal estate divided between my children giving POLLEY
L. REGINS eight pounds.

Appoint THOMAS PISTOLE and HENRY WILKINSON executors.

THOMAS PISTOLE, SR.

Wit: THOMAS BROWN, JAMES H. PASS, BEZELEEL WER, SR., JOHN NEWBELL

CHARLES PISTOLE, ABRAHAM PISTOLE and THOMAS BROWN security for
executors.

Page 356-357
16 December 1807
Pr: 18 February 1811

LWT WILLIAM HARRISON

I desire my just debts paid and think it just that my children
should contribute towards this by equal ratio of what they have
received.

I confirm the gift I made my son ROBERT HARRISON except 50 acres
I had of him to accomodate Col. JOHN WILSON in consideration of
a negro I let him have, also give him five shillings as he has
had a great proportion of my estate.

I confirm the gift to my daughter SUSANNAH WARE wife of WILLIAM
WARE who is deceased and to WILLIAM WARE I give five shillings.

I confirm the gift to JANE STONE and give her five shillings, as
she has had her part in the possession of HENRY STONE.

I confirm the gift to ANNE COLEMAN wife of DANIEL COLEMAN except
the negro Jane who died before ANNE HARRISON married said DANIEL
COLEMAN, give ANNE five shillings.

I confirm the gift made POLLEY DILLARD HARRISON which is in her
possession.

157

HARRISON will cont'd:

I confirm the gift to WILLIAM PORTER HARRISON.

I confirm the gift to NATHANIEL HARRISON.

It is stated in my father's will that if any of his children die without an heir, their estate to be equally divided amongst the rest of his children. Should such an event happen I shall be entitled to my share and I bequeath it to my son NATHANIEL HARRISON.

Appoint sons NATHANIEL and WILLIAM PORTER HARRISON executors.

They are with the rest of my children to take particular care of their tender Mother who has many times contributed to their comfort.

WILLIAM HARRISON

This will to be recorded without witnesses as it is wholly written by my own hand.

Page 357-358
17 January 1811
Pr: 18 March 1811

LWT WILLIAM HAYMES low in health but sound of mind.

To my beloved wife JILICO six negros: Grace, Ceasar, Sarah, Jerre, Winney and John, the land where I now live and the livestock, furniture, my still and oxcart during her natural life.

After the death of my wife all property to be sold and divided between my children: MARY PACE, SUSANNAH PACE, WILLIAM HAYMES, JR., JOSHUA HAYMES, NANCY HOLLAND, ROBERT HAYMES, DAVID HAYMES and DANIEL HAYMES. My two old negros Sarah and Grace to choose their masters.

To my son DANIEL the old tract known as Purnell's tract and the small tract taken from Goodman's, a negro Jim, bed and furniture, livestock and a mare.

To my son WILLIAM negro Tabb.

To my son JOSHUA negro Henry.

To my son ROBERT negro Joel.

To my daughter NANCY HOLLAND my negro Hannah.

To my son DAVID my negro Garland, a cow and calf, a sow and pigs.

To my daughter MARY PACE negro Grace.

To my daughter SUSANNAH PACE negro Silvey.

To my daughter ELIZABETH BOATMAN $10.00.

Appoint sons WILLIAM and DANIEL HAYMES executors.

WILLIAM (X) HAYMES

158

HAYMES will cont'd:

Wit: WILLIAM SHELTON, GILES PAYNE, WILLIAM NELSON alias BOWING, ELIZABETH NELSON alias BOWING.

THOMAS B. JONES, BENJAMIN SHELTON, THOMPSON ROBERTSON, OBEDIAH TAYLOR, ROBERT LOVE, JOSEPH HOLLAND and ROBERT HAYMES security.

Page 358
7 November 1810
Pr: 20 May 1811

LWT THOMAS WATSON being weak in body but of sound mind.

I give unto my wife ELSE all that I possess during her lifetime.

To EADY RUMBLY my grand daughter $50.00

To POLLY RUMBLY $50.00

To CANNON RUMBLY $50.00

At the death of my wife, my estate to be equally divided among my children: daughter JERUSHA JONES an equal part during her life and then to her heirs; to daughter GRESSELL HILL one part; to son JOHN WATSON one part; to son GEORGE WATSON one part; to son AMOS WATSON one part; to son SHEMEIAH WATSON one part; to my daughter ANNE WATSON one part during her life and then to her heirs; to son THOMAS WATSON one part.

Appoint sons JOHN and THOMAS WATSON executors.

THOMAS (X) WATSON

Wit: THOMAS EASLEY, WILLIAM FERGUSON, STEPHEN GILES.

JOHN WATSON, SR., SAMUEL CALLAND and RICHARD JOHNSON security for executor.

Page 360
27 July 1810
Pr: 20 May 1811

LWT THOMAS FARMER being in my proper sense.

I lend to my beloved wife JENE FARMER all that I possess during her life or widowhood.

To my son JAMES FARMER thirty pounds.

To my son LABAN FARMER the land he lives on.

To my daughter MARY PRQUAL(?) thirty pounds.

To my son JOHN FARMER negro Nancy.

To my son ROBERT negro Chana.

To my son SAMUEL FARMER negro Sarah.

FARMER will cont'd:

The rest of my estate, after the death of my wife, to be divided as named equal: WILLIAM FARMER, JOHN FARMER, ROBERT FARMER, SAMUEL FARMER, SALEY BELLSTON, ANNE IRBY, LUCY FARMER, MILY FARMER, SUSANNA FARMER.

Executors LABAN FARMER, ROBERT FARMER and JOHN FARMER.

THOMAS FARMER

Wit: CHARLES CLEMENT, ADAM CLEMENT, JR., THOMAS EAST.

Court 18th November:
JOHN and LABAN FARMER executors with ROBERT FARMER, FRANCIS ABSTON, DANIEL FARMER, SUSANNAH FARMER, LABAN HARMAN, JAMES BRUCE their security.

Page 360
10 February 1810
Pr: 16 September 1811

LWT CHARLES MC LAUGHLAN, SR. weak in body yet of sound mind.

I give my land to my son HENRY MC LAUGHLAN and my son CHARLES MC LAUGHLAN.

To my daughter PATIENCE MC LAUGHLAN the choice of bed and furniture, a mare and saddle, chest and one cow.

To my daughter POLLY bed and furniture, cow and calf.

To my daughter SARAH bed and furniture, cow and calf, chest, saddle and wheel.

Appoint my sons HENRY and CHARLES executors.

CHARLES MC LAUGHLAN, SR.

Wit: DAVID TERRY, BARTON TERRY, SR., MOSES TERRY.

JAMES M. WILLIAMS and DAVID C. WILLIAMS security for executors.

Page 361-362
14 February 1811
Pr: 21 October 1811.

LWT RICHARD BENNETT, SR. being weak in body but of sound mind.

After my decease LOUVISA COCKRAM to have two feather beds & furniture, two cows and calves, a horse, saddle, bridle and a negro Dan, during her natural life and to have the priviledge to live on the plantation as long as she lives, free from molestation.

To CHARLES W. BOBBETT the land and plantation where I now live, negros George, Sarry, Winston, Easter, Lucy, and Howard, furniture, and balance of livestock.

At the death of LOUVISA COCKRAM the part lent her to CHARLES W.

160

BENNETT will cont'd:

BOBBETT.

Appoint friends PEYTON GRAVES and CHARLES W. BOBBETT executors.

RICHARD (X) BENNETT

Wit: JOHN SMITH, ELIJAH TOWLER, RALPH SMITH, WILLIAM MITCHELL,
WILLIAM THOMPSON.

Memorandum:

RICHARD BENNETT and CHARLES W. BOBBETT agree that in addition to
what the Will specifies, that LOUVISA COCKRAM is to have my walnut chest, walnut table, the use of my kitchen furniture during
her life and maintained as usual out of my crops, this in addition to what has been mentioned in the will, and at her death to
CHARLES W. BOBBITT.

RICHARD BENNETT, CHARLES W. BOBBITT.

Wit: JOHN SMITH, WILLIAM GRAVES, JOHN GRAVES.

WILLIAM WITCHER and CHARLES WALDEN security for the executors.

Page 362-363
28 January 1811
Pr: 21 October 1811

LWT THOMAS PULLIN being weak in body but of sound mind.

To my two grandsons THOMAS and JOHN MITCHELL 1/7th part of my remaining estate to be equally divided between them.

To my two grand daughters MARY and PEGGY PRESTON 1/7th part to
be equally divided between them.

To my daughter SARAH WRIGHT 1/7th part.

To my daughter HULDAH WRIGHT 1/7th part.

To my daughter PEGGY TOWLER 1/7th part.

To my daughter SENNA DALTON 1/7th part.

To my daughter PATSEY BENNETT 1/7th part.

To my son WILLIAM my large bible, dictionary and geography.

To my daughter WINIFRED JARVIS five shillings.

Appoint STEPHEN PRESTON, SAMUEL MITCHELL, THOMAS WRIGHT, WILLIAM
WRIGHT and STEPHEN TOWLER executors.

THOMAS PULLIN

Wit: GARLAND HURT, DAVID PARKER, RICHARD (X) FREEMAN, WILLIAM (X)
FREEMAN.

WILLIAM SWANSON, JR. and BENJAMIN RICE security for SAMUEL MITCH-
ELL and THOMAS WRIGHT.

161

Page 363-364
21 June 1811
Pr: 21 October 1811

LWT JOHN WADDELL of sound mind and memory.

I lend to my beloved wife during her natural life negros: Sylva, Betty, Jim and Phill.

My daughter NANCY to have a young negro at the age of 18 years.

To my son NOELL WADDELL, the next increase of the above negros when he comes of age.

To my son MARSHALL the next increase of the negros when he comes of age.

Should my wife marry or die before my children come of age, the negros to be hired out to support the said children.

When my youngest son comes of age the negros to be equally divided between them.

My wife's father and RICHARD MARSHALL to manage my estate.

Appoint DEVERAUX HIGHTOWER, MATHEW FITZGERALD and CHARLES WADDELL executors.

JOHN WADDELL

Wit: CHARLES ANDERSON, THEODOSIA WILSON.

CHARLES ANDERSON, THOS. WOODY and WILLIAM RICHARDSON security for MATHEW FITZGERALD.

Page 364
24 October 1810
Pr: 16 September 1811

LWT GEORGE SHELTON being low in body but of perfect mind and of memory.

Lend unto my beloved wife MARY during her lifetime or widowhood all my estate to maintain and educate my young children. Should she marry the estate to be equally divided among my children having regard to what I have advanced my son LEVI and daughter ANNA.

Appoint my wife MARY SHELTON executrix.

GEORGE SHELTON

Wit: WILLIAM WHITE, JEMIA (X) SHELTON.

PEYTON KING, ORLANDO SMITH and JOHN PATTERSON security for executrix.

Page 364-365
6 September 1811
Pr: 18 November 1811
(cont'd next page)

162

LWT GEORGE COX being weak in body but of sound mind.

To my beloved wife PATSEY COX during her life or widowhood, all
my estate excepting what has already been given to my children.

At the death or marriage of my wife, my estate be sold and the
money be equally divided among my children except my son JOSIAH
COX who has received his share.

Also my sons WILLIAM COX, ISHAM COX and THOMAS COX have received
$10.00 each, which is to be deducted, then an equal division be-
tween them and JOSIAH COX, GEORGE COX, JR., ELIZABETH COX, POLLY
COX, and SALLY COX.

Appoint my sons ISHAM, THOMAS, JOSIAH and GEORGE COX executors.

                                        GEORGE (X) COX

Wit: RALPH SMITH, WILLIAM IRBY, PATSY BARBER, FRANCIS ABSTAN.

ISAAC MILLER, JOHN S. ADAMS and GEORGE COX security for JOSIAH
COX.

Page 365-366
27 March 1802
Pr: 21 October 1811

LWT BENJAMIN BRAWNER being in health and sound mind.

To my wife MARY BRAWNER land and house where I now live during
her lifetime with one third part of my household furniture, livestock and one third of the value of the labour of my negros Jacob and Ranney.

The remaining two thirds be sold at my death and out of this pay
my daughter MARY DOUGLASS $50.00 the balance divided between my
children, the other third left my wife, at her death, divided between my children.

The remaining part of my land where WILLIAM ROGERS lives, to be
rented out.

To my daughters MILLEY NELSON, MARY DOUGLASS and NANCY ROGERS the
whole of my land to be equally divided.

Appoint my friends JAMES NELSON, JOHN DOUGLASS and WILLIAM ROGERS
as executors.

                                        BENJAMIN (X) BROWNER

Wit: WILLIAM MC DANIEL, MARTHA MC DANIEL, BETSEY W. MC DANIEL.

JOSEPH ROGERS, REUBEN ROGERS and JEDUTHUN CARTER security for WIL-
LIAM ROGERS.

Page 367-368
30 November 1805
Pr: 16 December 1811

LWT JESSE CARTER being sick and weak in body but of perfect mind.

CARTER will cont'd:

To my son THOMAS C. CARTER 50 acres on Banister River together with what I have given him.

To my daughter SARAH CARTER, wife of JEDUTHUN CARTER, 200 acres at the upper end of my tract with what I have given her.

To my daughter PEGGY THOMPSON, wife of SAMUEL THOMPSON, the property I formerly gave her and negro Else.

To my son JOSEPH CARTER the balance of my tract on the south side of Banister River including the plantation whereon I now live, and the north side after what I have given my son THOMAS and my daughter SARAH is taken off, the balance being 852 acres with negros: Isaac, Ned, George, Milly, James and Letty.

To my grandson JAMES HOPKINS negro Braiston.

To my grandson ROBERT CARTER, son of my daughter MARY HOPKINS, a negro Phil.

To my loving wife MARY CARTER negros: Anthony, Peter, Hannah, Abigal, Charlott, Winney, Murrier, Matilda, and Stephen, during her natural life and at her death to be equally divided between my children: THOMAS C. CARTER, SARAH CARTER, MARY HOPKINS, JESSE CARTER, JOHN CARTER, JOSEPH CARTER and PEGGY THOMPSON.

The residue of my property to my son JOSEPH CARTER.

JESSE CARTER

Wit: WILLIAM NELSON, WELCOME WILLIAM ALLEN, CALEB ANGLIN, ROBERT LEFTWICH, RAWLEY WHITE, WASHINGTON THOMPSON, WADDY THOMPSON, JENNINGS THOMPSON.

JOHN CARTER, JESSE CARTER, JEDUTHUN CARTER, SAMUEL THOMPSON and JAMES HOPKINS security for JESSE CARTER.

Page 368-369
17 October 1808
Pr: 16 December 1811

LWT JOHN HARMON being very sick and weak but of perfect mind and memory.

To my dearly beloved wife MOLLY HARMON who with SOLOMON HARMON and THOMAS HARMON my sons, executors of my will, all my estate real and personal, during her lifetime or widowhood.

My daughters to have the privilege of enjoying the lands during their single life.

At the decease of my wife, all my estate divided between my children.

JOHN HARMON

Wit: CHARLES SHELTON, HENRY SHELTON, MARY F. BEAVERS.

PEYTON KING, BARRETT BURNETT, THOMAS HARMON, JEDUTHUN CARTER, JR.

HARMON will cont'd:

and JESSE RICHARDS security for SOLOMAN HARMON.

THOMAS HARMON refused to be executor and MOLLY HARMON, widow with
her securities: THOMAS HARMON, SOLOMON HARMON, NICHOLAS HARMON,
SAMUEL HARMON, PATSEY HARMON, POLLEY HARMON and NANCY K. HARMON.

Page 369-370
20 September 1810
Pr: 19 February 1811

LWT WILLIAM WRIGHT being sick and weak but of perfect sense.

Three or four years ago I made a power of attorney to JAMES WOODY
which is recorded for the purpose of collecting money owed me by
the executors of THOMAS POLLARD, late of the county of Amelia,
and the said JAMES WOODY is to pay me $120.00 I have also recov-
ered a judgement in the county of Caswell against JOSIAH EASP(?)
of one hundred forty pounds of North Carolina money which I have
not received.

I give to the children of my first wife one shilling and the same
to my children: MARTHA, RUSSEL, RICHARD P., ROSAMOND, PALLON, LA-
BON and WILLIAM, and having considered my wifes departure as an
elopement, have taken steps to bar her from any part of my estate.

To my son ROBERT WRIGHT $120.00 in the hands of JAMES WOODY also
the money of the other judgement with all my other property.

Appoint my son ROBERT and friend HENRY WILSON executors.

W. WRIGHT

Wit: DANIEL BRYANT, WILLIAM HUGHES (X) WHITE.

JAMES WOODY and JOHN WILKINSON security for executor.

Page 370-371
19 December 1811
Pr: 20 January 1812

LWT JAMES SUTHERLIN

My wife PATSEY SUTHERLIN, mother of my two children: FANNY JEF-
FERSON SUTHERLIN and JAMES MADISON SUTHERLIN, to have reasonable
support out of my estate during her natural life.

To my daughter FANNY JEFFERSON SUTHERLIN half my personal estate
and half of my real estate.

To my son JAMES MADISON SUTHERLIN the other half of my estate.

Appoint my friends JOHN WALTON and NATHANIEL WILLIAMSON executors.

JAMES SUTHERLIN

Wit: JAMES D. PATTON, ROBERT GLASCO, JOHN (X) WARE, SAMUEL MC COL-
LOUGH.

Page 371 (cont'd next page)

25 February 1812
Pr: 16 March 1812

This is to certify the request of WILLIAM EASLEY before his death
in the presence of STEPHEN GILES, NANCY GILES and ELIZABETH EAS-
LEY, they heard him say he wished his son THOMAS EASLEY to have
all the property which he died possessed of, with all debts due
him, except the land in Mecklenburg which is to be sold and part
of the money given to his daughters.

STEPHEN GILES, NANCY (X) GILES, ELIZABETH (X) EASLEY.

Wit: WILLIAM FERGUSON.

ANTHONY P. LIPFORD, THOMAS WILSON and BENJAMIN WILSON security
for THOMAS EASLEY.

Page 371-372
30 January 1812
Pr: 18 May 1812

LWT PETER DUPUY in perfect health and sound mind.

I desire my wife ELIZABETH DUPEY remain upon my plantation with
all negros except Nancy and all other personal estate except what
I willed to SARAH DUPUY.

To my son JESSE DUPUY eighty five pounds.

I lend to my daughter SARAH DUPUY 200 acres on Shoco Creek, negro
Nancy, bed and furniture, a mare, cow and calf, sow and pigs, and
her heirs, if none to the following legatees: STEPHEN DUPUY, WIL-
LIAM DUPUY, ROBERT DUPUY, JESSE DUPUY, MARY ELLINGTON and ELIZA-
BETH MOTLEY.

One childs part to be divided between my grand daughter MARY KEE-
SEE and ELIZABETH MOTLEY.

The balance of my estate to be equally divided between my beloved
children: STEPHEN DUPUY, WILLIAM DUPUY, ROBERT DUPUY, JESSE DUPUY,
MARY ELLINGTON, ELIZABETH MOTLEY and SARAH DUPUY.

Appoint my son ROBERT and JOEL WILLIS executors.

                                        PETER DUPUY

Wit: J. LANSDOWN, BRYANT THOMPSON.

DAVID C. WILLIAMS, WILLIAM VADEN, JOHN ADAMS, CREED TANNER, ALLEN
WOODSON, and JOHNSON LANSDOWN security for executors.

Page 374
12 February 1810
Pr: 21 April 1812

Nuncupative will of GRACE KING made before BARTON TERRY, SR.,
DAVID TERRY and SUSANNAH FITZGERALD.

Her will and desire was for ELIZABETH TERRY, daughter of BARTON
TERRY, to have all of her estate.

KING will cont'd:

GRACE KING departed this life 19 November 1811 at two or three o'clock in the morning.

RACHEL MADDING made oath that she had heard GRACE KING state that she wanted ELIZABETH TERRY to have her estate.

JAMES M. WILLIAMS security for BARTON TERRY, SR.

Page 374
29 January 1812
Pr: 20 July 1812

LWT BENJAMIN RIDDLE being weak in body but sound mind and memory.

My wife NANCY to have the use of my whole estate during her life.

At the decease of my wife, my estate is to be divided between my children: BURGES, FANNY, WILLIAM, SUSANNAH, LENTON, REUBIN, ELIZ- ABETH and LEWIS.

Appoint my wife and my father ZACHERIAH RIDDLE executors.

                                        BENJAMIN RIDDLE

Wit: JEDITHUN CARTER, SR., HARTWELL ALLEN, GEORGE GILES, EPHRAIM GILES.

Page 374-375
17 October 1810
Pr: 13 June 1812

LWT JOHN KEESEE weak in body but of perfect mind.

To my beloved wife MARY KEESEE I lend one third part of my estate both real and personal during her natural life.

My three sons: JOHN, CHARLES and BLACKWELL KEESEE my lands in Pittsylvania and Halifax Counties, equally divided.

The remainder of my estate to be divided between all my children: NANCY TALBOT, MILLY MILLET(?), JOHN KEESEE, CHARLES KEESEE and BLACKWELL KEESEE.
Appoint my friends CHAMPNESS TERRY and JEREMIAH TERRY executors.

                                        JOHN KEESEE

Wit: WILLIAM HALL, WILLIAM WALRAND, JESSE WILSON.

JOSEPH TERRY, WILLIAM WIMBISH, WILLIAM ECHOLS and JOHNSON LANS- DOWN security for CHAMPNESS TERRY.

Page 375-376
10 August 1812
Pr: 21 September 1812

LWT JESSE WALRAND being low in body but in perfect memory.

WALRAND will cont'd:

To my sister ANNA WALRAND fifty pounds.

To PATSY WALRAND, daughter of REUBIN WALRAND, my negro Milley, should she die without issue, the negro to go to the children of JOHN WALRAND, that he has by his present wife.

To GINNEY WALRAND, wife of JOHN WALRAND, a negro James, also to the children of JOHN WALRAND, negros: George, Abraham, Isaac, Jacob and Hester. The balance of my estate to his children also.

JESSE WALRAND

Wit: JERRY TERRY, NATHAN PEARMAN, D. C. WILLIAMS.

CHAMP TERRY, JOHN BENNETT and HENRY GLASS security for JOHN WALRAND.

Page 376-377
2 November 1812
Pr: 21 December 1812

LWT JOHN STAMPS, SR. being of sound mind.

I lend to my beloved wife LEANNA STAMPS all my estate both real and personal, during her natural life and afterwards to be disposed of as follows:

To my daughter MOLLEY ECHOLS a horse.

To my daughter AMY DODSON my most valuable horse.

To my daughter LYDDA STAMPS negro Eve and Rainey, cow and calf, furniture.

I desire my stock to be sold and the money divided between my 5 daughters: MOLLEY ECKHOLS, NANCY DODSON, RHODA WILSON, CATHERINE WALTERS and LYDDA STAMPS.

To my two sons THOMAS and JOHN STAMPS, JR., my land being five tracts by survey 319 acres.

My negros George, Harry, Milly, Ritter and Rachel and the household furniture to be sold and the money divided between my children: MOLLEY ECKHOLS, NANCY DODSON, WILLIAM STAMPS, RHODA WILSON, CATHERINE WALTERS, TIMOTHY STAMPS, THOMAS STAMPS, JR. and LYDDA STAMPS, if she should loose her negros.

Sons WILLIAM and THOMAS STAMPS executors.

JOHN STAMPS

Wit: JOSEPH HATCHETT, MATHEW FITZGERALD, CHARLES WADDELL.

CREED TANNER, SAMUEL FLIPPEN, MATHEW FITZGERALD and CHARLES WADDELL security for the executor WILLIAM STAMPS.

18 January 1813

THOMAS STAMPS had as his security JOSEPH FLIPPIN, JAMES M. WIL-

LIAMS and CREED TANNER.

Page 377-378
14 December 1811
Pr: 21 December 1812

LWT ELIZABETH MOTLEY of perfect mind and memory.

To JOSEPH MOTLEY TANNER my adopted son, my grey horse, saddle and bed and furniture.

To my niece ELIZABETH IRBY, daughter of EDMOND IRBY, a bay mare also a bed and furniture.

To my nephew BASTER IRBY, son of CHARLES IRBY, a bay horse.

The balance of my estate to be sold and the money divided between JOSEPH MOTLEY TANNER and ELIZABETH IRBY.

Appoint my friend CHAMPNESS TERRY executor and that he shall not call on my brother WILLIAM IRBY for any debts he may owe me.

                                        ELIZABETH (X) MOTLEY

Wit: WILLIAM HALL

WILLIAM HALL and WILLIAM ECHOLS security for the executor.

Page 378-379
1 January 1805
Pr: 19 April 1813

LWT WILLIAM YOUNG being infirm in body but of perfect mind and memory.

To my beloved wife ELIZABETH YOUNG during her natural life or her widowhood my land and plantation.

To my daughter FRANCES RAMSEY five shillings besides what I have already given her.

To my son ARCHIBALD YOUNG the same.

To JOEL ADKINS five shillings.

To my son MILTON YOUNG five shillings besides what he has already received.

To my son MERLIN YOUNG, likewise five shillings, besides what he has received.

To my son PEYTON YOUNG the tract of land where he now lives.

To my son WILIE YOUNG five shillings besides what he has received.

To my son GEORGE YOUNG the land and plantation where I now live and after the death or marriage of my wife, with all the stock and household goods.

To my son SAMUEL YOUNG five shillings besides what he has already received.

                            169

YOUNG will cont'd:

To my daughter JUDITH VANCE 20 acres where they now live.

Appoint my wife and Major JOHN SMITH and GEORGE YOUNG executors.

                                        WILLIAM YOUNG

Wit: WILLIAM THOMPSON, JOHN THOMPSON, ABRAHAM C. SHELTON.

HEZEKIAH GILL, PEYTON YOUNG and ELIJAH TOWLER security for the executors.

Page 380
5 April 1812
Pr: 21 June 1813

LWT THOMAS BOAZ of perfect mind and memory.

To my nephew BOAZ FRIZZEL, son of ISAAC FRIZZEL, half of my estate.

To my nephew JAMES BOAZ, son of DANIEL BOAZ, the other half of my estate.

This is subject to my mother's dowery of land during her life.

Appoint ISAAC FRIZZEL and JAMES BOAZ executors.

                                        THOMAS BOAZ

Wit: SAMUEL BECK, WILLIAM BECK, JOHN MARTIN.

WILLIAM BECK and LEROY SHELTON security for executors.

Page 380-382
13 September 1810
Pr: 17 August 1813

LWT ISAAC COLES

To my wife CATHERINE COLES during her natural life, my land on Georges Creek and negros: Billy, Tom, Abram, Peter, Ben, Nicholas, Landon, Madge, Suckey, Henry, Flora, Edward, Nicholas (2d?) Robert, Clementina, Dicey, Betty, Helen, Becky, Lawney, Betsey, Caroline, Jack, with household furniture, my carriage and stock of every kind, subject to the legacies given hereafter. My wife is to dispose of the above negros to my children.

I desire my estate to be kept together till my children come of age. My children to be educated in a liberal manner.

The furniture and stock, at the decease of my wife, to be divided between the children.

To my son WALTER COLES, all my land on Whitethorn Creek with negros: Phil, Lewis, Tom, Sally, Moses, Polydare, Betty, Lucretia and Lagavina, furniture and livestock.

COLES will cont'd:

To my daughter CATHERINE COLES the tract on Banister River and negros: Meania, Randolph, Landa, Coleman, Nancy, Carter, Hampton, Westley, furniture and livestock.

To my son JAMES THOMPSON COLES my mill tract, 700 acres of the Meadow tract, negros: Jane, Lewis, Henry, Calland, Polley and her five children, furniture and livestock.

To my son JOHN COLES my Meadow land with seven negros, livestock and furniture.

To my son ROBERT THOMPSON COLES my land on Whitehorn Creek, tract of 864 acres, seven negros, furniture and livestock.

To my daughter MARY the remaining part of the land on Banister River with six negros, furniture and livestock.

To my son JACOB THOMPSON COLES the land lent his mother, seven negros, furniture and livestock.

To my son ISAAC COLES twenty five pounds as he has received his share.

Appoint my wife, friend JAMES BRUCE, nephew ISAAC COLES and my sons ISAAC and WALTER executors.

                                        ISAAC COLES

Wit: none

Page 382-383
22 November 1813
Pr: 21 December 1813

LWT JOHN TURLEY, farmer, being sick and weak but of perfect mind and memory.

To my daughter JANEY RUSSELL a bed and sheets.

To my daughter NANCY BARBER pewter dishes.

To my son JAMES TURLEY my black walnut cupboard.

To my daughter PATSY TURLEY my pine chest.

To my son RIER TURLEY my stock of hogs, sheep, two cows, one mare, walnut table, one bed and corn crop, potters wheel, pots.

To MOLLEY STANDEFORD the bed she lay upon while in my service and my cotton cards.

Appoint worthy friend PLEASANT PHARIS executor.

                                        JOHN (X) TURLEY

Wit: GEORGE RORER, THOMAS (X) WRIGHT, JOSEPH TAYLOR

GEORGE DASHT and THOMAS WRIGHT security for executor.

Page 383-384
23 January 1799
Pr: 17 January 1814

LWT EDWARD BURGESS being weak of body but disposing mind and of sound memory.

To my son BENJAMIN BURGESS five shillings.

To my daughter MARY CLARK, SARAH BURGESS, MORDIEA BURGESS, JANE PREWITT, JAMES BURGESS, JOHN BURGESS and MILLY WILSON five shillings each having given them all I intended.

To my daughter VERLINNA BURGESS bed and furniture, cow and calf, one third part of my furniture.

To my beloved wife MARGARET BURGESS residue of my estate.

I give my son WILLIAM BURGESS the land where my son, BENJAMIN BURGESS lived.

My looms, cards and wheels to my daughter VERLINNA after death of my wife.

Appoint my wife MARGARET BURGESS and WILLIAM BURGESS executors.

EDWARD (X) BURGESS

Wit: HALCOTT TOWNES, GEORGE SPRATLIN, JASSHETH PREWITT, MATHEW FITZGERALD, WILLIAM SNODY.

Page 384-386
20 July 1813
Pr: 21 March 1814

LWT JOHN WORSHAM being of sound mind.

To my beloved wife MARY WORSHAM all my land, negros, furniture and some livestock during her natural life, one hundred pounds.

I devise to my friend THOMAS STEWART of Danville, 100 acres of land joining JAMES D. PATTON.

To my brother THOMAS WORSHAM two horses, negros Esaw and Jacob.

To my brother DANIEL WORSHAM fifty pounds.

I desire my three old negros James, Philly and Jenny be set free after the death of my wife and for their support I leave them a tract of land, 100 to 200 acres, in Caswell County, North Carolina, a horse, livestock, spinning wheels, and tools. On death of these three, the property to revert back to my estate.

After the death of my wife, all remaining property to be sold and the money divided between THOMAS STEWART, LUDWELL WORSHAM and the legitimate children of my brothers ROBERT WORSHAM, and JOSHUA WORSHAM, who are deceased, THOMAS WORSHAM, my sister MICHAEL FERGUSON and PHOEBE WYNNE (which last is also dead) share and share alike.

Appoint my wife, my brother THOMAS, my friends THOMAS STEWART and

WORSHAM will cont'd:

JAMES D. PATTON executors.

JOHN WORSHAM

Wit: FR. DABNEY, WILLIAM DODSON, DANIEL L. COLEMAN.

NATHANIEL WILSON, FRANCIS DABNEY, THOMAS STEWART, WILLIAM DODSON, JOHN ROSS, SILBY BENSON security for JAMES D. PATTON.

Page 386-387
8 February 1814
Pr: 20 June 1814

LWT JAMES BRUCE being weak and in a low state of health.

I desire the land where my son WILLIAM BRUCE's family now live and that where CLEBON SHELTON formerly lived, to be sold to pay my just debts. Should there be a surplus, to be applied towards the support of my wife and children.

Appoint JESSE KEESEE, GRIFFITH DICKINSON and EVERY MUSTIEN executors.

To my beloved wife TABITHA BRUCE, my land and the home where I now live with the household furniture.

At the decease of my wife, executors to sell the property and the money equally divided amongst my children. Some of the children have received certain property as follows:

My son WILLIAM BRUCE, 117.0.3

My daughter CATHERINE DOVE, 19.12.0

My daughter SALLY COX, 43.12.0

My son THOMAS BRUCE, 28.12.0

My son FREDRICK BRUCE, 21.12.0

My daughter WINNEY SIMPSON, 13.12.0

The children who have received no part are: ELIZABETH BRUCE, TABATHA BRUCE, JAMES BRUCE, ANSELM BRUCE, SUSANNA BRUCE.

JAMES (X) BRUCE

Wit: JACOB MILLER, GEORGE CAMP, NEVIN STEWART.

JOSHUA STONE, SR., NELSON TUCKER, PHILIP L. GRATSY security for SAMUEL STONE.

Page 388-389
12 July 1813
Pr: 20 June 1814

LWT JAMES HARP in a low state of health.
(cont'd next page)

173

HARP will cont'd:

To my beloved son PHILIP all my land and plantation whereon I now live, being 70 acres more or less, but it to be a home to my beloved wife MARY during her natural life.

To my beloved daughter SARAH CAMMIL five dollars.

To my beloved daughter ELIZABETH GAMMON five dollars.

To my beloved daughter JINCEY BARKER five dollars.

To my beloved daughter RACHEL BOOTHE five dollars.

To my beloved daughter SUSANNA HARP five dollars.

At the death of my wife, the personal estate to then be divided between my son PHILIP HARP and my daughter SUSANNA HARP.

Appoint my friend JAMES WATKINS executor.

JAMES (X) HARP

Wit: JOHN (X) O'DONEAL, STEPHEN O'DONEAL, ANN (X) O'DONEAL.

ICHABOD THOMAS security for executor.

Page 389-390
2 December 1813
Pr: 21 June 1814

LWT JOHN HODGES being weak in body but of sound mind.

To my beloved daughter ELIZA HUBBARD negros: Harry, Delila, Natt, Rachel, Isham, Lucy, Soloman, and Patty, and the other property given her at her marriage.

I lend to my beloved daughter MARY JONES during her natural life, all the tract of land whereon I now live on Bearskin Creek and negros: Nel, George, David, Judy, Amos, Jenny, Aron, Margary and Nathan, all stock and household furniture. At her decease, the land and other property to be divided between her heirs. None of the above property to be used to pay the debts of her husband.

Appoint my friend MOSES HUBBARD and HUGH REYNOLDS executors.

JOHN HODGES

Wit: SAMUEL MITCHELL, JAMES A. MITCHELL, JOHN MITCHELL.

Page 390-391
30 March 1814
Pr: 20 June 1814

LWT CORNELIUS MC HANEY of sound mind and memory.

To my son JOHN MC HANEY a tract of 350 acres, 100 acres, 145 acres, 152 acres, and 50 acres of land.

To my son CORNELIUS MC HANEY the tract whereon I now live 150 ac. and 106 acres that I purchased of JESSE EDDS; the tract on little

MC HANEY will cont'd:

.....Stone Creek; part of the Arnold tract.

The remainder of my land not before given, I give to my three living daughters: POLLY HUBBARD, MARY GILBERT and LELIA GEORGE and
the children of my deceased daughter FRANKY TURNER.

The remainder of my personal estate to be equally divided between
my children.

Appoint my son-in-law GEORGE GILBERT, my friend SAMUEL PANNILL,
my son CORNELIUS MC HANEY executors.

                                          CORNELIOUS MC HANEY

Wit: JAMES H. MITCHELL, JAMES DEGARNETT.

CORNELIOUS MC HANEY and GEORGE GILBERT, security for SAMUEL PAN-
NILL.

Page 392-393
1 September 1806
Pr: 20 June 1814

LWT THOMAS BLACK

I gave my daughter ELIZABETH MITHCELL, when she married, a negro
Agnes and other personal property.

I gave my son SKIPP RITCHERSON BLACK a negro named Sam and other
personal property.

I gave my daughter SARAH DEWS a negro Molley and other property.

I gave my son THOMAS BLACK negro Dolla and other property.

I desire the balance of my estate both real and personal be left
in the care of my wife SUSANNAH BLACK during her lifetime and for
the support of my five children who are not married: ABSALEM,
NATHANIEL, JOHN, SUSANAH and POLLEY.

I desire my last children when they come of age or marry, to have
equal value with the others.

At the decease of my wife, my estate to be sold and the money divided between my children so that the last ones have equal with
the first ones.

Appoint my son THOMAS BLACK, WILLIAM MITCHELL and PETER BARKSDALE
(in Halifax) executors.

                                          THOMAS BLACK

Wit: JOHN B. DAWSON

JONATHAN B. DAWSON, JOHN BLACK, SR., JOSIAH RICE and JOHN FARRIS
security for THOMAS BLACK.

Page 393-394 (cont'd next page)

4 June 1814
Pr: 21 November 1814

LWT SHERAD NOWLIN

To my brother SAMUEL NOWLIN all the money belonging to me, and
my horse and saddle, and my negro Branser.

My wearing apparel to be given to BRYAN W. NOWLIN, son of DAVID
NOWLIN.

I desire anything else belonging to me to go to SAMUEL NOWLIN.

Appoint my brother SAMUEL NOWLIN executor.

                                            SHERAD NOWLIN

On the oaths of JOHNSON LANDSDOWN, RICHARD JONES and GEORGE BUR-
GESS, that this is the handwriting of the said SHERAD NOWLIN, to
be entered into the record.

Page 394
6 June 1814
Pr: 23 November 1814

LWT JOHN DANGERFIELD in perfect health.

Lend to my beloved wife ELIZABETH DANGERFIELD all my estate, both
real and personal, during her natural life.

At the decease of my wife, to be divided between my eight child-
ren: DOLLY P. DANGERFIELD, ELIZABETH DANGERFIELD, JOHN DANGER-
FIELD, CATY DANGERFIELD, LEONARD H. DANGERFIELD, GINSEY DANGER-
FIELD, ALEXANDER DANGERFIELD and WILLIS R. DANGERFIELD.

I have given my daughter NANCY T. HUFFMAN and my son WILLIAM DAN-
GERFIELD as much as I intended.

Appoint my wife ELIZABETH DANGERFIELD executrix.

                                      JOHN (X) DANGERFIELD

Wit: JAMES NOWLIN, MATHEW NOWLIN, RANEY NOWLIN, DAVID (X) MC NEAL-
EY.

Page 395
13 August 1814
Pr: 16 January 1815

LWT JOHN MADDING being in perfect health.

To my sister SALLY MADDING the right of living on my land on the
old river road as long as she remains single.

I give 90 acres on Double Creek to my two sons SMITH H. HENDRICK
and JOHN H.HENDRICK, sons of POLLY HENDRICK and my personal estate as follows: my household furniture to POLLY HENDRICK during
her single life to raise and support my two sons and after her
death to them. My sorrel horse and livestock treated in the same
manner.

MADDING will cont'd:

My bonds to be put out to interest until my first son comes of age, then equally divided between my sons.

I appoint LARKING MADDING my executor.

                                        JOHN (X) MADDING.

Wit: ALLEN C. TANNER, SELVANG GARDNER, CREED TANNER.

THOMAS SHELTON security for executor.

Page 395-396
...........1813
Pr: 16 January 1815

LWT THOMAS JAMES

To my wife NANCY JAMES all my estate both real and personal to act with as she may think proper, but she is not to prevent WILL-IAM JAMES from settling on some part of the land. At the death of my wife my tract of land to WILLIAM JAMES.

To ALLEN and NANCY JAMES, two children my daughter (?) MATHEW JAMES her part of my estate and also to ALLEN JAMES one year of schooling.

After the death of my wife, my estate be equally divided between my children, only JOSEPH BLANKS and THOMAS HARN to have $10.00 less as they have had more.

                                        THOMAS (X) JAMES

Wit: HUBBARD FARMER, CATHERINE JENKINS, JAMES (X) LANDERS.

HUBBARD FARMER security for ANSWORTH HARRISON.

Page 396

Nuncupative will of SAMUEL FARMER made whilst he was in the military service and directed if he should die that his negro Sarah willed to him by his father, in which his mother has a life estate, should at her death go to his brother JOHN FARMER.

LABAN FARMER, THOMAS DAVIS, ROBERT TANNER.

Court of 19 June 1815, the will was presented and ordered recorded.

Page 396-397
13 February 1813
Pr: 20 March 1815

LWT ALEXANDER MAHAN being in my perfect will and sense.

My sons JOHN and WILLIAM have had their share of my estate.

My estate to be kept together for the support of my children not

                        177

MAHAN will cont'd:

provided for and as each child marries or comes of age, to have their share.

My wife CATHERINE, as long as she remains my widow, to keep any or all of my estate for her comfort.

Appoint my sons JOHN and WILLIAM as executors.

ALEXANDER MAHAN

Wit: FRANCIS DADE

HUGH REYNOLDS security for the executors.

Page 397-398
17 February 1800
Pr: 19 April 1815

LWT JAMES ROBERTSON in a low state of health but sound mind.

Lend to my beloved wife MARY ROBERTSON all my tract of land where I now live and all other personal estate during her natural life to support her and the children.

At the decease of my wife, any estate left be sold and the money divided between the children I have or may have and the children by my first wife CATHERINE ROBERTSON, deceased.

My wife is to let my son WILLIAM ROBERTSON have a place on my.... tract to live upon, rent free, only pay her annually one year of corn.

Appoint my wife executrix.

JAMES ROBERTSON

Wit: W. HARRISON, WALTER GUILD, ISAAC POTTER.

17 April 1815

W. HARRISON is now dead, WALTER GUILD and ISAAC POTTER are out of the state.
JOHN WILSON and WILLIAM TUNSTALL make oath that the will is the handwriting of JAMES ROBERTSON.

Page 398-399
19 January 1815
Pr: 19 June 1815

LWT JOHN ADAMS

I desire as much as needed of my personal estate to be sold to pay my just debts. If my negro Jesse wishes to be sold, sell him in place of the personal property.

I give HARRISON WILLIAMS my horse and saddle.

I desire my negros Abraham and Jesse and other personal property

178

ADAMS will cont'd:

be left in the hands of my son JOHN ADAMS for the benefit of my
daughter ELIZABETH WILLIAMS.

My son JOHN ADAMS to hire out the negros and use the money for
ELIZABETH WILLIAMS. At the death of Elizabeth the property to be
sold and the money divided between her children: LUCY, POLLY,
NANCY, ROBERTSON, WILLIAMSON, JACKSON, ELIZABETH HARRISON and
WILMOTH WILLIAMS.

                                             JOHN ADAMS

Wit: JAMES H. STONE, WILLIAM LINDSEY, LEWIS HAGWOOD.

THOMAS WOODING and WILLIAM CLARK security for the executor.

Page 399-400
6 January 1812
Pr: 13 May 1815

LWT PRESLEY THORNTON being of good health and perfect mind.

I lend to my beloved wife MARY THORNTON one third of my estate
during her life, then to be divided among the heirs of her body.

To my son ZACHARIAH THORNTON one equal share of my estate.

To my son BOLEN THORNTON the same.

To my son MOSES THORNTON the same.

To my daughter ELIZABETH NANCE the same.

To my daughter JANE WILSON the same.

To my son JOHN THORNTON the same.

To my son WILLIAM THORNTON forty pounds.

To my daughter FANNY OAKES forty pounds.

To my son PRESLEY THORNTON one shilling.

To my daughter BARBARY JONES one shilling.

To my daughter SUSANNAH WATTS one shilling.

To my daughter LARARY BARNETT one shilling.

Appoint my sons ROWLAND and MOSES THORNTON executors.

                                      PRESLEY (X) THORNTON

Wit: CLEMENT WILSON, AGNATIUS WILSON, MARY WILSON.

ELLIS WILSON and RANDOLPH MC DANIEL security for executors.

Page 401
10 January 1815 (cont'd next page)

Pr: 20 March 1815

LWT WILLIAM TERRY being very sick and weak but of perfect mind.

To my beloved wife PATSY TERRY all my estate, both real and personal, during her natural life or widowhood.

Provided my wife does not marry, she may dispose of my property to my children as she thinks proper.

Appoint my wife and her brother STEPHEN FARMER executors.

WILLIAM TERRY

Wit: JOHN JENKINS, JOSIAH RICE, ABSOLAM FARMER.

HAYNES MORGAN, JOSIAH RICE, ISHAM FARMER and ROBERT TOWNES security for the executors.

Page 402-403
8 October 1814
Pr: 20 February 1815

LWT WILLIAM SLAYDON (SLAYDEN) being very sick and weak but of perfect mind.

I lend to my beloved wife NANCY SLAYDEN my land, plantation and household furniture during her natural life, also two horses and livestock.

I will to my youngest children: WILLIAM SLAYDEN, JAMES SLAYDEN and NANCY SLAYDEN to be raised to an equality with the rest of my children that have left me.

The remainder of my estate to be equally divided between my seven children: THOMAS SLAYDEN, DANIEL SLAYDEN, JAMES SLAYDEN, WILLIAM SLAYDEN, SALLY SCOTT, LUCY DODSON and NANCY SLAYDON except my negro Margaret and her children who are to stay with my wife. After the death of my wife, the part lent her to be divided between all the children.

Appoint my son THOMAS SLAYDON executor.

WILLIAM (X) SLAYDEN

Wit: THOMAS RICHARDSON, PHILIP CALLIE, MARGARET DODSON.

THOMAS SHELTON and DANIEL SLAYDON security for the executor.

Page 403
13 December 1814
Pr: 21 February 1815

LWT SALLY HUGHES being weak in body but of sound mind.

To my nephew WILLIAM WASHINGTON ARNETT $150.00 to be paid him at my mothers death.

The rest of my property I give to my beloved brother JOSEPH W. W. ARNETT.

HUGHES will cont'd:

Appoint my brother JOSEPH (ARNETT) executor.

                              SALLY (X) HUGHES

Wit: FRANCIS SMITHSON, OBEY BROWN, KEZIAH (X) BOOTHE.

FRANCIS SMITHSON security for JOSEPH W. W. ARNETT.

Page 404
3 September 1814
Pr: 20 February 1815

Whereas I am about to take a tour of military duty, I leave in
the care of my grandfather JOHN BALINGER the following notes:
HENRY MOTLEY $65.00; DANIEL JOHNS $21.50; JOHN CLARK $21.50; a
bank note for $20.00.

All of which I give to my sister NANCY CLARKE if I should not return.

                              THOMAS CLARKE

Wit: N. TUCKER, GEORGE BOYD.

GEORGE BOYD security for NELSON TUCKER.

Page 404-405
23 January 1815
Pr: 20 February 1815

LWT WILLIAM JAMES

My wife CHARITY JAMES to have all my property, real and personal,
during her life or widowhood.

At her death or marriage, my son CHRISPIN JAMES to have my tract
of land. The land to be for the support of all my children until
the youngest comes of age. The balance of my estate, at the decease of my wife, to all my children.

JOHN LOGAN to be executor.

                              WILLIAM (X) JAMES

Wit: HUBBARD FARMER, JOSEPH BLANKS, WM. L. GLASCOCK.

JOSIAH RICE security for executor ANSWORTH HARRISON.

Page 405-406
8 April 1814 Friday
Pr: 17 July 1815

LWT MATTHEW CLAY in good health and of sound mind.

To my sons JOSEPH CLAY and MATTHEW CLAY all the lands which I own
or claim, lying out of the state of Virginia.

181

CLAY will cont'd:

To my daughter AMANDA ANN S. CLAY all the lands I own in Virginia.

The residue of my estate to be equally divided between my three
children: JOSEPH, MATTHEW and AMANDA ANN L., except the legacies
herein after mentioned.

To WILLIAM PENN, who is now 14 years of age, he shall be clothed,
boarded and schooled until he acquires a good English education,
then bound out to learn a trade until he is 21 years of age, then
my executors are to pay him $1,000.00, also a horse, saddle and
bridle, and a good suit of clothes.

My executors to take the three mullatto girls, now about 8 years
of age: Adelia, Eliza and Ellen, out of the state of Virginia to
some other state, emancipate them, cloth, board and school them
until they are 18 years of age and then pay each of them $500.00
and give them a good suit of clothes.

Appoint my sons JOSEPH CLAY and MATTHEW CLAY executors.

MATTHEW CLAY of
Lavallee

OBEDIAH P. TERRY, JOHN BENNETT, JOEL TANNER, WESTLY SHELTON, TUN-
STALL SHELTON, DANIEL SHELTON, SAMUEL CALLAND and JOHN J. OLIVER
security for the executors.

Page 406-409
26 November 1810
Pr: 17 July 1815

LWT JAMES MITCHELL being sick and weak of body but of sound mind.

Lend to my well beloved wife WINIFRED MITCHELL the tract of land
whereon I now live during her life or widowhood.

Also negros: Charles, Phill, Dinah, Jude, Isaac, Milly, David,
Stepney, Isaac, household furniture. Should my wife marry then
one half the property be given up and divided between my children, at her death the balance to them.

To my well beloved son WILLIAM C. MITCHELL negros: Rachel and Joe

To my beloved daughter SALLY C. LOVELACE negros: Liz and Aggy and
at her death to her children should she have any, if not to the
rest of my children. Not to be used by her husband for debts.

Appoint WILLIAM C. MITCHELL, THOMAS LOVELACE, JAMES LOVELACE and
JOHN MC HANEY executors of this legacy.

I lend my beloved daughter NANCY LOVELACE negros Amy and Charlotte, subject to same conditions of above with WILLIAM C. MITCH-
ELL, JAMES LOVELACE and NATHANIEL LOVELACE executors of this legacy.

To my beloved daughter POLLEY LOVELACE half of my King tract and
lend her negros Abram and Pat under the same conditions as above.

I lend to my beloved daughter BETSEY MC HANEY negros Violet and

182

MITCHELL will cont'd:

York under the same conditions stated above.

To lend my beloved daughter SUSANNAH P. MITCHELL negros Luce, Ennis and Fanny under the same conditions above stated.

I give her (Susannah) the balance of my King tract, horse and a saddle, furniture.

To my beloved son JAMES H. MITCHELL the tract where I now live at the marriage or death of his mother also a negro Land and Hannah, furniture, horse and saddle.

Appoint WILLIAM C. MITCHELL, NATHANIEL LOVELACE, THOMAS LOVELACE, JAMES LOVELACE and JOHN MC HANEY executors.

JAMES MITCHELL

Wit: JAMES M. GEORGE, WILLIAM CRADDOCK, FRANCIS LUCK, JAMES A. LUCK.

JAMES M. GEORGE and WILLIAM CRADDOCK are deceased; FRANCIS LUCK is a legatee; JAMES A. LUCK acknowledged the signature to be that of JAMES MITCHELL.

THOMAS B. JONES, DAVID NOWLIN, JOHN MC HANEY and FRANCIS LUCK security for the executors.

Page 410-411
4 March 1807
Pr: 21 August 1815

LWT EZEKIEL CHANEY, SR. being in my perfect senses.

To my loving wife LETTY CHANEY the land and plantatioin where I now live during her natural life, bed and furniture, and two cupboards, two cows and horses and the mountain orchard. The plantation and the cupboards go to my son JOSEPH CHANEY at her death.

The orchard mountain tract be sold and the money to my two daughters RHODA and SALLEY.

At my death I give my son JOSEPH the plantation I bought of DANIEL REAVES, 61 acres and a colt.

To my daughter RHODA CHANEY a cow, bed and furniture and a chest.

To my daughter SALLEY CHANEY a cow, bed and furniture, and chest.

I have given my three sons WILLIAM, EZEKIEL and THOMAS CHANEY all that I intended them to have.

I have given my three daughters MARY MABREY, BETSEY MABREY and NANCY WALTERS all I intended to give them.

Appoint my sons EZEKIEL and THOMAS my executors.

EZEKIEL (X) CHANEY

Wit: LEMUEL HEADSPETH, HEATH GARDNER, JONATHAN GARDNER.

183

CHANEY will cont'd:

THOMAS SHELTON security for the executors.

Page 411-413
28 August 1815
Pr: 18 September 1815

LWT THOMAS SIMPSON being indisposed but of sound mind.

To my beloved wife MARY SIMPSON all my estate during her natural life under the management of my son WILLIAM SIMPSON.

My daughter HANNAH to have use of the property as long as she is single.

At the death of my wife, the plantation to my son WILLIAM SIMPSON.

To my son JOHN SIMPSON 50 acres where he now lives.

To my son THOMAS SIMPSON 50 acres.

The balance of land I give my son WILLIAM SIMPSON; at the death of my wife he is to pay my son FRANCIS SIMPSON $50.00 instead of giving him land.

The personal property I loaned AZARIAH DOSS when he married, I give him and no more.

Appoint my son WILLIAM SIMPSON my executor.

THOMAS (X) SIMPSON

Wit: ABRAHAM C. SHELTON, LEONARD (X) DOVE, DANIEL SANDERS.

JOHN WEST and ABRAHAM C. SHELTON security for the executor.

Page 413-415
27 February 1815
Pr: 18 September 1815

LWT JACOB FARIS

To my beloved wife PRISSILA FARIS the use of part of my planta- tion and house, my negro Spencer, and a reasonable amount of the furniture and stock for her use during her natural life.

The remaining part of my estate to be sold and the money divided between my children: JURIAH, NATHANIEL, UNISY, STEPHEN, NANCY, SELUDY except a bed and furniture to NANCY if she is living when my wife dies.

To my daughter JURIAH a chest and a negro girl Rachel.

To my beloved son NATHANIEL 200 acres, part of the tract where I live provided he pays my daughter UNISY ROWLAND sixty pounds, a part of her legacy.

To my beloved son STEPHEN 100 acres, a part of the tract where I now live.

FARIS will cont'd:

To my beloved daughter NANCY PATERSON 100 acres joining STEPHEN
and NATHANIEL, during her widowhood. Should she marry or die, the
land to my son STEPHEN and he is to pay EDWARD and CHARLES PATER-
SON, sons of NANCY, twenty pounds each.

To my beloved daughter SELUDY FARIS, a horse, bed and furniture,
a desk, a negro Fanny and a cupboard.

I give to ELIZABETH FARIS, daughter of UNISA ROLAND, a bed and
furniture.

To WILLIAM ROACH, son of my daughter STACY, deceased, five pounds.

I give to JOHN ROACH, son of my daughter STACY, deceased, five
pounds.

After my wife has been alloted as much stock as she thinks is necessary the balance divided between: JURIAH FARIS, UNISA ROLAND,
SELUDY FARIS and STEPHEN FARIS.

Appoint my beloved son NATHANIEL executor.

                                          JACOB FARIS

Wit: HENRY GOSNEY, BENJAMIN GOSNEY, JOEL SHELTON.

Memorandum:
I JACOB FARIS amend my will as to the land left NANCY PATTERSON,
my daughter to be that at her death the 100 acres to go to her
sons EDMUND and CHARLES and her daughter SELUDA PATTERSON to be
divided between them.

31 May 1815
JACOB FARIS

Wit: ABRAHAM SHELTON, HENRY H. GOSNEY

BENJAMIN GOSNEY, HENRY GOSNEY and ABRAHAM SHELTON security for
the executor.

Page 415-416
4 December 1809
Pr: 20 November 1815

LWT WILLIAM PRICE being in my perfect mind.

I give all my children all the property which they have received
from me.

To my son CUTHBIRD PRICE the tract of land where he now lives,
220 acres, also a tract of 40 acres.

I give my son-in-law WILLIAM MC DANIEL $1.00.

To my beloved wife SUSANNAH PRICE the rest of my estate, both
real and personal during her natural life, but she cannot dispose
of any part during her lifetime, but at her death she may give
the estate to my children or grandchildren.

PRICE will cont'd:

I appoint my sons DANIEL PRICE, MARADAY PRICE and MAJOR PRICE executors.

                              WILLIAM PRICE

Wit: JAMES MATNEY, LEROY SHELTON, ADIN GRAY, JOSEPH TAYLOR.

DANIEL COLEMAN, WILLIAM LINN, WASHINGTON THOMPSON, and LEWIS B.
ALLEN security for DANIEL PRICE, MEREDITH PRICE and MAJOR PRICE.

Page 416-417
4 August 1808
Pr: 20 November 1815

LWT HANNAH HOSKINS being of sound mind and memory.

To my daughter HANNAH HOSKINS my mullatto man Jesse, two horses,
half my livestock and furniture and lend her half of my land including the dwelling house during her lifetime. Should she marry
I give the land to her children.

To my grand daughter TABITHA CURRY(?) HOSKINS, daughter of my
son JOHNSON HOSKIINS, my mare Fortune, bed and furniture.

The residue of my estate I lend my son JOHNSON HOSKINS during his
natural life, should his wife REBECCA survive him she may live
on the property during her lifetime. But at their death to go to
their children.

Should my daughter HANNAH die without issue, her part to go to
the children of JOHNSON HOSKINS.

My children: THOMAS HOSKINS, JOHN HOSKINS, MARTHA HOSKINS, ELIZ-
ABETH HART and MARY WILLIAMS to have no part of my estate as I
have already given them what I intended.

Appoint friends THOMAS B. JONES and THOMAS H. WOODING executors.

                              HANNAH HOSKINS

Wit: WILL TUNSTALL, FRANCIS DABNEY, JOHN J. OLIVER, EDWARD CARTER

Page 418-419
6 January 1815
Pr: 20 November 1815

LWT JOSEPH TERRY being weak in body but of perfect mind.

To my son CHAMPNESS TERRY my tract of land called Turners and also half the Sparks tract.

To my son JEREMIAH TERRY a tract called Dupuys and also half the
Sparks tract.

To my son JOSEPH B. TERRY all the land on the north side of Elkhorn Creek and that part of the Bell tract on the right hand side
of the road by JAMES JOHNSON to the Lynchburg Road.

TERRY will cont'd:

To my son WILLIAM L. TERRY all my land on the south side of Elkhorn Creek including my mansion house.

The balance of my land: the McDaniel tract, Manns tract, Clay-
brooks, the balance of the Bell tract and lots 1,2, and 3, also
the Courthouse tract to be sold. The money arising from the sale
to be equally divided between CHAMPNESS TERRY, JEREMIAH TERRY,
ELIZABETH ECHOLS, JOSEPH B. TERRY, WILLIAM L. TERRY, and SARAH
VAUGHAN. Also the balance of my estate not given to be divided
between the above mentioned.

I leave in the hands of my executors seven hundred pounds to be
for the use of NANCY ARNOLD during her life and at her death the
remainder divided between her children.

Appoint my sons CHAMPNESS TERRY and JEREMIAH TERRY my executors.

                                        JOSEPH (X) TERRY

Wit: GEORGE TOWNES, ABRAM SYDNOR, EP(?) Y. WIMBISH.

ABRAM SYDNOR, BENJAMIN TERRY, JR., DANIEL COLEMAN, DAVID C. WIL-
LIAMS, WILLIAM ECHOLS, ROBERT DUPUY, JOHN HENRY, WILLIAM L. TERRY
WILLIAM B. VAUGHAN and JOSEPH B. TERRY security for the executors.

Page 419-420
17 July 1815
Pr: 20 November 1815

LWT GEORGE BURTON in a very low state of health but sound mind.

My executor to sell all my land, two tracts, and the money used
to support my wife and children and educate them. When the youngest comes of age the money to be divided between them, at this
time there are six children.

I desire my negros and personal property be kept together for the
use of my family until the youngest comes of age and then divided between the children, with my wife having an equal share with
the children.

My family desires to move to the Western Country.

At the death of my wife what estate left her be divided between
my children.

My daughter ELIZABETH to have my horse called Drury.

To my son EDMUND a sorrel colt.

To my daughter LYDIA a mare called Eagle.

Appoint my friends JOSEPHUS CONN and JOHN BROWN executors.

                                        GEORGE BURTON

Wit: BENJAMIN WATKINS, SUSAN WATKINS, THOMAS SPARKS.

STEPHEN BEASLEY and DAVID BEASLEY executor for WARNER BEASLEY.

187

Page 420-421
13 April 1815
Pr: 20 November 1815

LWT JOEL R. WILKINSON being sick and weak in body but of sound mind and disposing memory.

To JOHN P. WILKINSON my mill and the lands adjoining by his paying NATHANIEL WILKINSON $50.00.

To NATHANIEL WILKINSON my saw mill tract that joins Nathaniel and THOMAS WILKINSON, SR.

I desire my estate both real and personal and after a final settlement of my fathers estate, be delivered to JOHN P. WILKINSON my executor and to be equally divided between himself and NATHANIEL WILKINSON.

My part of my mothers dower after her death, be divided between JOHN and NATHANIEL.

                                        JOEL R. WILKINSON

Wit: MICHAEL MITCHELL, THOMAS WILKINSON, MOSES (X) BARKER.

NATHANIEL WILKINSON, STOCKLEY TURNER, MICHAEL MITCHELL security for JOHN P. WILKINSON.

Page 421-422
5 May 1815
Pr: 18 December 1815

LWT WILLIAM VAUGHAN

I desire the perishable part of my estate sold immediately except my horse and the money used to pay my just debts. If not sufficient sell my man Davy.

To my wife MARTHA VAUGHAN, Tamer and her children: Fanny and Lucinda, during her life or widowhood. At her death to be sold and the money equally divided between my children.

To my son JEDIAH VAUGHAN my mare Diameed.

To my son GEORGE VAUGHAN my mare Silva.

To my son JAMES VAUGHAN my colt Knowsley.

I desire my land not be sold until my son JAMES comes of age, and then sold and the money equally divided among all my children.

Appoint sons THOMAS T. VAUGHAN and WILLIAM B. L. VAUGHAN executors.

                                        WILLIAM VAUGHAN

Wit: SAMUEL NOWLIN, SHERAD NOWLIN.

WILLIAM WORSHAM, JOHN WORSHAM, HENRY WORSHAM, JESSE PITTS and GEORGE VAUGHAN security for WILLIAM B. L. VAUGHAN.

Page 422-423
27 December 1815
Pr: 15 January 1816

Nuncupative will of DAVID NEAL

He called on VINCENT DICKENSON and asked him to take charge of
his family, continue them together and make no sale or division
except if MRS. NEAL should marry. He further asked Mr. Dickenson
to take charge of his ..... THOMAS particularly his educatioin
and desired the overseer then employed be continued. He desired
Mr. Dickenson pay his debts out of the tobacco crop.

Wit: DAVID C. (X) WILLIAMS, JOHN (X) POLLARD, JOHN (X) BAYS, SAL-
LEY (X) BAYS.

GRIFFITH DICKENSON, DAVID C. WILLIAMS and WALTER COLES security
for VINCENT DICKENSON.

Page 423-424
8 November 1815
Pr: 19 February 1816

LWT SAMUEL HARRIS being in a low state of health and weakness
of body but of sound mind.

I desire my debts be paid out of the bonds due me from Maj. JOHN
BENNETT, one of the bonds due 25th December 1816 for one hundred
thirty three pounds eighteen shillings, another for the same sum
due 25th December 1817. The balance left from the bonds be divided as I will hereafter mention.

My estate, real and personal, be kept together in the hands of
my wife ELIZABETH HARRIS for the benefit of my children until my
son MANDLEY WINSTON HARRIS shall become 21 years of age, then
be equally divided between my beloved wife ELIZABETH HARRIS and
my five children: MARGREATE HARRIS, JEAN HARRIS, ELIZA Z. HARRIS,
SUSANNA HARRIS and MANDLEY W. HARRIS.

Appoint my friend Maj. JOHN BENNETT, FRANCIS SMITHSON and my wife
executors.

                                        SAMUEL HARRIS

Wit: ROBERT WORSHAM, JOHN NEWBELL, JAMES GLASGOW.

JOSEPH MOTLEY, CHAMP TERRY, LEONARD CLAIBORNE, ALLEN C. TANNER
security for ELIZABETH HARRIS and JOHN BENNETT.

Page 424-425
24 November 1815
Pr: 19 February 1816

LWT HENRY WORSHAM, SR.

My wife AGNES WORSHAM to have my tract of land whereon I now live
with other property during her natural life.

My three sons JOHN, HENRY, and DAVID pay my just debts and at the
death of my wife my land be equally divided between them.

189

WORSHAM will cont'd:

My son JOHN is to take care of my youngest daughter until she comes of age.

To my daughter NANCY a feather bed.

The remainder of my property at the death of my wife, to be divided between my three youngest daughters: AGNES, SALLY and PAMELIA.

I have given my three oldest children BETSY EAST, WILLIAM WORSHAM and PATSY BILEY all they are entitled to.

Appoint my sons JOHN and HENRY WORSHAM executors.

HENRY (X) WORSHAM, SR.

Wit: CORNELIUS TURNER, WILLIAM B. L. VAUGHAN, JOHN TURNER.

Page 425-426
21 October 1815
Pr: 20 November 1815

LWT JOHN MATTON being weak and in an imperfect state of health but of sound mind.

To my beloved wife POLLY MATTON all my real and personal estate during her life or widowhood.

I desire that the negro Fanny and her child Rainey, the property of my mother during her life, to return to my estate. The negros be valued and the valuation divided between my wife and brother GEORGE MATTON. My brother at the same time settling according to an instrument of writing in the hands of Maj. ARMISTEAD SHELTON for that purpose.

Should my wife marry it is my desire that she retain one third of my estate during her lifetime.

Appaoint THOMPSON ROBINSON, AVERY MUSTAIN and JOSEPH BLANKS executors.

JOHN (X) MATTON

Wit: LEWIS (X) DALTON, SOLOMON (X) PICKEREL.

YOUNG SHELTON and JAMES ADAMS security for THOMPSON ROBERTSON.

Page 426-428
.........1813
Pr: 19 February 1815

LWT PYRANT EASLEY being in good health and disposing mind.

To my beloved wife MOLLY EASLEY negros: Suckey, Maria, Isaac, one fourth part of my household furniture, livestock. I lend my wife during her lifetime my negro Dick, my tract of land where I live. Should she marry, I lend her the Short tract during her lifetime. The loan of my home tract and the use of my negro Dick will cease

EASLEY will cont'd:

if she marries.

To my son JOHN EASLEY the land on Cherry Stone Creek...which I bought of WILLIAM WATSON, JOHNSON & HURTON and ANTHONY D. HADEN.

To my son PYRANT EASLEY my tract where I now live also the Short tract reserving to my wife the loan of the property.

My sons JOHN and PYRANT are not to clear the land until they come of age.

To my daughter SALLY EASLEY the 415 acre tract I purchased from WILLIAM DABNEY and 15 acres adjoining.

After the one fourth of my stock is layed off to my wife, my executors to sell the remaining and give my daughter SALLY EASLEY two hundred pounds in order to make her legacy equal to my sons.

To my daughter SALLY and my sons PYRANT and JOHN the balance of my negros and the residue of my estate equally divided between them on my son John coming of age or my daughter marrying.

To my friend JENNINGS THOMPSON fifty pounds which he owes me.

Appoint my wife and my friends THOMAS H. WOODING, WILLIAM TUN-STALL and JENNINGS THOMPSON executors.

PYRANT (X) EASLEY

Wit: W. BEAVERS, THOMAS RAGSDALE, NATHN. WILSON.

MOSES HUTCHINGS, SAMUEL THOMPSON and JOSEPH CARTER security for WILLIAM TUNSTALL and JENNINGS THOMPSON.

Page 428-429
29 January 1816
Pr: 19 February 1816

LWT ADIN GRAY in a low state of health but of sound mind and of memory.

To my beloved wife ELIZABETH GRAY during her natural life, all my estate both real and personal. At her death, my wife may dispose of half the property as she desires.

To the heirs of JOHN PIGG, deceased, after the death of my wife, my negro Joe which I purchased of said Pigg.

To REBECAH PIGG, daughter of CLEMONS PIGG, after the death of my wife, my negro girl Tempy.

It is my will and desire that the balance of my estate after the death of my wife, be applied as though this declaration had not been made.

Appoint my wife executrix.

ADIN GRAY

(cont'd next page)

GRAY will cont'd:

Wit: WILLIAM WALTON, ALLEN CHANDLER, REBECAH (X) PARRISH, JOANNA (X) PARRISH.

Page 429-430
2 November 1815
Pr: 19 February 1816

LWT JOHN PIGG being weak in body but of perfect sense.

My beloved wife POLLY PIGG to have exclusive of her third part, the household furniture, all my stock, my crops, negros Lile and Wise for the support of her and the family during her lifetime.

To my oldest son PAYTON the negro George when he comes of age.

To my second son CLEMONS a negro Randle when of age.

To my third son HESEKIAH the negro Major when of age.

To my daughter ELIZABETH a negro called Sindy when she marries or comes of age.

To WILLIAM my fourth son, a negro girl when he comes of age called Chaney.

To my fifth son JOHN WALKER the negro Patty when he comes of age.

I desire my children to have a good liberal English education..

The balance of my estate to be divided between my six children as they come of age.

I appoint my wife and ADIN GRAY executors.

                                        JOHN PIGG

Wit: W. NASH, ADIN GRAY, CLEMENT PIGG.

JAMES ADAMS, SAMUEL CALLAND, NATHAN HUTCHERSON, JAMES HART and CLEMENT PIGG security for the executrix.

Page 430-431
20 January 1816
Pr: 19 February 1816

LWT JESSE HODGES

To my beloved wife during her natural life, my estate.

After her death to be equally divided between my seven children and POLLY's son WADE now about 2 years old; DORCAS PARRISH, SU-SANNAH GRUBS, POLLY, NEPHANAH BOWLING, NANCY HUNDLEY, JAMES and SALLY GRUBS.

Appoint my wife and son JAMES and WILLIAM BOWLING who married my daughter NEPHANAH as executors.

                                        JESSE (X) HODGES

HODGES will cont'd:

Wit: JAMES HART, MOSES HODGES, JEREMIAH W. WALKER.

MATHEW PARISH, RICHARD PARISH, ALLEN PARISH and JABEZ SMITH security for JAMES HODGES.

Page 431-432
2 February 1816
Pr: 19 February 1816

LWT VINCENT WALKER being very sick and weak of body but of perfect mind.

After my debts are paid, the balance to my beloved wife ELIZABETH WALKER during her life. At her decease to be equally divided among my lawful heirs.

Appoint JAMES G. KEATTS and RICHARD KEATTS executors.

                                        VINCENT WALKER

Wit: JOHN L. GLENN, WILLIAM DENNING.

WILLIAM S. CLARK and WILLIAM CLARK security for SAMUEL STONE.

Page 432
3 September 1813
Pr: 18 September 1815

LWT PHEBE COUSINS

I give my nephew WILLIAM BEAVERS all my estate including my seven negros: Betty, Peter, Dick, James, Sally, Fanny and Mary and appoint him executor.

                                        PHEBE COUSINS

Wit: JAMES D. METTON, WILLIAM DODSON, ELIZABETH FOUNTAIN, CHLOE COLEMAN.

Page 432-434
16 August 1804
Pr: 17 June 1816

LWT JAMES BARNETT, SR. being advanced in years but of sound mind.

To my beloved wife ANN BARNETT, I lend her six negros: Old Peter, James, Violet, Judith, Patty and Little Jim with all my household furniture, two horses and cattle.

At the death of my wife, my son WILLIAM BARNETT is to have Little Jim.

To my son THOMAS BARNETT my horse Dabsten.

The residue of my estate to be equally divided between my five children: JOHN BARNETT, WILLIAM, THOMAS, BETSY WOODFOLK and NANCY CAMPBELL.

193

BARNETT will cont'd:

To my son JOHN BARNETT I lend at my death four negros: Old Glouster, Cloe, Graybeal and Jinney and at his death to his children
and a mare called Bald.

To my son WILLIAM BARNETT I lend negros: Little Glouster, Young
Peter and Ran and at his death to his children, and a horse called Maz and a set of blacksmith tools.

To my son THOMAS BARNETT I lend negros: Sue, Charles, Hezekiah
and Milly, and at his death to his children and a still.

To my daughter BETSEY WOODFOLK five negros: Nick, Patrick, Mary,
Sally and Wilson and at her death to her children.

To my daughter NANCY CAMPBELL I lend negros: Harrison, Sauc...?,
and Ritta and at her death to her children.

The money MICAJAH DAVIS of Richmond is endebted to me be equally
divided between JOHN BARNETT, WILLIAM BARNETT and BETSEY WOOL-
FORK.

Appoint my sons JOHN BARNETT, WILLIAM BARNETT and THOMAS BARNETT
executors.

                                         JAMES BARNETT

Wit: ROBERT PAYNE, WILLIAM CLARKE, CUR... BARNETT.

In addition to the above, money due from land accounts to be for
the use of my beloved wife ANN BARNETT.

9 September 1804, JAMES BARNETT.

Wit: CUR... BARNETT, WILLIAM (X) QUINIALY, JOHN (X) QUINIALY.

Caswell County, North Carolina.
Proved by the witnesses and ordered to be recorded.
23 May 1816.

Recorded in Pittsylvania County, Virginia, 17th June 1816. ADAM
SUTHERLIN and PEYTON LUMPKIN security for JOHN BARNETT.

Page 435-439
1 August 1811
Pr: 19 August 1816

LWT   JOHN LEWIS of sound mind.

The tract of land whereon I now live on Dan River, being about
1300 acres, to my brother CHARLES LEWIS for his lifetime and at
his death to his son NICHOLAS MEREWETHER during his life and at
his death to his sons to be equally divided between them. Should
NICHOLAS MEREWETHER die without a son and should my brother CHAR-
LES have a second son, then at the death of Nicholas, I give the
tract to the second son of my brother Charles for and during his
life then to his sons. Should my brother Charles die leaving no
sons, I give the tract to the three sons of my deceased brother
ROBERT during their lives, to wit: JOHN EVIN, ROBERT HENRY and
MEREWETHER WARNER and at their deaths to their sons. Should there
be no heirs, then to the sons of my sister JANE READ.

LEWIS will cont'd:

To the sons of my brother ROBERT, I give my 1400 acre tract in Halifax County on the Dan River for life, then to their sons. But should they die without sons then to the sons of sister MARY WILLIAMS. This land to be under the management of my executors until the sons of my brother Robert come of age.

My sister JANE READ to have the use of the house where she now lives and the plantation and part of another on Stoney branch as long as she remains unmarried.

My tract in Person County, North Carolina, 450 acres, to the four children of my brother Robert: JOHN ERVIN, ROBERT HENRY, NANCY SUSANNAH and MEREWETHER WARNER.

The tract I purchased of DURETT RICHARDS on Dan River, 200 acres, to my brother CHARLES LEWIS, my sisters JANE READ, MARY WILLIAMS and ELIZABETH HOPSON.

My negros to be divided into 27 parts to be given as follows: to my brother Charles, four parts; to my sister Jane Read eight; to my sister Mary Williams nine parts; to my sister Elizabeth Hopson two parts; to the four children of my deceased brother Robert (John Ervin, Robert Henry, Nancy Susannah and Merewether Warner) I give the remaining four parts.

To my brother Charles, my mirror, my clock and family sword.

To my brother Charles and my sisters Jane Read, Mary Williams and Elizabeth Hopson, the residue of my estate.

Appoint my brother CHARLES LEWIS, WILLIAM WILLIAMS, husband of my sister MARY, Dr. CHARLES MEREWETHER, Dr. SAMUEL DABNEY, Capt. WILLIAM ROYALL executors.

                                        JOHN LEWIS

Wit: FRANCIS DABNEY, GEORGE DABNEY, PHL. THOMAS, JAMES DIX.

Codicil dated 27 July 1809:

I desire the two tracts I purchased of JOHN THOMAS' executors and one of THOMAS BOULDIN about 400 acres, to to to CHARLES LEWIS and my three sisters: JANE READ, MARY WILLIAMS and ELIZABETH HOPSON. To the three sons of my deceased brother ROBERT: JOHN ERVIN, ROBERT HENRY and MEREWETHER WARNER a tract on Sandy Creek 275 acres more or less and they are to pay their sister NANCY SUSANNAH fifteen pounds each.

                                        JOHN LEWIS

Wit: FRANCIS DABNEY, GEORGE DABNEY.

I intend when WILLIAM K. HARRISON pays me six hundred twenty six pounds thirteen shillings with interest from 22 July 1811 to deed him the lands he sold me. The debt to be paid my heirs within one year after my death or my executors may sell the land, pay the above sum and give the said Harrison any surplus.

                                        JOHN LEWIS

Page 547
11 January 1811
WILLIAM K. HARRISON to JOHN LEWIS
Cash paid SAMUEL SMITH agreeable to your Deed of Trust to THOMAS
BOULDING and myself 452.0.0

22 July
Interest to date 15.2.9
To Clerk for recording Deed of Trust 0.3.0; cash paid trustees
charges 1.1.7; bond dated 16 April 1804 100.8.7; interest from
1804 to 1811 43.18.7; to Clerk for recording deed 0.3.0; to Clerk
for recording release 0.6.0; six months interest 13.10.0

WARNER WILLIAMS, HOWEL S. READ, JAMES LANIER, THOMAS RAGSDALE,
GEORGE DABNEY, LEWIS B. ALLEN and WILLIAM H. SHELTON security for
SAMUEL DABNEY.

Page 440
13 July 1802
Pr: 19 August 1816

LWT WILLIAM G. PARHAM

To my dearly beloved mother all my estate real and personal during her life and at her decease to be equally divided among my
then surviving sisters.

                                        WILLIAM C. PARHAM

Wit: PHILIP L. GRASTY, BENJ. STONE.

JOHN LEWIS, JOSIAH CREWS and BENJAMIN STONE security for SUSANNAH
PARHAM.

Page 440-441
7 May 1816
Pr: 19 August 1816

LWT JOHN TURNER being sick and disposing mind and memory.

I lend my beloved wife one third part of my estate, real and personal, during her lifetime. At her death the land that was alloted her be sold and the money divided between my children: CORNE-
LIUS TURNER, JOHN TURNER, WILLIAM TURNER, ROBERT TURNER, and MARY
TURNER. The other property lent my wife be sold and money divided
between the children of my last wife: ANNA HENRIETTA, HENRY HOW-
ARD, RICHARD, KITTY, NANCY, GEORGE and JOSEPH.

The balance of my estate to be sold and the money from such pay
my sons JOHN TURNER and WILLIAM TURNER ten pounds each in lieu
of bed and furniture. Then pay my seven youngest children: Anna
Henrietta, Henry Howard, Richard, Kitty, Nancy, George and Joseph
one hundred pounds each and the balance between all my children.

To my son JOSEPH an extra legacy, a colt.

It is my desire that my sons be put to some trade and if conven-
ient for HENRY and RICHARD with the same man and my son GEORGE
and JOSEPH with the one man.

196

TURNER will cont'd:

Appoint my friend WILLIAM SMITH executor.

                                            JOHN TURNER

Wit: JOHN HUNT, DAVID (X) WORSHAM.

KITTY TURNER, widow, relinquishes any claim to administer the estate of her deceased husband.

CORNELIUS TURNER and JOHN TURNER security for executor.

Page 442-443
12 April 1816
Pr: 16 September 1816

LWT JAMES HINTON

All my perishable estate to be sold to pay my just debts.

I give to my half sister and brothers: LEAN D. JOHNSON, NANCY W.
JOHNSON, MARY P. JOHNSON, RICHARD JOHNSON and JAMES F. JOHNSON
children of my mother LETTICE JOHNSON and her husband, RICHARD
JOHNSON, the following negros: Betty, Peter and Anthony, to be
divided when James comes of age, Said negros to remain with my
mother to help educate my half sisters and brothers as my executor will direct.

To my mother LETTICE JOHNSON my bond on DANIEL MOTLEY, deceased,
which was due 1 April 1816 for $630.00.

Also to my mother any money that is due me.

I appoint my step-father RICHARD JOHNSON my executor.

                                            JAMES HINTON

Wit: WM. SHELTON, JAZ. FURGUSON, JR., JER. WHITE, WM. RAWLINS.

Page 443
12 June 1816
Pr: 19 August 1816

LWT MARTHA LAWSON weak in body but full presents (sic) of mind.

To my grand daughter SALLY HENDRICK all my household and kitchen
furniture and a negro woman Dils and her child Richard, all my
stock.

Appoint SALLY HENDRICK my executrix.

                                            MARTHA (X) LAWSON

Wit: ERASMUS STIMPSON, JR., ERASMUS STIMPSON, BENJAMIN SADLER.

ERASMUS STIMPSON, JR., JOHN M. DIX and BENJAMIN SADLER security
for executrix.

Page 444-446 (cont'd):

23 May 1816
Pr: 21 October 1816

LWT THOMAS MOORE in a perfect state of health and sound mind.

I desire my tract of land whereon I now live be sold if it is the desire of my wife and the money used to purchase other land of her choice during her natural life. Also any money due me at my death for the benefit of my wife NANCY. This property, after her death, to five of my children: TERRY, MERRIMAN, MATHEW, ANNA and POLLY.

My wife to have negros: Peter, Betty, Tener and her child French during her lifetime and reserving Betty that she may dispose of at her discretion. My wife is to have the use of all my livestock during her lifetime.

I lend to my daughter ANNA negro Lucy during her life for her to dispose of within the family, a feather bed and furniture, cow and calf, and a horse.

To my daughter POLLY, during her lifetime, my negro Cate and the same as my daughter Anna.

To my son JAMES the tract of land where he now resides and thirty five pounds.

To my son WHALEY my negro Nance of Ephraim, and should he have no heirs, then Nance to return to the family.

To my son THOMAS my negro girl Patty.

To my daughter SALLY my negro girl Juno.

To my daughter PENELOPHE HOPWOOD, $350.00 exclusive of what she has received.

To my son MATHEW B., my negro girl Kason, a horse and money for three years tuition and at the death of my wife, my negro Peter, bed and furniture. Should he die without heirs his part to return to the estate.

After giving my son VINCENT the 100 acres where he lives, then the balance to my son LEVI. If Levi should die without an heir the property to return to the family.

My Long tract to be sold to discharge the legacy to my daughter PENELOPHE HOPWOOD and to my son JAMES and the balance if any be divided between my three children: SALLY HAYMES, WHALEY & THOMAS.

Whatever remains after the death of my wife, not before given, shall be equally divided amongst my children.

My son VINCENT to hold and enjoy the place where he now lives and to include 100 acres, to have my negro Nelson. Should Vincent die without issue, the property to revert to the family.

To my son LEVI my negro Simon with the conditions above stated.

To my son JERE my negro Gabriel and at the death of my wife to have negro French, and at my death, a feather bed and furniture.

MOORE will cont'd:

To my son MARRIMAN my negro Anthony, a bed and furniture. Should
he have no heirs, the property to return to the family, also a
horse and at the death of my wife, to have the negro Tena.

Appoint my sons MERRIMAN, JERRE(?), and JAMES ADAMS as my executors.

THOMAS MOORE

Wit: JOHN LINDSEY, JOHN PARSON, LITTLE B. LEWIS, CRISPEN DICKER-
SON, YOUNG SHELTON.

SAMUEL CALLANDS and WILLIAM ECHOLS security for JAMES ADAMS.

16 May 1818
MERRIMAN MOORE, MARY MOORE, ANNE MOORE, NANCY MOORE security for
JEREMIAH MOORE one of the executors who entered into bond.

Page 446-447
20 May 1816
Pr: 21 October 1816

LWT JAMES DOUGLASS being of sound and perfect understanding.

My executor to sell all my estate at twelve months credit except
my negro man John is not to be sold out of the family. The money
from the sale to be divided equally between my wife PATSEY DOUG-
LASS and my son JAMES A. DOUGLASS. Should my wife be with child,
then the division to be a third each.

Should my wife desire to move out of the state, my executor may
pay the whole amount without taking on the guardianship of the
child.

To my wife PATSEY all the bedclothes, not to be sold with other
articles.

Appoint JOHN DOUGLASS executor.

JAMES DOUGLASS

Wit: JAS. E. HAILEY, JAMES DOSS, WILLIAM W. HAILEY.

EDWARD DOUGLASS and CHARLES S. ADAMS and JAMES DOSS security for
the executor.

Page 447-448
4 January 1817
Pr: 17 February 1817

LWT JAMES MEADE

I give unto MARLEY ADAMS nothing more than I have heretofore giv-
en her.

To my son MEREDITH MEADE all my wearing apparel.

To my daughter LUCY DAVIS $20.00

199

MEADE will cont'd:

To my daughter SALLY ADAMS $30.00.

To my son MEADY my shotgun.

To my beloved wife ROSAMON all and every part of my estate during her lifetime. At her death to my children equally: TALELET MAHO MEADE, MIDDLETON MEADE, EDITH MEADE, MORRISON MEADE, BETSY MEADE and MEADDY MEADE.

Appoint my wife ROSAMON MEADE and JAMES ADAMS executors.

                                        JAMES (X) MEADE

Wit: ROBERT DEVIN, JAMES BLAKELY, TALIFAFERRO HAMMACK, GREENWOOD ADAMS, WILLIAM (X) ELLIOTT, SR.

JAMES BLAKELY and NATHAN ADAMS security for the executors.

Page 448-449
6 November 1809
Pr: 18 November 1816

LWT ABRAM PARRISH in perfect health and sound mind.

To my beloved wife during her natural life and after her death I give to WILSON PARRISH the tract of land I bought of NICHOLAS PARRISH. I also lend my wife SUSANNAH PARRISH my three negros: David, Hager and Selvah during her life then equally divided between Wilson and all the children the said Susannah may have begotten by me.

Appoint SUSANNAH PARRISH executrix.

                                        ABRAM PARRISH

Wit: EDWARD NUNNELLE, JAMES EDWARDS, WILLIAM HANKINS, MORTON WARREN.

JOHN GILES, JAMES GILES and THOMAS RIDDLE security for the executrix.

Page 449-452
18 July 1804
Pr: 18 November 1818

LWT THOMAS WRIGHT being sick and weak in body but of sound memory.

To my beloved wife HANNAH WRIGHT all my personal estate together with the land whereon I now live on Sandy River that joins DANIEL PRICE, WILLIAM BATES, WILLIAM ASTIN, THOMAS WRIGHT, DANIEL WRIGHT and after her death to be disposed as hereinafter mentioned.

To my son THOMAS WRIGHT a tract on Mill Creek.

To my son JOHN WRIGHT a tract whereon he now lives.

To my daughter ELIZABETH EARP wife of ABEDINGO EARP $2.00.

WRIGHT will cont'd:

To my son DANIEL WRIGHT part of a tract joining JOHN WRIGHT on Mill Creek and THOMAS WRIGHT.

To my daughter SALLY WATTS wife of JOSHUA WATTS, the priviledge of living on the land where they now live as long as they wish or until Daniel Wright and John Wright sell the property at which time they are to pay Sally Watts five pounds.

To my son JAMES WRIGHT the tract where Thomas Wright lives.

To my daughter NANCY WRIGHT a bed and furniture.

The land where I live, afer the death of my wife, I give to ..... when he comes of age and the personal property left my wife.

I appoint my wife and GEORGE ADAMS executors.

THOMAS (X) WRIGHT

Wit: BEN WRIGHT, JESSE (X) KEESEE, WILLIAM (X) CARTER.

Page 452-453
19 December 1816
Pr: 20 January 1817

LWT JOHN FARMER being sick and weak in body but of perfect mind and memory.

To my brother LABAN FARMER my negro Nancy.

To my brother ROBERT FARMER my negro Sarah.

To my sister SUSANNA FARMER twenty pounds out of the legacy coming to me from my Father.

The balance of my legacy coming to me to be equally divided between my brother LABAN and my brother ROBERT together with all else I may possess.

JOHN FARMER

Wit: THOMAS (X) BRUICE, WILLIAM (X) CREWS, JOHN ABSTON.

JOHN ABSTON and FRANCIS ABSTON security for LABAN FARMER, executor.

Page 453-454
8 January 1816
(No other date)

Personally appeared before me WILLIAM DODSON and RHODA DODSON and made oath that GEORGE DODSON called upon them at their house and stated that he wanted the land where he now lives divided between his three sons: THOMAS, GEORGE and EASLEY DODSON after the decease of his wife, and a cow to his son Thomas, a colt and sow to Easley, the crop now made for the use of his wife and family.

To his daughter FRANKY, two beds and furniture, a colt, side sad-

DODSON will cont'd:

dle, cow, trunk, a little wheel at her mothers decease.

At the decease of his wife, the remainder of his estate divided
between all his daughters.

WILLIAM   (X)   DODSON,
RHODA (X) DODSON

Sworn to before JOHN WILSON.

Recorded 20 January 1817.

Page 454-456
8 September 1816
Pr: 20 January 1817

LWT LARKIN DIX being sound of mind.

To my beloved wife JENNEY DIX my land, house, furniture and livestock during her natural life except such parts hereinafter given.

To my son JOHN DIX 120 acres on Old Ferry Road on the south side,
bed and furniture.

To my son LARKIN DIX 80 acres being the place where I live and
part of the same tract where my son JOHN's part is layed off after the death of my wife.

To my sons THOMAS and WILLIAM DIX the residue of my land equally
divided, with William having the liberty of having the part where
he now lives, after the death of my wife.

To my daughter SUSANNA WILKINS my negro Milley.

To my son-in-law JOHN LUMPKINS my negro Lewis after the death of
my wife.

My negro woman Tabby with the increase of Milly to my daughter
SUSANNA WILKINS and my son-in-law JOHN LUMPKINS after the death
of my wife.

My negro Daniel to be sold and the money divided between my four
sons: THOMAS, JOHN, WILLIAM and LARKIN DIX.

After the death of my wife all the personal property be divided
equally between my four sons: THOMAS, JOHN, WILLIAM and LARKIN
DIX, my son-in-law JOHN LUMPKIN and my daughter SUSANNA WILKINS.

Should my two old negros Peter and Tener outlive my wife, they
are to be taken care of by my executors out of my estate.

Appoint my son-in-law JOHN LUMPKIN and my sons THOMAS and JOHN
DIX executors.

LARKIN DIX

Wit: JAMES D. PATTON, LEVIN CARTER, BENJAMIN (X) RATLIFF, JOHN
D. DIX, WILLIAM P. DIX, JOHN LUMPKIN, H.... WILKINS.

JAMES D. PATTON, LEWIS B. ALLEN, BENJAMIN RATLIFF and LARKIN DIX

DIX will cont'd:

security for JOHN P. DIX.

Page 456-457
7 September 1816
Pr: 17 March 1817

LWT POLLY CALLAWAY being sick and weak in body of sound mind.

I desire the perishable part of my estate to be sold reserving the best bed and furniture and one half dozen teaspoons. Money from the sale to pay my just debts and funeral expense.

I give my daughter MARTHA ANN the residue of my estate. Should she die without an heir, then my sister SALLY ANDERSON's daughters should have my estate.

Appoint my brother CHARLES CALLAWAY executor.

POLLY CALLAWAY

Wit: JAMES CALLAWAY, CHARLES CALLAWAY, SR., CHARLES CALLAWAY, JR.

Page 457-460
31 October 1816
Pr: 18 November 1816

LWT STEPHEN WILKINSON being of sound mind and disposing memory.

After my death, the following negros be sold: Spencer, Peter, Lewis, Adam, Garland, Viney, Linney, Edmund and Martha also my perishable property and every part of my estate not hereinafter given. Out of the money, I want my just debts paid and the balance divided between my children as follows: to each of my daughters and their heirs one hundred pounds, in lieu of land.

The residue I wish divided between my five children: SAMUEL, SELVEY, PATTEY, BETSEY and FREDERICK.

To my beloved wife SALLY WILKINSON the following negros: Chaney, Gerald and Polley, a horse, saddle and bridle, and livestock and furniture and ten pounds in cash. I lend her during her natural life or widowhood 283 acres including the mansion and the other houses of the west end of the tract where I now reside (being the balance of the tract after giving my son SAMUEL 250 acres) also lend my wife two negros Davy and Annaka.

To my son JOHN WILKINSON negros Sippier and Jude, now in his possession, a silver teaspoon and ten pounds.

To my son SAMUEL WILKINSON negros Will and Phill, now in his possession, bed and furniture, silver teaspoon and ten pounds and 250 acres.

To my daughter SILVEY MOORE negros Bett, Clarisa and Mary, and a silver spoon.

To my daughter POLLEY R. KENT negros Elijah, Fanny and Jinney, a horse, saddle and bridle, bed and furniture, silver spoon.

203

WILKINSON will cont'd:

To my daughter BETSEY R. BURTON negros Sooky, Lucy, Armstead and
George, horse, saddle and bridle, bed and silver spoon.

To my son FREDERICK T. WILKINSON negros Jim, Charles and Nancy,
a horse, saddle and bridle, bed and furniture, silver spoon and
at the death of his mother, I give him the 283 acres of which I
loaned my wife with the negro Annaka.

Should my daughter BETSEY R. BURTON die without issue, her legacy
returned to my estate for FREDERICK WILKINSON.

At the death of my wife, the negro David to be sold and the proceeds divided between: SAMUEL, SILVEY, POLLY, BETSEY and FREDER-
ICK.

It is my desire that the negros sold be purchased by my children.

Appoint my friend STEPHEN KENT, DANIEL W. FOURGUREAN and WILLIAM
H. SHELTON executors.

                              STEPHEN (X) WILKINSON

Wit: T. WILKINSON, JR., JERALD (X) FORD, RICHARD STONE.

THOMAS WILKINSON, JOHN M. DIX, THOMAS CHANEY, JOHN DODOSN, AZA-
RIAH MOORE, ARCHER WALTERS, JOHN P. WILKINSON, MATHEW PARRISH and
EZEKIEL CHANEY security for DANIEL FOUGUNEAN.

Page 460
26 November 1816
Pr: 20 January 1817

LWT ADAM CREEL

I want my horse and cow sold to pay my debts and after that, I
want RUTH EVINS to have a pot, SAM BEACH a pot, sister LUCE the
wheel and cards and the old womans wearing clothes. JOSEPH HILL
all that is at my new place, corn and all the rest of my property
to be equally divided between SAMUEL BEACH and sister LUCY and
JOSEPH HILL.

I want JOSEPH HILL to settle and divided according to my wishes.

                              ADAM CREEL

Wit: DAVID FITZGERALD

WILLIAM H. SHELTON security for executor.

Page 461-463
7 May 1817
Pr: 21 July 1817

LWT WILLIAM WALKER, SR. being weak of body and very sick but of
perfect mind and memory.

All my property divided as follows: to my daughter POLLEY NIGHT
the lawful interest of $280.00 per year as long as she lives, at

WALKER will cont'd:

her death, the principal to her heirs, which will be in the hands of my son JOSEPH WALKER.

To my daughter SUSANNA H. ESTES, the negros in her possession: Nance, Alex, George, Claiborne and Harry.

To my son JEREMIAH W. WALKER, 185 acres, negros Isaac, Sile and Matilda.

To my son WILLIAM WALKER, 430 acres which he sold RALPH SMITH, a negro Sampson, a wagon, horse and eight dollars which property he has received.

To my son JOSEPH WALKER, 250 acres, negros Sally and Harry, bed and furniture.

To my daughter ANNE W. FINNEY, six negros: Eave, Febby, Ben, Lewis, Darkis and Joannah, which she has in her possession except Ben.

To my son THOMAS WALKER, 175 acres where I now live, the negros: Thomas, Silvey and Bob and two old wenches Dinah and Jeany, which he is to keep and maintain during their lifetime; a bed and furniture.

To my daughter ELIZABETH ESTES, negros: Joice, Dave, Letty and Charity.

To my loving wife CATHARINE, negros: Abb, Anthony and Peter, a tract of land that I have BURWELL WALKER's title bond for a right being 200 acres, beds and furniture, a horse, saddle, bridle, and other furniture and livestock. To be only for her widowhood, then to go to her child if she has one by me. If not, to return to my estate.

To my two youngest sons JOSEPH WALKER and THOMAS WALKER, the balance of the household, excepting the household and kitchen furniture, my wearing clothes and cows and sheep.

My negro Parton with the balance of my estate be sold and then the money divided between my seven children: SUSANNAH H. ESTES, JEREMIAH W. WALKER, WILLIAM WALKER, JOSEPH WALKER, THOMAS WALKER, ANNA W. FINNEY and ELIZABETH ESTES.

Should my wife not have a child, the property she hath must return to my seven youngest children above named.

Appoint my son JOSEPH WALKLER and PETER FINNEY and my son THOMAS WALKER, executors.

                              WILLIAM WALKER

Wit: JESSE ESTES, JOHN (X) BOSWELL, POLLEY HUNDLEY.

JOHN SMITH, JABEZ SMITH and JOHN BOSWELL security for the executors.

Page 463-466
28 March 1814
Pr: 17 January 1817

LWT SHERWOOD PEIRSON being of perfect health and memory.

To my son RICHMOND PEIRSON a negro Soloman, a tract of land in Greene County, Kentucky of 300 acres more or less.

To my son MASTIN PEIRSON, a negro Peter, and $90.00 due him for services rendered.

To my son THOMAS PEIRSON a negro Abram.

To my son DOCTOR PEIRSON a negro Yorrick.

To my son CHARLES PEIRSON a negro Randolph.

I lend to my daughter ELIZABETH LACY the negros: Ailey, Marie and Jesse, they are not to be sold.

I lend to my daughter POLLEY PEIRSON, a negro Amey and her child, but not to be sold; also two cows and calves, a horse, bed and furniture, and a table.

To my son WILLIAM PEIRSON, negros George and Milley.

To my grand daughter ELIZA PEIRSON, $200.00 when she comes of age or marries.

I have given heretofore my son SHERWOOD PEIRSON, deceased, his full portion, therefore I leave to his children when they come of age, twenty shillings each.

Should any of my children die without issue, their portion to return to my estate.

I lend my well beloved wife ELIZABETH PEIRSON during her natural life, under the management of MASTIN PEIRSON, the tract where I now live, furniture, stock and slaves: Easther, Miner, Isaac, Lucy, Squire, Jug, Patience, Lydia, Luris, Seney and Dick, livestock for the maintenance of my wife and youngest children. And should my wife die before the youngest son WILLIAM comes of age, the property to be held by MASTIN until WILLIAM comes of age.

All the property I have lent my wife, at her death to be divided between my sons: RICHMOND, MASTIN, THOMAS, DOCTOR, CHARLES and WILLIAM PEIRSON.

I desire my son WILLIAM be sent to school until he is capable of working interest.

At the division of my property, the tract where I now live, 549 acres more or less, be divided between my sons: MASTIN, THOMAS, CHARLES and WILLIAM.

Should my daughter POLLEY not marry before this division takes place, that my sons Thomas, Mastin, Charles and William attend her welfare.

My negro woman Easter may live with whom she thinks proper.

Appoint my wife ELIZABETH PEIRSON executrix and MASTIN PEIRSON, THOMAS PEIRSON, CHARLES PEIRSON and WILLIAM PEIRSON executors.

SHERWOOD PEIRSON

206

PEIRSON will cont'd:

Wit: JABEZ SMITH, JOHN SMITH, JR., ALLEN (X) WRAY,JAMES THOMAS.

JABEZ SMITH, JOHN SMITH, JR. and SAMUEL CALLAND security for executors MASTIN PEIRSON and THOMAS PEIRSON.

Page 466-467
9 October 1813
Pr: 21 April 1817

LWT MARY HENDERSON being in great pain and affliction of body
but of sound mind.

To my grand daughter TABITHA JENKINS a horse.

The balance of my estate be divided among all my children, male
and female, or their heirs.

Appoint my friend WILLIAM SMITH executor.

                                        MARY (R) HENDERSON

Wit: JOSHUA STONE, BENJA. STONE, WM. TERRY, THOMAS BLACK, SR.

JESSE BUCKLEY and JOHN CHISNHALL security for executor.

Page 467-470
16 September 1803
Pr: 18 August 1817

LWT THOMAS CARTER in my usual health.

I lend my loving wife WINIFRED CARTER during her natural life the
tract where I now live, my Green Rock tract and the use of the
following negros: Peter, Daniel, Sam, Bob, Juda, Lee, Rachel, Lucy, Molley, Fanny, Cintha, Jack, Jonathan, Rhoda and Abram. To
also have the use of my personal estate except a bed and furniture I give my daughter JOANNA CARTER and the bed and furniture
I give to each of my sons: EDWARD CARTER, LAWSON HOBSON CARTER,
CHRISTOPHER LAWSON CARTER and RAWLEY WILLIAMSON CARTER.

To my daughter JOANNA CARTER my negro Nancy.

To my daughter ELIZABETH CARTER a negro Abbey.

To my daughter SALLY LOVELL a negro woman.

To my son JESSEE CARTER the tract of land where he now lives and
my negro Ellinor.

To my son EDWARD CARTER my negro Stepney.

To my son THOMAS CARTER half the tract where he and his brother
JEDUTHAN CARTER at present carries on the sadlers business also
my tract on the south side of Hickeys Road and negro Robin.

To my son JEDUTHAN CARTER half the tract with Thomas and half the
tract on the south side of Hickeys Road and negro Katy.

CARTER will cont'd:

To my son LAWSON HOBSON CARTER my tract called Rigneys and negro Anna.

To my son CHRISTOPHER LAWSON CARTER part of the tract where I now live, lines of JOHN GILES, deceased, but not to possess the land while his mother lives and a negro Micka.

To my son RAWLEY WILLIAMSON CARTER the residue of my tract where I live at the death of his mother, also negro Abbey, daughter of Lucy.

To my daughter JOANNA CARTER and my daughter ELIZABETH CARTER, all my Green Rock Tract after the death of my wife.

The personal property I have lent my wife during her life, at her death be equally divided between my children: JAMES CARTER, ELIZ-ABETH CARTER, SALLEY LOVELL, JESSEE CARTER, EDWARD CARTER, THOMAS CARTER, JEDUTHAN CARTER, LAWSON HOBSON CARTER, CHRISTOPHER LAWSON CARTER and RAWLEY WILLIAMSON CARTER.

Appoint my wife WINIFRED CARTER executrix.

THOMAS CARTER

Wit: JEDUTHAN CARTER, WILLIAMSON CARTER, M. HUTCHINGS, WASHINGTON THOMPSON.

THOMAS CARTER, THOMAS C. CARTER, SAMUEL M. LOVELL, LAWSON H. CAR-TER, CHRISTOPHER L. CARTER and RAWLEY W. CARTER security for the executrix.

Page 470-471
10 January 1817
Pr: 20 1817

LWT HENRY BURNETT being weak in body but of sound judgement.

To my well beloved daughter ELIZABETH SMITH one third part of my estate both real and personal during her natural life and after her decease divided equally among her children.

The remaining two thirds of my estate to ELIZABETH SMITH's child-ren to be equally divided.

Appoint WILLIAM SMITH and SMITH FULTON executors.

HENRY BURNETT

Wit: WILLIAM O'BRYAN, GILBERT BURNETT, JR., THOMAS BURNETT, PAT-SEY BURNETT, JAMES BURNETT, GILBERT BURNETT.

THOMAS B. JONES and SAMUEL CALLAND security for WILLIAM SMITH.

Page 471-472
22 November 1816
Pr: 20 January 1817

LWT PETER BASS in a low state of health but of sound mind.

208

BASS will cont'd:

To my daughter SALLY one dollar.

I lend to my beloved wife SUSANNA all the remaining part of my estate during her lifetime or widowhood. Should she marry she is to take one third part for life.

The remaining part of my estate then to be equally divided between my daughters: SUSANNA, ANNE, CHLOE, ELIZABETH and DIANNA being the five daughters of my wife SUSANNA. Should my wife not marry, the whole of my estate to be divided between my daughters: SUSANNA, ANNE, CHLOE, ELIZABETH and DIANNA after paying my daughter SALLY the one dollar above mentioned.

Appoint BENJAMIN STONE executor.

                                        PETER BASS

Wit: BENJAMIN STONE, WILLIAM CREWS.

JOHN DICKENSON security for executor.

Page 472-473
11 August 1817
Pr: 15 December 1817

LWT THOMAS WORSHAM being of sound and disposing mind.

My beloved wife BETSEY WORSHAM shall remain in possession of my property real and personal during her natural life except what will hereinafter be disposed of.

To my son WILLIAM WORSHAM negros: Rawley, Leilla, and Cheasy; bed and furniture, cow and calf to take effect upon my death.

To my daughter SALLY STUBLEFIELD a horse.

To my daughter POLLEY WORSHAM my negro woman Aggy and her child Clary, a boy Adam, a horse, bed and furniture, and one cow and calf.

To my son THOMAS WORSHAM negros: Esau, bob, John and Frankey, a horse, bed and furniture, and cow and calf.

To my two sons WILLIAM and THOMAS WORSHAM the tract of land where I now live, to be divided equally, Thomas to have the upper end with the dwelling house. They are to share the bridge equall. To take effect after the death of my wife.

The residue of my estate, after the death of my wife, be equally divided between my six children: NANCY BENSON, JOSEPH WORSHAM, WILLIAM WORSHAM, SALLY STUBLEFIELD, POLLEY WORSHAM, and THOMAS WORSHAM.

Appoint my wife, my son WILLIAM WORSHAM, and my son-in-law PETER STUBLEFIELD executors.

                                        THOMAS (X) WORSHAM

Wit: JAMES D. PATTEN, ROBERT ROSS, JOHN ROSS.

                        209

Page 473-475
2 June 1817
Pr: 15 December 1817

LWT BENJAMIN TERRY, SR. being in my perfect sense and disposing memory.

To my daughter ELIZABETH D. MOTLEY one hundred fourteen pounds in property.

To my son BENJAMIN TERRY thirty six pounds in property.

To my son DANIEL TERRY one hundred seventy four pounds, but out of that he is to pay JEREMIAH TERRY the amount of a bond given by DAVID FUQUA in which I am bound, the balance to be in property. The balance as Daniel may think proper for the benefit of my daughter DRUCILLA FUQUA.

To my daughter POLLEY BENNETT one hundred seventy four pounds in property.

To my son NATHANIEL TERRY forty two pounds in property.

To my son OBEDIAH P. TERRY forty five pounds in property.

To my son DANIEL TERRY one hundred seventeen pounds in property.

To my daughter SALLY C. TERRY four negros: Isbel, Lippur, Chaney and Wilmouth.

To my daughter NANCY R. FONTAINE one hundred eight pounds in property.

To my son ROBERT TERRY sixty six pounds in property.

To my daughter LUCY G. TERRY five negros: Easter, Jesse, Matilda, Levina and Joseph, and eight pounds.

The balance of my estate to be divided as follows: one eleventh part to my son NATHANIEL TERRY's heirs. One eleventh part to DANIEL TERRY to sell or dispose of for the benefit of my daughter DRUSCILLA FUQUA; the balance divided between my children: ELIZABETH D. MOTLEY, BENJAMIN TERRY, POLLEY BENNETT, OBADEAH P. TERRY, DANIEL TERRY, SALLY C. TERRY, NANCY R. FONTAINE, ROBERT TERRY and LUCY G. TERRY.

Appoint my son DANIEL TERRY executor.

BEN. (X) TERRY

Wit: JESSE WOODSON, WILLIAM ANDERSON, ABRAM WHITE.

Page 475-476
18 June 1817
Pr: 21 July 1817

LWT TEMPLE HAILEY

Wife ELIZABETH to have all the property during her lifetime or widowhood. Should she marry, to have only what came to her, the other part of my estate to return to my father's estate at her

HAILEY will cont'd:

marriage or at her death.

Also the money due from him to negro woman Tempy should be paid to her and the sum of ten dollars and one dollar apiece to negros: George, Hui..y and Rachel.

Appoints his father JOSEPH E. HAILEY executor.

Wit: ROBERT H. SLAUGHTER, WILLIAM W. HAILEY, NANCY HAILEY.

Page 476-478
22 May 1806
Pr: 17 November 1817

LWT CHARLES LEWIS of Caswell County, North Carolina.

My executors to sell what part of my estate necessary to pay my just debts, if necessary my house in Milton. Should it be necessary to sell some of the slaves, do not seperate the small children from their mothers.

I lend to my loving wife GATIE HOOD(?) during her widowhood one third part of my land layed off the lower end to include the mansion house; all furniture and her choice of a third of my negros.

To my son NICHOLAS land on Dan River.

To my daughters ELIZABETH and LUCY the balance of my land.

To my son NICHOLAS one fourth of my negros, with the other fourth to my daughters ELIZABETH and LUCY. After the death of my wife, NICHOLAS to have my desk and bookcase.

The balance of my estate divided between NICHOLAS, ELIZABETH and LUCY, and after the death of my wife, her third to be divided between the three children.

Appoint SAMUEL DABNEY, and Capt. JAMES WISE and ASA THOMAS, ANDREW HARRISON, JR., JOHN STAMPS, JR. as executors.

CHARLES LEWIS

Wit: GEORGE DABNEY, WILLIAM BOULTON, DANIEL FARLEY, CHARLES HARRISON.

Codicil:
Makes corrections to the dividing lines of the property given his children.

To NICHOLAS my old clock and $600.00.

To my daughter LUCY my new clock and $1200.00.

To my beloved wife $1200.00.

To my son-in-law WARNER WILLIAMS enough land to make a mill race.

Revoke executors SAMUEL DABNEY, JAMES WISE, ASA THOMAS and JOHN STAMPS. I appoint my son-in-law WARNER WILLIAMS & WILLIAM STAMPS

211

LEWIS will cont'd:

as my executors.

CHARLES LEWIS
20 October 1817

Wit: ANDREW HARRISON, JR., JOHN RUSSELL, WM. WALTERS.

WALTER COLES, JAMES M. WILLIAMS, JOHNSTON LANSDOWN, EUSTACE HUNT and WILLIAM ROBERTSON security for WARNER WILLIAMS.

Page 479
15 December 1815
Pr: 17 November 1817

LWT ANN BARNETT of Danville, Virginia.

To my grandson WILLIAM BARNETT, son of my son WILLIAM BARNETT, the house and lot where I now live by paying my son JOHN BARNETT $250.00.

To my grand daughter LUCY BARNETT, daughter of my son JOHN BAR- NETT; WILLIAM BARNETT, son of my son WILLIAM BARNETT; ALEXANDER A. CAMPBELL, son of FRANCES CAMPBELL, the balance of my property.

Appoint my grandsons WILLIAM BARNETT and ALEX A. CAMPBELL executors.

                                        ANN BARNETT

Wit: JAMES D. PATTEN, DAN. SULLIVAN, SELBY BENSON.

Page 480
28 January 1809
Pr: 19 October 1812
Pr: 20 July 1818

LWT JAMES CURRY being weak in body but in perfect mind.

To my wife PEGGY CURRY all my household furniture and livestock to use during her natural life.

To my son JAMES CURRY the tract of land whereon I now live being 273 acres. He is to give me and my wife a comfortable maintenance during our natural lives.

                                        JAMES CURRY

Wit: WM. MURPHY, LEWIS MURPHY

Page 481
24 May 1813
Pr: 19 January 1818

LWT ANN HALEY being of sound and perfect understanding.

To my two grand daughters POLLEY HAILEY and PATSEY HALEY of Ten- nessee, daughters of PLEASANT HALEY what money I have in the hand

HALEY will cont'd:

of JOSEPH E. HALEY, fifty pounds twelve shillings and ten pence, if I do not use this during my lifetime.

To my son JOSEPH E. HALEY the part of the estate of THOMAS HALEY which is coming to me after the death of his widow. My part and my son PLEASEANT HAILEY's part which I am entitled to by a power of attorney from him.

To my grand daughter BYRAN W. HAILEY my bed and furniture.

My sons WYATT and RICHARD and my daughter POLLEY I have given all I intend.

I appoint JOSEPH E. HAILEY executor.

ANN HALEY

Wit: TEMPLE HAILEY, WILLIAM W. HAILEY.

(N. B. There are three spellings of the name HALEY, HAILY, HAILEY used in this will.)

Page 482-483
22 January 1803
Pr: 1 February 1818

LWT WILLIAM PAYNE being of sound mind and memory.

I lend my beloved wife SARAH PAYNE my plantation where I now live and a bed and furniture, 2 cows and calves and a horse.

To my daughter MARY HUTCHESON five shillings.

To my daughter SARAH WILLIS five shillings.

I lend my daughter SUSANNAH JOHNSON a tract of 100 acres bounded by WILLIAM PAYNE, JAMES JOHNSTON, WIDOW BOATMAN and ARMSTEAD SHEL-TON and the improvements made by PHILEMON JOHNSON, husband of the said SUSANNAH during her life and at her death to be sold and equally divided between her children.

To my daughter ANNY WILLIS five shillings.

To my son GILES a bed and furniture.

To my son WILLIAM the tract of land and plantation where I now live, at the death of my widow also my negro Betty, all my stock and furniture. Should my son WILLIAM die without an heir, all I have given him to be divided between all my grandchildren.

I appoint my sons GILES and WILLIAM executors.

WILLIAM PAYNE

Wit: ARMSTEAD SHELTON, BEVERLY SHELTON, STEPHEN SHELTON.

GILES PAYNE and JOHN K. GREGORY security for the executor.

Page 483-484 (cont'd next page)

25 February 1815
Pr: 16 March 1818

LWT JOAB MEADOR being of perfect mind and memory.

To my grand child, a son of NANCY FLIPPEN, twenty five pounds at
the decease of my wife.

I lend to my beloved wife SARAH MEADOR during her life or widowhood, the tract whereon I now live except the part I give my son
SAMUEL MEADOR after the decease of my wife. I lend my wife negros: Lucy, Agnes, Isaac, Jenney, Johnson, Lindy, Charles, Joe,
David, Sirus, Rawley, James and Bob. After the death of my wife,
my estate to be sold and equally divided among all my children:
JAMES, LIDIA, FRANCIS, SAMUEL and SARAH.

I appoint my wife and my friends JOEL WILLIS, BENJAMIN DAVIS and
THOMAS DAVIS my executors.

JOEL MEADORS

Wit: WILSON VADEN, HAML. WHITE, SAMUEL MEADOR

THOMAS RAGSDALE, EDWARD ROBERTSON, SR., WILLIAM HUTCHINGS, THOMAS
H. WOODING, RAWLING WHITE, JR., MARTIN FARMER, JOSIAH ATKINSON,
HAMILTON WHITE, SAMUEL MEADOR and JAMES MEADOR, security for BEN-
JAMIN DAVIS, THOMAS DAVIS and JOEL WILLIS.

Page 484-485
9 March 1818
Pr: 16 March 1818

Nuncupative will of REBECCA MARLOW.

REBECCA MARLOW in her right mind and memory made the following
verbal will:

To WILLIAM R. IRBY a cow and calf.

To NATHAN CLEMENT, son of DANIEL CLEMENT, one pot and oven.

To GEORGE CAMP, JR., one bed and furniture.

To NANCY C. CAMP, nine shillings.

To FRANCES H. CAMP, six shillings.

To JAMES M. CAMP, six shillings.

To ELIZABETH GRANT, one cotton wheel and cards.

To MARY GRANT one flax wheel and a chest.

To SARAH GRANT one loom and one chest.

To ANNA GRANT a mare and one bason (basin).

To PATSEY MUSTAIN (Widow) one bason (basin).

To AMEY IRBY one bason (basin).

MARLOW will cont'd:

To PRUDENCE IRBY three dollars.

The balance of her estate be sold and the money divided between the following: MARY CAMP, AMEY IRBY, ANNE GRANT and MARY ROBERTS. Also the land to be sold and the money divided between the four above named.

GEORGE CAMP, SR. to act as executor.

Wit: FRANCES CAMP, NANCY CAMP, ELIZABETH GRANT.

JOHN L. ADAMS security for the executor.

Page 485-486
22 February 1818
Pr: 16 March 1818

LWT WILLIAM PARSONS being advance in life but of sound mind.

To my beloved wife MARY PARSONS the whole of my estate during her natural life. After the decease of my wife, I give the whole of my land viz: 50 acres, to my son RICHARD PARSONS.

My unfortunate son HENRY PARSONS shall be supported out of my perishable estate.

To the rest of my children, I give one dollar with what else they have received.

Appoint RICHARD JONES executor.

WILLIAM (X) PARSONS

Wit: WILL LEFTWICH, RACHEL (X) PARSONS, DOLLEY (X) FARTHING.

RICHARD JONES refused to take the executorship and MARY PARSONS the widow with JAMES BURNETT, ABNER FARTHING, and RICHARD PARSONS entered into bond.

Page 486-488
3 March 1818
Pr: 18 May 1818

LWT SAMUEL CALLAND

The residue of my store containing dry goods, groceries and my wagon and team, one horse be immediately sold after my decease. The accounts due me and the bonds be collected and the monies be used to pay my just debts. Should this not be sufficient, my executor is to sell the tract I purchased of ROBERT KING and HARDY and my interest in the tract whereon ELIZA CALLAND now resides, the tract I purchased of ROBERT DEVIN and Trustees of JAMES TOMPKINS.

To my wife ELIZA CALLAND one third part of the tract whereon we now live and negros: Daniel, Linday, Harry, Nat, John, Jack, Molley, David and Lucinda during her naturl life. After her death the negros to my children hereinafter mentioned equally divided.

215

CALLAND will cont'd:

Also to my wife all the household furniture and livestock.

To my daughters LETITIA, ELIZA, ANN, ELVIRA and JANE CALLAND, the following slaves: Lucinda, Iverson, Jinsey, Hampton, Fan, Frederick, Patsey, Sam, Lucy, Turner, Becky, Andrew, Milley, Moses, Betty, Christopher, Moriah, Augustine, Nancy and Lucinda also the tract of land where I now reside.

To JESSE CARTER a horse, saddle and bridle.

I desire my daughters to be educated at the common schools in the neighborhood, after which to be sent to some female academy for 12 months each.

My mill is to be rented out until my youngest daughter is of age or married.

I desire all the land I own or have an interest in lying in the state of Kentucky as a legatee of SAMUEL CALLAND, deceased, or RALPH S. CALLAND, deceased, shall be sold when the other legatees to this property shall sell their interest.

The land that is unsold, all money remain on hand until my youngest daughter is of age and then to them.

Appoint my wife ELIZA CALLAND and my mother ELIZA CALLAND executrixs, RALPH SMITH and JABEZ SMITH executors.

SAMUEL CALLAND

Wit: BOWKER S. CALLAND, MARY WAUGH, JOHN SMITH, JR.

WILLIAM S. CLARK, JOHN SMITH, JR., RICHARD JONES, ROBERT WILSON and BOWKER S. CALLAND security for JABEZ SMITH and RALPH SMITH.

Page 488
28 November 1817
Pr: 19 January 1818

LWT MARY HODNETT being very sick but of sound mind and memory.

To my daughter LUCY DAVIS, wife of JOSEPH DAVIS, all my part that is coming from my son JAMES HODNETT's estate together with what I had when I went to live with JAMES HODNETT, my son.

MARY (X) HODNETT

Wit: JER. WHITE, JESSE WOODSON

JOEL WILLIS and AYRES HODNETT security for WILLIAM DAVIS.

Page 489-490
25 January 1818
Pr: 13 June 1818

LWT JOHN DOUGLASS being afflicted in body but of sound mind.

Lend to my beloved wife MARY DOUGLASS all my estate during her

DOUGLASS will cont'd:

natural life except what is needed to school my children in the
following manner: My sons HARRISON DOUGLASS, SMITH DOUGLASS and
ASA DOUGLASS one year each; my son SAMUEL DOUGLASS one and a half
year; my daughter NANCY DOUGLASS two years. The schooling they
are to receive to make them equal with what I have given my former children.

At the death or marriage of my wife, give to my children: REBEC-
CA DOUGLASS, TABITHIA DOUGLASS, HARRISON DOUGLASS, SAMUEL DOUG-
LESS, SMITH DOUGLASS, ASA DOUGLASS and NANCY DOUGLASS, each to
have a horse.

At the death of my wife, to my children: ROBERT DOUGLASS, REBEC-
CA DOUGLASS, TABITHIA DOUGLASS, HARRISON DOUGLASS, SMITH DOUG-
LASS, SAMUEL DOUGLASS, ASA DOUGLASS and NANCY DOUGLASS the bal-
ance of my estate divided between them.

Appoint my wife MARY DOUGLASS executrix.

                                        JOHN DOUGLASS

Wit: WILL ECHOLS, WILLIAM ROGERS, NANCY ROGERS.

Page 490
8 March 1818
Pr: 15 June 1818

LWT LUCY FONTAINE

To my sister TABITHIA FONTAINE all the land now alloted to me ...
(being my part of two thirds of the land whereon my father lived
and died), also my negro Mintay, a bed and furniture, and a bur-
reau and all monies on hand and due me.

To my sister BETSEY BEAVERS all my interest in my mother's dower
land also my saddle, bridle and a counterpain.

To my brother WILLIAM FONTAINE all my interest in a tract of land
in Kentucky on the waters of Raven Creek, one hexagen bed quilt.

Appoint TABITHIA FONTAINE and JAMES D. PATTON executors.

                                        LUCY FONTAINE

Wit: JAMES D. PATTON, CHRISTOPHER CONWAY, ROBERT B. FONTAINE.

WILLIAM BR..... and JAMES SOYARS security for the executors.

Page 491-492
3 June 1818
Pr: 15 June 1818

LWT JAMES PARRISH being sick of body but of perfect mind and of
memory.

I lend to my beloved wife MARY PARRISH during her natural life:
negros Jere, Betty and Scot, and 100 acres of land where I now
live, two feather beds, furniture, two horses and livestock.

PARRISH will cont'd:

To my friend JOAB SIKES $150.00 that I lent him, negros Orange, Rachel and Caroline, and a bed.

Tomy friend EATON BAYNES negros: Caleb, Tom and Lucy; the land where I now live to him after the death of my wife.

To POLLEY DAVIS, wife of WILLIAM DAVIS, negros: Hannah and Stephen and two horses during her natural life then to her heirs, should she die without issue, then to the heirs of my friend EATON BAYNES.

After the death of my wife, the personal property lent her to be equally divided between JOAB SIKES, EATON BAYNES and POLLEY DAVIS.

Appoint EATON BAYNES and DEVAUREX HIGHTOWER executors.

                                        JAMES PARRISH

Wit: BAXTER IRBY, THOMAS BENNETT, JULIUS TERRELL.

WILLIAM H. SHELTON, JOSHUA DODSON, RAWLEY WHITE, THOMAS SHELTON and THOMAS CHANEY security.

Page 492-493
13 June 1818
Pr: 2 August 1818

LWT WILLIAM DAVIS, JR. of sound mind and memory.

To my beloved wife MARY DAVIS a negro Celah during her natural life. At the death of my wife, the negro to be sold and one half the money divided between my sisters and brothers. The other half my wife may dispose of as she thinks fit.

To my beloved wife all my personal estate.

                                        WILLIAM (X) DAVIS

Wit: TIMOTHY STAMPS, WILLIAM (X) DAVIS, ELIZABETH BOHANNAN.

JOSEPH FLIPPEN and THOMAS CHANEY security for TIMOTHY STAMPS.

Page 493-494
27 December 1817
Pr: 17 August 1818

LWT WILLIAM RICHARDSON, SR. being in perfect mind and memory.

I lend my beloved wife FRANCES RICHARDSON during her natural life the use of my personal estate with negros: Joe, Hannah, Martha, John and Leeve, and half the land in my possession with the manor house.

At the death of my wife I give the land to my son EDMUND RICHARDSON. Should my wife marry, she is to be made equal to a childs part out of the property lent her.

RICHARDSON will cont'd:

At the decease of my wife the property lent my wife to be divided
to make my childrens portions equal with what the others have received.

I have given my daughter SALLY DODSON ninety nine pounds.

I have given my daughter ANN TALLOAH one hundred three pounds.

I have given my son JAMES RICHARDSON seventy eight pounds.

I have given my son WILLIAM RICHARDSON, deceased, ninety five
pounds in land.

I have given my daughter MARY HARRISON ninety seven pounds.

I have given my daughter ELIZABETH RICHARDSON eighty nine pounds.

I have given my daughter FRANCES LOVENS one hundred one pounds.

I have given my son EDMUND RICHARDSON, deceased, the upper half
of my land.

To THOMAS TALLOAH, four acres he purchased of my son WILLIAM.

Appoint my son JAMES and ANDREW HARRISON, SR. executors.

                                        WILLIAM RICHARDSON

Wit: JOSEPH DODSON, THOMAS TULLAH, WILLIAM ANDERSON.

Page 495-496
15 January 1811
Pr: 21 September 1818

LWT BENJAMIN WHITE being sick and weak in body but of sound mind
and memory.

To my beloved wife REBECAH WHITE all my real and personal estate
during her natural life or widowhood, except such parts hereinafter disposed of.

To THOMAS ZACHERY, son of my wife REBECAH WHITE, sum of twenty
five pounds when he comes of age provided he stays with his mother.

To SALLY PARKER, wife of JOHN PARKER, $1.00 with what else she
has received.

To RACHEL BENNETT, wife of WILLIAM BENNETT, $1.00 with what I had
given her previously.

To the lawful heirs of JOHN WHITE, deceased, $1.00 with what I
have given him.

To MOLLY PIERCE, wife of JOHN PIERCE, $1.00 with what I hereto-
fore have given her.

To ELIZABETH KIZZEE, wife of STOBALL KIZZEE, $1.00 with what else
I have given her.

WHITE will cont'd:

After the death of my wife the balance of my estate to go to JOHN
PIERCE, son of JOHN PIERCE.

Appoint ZADOCK PIERCE and GEORGE ADAMS executors.

                              BENJAMIN (X) WHITE

Wit: DRURY GAMMON, TALIFERIE CARTER, JOSHUA WATTS, THOMAS BARKER.

MAJOR RPICE security for ZADOCK PIERCE.

Page 496-498
18 September 1818
Pr: 19 October 1818

LWT JOHN EMMERSON being in a low state of health but of sound
mind and memory.

I have given my son JOHN EMMERSON a tract of land where he now
lives with other property this being his part.

I have given my son JAMES EMMERSON a tract of land whereon he now
lives except $100.00 to be paid and have given him other property
this is his full share.

I hve given my son HENRY EMMERSON a tract of land where he now
lives and a negro girl Bartheny to be delivered to him at his mothers death.

I have given my son WILLIAM EMMERSON a tract of land where he now
lives and he is to have the negro Lizza at the death of his mother.

I have given my daughter SALLY 50 acres together with other property and she is to have a bed.

I have given my daughter JUDITH 50 acres of land and at the death
of her mother to have a bed that my daughter ANNY can spare.

I lend my wife all my estate, except what has been given, during
her natural life.

To my daughter MARTHA, after the death of my wife, a certain lot
of land joining WILLIAM EMMERSON and a negro called Sooky, bed
and furniture, a chest and a large bible.

At the death of my wife, the residue of my estate real and personal to my daughter ANNA.

I appoint my sons HENRY and WILLIAM EMMERSON executors.

                              JOHN (X) EMMERSON

Wit: ALLEN CHANDLER, ISAAC STONE, THOMAS PARRISH.

ALLEN CHANDLER, JOHN HUTCHINGS and THOMAS PARRISH security.

Page 498 (cont'd next page)

220

29 September 1818
Pr: 19 October 1818

LWT WILLIAM LEFTWICH

My executors to sell the land I purchased of WILLIAM L. CLARK,
formerly the property of JAMES WITCHER, on Cherry Stone Creek,
being 142 acres, also sell my lots in Leaksville, North Carolina
and from the sales settle my just debts. Should this not be sufficient, my executors to sell my land in Rockingham County, North
Carolina on Hogins Creek.

I appoint JOHN SMITH and RICHARD JONES executors.

                                            WILL. LEFTWICH

Wit: A. C. SHELTON, JOHN WARD, JR., ALLEN CHANDLER.

ROBERT A. WARD and THOMAS B. JONES security for the executors.

Pagee 499-500
24 February 1816
Pr: 16 November 1818

LWT ROBERT FENDLEY, SR. being low in body but of sound mind and
memory.

To my son JOHN FENDLEY a horse, saddle, feather bed and furniture
which he has in his possession also he is to have 100 acres of
land when he has completed the payment on the land.

To my son ABRAM FENDLEY a bed and furniture and what else has already been given him.

To my son ROBERT FENDLEY a colt, bed and furniture, other property he has received.

To my daughter JANE FENDLEY bed and furniture now in her possession.

To my daughter MARY ANN FENDLEY bed and furniture when she thinks
proper.

To my beloved wife MARGARET FENDLEY the residue of my estate real
and personal to be disposed of as she thinks fit.

                                            ROBERT FENDLEY, SR.

Wit: WM. WALTON, EDMUND SPARKES, JAMES (X) MEADE, JAMES WILLIAMS

MARGARET FENDLEY executrix.

Page 500-501
4 September 1818
Pr: 16 November 1818

LWT BENJAMIN RATLIFF being weak in body but of perfect mind and
memory.

I lend my beloved wife my estate and at her decease to be divided

RATLIFF will cont'd:

between my surviving children.

I appoint my wife and my son JOHN RATLIFF executors.

                              BENJAMIN (X) RATLIFF

Wit: SIMON ADAMS, JOSEPH MOTLEY, JAMES (X) WOLF

Proved again 16 August 1819 with JOHN M. DIX and JOSEPH FERGUSON
security for JOHN RATLIFF.

Page 501
14 November 1818
Pr: 15 February 1819

LWT JOHN GRIGGS, SR. being weak in body but in perfect memory.

To AXCY GRIGGS my cow and calf for her service to me.

To REBECCA BURGESS my bed and furniture for her service.

I give JAMES GRIGGS, PETER GRIGGS, PENDLETON BURGESS, MICHAEL
GRIGGS, GEORGE GRIGGS, THOMAS WILKINS, JOHN GRIGGS, JR. and DAVID
ARTHUR the rest of my property divided equally between them.

I give ROBERT GRIGGS $50.00 which he owes me.

I give SARAH GOVERS bodily heirs one share of the above property.

Appoint MICHAEL GRIGGS executor.

                              JOHN (X) GRIGGS

Wit: WM. HAIZLIP, PARMANAS LANSFORD, MARTHA DAVIS.

ROBERT B. BECK and JAMES WOODALL security for executor.

Page 502-503
18 January 1819
Pr: 15 February 1818(as written)

LWT ARTHUR EANES, SR. being very sick and weak but of perfect
mind and memory.

I lend my whole estate both real and personal to my beloved wife
ELINOR EANES during her lifetime or widowhood. At her death all
my land to my sons JOSEPH H. EANES and ARTHUR EANES, JR.

When my single children: JOSEPH H. EANES, ARTHUR EANES, MARTHA
EANES and REBEKAH EANES when they leave my wife, they are to have
as much as my four married children.

At the death of my wife what estate is left is to be divided be-
tween all my children: SARAH EANES, MARY BARDING, JOSIAH EANES,
NANCY SIMMONS, JOSEPH H. EANES, MARTHA EANES, ARTHUR EANES and
REBECKAH EANES.

I desire Squire be sold and the money used to purchase a negro

EANES will cont'd:

for my family.

I appoint JOSIAH and JOSEPH EANES executors.

THOMAS GARRETT, THOMAS SHELTON and JAMES ADAMS security for executors.

Page 503-504
14 October 1818
Pr: 18 January 1819

LWT JOSEPH SMITH being in a low state of health but of perfect mind and memory.

To JOHN MIDKIFF, JR. the whole of my estate consisting of a tract of land on the waters of White Thorn, a cow and calf, a bed and furniture with all other articles I possess.

                                    JOSEPH (X) SMITH

Wit: ELISHA WALDEN, JOHN MIDKIFF, SR., MARY (X) MIDKIFF.

Presented in Court 21 October 1820 by JOHN MIDKIFF, SR. with WILLIAM CLARK as his security.

Page 504
4 January 1819
Pr: 15 February 1819

LWT ARTHUR GOOLSBY being weak in body but of sound mind and perfect memory.

To my well beloved wife my lands, negros, money and livestock.

To my living brothers and sisters, I give them $2,000.00 to be equally divided between them.

I appoint Capt. WILLIAM PRITCHETT and Capt. JAMES LANIER my executors.

                                    ARTHUR GOOLSBY

Wit: WM. MURPHEY, WIATT BROWN, JOSIAH MORTON, ROBERT RITCHETT, ROBERT GOURLEY.

The executors refused to take the executorship and MARY C. GOOLSBY with WILLIAM PRITCHETT, JOSIAH MORTON and JAMES LANIER her security became executrix.

Page 504-505
17 July 1818
Pr: 15 February 1819

LWT SARAH HERNDON being in a low state of health but of sound mind and memory.

To MARY WITCHER, wife of WILLIAM WITCHER, SR., my negro Malindy

HERNDON will cont'd:

until she comes of age, then be freed; also to MARY WITCHER a bed and furniture.

To POLLEY WITCHER a cherry chest.

My negros Amanday, Tanday, Tassamus, Candice, Landy, Lanksford with the residue of my estate be sold and pay my just debts and what is left be divided between: ABEL HUTSON, DRURY HUTSON, SARAH WHEAT and ELIZABETH RAZOR's children, she the wife of GEORGE RAZ- OR.

My negro Mary is not to be sold but to have the liberty of going with her children.

I appoint JOHN WITCHER, JR. and WILLIAM GRAVES my executors.

                                        SARAH HERNDON

Wit: VINCENT WITCHER, JOHN KEIN, WILLIAM WITCHER, JR.

WILLIAM WITCHER, SR. and CHARLES W. BOBBETT security for the exe- cutors.

Page 505-506
15 January 1815
Pr: 15 February 1819

LWT WILLIAM DODSON being in perfect health and sound mind and memory.

I desire my estate not otherwise given be sold, my just debts to be paid, and my funeral expense paid.

To my cousin EDWIN R. BEAVERS, son of MAJOR WILLIAM BEAVERS and ELIZABETH his wife, a negro named Brister.

My wife MARY DODSON is to have one third of the value of what is left after my debts are paid.

To my brothers EDWARD DODSON and STEPHEN DODSON and all my sis- ters that should be single at my death I give the balance of my estate.

I appoint my friend WILLIAM BEAVERS and my brother EDWARD DODSON executors.

                                        WILLIAM DODSON

Wit: NATHANIEL W. PASS, HOLLAWAY PASS.

JAMES SOYARS, WILLIAM ROBERTSON security for WILLIAM BEAVERS.

Page 507-508
27 February 1819
Pr: 19 April 1819

LWT JAMES BLEAKELY (BLEAKLEY) being in a low state of health but of sound mind.

BLEAKELY(BLEAKLEY) will cont'd:

I desire my household furniture and the land I bought of BENJAMIN
BLEAKLEY sold and my just debts be paid.

In a will written 16 March 1816 I did devise and give my wife,
ELIZABETH, then living, certain property and before her death she
requested it should be given to the persons herein named: JOSEPH
SMITH, brother to my wife, negros: Ned and negro Fann except her
son Richmon. To BETSEY SMITH, daughter of JOSEPH SMITH, a horse,
saddle and bridle. To BETSEY NANCE, daughter of ISAAC NANCE, a
negro boy Richmond.

My negro boy Isaac, for his dutiful and faithful service while
my wife was sick and in my calamity, shall be freed.

To JAMES B. SMITH, son of WILLIAM SMITH, after my debts are paid,
the residue of my estate to be under the direction of my executor
until he comes of age. Should JAMES die before he comes of age
then the property to go to all the children of the said father
WILLIAM SMITH by his present wife.

I appoint my friends WILLIAM C. HURT and SAMUEL BECK executors.

                                        JAMES BLEAKELY

Wit: ROBERT DEVIN, LEWIS (X) ADAMS, THOMAS PARRISH, JOHN EMMERSON

ROBERT DEVIN, THOMAS PARRISH and JAMES BECK security for executor

Page 508-509
22 August 1818
Pr: 19 April 1819

LWT DANIEL WORSHAM in a low state of health but of sound mind
and memory.

All my property after my just debts are paid to remain with my
beloved wife ELIZABETH WORSHAM during her natural life.

At the death of my wife the land whereon I now live I give to my
son GEORGE WORSHAM also a bed and furniture, cow and calf and a
horse.

The remaining property divided among all my children with the exception of GEORGE WORSHAM.

I appoint my wife ELIZABETH WORSHAM and FRANCIS SMITHSON as my
executors.

                                        DANIEL WORSHAM

Wit: FAUNTLEROY ALLEN, STEPHEN WOODSON, JOHN M. DIX.

DANIEL SUTHERLAND, JOHN M. DIX, and HEZEKIAH P. SMITHSON security
for FRANCIS SMITHSON.

Page 509-510
20 March 1819
Pr: 17 May 1819

LWT HUBBARD FARMER being in a low state of health but of sound

FARMER will cont'd:

mind and memory.

To my beloved wife POLLEY FARMER all my estate during her natural life and one half of my perishable and personal estate for her to dispose of as she desires.

I desire that LUCINDA DAVIS and JANE BRUISE children that we have ratly raised shall half my personal and perishable property.

At the death of my wife I give LUCINDA DAVIS all my real property.

STEPHEN COLEMAN to be executor and guardian for LUCINDA DAVIS and JANE BRUISE.

HUBBARD FARMER

Wit: JOHN WHITE, JOSEPH BLANKS, STEPHEN FARMER

DANIEL PRICE security for the executor.

Page 510-513
22 October 1815
Pr: 17 February 1817

LWT   JAMES JOHNSON being of sound mind.

To my beloved wife JANE JOHNSON during her widowhood the follow- ing slaves: Rawley, George, Eve, Cooty, Jourdon and Little George two beds and furniture, horse and saddle, table and chairs and livestock. At her death or marriage, the property aforesaid ex- cept the horse, chairs and livestock which is to go into the res- idue be given to my deceased son FULLINGTON's children as follows -the negros Cooty and Jourdan to my grand daughter JANE H. JOHN- SON. The other part divided between the sd JANE H. and the other children of FULLINGTON. I give to the six children left by my son FULLINGTON: JANE HAMILTON, GEORGE WASHINGTON, LETTY SHEPHERD, NAN- CY, JAMES, RICHARD and JEREMIAH FULLING, the following slaves: Lucinda, Polley, Petitha, Moris, Sirus alias Tim, Dick, Peter, Pindar, Phill, Hannah and Patrick, the said slaves to be under the management of the mother of the said children NANCY JOHNSON and no division made until the death of my wife or the marriage of my daughter-in-law.

To my three grandsons GEORGE WASHINGTON, JAMES and JEREMIAH FUL- LINGTON, my land of 300 acres it being the land I got of my son RICHARD who has not made me a right to, should he not do so, I give them the land on Cherry Stone Creek, should he do so I de- vise my grandson GEORGE WASHINGTON JOHNSON this last mentioned land together with the following slaves: Miller, George, David, Shadrack, Nancy, Lucy, Young Beck and Viney which I give him in confidence that he will manage them in such a manner as will con- tribute to the support and maintenance of my two grandsons RICH- ARD and JAMES FULLINGTON JOHNSON, sons of RICHARD JOHNSON, and at the death of my son RICHARD JOHNSON or his wife LETTICE then the property be divided between my two said grandsons. But should either die without issue then divided amongst RICHARD's living children.

To my three grandsons JEREMIAH FULLINGTON JOHNSON, JAMES FULLING- TON JOHNSON and JAMES FULLINGTON JOHNSON SHELTON my mill and one

JOHNSON will cont'd:

acre plus one acre on the opposite side on White Thorn Creek. If JAMES FULLINGTON JOHNSON SHELTON dies before he comes of age then LANGSTON SHELTON is to have his part of my mill. Should my grandson JAMES FULLINGTON JOHNSON die before he comes of age then RICHARD JOHNSON, son of RICHARD JOHNSON, should have his part of the mill. Should my grandson JEREMIAH FULLINGTON JOHNSON die before he comes of age his part to JAMES JOHNSON SHELTON.

To my grandson GEORGE WASHINGTON JOHNSON the negros Carmey and Surry with the remainder of the tract of land on both sides of White Thorn Creek, the house and furniture on the said land with the understanding he will manage the same as to contribute to the support of my daughter ELIZABETH C. SHELTON and her children during his life and at her death the same be equally divided among the children of ELIZABETH that may be living.

To my beloved grand daughter JANE H. JOHNSON my Alderman mare, saddle and bridle, bed and furniture, and this exclusive of her equal share of all other estate which I may direct be divided as equal among the children of my deceased son FULLINGTON.

To my niece MARTHA HOSKINS a bed and furniture.

The balance of my estate to be divided into three parts, 2/3's of which I give my grandson GEORGE WASHINGTON JOHNSON, one third in trust for the use of the children of my son RICHARD JOHNSON, one third in trust for the use of the children of my daughter ELIZABETH C. SHELTON, the other third to the children of my deceased son FULLINGTON JOHNSON.

I appoint my grandson GEORGE WASHINGTON JOHNSON executor.

                                        JAMES JOHNSON

Wit: JERE. WHITE, GEO. FACKLER, LETTICE WHITE, POLLEY FACKLER.

The executor is not of full age, the widow JANE JOHNSON becomess executrix with THOMAS H. CLARK, WILLIAM CLARK & WILLIAM L. CLARK her security.
19 May 1819, presented in Court and GEORGE W. JOHNSON becomes executor.

Page 514-515
17 April 1819
Pr: 21 June 1819

LWT LEONARD DOVE

The land whereon I now live to my two sons-in-law HEZEKIAH RIPLEY and DANIEL SAUNDERS, Ripley to have the land on the south side and Saunders to have the land with the house. My wife is to have the priviledge of living in the house during her lifetime, should she see cause she may have one third part of the land to include the house and have use of it during her lifetime.

To H. REPLEY and D. SAUNDERS my blacksmith tools, my wagon, gears and horses jointly.

To my daughter SALLY SAUNDERS my cupboard.

To my beloved wife HANNAH DOVE two beds and furniture and kitchen

DOVE will cont'd:

furniture during her life and at her death to be equally divided between the aforesaid Repley and Saunders.

The balance of my estate to my sons-in-law HEZEKIAH REPLEY and DANIEL SAUNDERS and my beloved wife HANNAH DOVE.

I appoint HEZEKIAH REPLEY and DANIEL SAUNDERS executors.

LEONARD (X) DOVE

Wit: ABRAHAM C. SHELTON, FLEMING MAYS

Page 515-516
15 June 1819
Pr: 19 July 1819

LWT HUGH GEORGE being sick and weak of body but of sound mind and disposing memory.

To my well beloved wife LELA GEORGE the land whereon I now live and all the negros except one that I give to JOHN GRAVES and my daughter MILLEY, named Rachel.

All my personal property to my wife during her natural life. At her decease equally divided among all my children. Should she die before the children are all of age, some of the estate be allowed to raise them.

To JOHN GRAVES and his wife MILLEY, part of my tract of land on Staunton River.

To my son JAMES H. GEORGE 250 acres joining GRAVES.

The balance of that tract divided between my four daughters: LELA GEORGE, BETSEY GEORGE, ELLISE GEORGE and MARTHA GEORGE.

To my two sons CORNELIUS M. GEORGE and JOHN GEORGE the tract of land where J..... live, equally divided.

The rest of my estate to be divided amongst all my children be-fore named.,

I appoint my wife and JOHN GRAVES executors.

HUGH GEORGE

Wit: PETER H. CLARK, FRANCIS MC CLANNAHAM, JOHN MC CLANNAHAM.

PEYTON GRAVES, PETER CLARK and FRANCIS MC CLANNAHAM security for the executors.

Page 516-517
1 November 1812
Pr: 19 July 1819

LWT AMBROSE HAWKER very sick and weak of body but of full mind and memory.

To my son AMBROSE HAWKER my riding beast.

HAWKER will cont'd:

To my grand daughter POLLY BUTT a cow.

To my sons WILLIAM HAWKER and PHILIP HAWKER tract of land whereon
I now live being 144 acres, all my stock not before given and the
balance of my estate not hereafter given. Must maintain their mother during her life.

To the heirs of DRUSILLA BUTT, PRISCILLA CLARK, BASIL HAWKER and
unto DARCAS RICE, SARAH RIDDLE, MARY THOMPSON, ELIZABETH SEAL,
ANNA BUTT, LYDA RICE and DEBORAH EARP each one shilling.

                                        AMBROSE (X) HAWKER

Wit: WILLIAM SIMPSON, THOMAS STIMPSON, WILLIAM SNODY.

Page 517-518
18 March 1819
Pr: 19 April 1819

LWT JOSEPH SLAYDEN being weak of body but of full mind and memory.

To my beloved wife MILLEY SLAYDEN all my land, negros, household
furniture and livestock during her natural life. After her death
to my son WILLIAM SLAYDEN $50.00.

To my son ARTER SLAYDEN $50.00.

To my son OBADIAH SLAYDEN $50.00.

To my son JOHN SLAYDEN $1.00.

To my daughter RACHEL SLAYDEN $1.00.

To my daughter SALLY HENLEY $1.00.

To my daughter FRANCES SIMPSON $50.00.

To my daughter AGNESS WIER $1.00.

To my four sons: JOEL SLAYDEN, SHOCKELEY SLAYDEN, BENJAMIN SLAY-
DEN and TOLBERD SLAYDEN the legacy which I have coming to me at
the death of MARY DURRETT which I bought of EPPA EVERITT.

I give to the children now living with me: WINSTON SLAYDEN, PEGGY
SLAYDEN and LENCY SLAYDEN at the death of their mother the balance of my estate after paying the amounts willed above.

I appoint my son WINSTON executor.

                                        JOSEPH SLAYDEN

Wit: WILLIAM SIMPSON, JAMES SLAYDEN, THOMAS HARDEY.

WILLIAM SIMPSON and THOMAS HARDEY security for executor.

Page 518-519
2 June 1819
Pr: 20 October 1819

LWT JOSIAH NUCKOLDS being sick and weak but of perfect mind &

229

NUCKOLDS will cont'd: memory.

To my beloved wife MILLEY NUCKOLDS my whole estate during her natural life.

At the death of my wife, all my lands to my two sons: LEVE NUCKOLDS and JOHN NUCKOLDS.

At the death of my wife the remaining property equally divided between my children: LEVE NUCKOLDS, CATHARINE NUCKOLDS, ELIZABETH NUCKOLDS, JOHN NUCKOLDS, MARTHA NUCKOLDS, and MORNING NUCKOLDS.

I appoint my wife and son Leve executors.

To my son JOHN a horse, saddle and bridle.

                                          JOSIAH (X) NUCKOLDS

Wit: JAS. H. EANES, JAS. H. EANES, WM. DUNN, RICHARD DUNN.

THOMAS PARRISH and JAMES THOMAS security for executors.

Page 520
4 June 1817
Pr: 18 October 1819

LWT THOMAS HOLLEY weak in body but of perfect mind and memory.

To my son LEONARD HOLLEY the whole of my stock, my cart, my plantation tools as his full part.

To my beloved wife MILLEY HOLLEY the whole of my household furniture during her natural life and at her death to be sold and divided between my children: ANNE O'NEAL, JAMES HOLLEY, JOEL HOLLEY, WILLIAM HOLLEY and LEWIS HOLLEY according to what they have heretofore received (one of my executors has an account).

I appoint WILLIAM MORRIS, SR. and WILLIAM BECK, SR. executors.

                                          THOMAS (X) HOLLEY

Wit: JAMES WILLIAMS, MARTHA (X) BUTCHER, ELIJAH (X) MORRIS.

SAMUEL BECK security for WILLIAM BECK.

Page 521-523
10 July 1818
Pr: 15 November 1819

LWT JOSEPH TOWLER being sick and weak but of perfect mind and memory.

To my beloved wife FRANCES TOWLER, during her natural life, the dwelling plantation where I now live and after her decease to my son ABSALOM TOWLER. To my wife negros: Charles, Wiatt, Mary, Bob and Old Hannah. At her death the negros equally divided between my children.

To my beloved son WILLIAM TOWLER the plantation whereon he now lives and negros: Betty and Sally (Daniel's daughter).

To my beloved daughter SALLY GOAD the tract of land whereon she

TOWLER will cont'd:

now lives on Lynchs Creek and negros: Stephen, Sarah and Edy. At
her death this property to be equally divided among her children.

To my beloved daughter ELIZABETH SHOCKLEY the tract of land where
she now lives and negros: Nan, Walter and Rodah and at her death
to her children.

To my beloved daughter MORNING ROBERTSON the land she now lives
on and negros: Lette, Hannah, Fanny, Armstead and Ben and at her
death to her children.

To my beloved daughter MARY BENNETT the tract of land where she
now lives and negros: Aggy, Lazenberry, Locky and Lassy and at
her death to her children.

To my beloved son ELIJAH TOWLER the tract of land I purchased of
WILLIAM YOUNG and AUGUSTINE SMITH and negros: Big Ned, Clary and
child, and Gilley and at his death to his children, but should
his wife outlive him, to remain with her as long as she lives or
during her widowhood.

To my beloved daughter NANCY GOAD the tract of land in Bedford
County called Goads Tract and negros: Rachel and Little Ned and
at her decease to her children.

To my beloved son JAMES TOWLER a tract of land in Bedford County
on Staunton River with negros: Emanuel and Ewel.

To my beloved son ABSALOM TOWLER at the death of his mother the
tract given her and negros: D..., Hannah (his wife), Charity and
Richmond. Absalom has the liberty of settling on some part of the
estate but not to interrupt his mother.

To my beloved daughter JENNY THOMPSON a tract of land on Kemps
Creek and negros: Lucinda, Tildy and John and at her death to her
children, should she die without an heir, then to her brothers
and sisters children.

I appoint JOHN WARD, JR. to sell the land not given and out of
this give JOHN SHOCKLEY $200.00, the balance divided between all
my children. John Ward, Jr. to be executor.

                                              JOSEPH TOWLER

Wit: ABNER SNOW, EDMUND PEMBERTON, JOSEP. (X) BARBER

JOHN WARD, SR. and ROBERT A. WARD security for executor.

Page 523-524
2 May 1819
Pr: 15 November 1819

LWT RICHARD ROYALL being in a low state of health but of sound
mind.

I lend to my beloved wife ELIZABETH ROYALL my whole estate real
and personal during her life.

Should there be any spare money, it is to be used to educate my
two sons NATHANIEL and JOHN ROYALL.

ROYALL will cont'd:

At the death of my beloved wife ELIZABETH M. ROYALL I wish the balance of my estate divided between all my children: NATHANIEL ROYALL, JOHN ROYALL, SUSANNAH R. ROYALL, ELIZABETH ROYALL, MARY ROYALL, JUDITH ROYALL, SARAH ROYALL, NANCY ROYALL and CAROLINE ROYALL.

Should any of my negros behave rudely, my executors to sell same. Should my wife not wish to remain here, my executors to sell the land and the money for the use of my wife and family.

I appoint my wife and WILLIAM BAILEY of Halifax County and THOMAS SHELTON executors.

RICHARD ROAYLL

Wit: JOSIAH EANES, ELIJAH ROBINSON, JOHNA. B. ROYALL.

WILLIAM BECK, WILLIAM PAYNE, JOSIAH EANES and GEORGE T. LANDS-DION security for ELIZABETH M. ROYALL.

Page 524-526
3 January 1818
Pr: 13 November 1819

LWT THOMAS SUTHERLIN of sound mind and memory.

To my three sons GEORGE, JOHN and THOMAS the land whereon I now live. My wife is to live where she does during her natural life. My son THOMAS is to have any part of the wood land when he comes of age.

To my daughters NANCY and FRANCES all the parcel I bought of AL-LEND LEV(?) and WILLIAM PAYNE.

To my daughter SUSANNA WILLIAMSON my negro Phebey; to my ....MARY BARNETT the negro girl Sary; to my daughter ELISABETH BARNETT my negro Priss; to my son JOHN SUTHERLIN my negro Joseph; to my son GEORGE L. SUTHERLIN my negro Antenney; to my daughter NANCY my negro Ann; to my daughter FRANCIS SUTHERLIN my negro Nell; to my son THOMAS SUTHERLIN my negro Ruben; the balance of my estate not given I give my wife during her lifetime.

I appoint my sons JOHN and GEORGE SUTHERLIN executors.

THOMAS SUTHERLIN

On the oaths of ROBERT ROSS and JOHN SNEED that this is the hand writing of THOMAS SUTHERLIN ordered to be recorded. CHRISTOPHER CONWAY, HALLAWAY PASS, OBADEAH HAIN, WILLIAM SIMM, HEZEKIAH P. SMITHSON and LEVEN CARTER security for the executors.

Page 526-527
Pr: 20 December 1819

LWT WILLIAM IRBY, SR. in health of body and sound of mind.

To my niece ELIZABETH IRBY three negros: Big Jude, Milley and Joe.

To my sister NANCY IRBY the rest of my negros, my furniture, my

232

IRBY, SR. will cont'd:

stock and farming tools; I lend her my houses and plantation with
all my lands to live on during her natural life; after her death
I give the said land and plantation to my nephew WILLIAM HALL.

I apoint WILLIAM HALL my executor.

WILLIAM IRBY

Wit: WADE NOWLIN, THOMAS W. JONES, TERRY SLAYDEN.

WILLIAM M. WILLIAMS, DAVID C. WILLIAMS, MARTIN FARMER, JOHN WAL-
RAND and REUBEN WALRAND security for the executor.

Page 527-528
14 November 1819
Pr: 20 December 1819

LWT   THOMAS PAYNE being unwell but of sound mind and disposing
memory.

I lend my beloved wife during her life or widowhood my negro wom-
an Juney and my other property. At the death of my wife my negro
Juney be sold and the money divided between my daughters JANE B.
PAYNE and MILLEY PAYNE.

The balance of the property loaned my wife to be sold and divided
between my three daughters: FANNY SHELTON (wife of TUNSTALL SHEL-
TON), JANE B. PAYNE and MILLEY PAYNE.

To my son LEROY PAYNE the upper part of my land joining RICHARD
JONES of 94 acres; to my son JOHN L. PAYNE the upper part of my
land of 94 acres more or less; to my two other sons BENJAMIN and
REUBON PAYNE the balance of my tract of land of 188 acres more
or less.

I appoint LEROY PAYNE and JOHN L. PAYNE and TUNSTALL SHELTON ex.

THOMAS PAYNE

Wit: THOMPSON ROBERTSON, JOHN KEATTS, WILLIS SHELTON.

LEROY SHELTON, JOHN KEATTS, VINCENT H. SHELTON and RICHARD G.
KEATTS security for TUNSTALL SHELTON and LEROY PAYNE.

Page 528-529
2 September 1818
Pr: 21 February 1820

LWT   HENRY WORSHAM

All personal estate except one horse, be sold and my just debts
paid. To my brothers JOHN and DAVID WORSHAM all the land that may
fall to me fromt he estate of my deceased father HENRY WORSHAM.

To my brother JOHN WORSHAM a bond executed by himself and WILLIAM
WORSHAM for $104.00.

To my sister PAMELA WORSHAM a bay horse.

I desire any excess money arising from the sale of my perishable

WORSHAM will cont'd:

estate be equally divided between my brother WILLIAM WORSHAM and
my sisters ELIZABETH EAST, MARTHA BYBE, NANCY WORSHAM, SALLY WOR-
SHAM and AGNES WORSHAM. Should their part not equal $20.00 then
my brothers JOHN and DAVID WORSHAM to pay them taht amount.

Appoint JOHN WORSHAM executor.

                                          HENRY (X) WORSHAM

Wit: GEORGE DEJARNATT, JOHN HUNT, WILLIAM B. L. VAUGHAN, GEORGE
VAUGHAN.

WILLIAM WORSHAM security for the executor.

Page 529-530
22 April 1818
Pr: 15 May 1820

LWT JAMES SANDS, SR. of sound mind and memory.

To my sons JAMES SANDS, JR. five shillings; to my daughter MAR-
GARET MURPHEY the bed and furniture in her possession.

To my daughters ELIZABETH SANDS and MARY SANDS the beds and furniture they now have in possession. Also to ELIZABETH and MARY the
money from the sale of three years ago and the sale of land to
LEWIS HAGOOD amounting to $400.00.

I appoint my son-in-law JAMES MURPHEY my executor.

                                          JAMES SANDS, SR.

Wit: THOS. H. CLARK, WM. CLARK, WILL. L. CLARK.

WILLIAM SMITH security for executor THOS. H. WOODING.

Page 530-531
3 May 1819
Pr: 19 June 1820

LWT WILLIAM INGRAM being weak in body but of disposing mind and
memory.

To my well beloved son LARKIN INGRAM 84 cents in addition to what
he has received; to my beloved son TAPLEY INGRAM 84 cents in ad-
ditin to what he has received; to my beloved son GARLAND INGRAM
84 cents in addition to what he has received; to my beloved son
GEORGE INGRAM 84 cents in addition to what he has received; to
my beloved daughter LETTY MAYS 84 cents in addition to (ditto);
to my beloved daughter EUTALLEY WALTERS 84 cents (ditto); to my
beloved daughter MARGARET SHELTON 84 cents (ditto); to my beloved
daughter RHODY INGRAM all the remaining part of my estate real
and personal. I have conditionally sold my land to HEZEKIAH P.
JACKSON should he comply with the purchase the money to my daughter RHODY INGRAM.

Appoint my friend SHOCKLEY TURNER executor.

                                          WILLIAM (X) INGRAM

Wit: JOSEPH H. TURNER, NANCEY A. STONE, WILLIAM STONE.

INGRAM will cont'd:

RAWLEY WHITE and JAMES CONNER security for the executor.

Page 532-533
2 November 1819
Pr: 17 July 1820

LWT ELIZABETH PARHAM being very sick and weak but perfect mind and memory.

I lend my well beloved sister REBECKA LEWIS, wife of JOHN LEWIS, a part of my land. I lend to my well beloved sister CRESCHANCEY CREWS, the wife of JOSIAH CREWS, three negros: Sarah, Joseph and Ransom and at her death to her children. To my beloved sister, ARCHER STONE, wife of BENJAMIN STONE, the part of my land on the south side with negros: Moriah, Frank and Patty during her life and then to her children. I give my sister REBECKA LEWIS' children the land lent her.

The residue of my estate to be sold and the money arising be divided between my three sisters: REBECKA LEWIS, CRESCHANEY CREWS and ARCHER STONE.

I appoint BENJAMIN STONE my executor.

ELIZABETH (X) PARHAM

Wit: JOHN W. FLETCHER, ADAM MC CUNE, NANCY (X) FLETCHER, WILLIAM KEATTS.

JAMES H. STONE, WILLIAM SMITH and WILLIAM LEWIS security for exs.

Page 533-534
12 January 1819
Pr: 21 August 1820

LWT SALLY WILKINSON being in a low state of health but of sound mind and memory.

My son FREDERICK WILKINSON to pay my just debts in as much as I hereinafter take the same into consideration.

To my beloved daughter BETSEY BURTON during her life and at her death to her children the following: negro Charity, a dressing table, livestock, chest and my wearing apparel.

To my beloved son FREDERICK WILKINSON the negro Gerrald, my horse and a table, turn, livestock, quilts and my crop of tobacco.

I desire my girl Polley to be sold and bought either by Elizabeth or Frederick. The balance of my estate be sold and the money divided between Elizabeth and Frederick.

SALLY (X) WILKINSON

Wit: WILL. H. SHELTON, WILLIAM BURTON, KIBBLE DANIEL. WILLIAM H. SHELTON and DANIEL W. FAURGURAN security for executor.

Page 534-537
23 January 1820
Pr: 21 August 1820

To my wife MARY WILSON during her life the whole of my tract of
land on the north side of Dan River where I now reside, my grist
mill on Sandy River, my household furniture, stock of all kinds
and slaves: Abel, Cate, Stepney, Nancy, Paul Charlotte, Harris,
Stephen, Squire, Charity, Big Dick, Ben, Dick, Edy, George, Luffa, Chloe, Pompey, Elias, Silvy, Queen, Silvy Ates, Bob, Curtis,
Old Polly, Jack the miller, Jenny, Tener, Kitt, Judy and Suckey.
At the death of my wife the aforesaid property to go as hereinafter directed. Also my wife is to have the dividend from my fifty
shares of Virginia Bank stock. At the death of my wife I give the
fifty shares of stock to my daughters: PATSY M. CUNNINGHAM and
NANCY R. BROADNAX. I also give my wife all my liquors and provisions of every sort and five hundred pounds in cash also the
following slaves: Oliver, Burrill, Sophy and her youngest child,
Smity, Polly, Barnett and Gracy.

To my son GEORGE WILSON all that part of land on the north side
of Dan River where I now reside which I purchased of JAMES and
ALLEN WILSON, also that part I purchased of my brother PETER WIL-
SON's executors, including the house where my brother PETER lived
also another tract on Sandy River 500 acres more or less which
I purchased of DANIEL JOHNSON. George is not to have possession
of the land on the north side until the death of my wife.

To my son ROBERT WILSON all my tract on the north side of the Dan
River where I reside not given George together with my dwelling
house, store house, lumber house and other houses. Also my land
on both sides of Sandy River (except the land I purchased of THOS.
GIVEN) including the bean garden and Bates tract and negros: Washington, Little Abel, Phill, Alley, Ben, Bates, Joe, John son of
Phillis, Allen, Anthony, Amey, John, Blacksmith, Edmund, Phillis
daughter of Queen, and her youngest child Hollaway, Custer, Ussey,
Lett and her child Chainey, Bratcher, Harry and Milley. But Robert is not to have the houses and land where I now reside during
the life of his mother.

To my son NATHANIEL WILSON a tract above the Sandy River bridge
being 300-400 acres called Booths Place.

To my daughter PATSEY M. CUNNINGHAM all my land on Sandy River
purchased of ASTIN, BOOTH & MC DANIEL, also a tract of 388 acres
on Sandy River purchased of THOMAS GIVEN, also negros: Rachel,
Little Cate, Goucester, Peter, Prisca, Reubin, Ellick, Stepney
son of Grace, Jim, Cyrus, Lavinia, Lucy, Rhoda, Saunders, Judy
and Sally and her two children Gabriel and Nelson.

To my daughter NANCY R. BROADNAX my water grist mill on the Sandy
River and the land adjoining, also a tract on the head of Sandy
River 325 acres called Ashes Meeting House Tract and negros: Filman, Cherry, Lyddy, Lethy, Anderson, Lewis and Else. Nancy is not
to have possession of the mill during the lifee of her mother.

To my grand daughters MARIA SIMS, MARY BAILEY and PHEBE BAILEY
a tract of land called Churchs, a tract of 75 acres I purchased
of Col. WM. HARRISON.

To my grand daughter MARIA SIMS a negro Esther; to my grand dau.
MARY BAILEY a negro Pearce; to my grand daughter PHEBE BAILEY a
negro Philada.

WILSON will cont'd:

To my sons GEORGE and ROBERT WILSON, my dau. NANCY R. BROADNAX, a tract of land on the Sandy River upwards of 500 acres including the Adams tract and also another tract I patented. To my son NA-THANIEL WILSON at the death of his mother, two slaves Stephen Harris and Suffa. To my daughter ISABELLA GLENN at the death of her mother, slaves: Judy daughter of Stepney and Big Dick. To my sons GEORGE and ROBERT and my daughters PATSEY M. CUNNINGHAM and NAN-CY R. BROADNAX at the death of their mother all the household furniture, stock of all kinds and all the slaves not heretofore given, and any residue of my estate. I appoint my son-in-law ROB-ERT BROADNAX and my sons GEORGE and ROBERT WILSON executors.

JOHN WILSON.

Wit: WILLIAM LEIGH, EDWARD T. BROADNAX, DANIEL TURNER.

EDWARD T. BROADNAX, NATHANIEL WILSON, WILLIAM TUNSTALL, MOSES HUTCHINGS, THOMAS RAGSDALE, JABEZ SMITH and GEORGE ADAMS, JR. security for the executors.

Page 537-538
23 May 1820
Pr: 21 August 1820

LWT JEREMIAH GREY being sick and weak of body but of sound mind and memory.

I lend my beloved wife NANCY GREY the tract of land on Sandy River where I live including the mill. At her death to be divided between my following children: JOHN GREY, CALVY GREY, SALLY GREY, ADIN GREY, BENJAMIN GREY and STEVEN GREY.

To my daughter REBECCA FISHER $1.00; to my son JOSHUA GREY $1.00. To the living children of my daughter ANEY PEARSON $1.00. To my daughter ELIZABETH WILLIAMS $1.00. To my son WILLIAM GREY a horse saddle and bridle, now in his possession; half my land on Beans Creek. To my son JEREMIAH GREY a filly now in his possession and the remaining half of my Beans Creek tract.

By the last will and testament of my brother ADIN GREY, at the death of his wife ELIZABETH GREY, he has willed me a part of his estate and I desire my wife NANCY GREY shall receive one third part and the other part be equally divided between the following children: WILLIAM GREY, JEREMIAH GREY, JOHN GREY, CALVY GREY, SALLY GREY, BENJAMIN GREY, ADIN GREY and STEVE GREY.

The balance of my estate to my wife NANCY to take care of the children underage and at her death the part of my brothers estate lent her for the children mentioned above provided they give an equal share for the care of my son JAMES GREY who is of unsound mind and that he shall remain with his mother during her life and then provided for by the other children..

I appoint my wife and son WILLIAM executors.

JEREMIAH GREY

Wit: JAMES TROTTER, DAVID R. BOAZ, JAMES BULLINGTON.
Court 21 August 1822, the executors refused to serve and sheriff ROBERT WALTERS was appointed executor.

Page 539-540
19 July 1820
Pr: 20 November 1820

LWT WILLIAM ROBERTSON in perfect health.

To my grandson CHRISTOPHER ORGAN my negro Bonaparte. To my dau.
DICY ORGAN my negro Tom also negros: Chany, Mickey and Thompson,
also $100.00 to be divided between the daughters of DICY ORGAN.

To my daughter ELIZABETH BOTTOM my negro Milly and her children
also the boy in her hands called Billy also the boy Thompson in
her possession.
I give to my son CHRISTOPHER's children: WILLIAM, JOSEPH, ENNIS,
PETER, HENRY and POLLY also to my son HENRY"s children: POLLY and
HENRY, my following negros and other property to wit: Crusie and
Poll my blacksmith, Rachel, George, Dick, John, Milley, Carson,
Edy, Nat, Lucy, Washington, Booker, Austin, Amy, Banks and Rich-
mond. Also to these grand children all my lands and all the other
property of every kind.

It is my desire my property be kept together for supporting the
said grand children, that is the children of my sons CHRISTOPHER
and HENRY. It is my desire that my two blacksmiths be hired con-
venient to their wives. It is my ardent wish and desire that my
negros be treated with utmost humanity.

I appoint my friends GEORGE GILES and RAWLEY W. CARTER executors.

                                        WILLIAM ROBERTSON

Wit: WESLEY SHELTON, JEDUTHUN CARTER, SER.

DAVID ECHOLS, JOHN H. LANIER, THOMAS RAGSDALE, JAMES SOYARS and
NATHAN HUTCHERSON security for executors. JEDUTHUN CARTER, SR.
is now deceased but the signature proved by other witnesses.

Page 541-542
15 November 1820
Pr: 20 November 1820

LWT JEDUTHUN CARTER, SR. being weak and low in body but of perfect mind and memory.

I lend my beloved wife SARAH CARTER my estate, both real and personal, during her life and at her decease I give to my friend Dr.
THOMAS ANDERSON the following negros: Letty, Henry and Armstead.

To my respected friend ELIZABETH TOWNES, consort of GEORGE TOWNES
my negro Rhener.

To my nephew REUBEN HOPKINS the entire tract of land where I now
live with the balance of my estate not before given and that he
will live on the property. I request REUBEN HOPKINS give to his
brother F. HOPKINS a negro.

I appoint Dr. THOMAS ANDERSON, WILLIAM CLARK and REUBIN HOPKINS
my executors.

                                        JEDUTHUN CARTER

Wit: RAWLEY W. CARTER, JAMES HOPKINS, MARY HOPKINS, EPHRAIM GILES

CARTER will cont'd:

NATHANIEL WILSON, GEORGE TOWNES, ROBERT WILSON, WILLIAM HALL and
JAMES HOPKINS security for the executors.

Page 541-542
26 September 1820
Pr: 16 October 1820

LWT CARTER MICKLEBOROUGH being sick and weak in body but of perfect mind and memory.

To my brother-in-law THOMAS DIX all my right and interest in the
land whereof my father HENRY MICKLEBOROUGH died seized. The balance of my estate to be sold by my executors and the money and
first $400.00 be used for the support of the Christian Religion
as my executors think fit.

To FUSHE CORNWAL, WILLIAM HARRIS and LARKIN CHEETHAM so much money equally divided between them as will make up the legacy of:
FRANCES CHEETHAM, left her by my father equal with the other legatees of his estate.

To my sister SALLY KIRBY so much as will make her equal to the
other legatees of my fathers estate. Should there be any surplus,
divided between all my living brothers and sisters.

I appoint my brother-in-law THOMAS DIX my executor.

                                        CARTER MICKLEBOROUGH

Wit: JAMES D. PATTON, ROBERT WHITE, GEO. T. LANSDOWN, THOMAS WIL-
SON. GEORGE T. LANSDOWN, WILLAM LINN, JOHN SUTHERLIN and JAMES
SOYARS security for the executor.

Page 542-543
8 March 1820
Pr: 16 October 1820

LWT MARY DEVERRETT

To my daughters RHODA DEVERRETT, ELIZABETH CARTER and MARY DOWNS
the sum of fifty pounds with interest computed from 1 Sept. 1793
until the day of my death. It being what my father left me after
the deceased of my husband WILLIAM DEVERETT. I give RHODA DEVER-
RETT a horse.

                                        MARY (X) DEVERETT

Wit: JAMES FARLEY, JOHN H. DAVIS, JOSEPH ARNETT. NATHANIEL WILSON
security for HEZEKIAJ P. SMITHSON.

Page 543-547
10 June 1819
Pr: 18 September 1820

LWT NATHANIEL KIRBY being weak in body but of sound and perfect
memory.

To my beloved brother MOSES KIRBY and mother SARAH KIRBY the following tracts of land and other property during their lifetime
and then to the legatees hereinafter named. One half the tract

on Pigg River and Snow Creek, 100 acres more or less, also half that tract on Pigg River formerly belonging to JOHN BOBBITT 100 acres more or less, also half the tract formerly belonged to AR-CHIBALD JEFFERSON 28 acres more or less, also half that tract of 100 acres more or less that Thompson formerly owned; also 280 ac. on the west side of Pigg River old road on Snow Creek and Turkey Cock Creek the tract that JOHN MISE formerly owned; also 319 ac. formerly belonged to JESSY PEAK on both sides of Long branch; al-so a part of a tract that was granted to my brother MOSES KIRBY 3 April 1783; also that tract in Franklin County on both sides of Mountain Creek 520 acres; also half that tract on both sides Big Turkey Cock Creek that formerly belonged to WILLIAM CRENSHAW deceased; also half the tract that formerly belonged to FRANCIS, deceased and being on both sides of Turkey Cock Creek; also half the saw mill and grist mill and half the profits arising from sd mills; also half the household furniture, plantation tools, wag-ons, carts, blacksmith tools, also ten negros: Dick, Daniel, Edy, Joseph, Lewis, Sam, Able, Carni, Ann and Clark; also half the ne-gros that formerly belonged to WILLIAM CRENSHAW, deceased named: Abby, Daniel, Jacob, Isaac, Jerry and Alex. I lend as is stated to my brother MOSES KIRBY and mother SARAH KIRBY all the above mentioned during their natural lives and at their decease to the legatees hereafter named.

I give to my beloved niece ELIZABETH HUDSON KIRBY the natural dau. of my brother MOSES KIRBY, who has always been recognised by him and raised in our family, the following tracts of land, houses and property viz: half the tract containing 100 ac. on Snow Creek also half the tract on Pigg River belonging to JOHN BOBBITT 100 ac. more or less; also half the tract formerly belonging to ARCH-IBALD JEFFERSON 28 ac. more or less; half the tract 100 ac. more or less that THOMPSON formerly owned; also 280 ac. more or less on the west side of Pigg River old road that formerly belonged to JOHN MUSE. To my beloved niece ELIZABETH HUDSON KIRBY the na-tural daughter of my brother MOSES KIRBY negros: Abel, Carine, ... and Clarka; also a negro Dick after the death of my sister JUDITH WALKER. Also the house whereon I now dwell with half the plantation tools, furniture, wagon, cart, blacksmith tools and stock.

To my nephews DAVID WALKER, NATHANIEL WALKER and MOSES WALKER the tract in Franklin County being 570 acres on both sides of Moun-tain Creek.

To my two nieces SUSANNAH EDES and CASSA WALKER, the following land: 319 ac. that formerly belonged to JESSE PEAK; also part of the tract that was granted my brother MOSES.

To my nephew HENRY WALKER half of that tract of 532 ac. on Little Turkey Cock Creek with half the saw mill and grist mill.

I lend my niece SUSANNAH CRENSHAW, wife of WILLIAM CRENSHAW, decd one third of the negros named: Aby, Daniel, Jacob, Isaac, Jerry and Alex; also a third of the land that formerly belonged Cren-shaw, dec'd, being 521 ac. more or less during her natural lfie and at her death or marriage to my two nieces SARAH WINSTON CREN-SHAW and POLLY WALKER CRENSHAW and to my nephew NATHANIEL KIRBY CRENSHAW. To my two nieces SARAH WINSTON CRENSHAW, POLLY WALKER CRENSHAW and my nephew NATHANIEL KIRBY CRENSHAW negro named Lewis when the youngest comes of age.

KIRBY will cont'd:

To my nephews HENRY WALKER and WILSON WALKER a negro Sam; to my nieces SALLY ALAN and JUDAH THOMAS three negros: Daniel, Edy and Joseph.

After the death of my mother SARAH KIRBY and brother MOSES KIRBY I lend my sisters JUDITH WALKER the house and plantation whereon I now dwell on Snow Creek and a negro Dick and to continue with my niece ELIZABETH HUDSON KIRBY until she comes of age, then my sister JUDITH to remove and go to the tract on Pigg River that JOHN BOBBITT formerly owned. Should I die, my brother, my mother and my sister JUDITH WALKER die before my niece comes of age my executors to rent out my slaves and land. Should my niece ELIZA- BETH HUDSON KIRBY die without issue the whole to then revert to my heirs-at-law the utter exclusion of her mother's family; and my estate to go to my nieces and nephews.

I appoint my brother MOSES KIRBY and Col. WILLIAM SWANSON and Col. GEORGE TOWNS executors.

                            NATHANIEL KIRBY

Wit: WILLIAM S. PEARSON, JOHN CAMPBELL, ALEXANDER JEFFERSON, SAM- UEL CAMBELL. JAMES NOWLIN, MARTIN PEARSON, WILLIAM ATKINSON, JOHN T. MUSE, HENRY S. MUSE and JAMES HOPKINS security for the execu- tors.

                    Deeds & Wills Book 10

Page 6-7
8 February 1794
Pr: 16 June 1794

LWT WILLIAM TWEDLE in my perfect sense, mind and memory.

To my loving wife ABIGAL TWEDLE the land and plantation where I now live, 200 acres, all the furniture and stock during her na- tural life. At the decease of my wife, the land and plantation to my son BENJAMIN TWEDLE provided he make his brother SILAS a title to the land where he lives, should he refuse then the land and plantation to SILAS.

To my wife ABIGAL a survey of 316 acres during her lifetime then to son BENJAMIN with the same proviso as aforesaid, 63 acres part of the last mentioned tract with lines of JAMES WOODY, WILLIAM WILKERSON, CHARLES HARRIS and 253 acres, the overplus I give to my son-in-law JAMES NELSON at the death of my wife.

To my son WILLIAM besides what he has received, 1 shilling; to my son SILAS 1 shilling in addition to what he has received; to my son JOHN 1 shilling with what else he has received; the resi- due of my estate, after the death of my wife, to my son-in-law JAMES NELSON.

Appoint JAMES NELSON and friend WILLIAM WILKERSON executors.

                            WILLIAM TWEDEL

Wit: WILLIAM DIX, W. WRIGHT, THOMAS WILKINSON. ABIA CHEATHAM and JOHN WIER security for the executors.

Page 35
13 December 1791
Pr: 21 July 1794

LWT BENJAMIN MORRIS being weak in body but of perfect mind and memory.

To my son SAMUEL MORRIS the land and plantation where he now resides and a saddle and bridle.

To my daughter ELIZABETH DONELSON the land and plantation where she now lives during her life then to her heirs.

I lend my beloved wife MARY MORRIS the land and plantation where I now live and half the stock and household furniture. At her decease that part be equally divided between MATHEW CREEL, MARY HEDGER and BENJAMIN MORRIS' children, that is in three parts.

To my son JOHN MORRIS the other half of the stock and furniture; to my son WILLIAM MORRIS the land where I live after the death of my wife.

Appoint my wife MARY and son SAMUEL executors.

                                    BENJAMIN (X) MORRIS

Wit: JOHN CHELTON, JOHN CREEL, MICAJAH CREEL.

Page 37-38
24 December 1793
Pr: 21 July 1794

LWT JAMES MC MURDY in perfect health and memory.

To my loving wife during her natural life or widowhood, the plantation and land where I now live. At her decease to my son-in-law RICHARD CHILDRUS and his wife MARY during their lives then to their children.

To JOHN HARRIS and wife, 5 shillings each.

To RICHARD and MARY CHILDRUS all the furniture, livestock and the plantation tools.

Appoint Richard Childrus executor.

                                    JAMES (X) MC MURDY

Wit: THOMAS DYER, JOHN (X) TURLEY, MARY (X) TURLEY, JAMES DYER.

Page 38-39
26 October 1790
Pr: 21 July 1794

LWT JOHN LEWIS, SR. being in perfect health and sound mind.

To my son JOHN LEWIS the land where I live on the north side of Dan River purchased of WILLIAM MC DONALD and JOHN LEWIS, JR. ... (Mountain) also the land on the south side of Dan River purchased of THOMAS MERIWETHER.

To my son CHARLES LEWIS the land on the north side of Dan River

242

LEWIS will cont'd:

purchased of JOHN MAYO.

To my son ROBERT LEWIS the land purchased of JOHN LEWIS, SR....
(Mountain) and ROBERT JONES and JOHN LEWIS, JR. (Mountain) on the
north side of the Dan River in Halifax County between Wolfhill
Creek and ALLEN CALDWELL, also the land on Cane Creek purchased
of JOHN MAYO.

To my grandson JOHN LEWIS READ, son of my daughter JANE and JONA-
THAN READ, a negro male about his age.

I desire two negro women and 11 children between the ages of 2
and 12 be taken out of my estate and divided between my son JOHN
and three daughters: JANE READ, MARY WILLIAMS and ELIZABETH HOP-
SON.

The residue of my negros, furniture and stock be divided between
my three sons and three daughters: JOHN, CHARLES, ROBERT LEWIS,
JANE READ, MARY WILLIAMS and ELIZABETH HOPSON. My daughters   are
not to sell their negros, they are to go to their heirs. Balance
of money to go to my daughters.

Appoint my three sons: JOHN, CHARLES and ROBERT LEWIS executors.

                                        JOHN LEWIS, SR.

Wit: PEYTON THOMAS, JACOB THOMAS, JOHN THOMAS. JONATHAN READ and
HAYMES MORGAN security for JOHN and ROBERT LEWIS.

Page 57-58
3 September 1794
Pr: 15 September 1794

LWT FRANCIS WISDOM

I have given my children at the time of their marriage an equal
part of my estate. My old negros Mill and Isabell are to go to
whichever one of my children or grandchildren as they please. To
Dr. CRAFFORD WILLIAMS negros: Lucy, George, Joe, Amy, Easter, Al-
by and Handy. The rest of my negros to go in families as follows:
Pheabe, Nat and
Ambrose to go together; Nell, Henry, Daniel, Aron, Cooling and
Shadrack in one lot; Harry, Toby, Mime, Rhoda and Winne in one
lot. My grandson THOMAS CRAG to have an equal share with Dr. Williams. My son THOMAS WISDOM's heirs to have a childs part with
the rest of my children. My grandson LEWIS WISDOM, son of THOMAS
WISDOM, to be paid twenty five pounds extra. The land and plantation where I live to be sold with the furniture, stock, crops.
Dr. WILLIAMS who is married to my grand daughter NANCY WISDOM,
is to be executor and move to my plantation and be paid 5 pounds
per month until he has settled my estate. All the money on hand
at my decease to the five children.

                                        FRANCIS (X) WISDOM

Wit: WLL. WHITE, LASARUS DODSON, JOHN HODNETT.
WILLIAM BARKSDALE, DAVID C. WILLIAMS, JAMES M. WILLIAMS, JESSE
SMITH, JOSEPH CARTER, JOHN WILSON, and WILLIAM WALTERS security
for the executor.

Page 73
15 September 1794
Pr: 20 October 1794

LWT HENRY BLANKS being weak in body but of sound mind.

To my beloved wife during her natural life or widowhood, the use of my plantation and the household furniture and livestock.

My sons JOHN BLANKS and JOSEPH BLANKS 210 acres where I now live on Banister River. My personal property to be divided between; JOHN BLANKS, JOSEPH BLANKS and my son-in-law WILLIAM PARSONS and his wife POLLY, WILLIAM FARTHING and his wife TABITHA.

My son JOHN BLANKS of Georgia to have the horse in his possession and my son WILLIAM BLANKS of Georgia to have the mare, cow and calf in his possession. My son-in-law BENJAMIN WATKINS and his wife SARAH, 5 shillings. To my son DANIEL BAYTS and his wife, EL-IZABETH, the cow and calf in their possession.

                                        HENRY (X) BLANKS

Wit: THOMAS ANDERSON, FRANCIS ANDERSON, RICHARD ANDERSON, ELKANAH ECHOLS.

The widow and relict NAOMI BLANKS has as her security JOHN BLANKS and JOSEPH BLANKS and JOHN OWEN.

Page 111
9 December 1794
Pr: 19 January 1795

LWT GEORGE HARDYE (HARDEY) being sick and weak of body but of perfect mind.

To daughter SARAH LEWIS a dutch oven, skillet, large pot, dish, 6 plates, chest, cow and calf; to son GEORGE HARDEY the land I now possess; to my son JOSHUA HARDEY the mare which he has in his possession; to ELIZABETH STRATTON, daughter of BENJAMIN and EL-LENDER STRATTON, a bed and furniture I give to my daughter ELLEN-DER STRATTON during her life then to ELIZABETH STRATTON.

To my daughter MARY HOLDER the bed and furniture in her possession.

Appoint JOHN LEWIS and my son GEORGE HARDEY executors.

                                        GEORGE HARDYE

Wit: CHARLES LEWIS, MARK SHELTON, WILLIAM LEWIS.

WILLIAM LEWIS and JOSEPH T. WILLIAMS security for executors.

LWT ANNE MC DANIEL

To my son JOEL MC DANIEL the plantation where I live three years from the first of January next. At the expiration of three years it is to be sold and the money divided among all my children: WILLIAM CLEMENT MC DANIEL, CHLOE, JAMES SMITH (MC DANIEL), COLLEN, NANCY, POLLEY and JOEL.

All the stock and moveable estate to be divided between the five

MC DANIEL will cont'd:

youngest children agreeable to the will of their late father. To
my daughter POLLY PRICE the part of such dividend as by the will
of their father aforesaid would fall to my son JAMES SMITH he being one of the five youngest children having bought his part of
the dividend and paid him.

To my son JOEL the stock of hogs and use of the horses for three
years, then to my son CLEMENT MC DANIEL.

To my grand daughter ANNE SMITH MC DANIEL, daughter of CLEMENT
MC DANIEL, my riding horse.

All the livestock to remain with JOEL for three years, then to
be divided among all the children.

Appoint son CLEMENT MC DANIEL executor.

                                        ANNE (X) MC DANIEL

Wit: JAMES MC DONALD, ABSALOM MC DONALD, ABSELM DONULED. DANIEL
COLEMAN and HOLCOTT TOWNES security for the executor.

Page 123-124
25 December 1794
Pr: 16 February 1795

LWT PETER IRBY being sick and weak of body but of perfect mind
and memory.

To my beloved wife ELIZABETH IRBY during her lifetime, the tract
of land where I now live, stock, plantation tools, furniture and
my negro John.

To my daughter MARY CEMP one shilling; to my son FRANCIS IRBY one
shilling; to my son DAVID IRBY one shilling; to my son ABRAHAM
IRBY one shilling; to my son SAMUEL IRBY one shilling; to my son
WILLIAM IRBY one shilling.

The residue of my estate, real and personal, after the decease
of my wife, to be equally divided between my daughters: AMEY IRBY,
REBECCAH IRBY, and ANNE GRANT and ZACHARIAH IRBY, son of MARTHIA
IRBY, deceased.

Appoint CRISPIN SHELTON and my son WILLIAM IRBY executors.

                                        PETER IRBY

Wit: JOEL SHELTON, STEPHEN CLEMENT, JOHN GRIGGORY, SHADRACK (X)
BARBER.

Page 137-138
15 January 1790
Pr: 20 April 1795

LWT HAYNES MORGAN in health and disposing memory.

The plantation I purchased of JOHN GEORGE on the road is to be
sold and the money divided as hereafter directed. The balance of
my estate, real and personal, be kept together for the support
of my wife and the education of my children until they come of

                          245

MORGAN will cont'd:

age or marry. At such time, to have a fourth part of the slaves
and personal estate. Should my wife live to the time my children
come of age, she is to have a fourth part of the personal estate
and slaves. But should she die before this, then the estate divided between the three children: HAYNES MORGAN, MARY THOMPSON
MORGAN and ELIZABETH LAURENCE MORGAN.

Half the land to my wife during her lifetime and at her decease,
my son HAYNES to have all the land upon paying his sisters fifty
pounds each.

My son HAYNES to have my library of books, my small sword and my
watch.

Appoint my wife, WILLIAM TERRY and JOSHUA STONE executors.

                                          HAYNES MORGAN

SAMUEL CALLAND and WILLIAM CLARK security for MARY MORGAN and
JOSHUA STONE.

Page 138-139
23 October 1794
Pr: 20 April 1795

Nuncupative Will of WILLIAM MOODEY a resident of Kentucky, who
died in Pittsylvania County, Virginia 22 October 1794.

To my beloved wife JUDITH MOODEY of Kentucky, all my lands and
goods which I received by her in right or consideration of our
marriage. To my sister MARY MOODEY of Kentucky, negros Charles
and Sue, also a horse at her marriage. To my honored mother ELIZ-
ABETH MOODEY one half of my estate (excepting legacies given),
during her lifetime and at her decease to my brothers and sisters
and my two daughters ELIZABETH BUFORD MOODEY and MARY MOODEY.

To my mother, the horse in her possession. I lend my wife JUDITH
the land with the balance of my estate to raise my two daughters
and at her decease to go to my two daughters. Any accounts that
may be due me from my brothers and sisters are voided. Appoint
my father-in-law WILLIAM BUFORD executor in Lincoln County, Kentucky.

Wit: BLANKS MOODEY, WILLIAM EASLEY, LITTLEBURY WELLS.

Page 160
18 February 1795
Pr: 20 April 1795

Nuncupative Will of WILLIAM EASLEY at his mansion in the presence
of ISAAC CLEMENT, JOHN WARD, JR. and DAVID HUNT.

WILLIAM EASLEY directed his whole estate remain with his wife,
SARAH EASLEY, for the use and support of his children during her
widowhood or lifetime.

At the decease or marriage of his wife, the estate to be equally
divided between the children. Appoint BLANKS MOODEY executor.

Wit: ISAAC CLEMENT, JOHN WARD, JR., DAVID HUNT.

Page 216
1 November 1791
Pr: 20 July 1795

LWT WILLIAM WADLOW being weak in body but of sound mind and memory.

To my dear loving wife MARY all the lands and all other estate to do with as she thinks proper.

WILLIAM (X) WADLOW

Wit: STEPHEN CORNWELL, ALICE CHURCH, JONATHAN MONTG. CHURCH. MARY WADLOW is executrix.

Page 245-246
3 September 1793
Pr: 21 September 1795

LWT ELIZABETH YEATES being sick and weak.

To my son JOHN YEATES and heirs a negro called Harry. To my son GEORGE YEATES and heirs a negro called Silvy. To my son ELIJAH YEATES and heirs a negro called Violet. To my daughter HANNAH, wife of WILLIAM SHELTON, a negro Delpha. To my daughter ANNA GIBSON, wife of RICHARD GIBSON, and her heirs, a negro called Jane. To my daughter MARTHA WATTS negro Annaca and a bed and furniture. The remaining part of my estate to be divided between the above named legatees. Appoint my sons JOHN and ELIJAH YEATES executors.

ELIZABETH (X) YEATES

Wit: GEORGE ADAMS, JONATHAN ELLIOTT, WILLIAM ROSS. JONATHAN ELLIOTT and DAVID OWEN security for the executors.

Page 237-238
11 March 1795
Pr: 21 September 1795

LWT JOHN KERBY

To my two sons NATHANIEL KERBY and MOSES KERBY all my lands, my land in Franklin County on Simmons Creek equally divided between them and my land where I now live equally divided between them also my stock, goods and chattels.

To my son NATHANIEL my negro Daniel. To my son MOSES the child my negro Charity is with now. To my daughter JUDITH WALKER I give a horse, saddle and one feather bed. I leave in care of my executors negros Charity and Rachel and their heirs to be divided between the children of my daughter JUDITH at her decease.

To my daughter SALLY CRENSHAW negros George and David, 1 feather bed and 1 cupboard.

Lend my beloved wife the land whereon I now live with personal estate during her lifetime or widowhood.

Appoint my wife and sons NATHANIEL and MOSES KERBY executors.

JOHN KERBY

KERBY will cont'd:

Wit: WILLIAM SWANSON, JOHN MUSE, FRANCIS HENRY, RICHARD COMER.
WILLIAM SWANSON and JOHN MUSE security for the executors.

Page 249-250
18 July 1795
Pr: 19 October 1795

LWT JAMES MITCHELL being very sick and weak.

To my beloved wife SARAH MITCHELL all my estate, both real and
personal, during her life or widowhood, or until the youngest of
the children arrives at lawful age. Then the estate to be sold
and the money divided between the children except the lawful part
belonging to my wife. My wife may dispose of her lawful part as
she thinks proper.

Appoint my wife SARAH MITCHELL executrix.

                                        JAMES MITCHELL

Wit: ROBERT DEVIN, WILLIAM DEVIN, JR., ELISHA WALKER, JOSEPH REY-
NOLDS, MOSES HUBBARD.

Page 250-251
4 September 1795
Pr: 19 October 1795

LWT CHARLES OAKES of sound mind and memory but weak of body.

To my beloved wife JEAN (JANE) OAKES all my estate real and personal during her life or widowhood. At her decease to be divided
between my son ISAAC OAKES and my daughter MARY THORNTON (except
I give my negro Jim to my son ISAAC).

Appoint my wife and son and daughter to be executors.

                                        CHARLES OAKES

Wit: DUTTON LAYNE, JOHN BRISCOE, WILLIAM (X) OAKES, ISAAC POTTER.

19 October 1795, HENRY LANDSFORD and DAVID HARRIS security for
JANE OAKES and ISAAC OAKES.

June 1802, ZACHARIAH THORNTON and his wife MARY THORNTON appeared
with PRESLEY THORNTON and RICHARD THORNTON as their securities.

Page 256
29 September 1794
Pr: 19 October 1795

LWT WILLIAM CLARK in perfect health.

To my beloved wife ANNA CLARK a bed, chest, a cow and calf fore-
ever. Also one half my land and goods and chattels and my negro
Annaka during her lifetime.

To my mother MARTHA CLARK the other half of my land and my negro
Reuben, a mare and the other half of my goods during her lifetime.

At the decease of my wife I give my negro Annaker to my sister

CLARK will cont'd:

ARCHER KEATTS.

Should I have an heir of my body, then to him or her, all that I possess in this world. If I should have no heir of my body, at the death of my wife and mother, I give to ROBERT C. WALLER, ANN WALLER, MARY PRICE and MARTHA TUCKER all my land and negro Reuben.

All my goods to be sold and the money divided between the four mentioned above.

Appoint YOUNG SHELTON and CHARLES KEATTS executors.

                                        WILLIAM CLARK

Wit: RICHARD KEATTS, EDMUND TAYLOR, DANIEL SHELTON. LEROY SHELTON and VACHEL CLEMENT security for executors.

Page 366-368
5 August 1795
Pr: 18 August 1796

LWT THOMAS WALTERS

To my beloved wife LUCY WALTERS the land and plantation whereon I now live and negros: Hector, Sam, Bett and Fillis, and half the furniture and stock except that which will hereinafter be given during her natural life or widowhood.

To my son CLEMENT WALTERS negro Cate. To my son WILLIAM WALTERS the land and plantation that joins CHARLES COOLEY, and negro Anthony. To my son ABRAHAM WALTERS negro Daniel, horse, saddle and after the decease of my wife the land and plantation where I now live. To my grandson JOHN WALTERS, son and heir of my son THOMAS WALTERS, deceased, 200 acres and the plantation that joins McMurrey, it being the land where the said Thomas, dec'd., formerly lived and a horse. Also the bond that is against me for his fathers effects. To my daughter MARGARET WALTERSZ a negro Pat, also a hors and saddle and one third part of the pewter, a bed, furniture, cow and calf, and a ten pound note on WALTER GOODING.

After the decease of my wife all my personal estate remaining to be divided between my children: JOHN, ROBERT, ARCHER, OBEDIAH, WILLIAM, ABRAHAM, WILMOTH SCOTT, AGATHA MATTHIS, LUCY WALKER and MARGARET WALTERS.

Appoint my sons JOHN and ROBERT WALTERS executors.

                                        THOMAS (X) WALTERS

Wit: GEORGE DODSON, JACKSON WALTERS, JOHN MADING.

Codicil:
It appears that negro Daniel, bequested to my son ABRAHAM WALTERS is at the point of death, should this happen, Abraham is to have the first child of either Betty or Fillis. 18 Feb. 1796. Thomas Walters.

WILLIAM RICHARDS, GEORGE DODSON, HENRY H. BARKSDALE security for the executors.

Page 368-369
22 August 1795
Pr: 18 April 1796

LWT JAMES SHOCKLEY, SR. being sick and weak but of sound mind
and memory.

To my loving wife MARGARET SHOCKLEY I lend her my land, house,
furniture, and chattels during her lifetime. At her decease to
go to my sons CHARLETON and JAMES SHOCKLEY, JR. as by deeds which
I make them.

To my son CHARLETON SHOCKLEY two heifers and a bed. To my son
JAMES SHOCKLEY, JR. a bed and all theother moveable property. To
my son LEVI SHOCKLEY one shilling. To my son DAVID SHOCKLEY one
shilling. To my daughter ELIZABETH one shilling. To my daughter
NANCY one shilling. To my son SALATHALL one shilling. To my dau.
PEGGY the property she holds on Long Branch, then to her children.

Appoint my son JAMES SHOCKLEY, JR. executor.

JAMES (X) SHOCKLEY

Wit: JOHN PEEK, JESSE PEEK, JR., DAVID PEEK, JOSHUA STONE, WILL-
IAM ATKINS.

Page 411
1 June 1795
Pr: 18 July 1796

LWT SAMUEL TOMPKINS

To my oldest son DANIEL, deceased, $1.00, he being my heir-at-
law. I appoint my sons JOHN and JAMES TOMPKINS executors to settle the accounts between my deceased son and SAMUEL CALLANDS.

SAMUEL TOMPKINS

Wit: JAMES BLAKLEY, JONATHAN (X) TOMMIS, JOSEPH DEVIN.

EDWARD NUNNELLE, STOOKLEY TURNER, NOEL WADDELL and JOHN COX security for the executors.

Page 420-421
21 May 1796
Pr: 18 July 1796

LWT JAMES DOSS, SR. being weak in body but of sound mind and of
memory.

Appoint my friends BENJAMIN CANNIFAX and NATHAN TURMAN, SR. executors. To JAMES DOSS, AMBROSE DOSS and DELILA PALEY(?) twenty
shillings at the death of my beloved wife ANNE DOSS. To my son
JOHN DOSS his bond I took in from ROBERT MC COY on his behalf.
To RACHEL RIGHT a cow in her possession. To my daughter MARY VEST
a cow. The land is to be sold by the executors and they are to
purchase 100 acres which I lend my wife during her natural life
and at her decease to my son SAMUEL DOSS.

The balance of money from the sale of my land to be used to purchase a negro for the use of my wife. My wife is to have the use
of any other part of my estate during her lifetime. Then at her

250

DOSS will cont'd:

decease to be divided between the following children: ANNE DOSS, AGNES DOSS, FANNY DOSS, SAMUEL DOSS, EDY DOSS and SARAH DOSS.

JAMES (X) DOSS, SR.

Wit: BENJAMIN CANNIFAX, ELIZABETH (X) CANNIFAX, JOHN PARROTT. BENJAMIN CANNAIFX security for the executors.

Page 432-433
11 October 1794
Pr: 19 September 1796

LWT GEORGE HOMES GEVIN, SR. being weak of body but of sound mind.

To my beloved wife ELIZABETH the plantation whereon I now live during her natural life also negros Philas and Amey and the stock and furniture. At the decease of my wife this to go to my son, THOMAS GEVIN. To daughter MARY LUMKINS negro Easter. To daughter MARTHA BOSTICK negro Lucy. To daughter NANCY SUTHERLAND the negro Hannah. To daughter ELIZABETH FALLEN negro Phillas. To my son JOHN GEVIN land on the south side of Sandy River and negro Joe. To my son JESSE GEVIN the land on the north side of Sandy River and negro Lucy and two horses. To my son HOMES GEVIN the negro Stephen. To my son LITTLEBERRY negro Roger. To my son JOSIAH negro Amey and the land on the south side of Sandy River below Birds shole (shoal). To my son THOMAS negros Jean and Sarah and all my land not given on Sandy River, all stock that I lent my wife at her decease as well as the furniture. The said Thomas is to pay all my just debts.

Appoint my sons JOHN and JESSE GEVIN as executors.

GEORGE HOMES GEVIN, SR.

Wit: THOMAS DUNCAN, JAMES ROBINSON, MATTHEW (X) SPARKS. ADAM SUTHERLIN, EDMUND FALLEN and JOHN SUTHERLIN security for the executors.

Page 434
4 April 1796
Pr: 19 September 1796

LWT THOMAS LINTHICUM, SR. in perfect health and good memory.

My estate both real and personal to be sold, my just debts paid and the balance divided between: THOMAS LINTHICUM miner, WILLIAM NEWTEN, THOMAS NEWTEN, JANE RIGNEY, and MARY RIGNEY when they come of age. My wife SARAH LINTHICUM to have possession of the land and plantation as long as she wishes, but if she removes it is to be sold with the rest of my estate.

Appoint my son THOMAS and JOHN BENNETT executors.

THOMAS LINTHICUM, SR.

Wit: THOMAS LINTHICUM, JR., JOHN BENNETT, DELILA NEWTON.

SARAH LINTHICUM came into court and desires to receive her dower, EDWARD HATCHETT, RICHARD JOHNSON, STEPHEN YATES and DAVID PARSONS are to lay off one third part. JOHN ADAMS and THOMAS B. JONES se-

LINTHICUM will cont'd:

curity for THOMA LINTHICUM.

Page 462-463
2 August 1796
Pr: 17 October 1796

LWT THOMAS HIGHTOWER being low and weak but of sound mind.

To my beloved wife ANN HIGHTOWER all my estate during her lifetime or widowhood. All my land to my three sons: JOHN, THOMAS and
WILLIAM after the decease of their mother. To sons STITH and to
GEORGE a horse, saddle and bridle, when they come of age. To my
four daughters: POLLY, ANN, CATHERINE and ELIZABETH, the rest of
my estate.

Appoint EDMUND FITZGERALD and THOMAS B. JONES executors.

                                        THOMAS HIGHTOWER

Wit: GEORGE ROBINSON, W. HAYMES, STITH (X) HIGHTOWER, GEORGE (X)
HIGHTOWER. WILLIAM HAYMES, GEORGE ROBINSON and BENJAMIN SHELTON
security fot the executors.

Page 468
20 April 1789
Pr: 18 October 1796

LWT LITTLEBERY PATTERSON in perfect sense and sound mind.

My executors to sell 200 acres at the upper end of where I now
live to pay my just debts. I lend my beloved wife NANNEY PATTER-
SON during her natural life or widowhood the remainder of land
and all moveable property. At the decease of my wife the balance
of my land and moveable property to be sold and the money divided
among my children: ELIZABETH PATTERSON, JOHN PATTERSON, AGATHA
PATTERSON, WILLIAM PATTERSON, EDWARD PATTERSON, ROBERT PATTERSON,
THOMAS PATTERSON, MILLEY PATTERSON and FANNY PATTERSON. My executors are to give my children a part of my estate as they come
of age or marry.

Appoint my wife, my brother JOHN PATTERSON and WILLIAM WARD executors.

                                        LITTLEBERRY (X) PATTERSON

Wit: WILLIAM (X) LUCUS, HENRY WARD, NANCY THOMAS.

Page 477-478
18 August 1796
Pr: 17 October 1796

LWT MOSIAS JONES weak in body but of sound mind and memory.

I appoint CLEMENT NANCE my executor who is to get a lawful title
to my land whereon I now live and sell sd property, out of which
he is to be paid for his trouble and expense.

To my three daughters: SUSANNAH JONES, MARTHA JONES and DEANITIA
JONES and grand daughter HENRIETTA JONES the balance of the price
of the land. To my daughter ELIZABETH JAMES one shilling. To my

JONES will cont'd:

daughter MARY NANCE one shilling. To my daughter WILMITH MASSEY
one shilling. To my son BUCKNER JONES one shilling. LYDDA CLARK
to have all my household furniture and goods.

MOSIAS (X) JONES

Wit: ISHAM LANSFORD, HENRY LANSFORD, JOHN (X) MAY, SAMUEL STRONG.
ISHAM LANSFORD security fot the executor.

Deed Book 29, pages 121-122
Record Book, page 89
At the November 28th, 1768 meeting of the Pittsylvania County Crt
the last Will and Testament of JOHN HANBY, deceased, was exhibited in Court and proved by the oaths of the subscribing witnesses there to be the act of deed of the sd JOHN HANBY and the same
is ordered to be recorded.
5 July 1768
Pr: 28 November 1768

LWT JOHN HANBY being very sick and weak but of perfect mind and
memory.

To my dearly beloved wife SUSANNA HANBY a bed and furniture and
other household goods she may choose, a horse and saddle, a cow
and calf and other necessaries during her lifetime.

To my sons JONATHAN HANBY and DAVID HANBY this improvement to be
equally divided and all other lands except a piece of land on the

Russells Creek which is to be equally divided between WILLIAM CAR-
TER and JONATHAN JENNINGS.

My sons JONATHAN HANBY and DAVID HANBY to have my three negros
and my real and personal property. To HANNAH CARTER the sum of
fifteen pounds. To SUSANAH JENNINGS, fifteen pounds.

JOHN HANBY

Wit: GEORGE CARTER, JAMES LYON.

Order Book 9, page 254
March Court 1800

Ordered that DANIEL MOXLEY executor named in the will of RICHARD
BAYNES be summoned and to show cause why he has not taken upon
himself the administration of the estate.

Deed Book 1, page 96
28 March 1766

LWT JOSEPH SPRADLING weak of body but of sound mind.

I lend to my beloved wife SUSANNAH SPRADLING all the household
furniture. The land where I now live to be divided between my two
sons JESSE SPRADLING and OBEDIAH SPRADLING after Odediah reaches
the age of 21 years. But my wife is to have the use of the said
property during her life or widowhood. Should my wife die or remarry I appoint DAVID TERRY and CHAMPNESS TERRY to take my children and bring them up and teach them to read and write.

Wit: THEOP. LACEY, JOSEPH TERRY, JOHN SNEED.

Deed Book 1, page 249
11 November 1768
Pr: 23 June 1769

LWT JOHN SLOAN

To my beloved wife ELENOR SLOAN my whole estate during her lifetime and at her decease the lands to my son JOHN SLOAN. My wife
to dispose of the moveable estate as she thinks fit. To my son
WILLIAM SLOAN one shilling. To my son JAMES SLOAN one shilling.
To my son THOMAS SLOAN one shilling. To my daughter MARY JUSTICE
one shilling. To my daughter ELENOR JOHNSON one shilling.

Appoint my wife executrix.

                                        JOHN (X) SLOAN

Wit: RICHARD HAMMOCK, MARY HAMMOCK, DANIEL (X) WITCHER.
JAMES SLOAN and DANIEL WITCHER security for the executrix.

Deed Book 2, page 67
23 October 1770
Pr: 29 November 1770

Inventory of the estate of GEORGE THOMAS, deceased.

Appraised by BENJAMIN LANKFORD, WILLIAM COLLINGS, WILLIAM CHEEK
for a total of Ƚ256.9.4.

Deed Book 1, page 439
23 March 1770

Inventory and appraisement of the estate of ELIJAH HARBOUR, decd.
Appraised by WILLIAM EDWARDS, JAMES EDWARDS and JULIUS SCRUGGS.

Deed Book 1, page 440
20 April 1770
Pr: 25 May 1770

Inventory and appraisement of the estate of SAMUEL NOWLING. By
BENJAMIN TARRANT, JEREMIAH WARD and EDWARD WADE total of forty
six pounds. 25 May 1770, add sixteen pounds.

Deed Book 1, page 77
16 September 1766
Pr: 27 November 1767

LWT PAUL PIGG of Halifax County, the parish of Antrim.

To my wife SARAH negro Phillis. To my son JAMES PIGG 200 acres
on Banister River. To ROBERT ADAMS 100 acres whereon he now lives.
To my son WILLIAM PIGG 200 acres on Great Cherrystone Creek and
my negros Darkus and Susey. To my son RICHARD PIGG the plantation
whereon I now live and the rest of the land after the decease of
my wife. My negros and moveable estate to be kept together during
the life of my wife SARAH PIGG. After the decease of my wife my
negros and the balance of my estate be divided between Sarah's
children: JAMES, WILLIAM, RICHARD, PATTEA, SARAH, ANN and MARY.

PIGG will cont'd:

To my son JOHN PIGG and my son PAUL PIGG 1 shilling each.
To my daughter ELIZABETH ASTON one shilling. To my three daughters PATTEA, SARAH, ANN and MARY (four) the remainder of my land
on the south side of Banister River be sold and the money divided
between the said Pattea, Sarah, Ann and Mary.

Appoint REUBEN PAYNE, HENRY MC DANIEL and JOHN ADAMS executors.

PAUL PIGG

Wit: WILLIAM GRIFFITH, ROBERT (X) ADDAMS, GEORGE PARSONS.
JOHN DONELSON security for executor HENRY MC DANIEL.

Will Book 1, page 1
13 February 1814
Pr: 21 November 1814

LWT BENJAMIN HOBSON being weak in body but of sound mind and of
memory.

I lend to my dearly beloved wife LUCEY HOBSON my whole estate,
real and personal, during her natural life. At the death of my
wife my land is to go to my two sons WILLIAM E. HOBSON and BEN-
JAMIN HOBSON and they are to pay my daughter POLLY W. HOBSON the
sum of $40.00 each. The balance of the estate to be divided be-
tween those three children.

BENJAMIN HOBSON

Wit: GEORGE SPRATLEN, BENJAMIN PRUITT, MASTIN PRUITT.

Will Book 1, page 2
4 July 1820
Pr: 16 October 1820

LWT FREDERICK SHELTON being very infirm but of sound mind and
memory.

I lend to my beloved wife POLLY SHELTON during her natural life
four negros: Edy, Lewis, Easter and Isaac, and the remaining part
of my estate. At the decease of my wife to my three children:
ROBERTSON SHELTON, PATSY LEWIS SHELTON and CHLOE ROBERTSON SHEL-
TON all the above property.

Appoint THOMPSON ROBERTSON and my son ROBERTSON SHELTON executors

(signed)   FRANCIS SHELTON

Wit: ARMISTEAD SHELTON, FREDERICK SHELTON, PATSEY SHELTON.

ARMISTEAD SHELTON and JOSIAH CREWS security for THOMPSON ROBERT-
SON.

Will Book 1, page 3
25 December 1820
Pr: 15 January 1821

Nuncupative Will of WILLIAM SNEED.

In his last illness at his place of residence he said his will
and desire was that ELIZABETH P. SNEED, dau. of HENRY P. SNEED,

255

SNEED will cont'd:

should have all the interest he then had in his late fathers estate. He wished his nephew DABNEY HILL SNEED, son of JOHN SNEED, to have his bay mare, saddle and bridle.

Appointed his brothers: DABNEY P. SNEED, JOHN SNEED and HENRY P. SNEED executors.

Wit: JOHN SNEED, NATHANIEL W. P...., NANCY (X) WILLIAMS.

JOHN SNEED and ROBERT HUTSON security for HENRY SNEED.

Will Book 1, pages 3-4
9 September 1820
Pr: 15 January 1821

LWT THOMAS C. CARTER being sick and weak but of sound mind and memory.

To loving wife ELIZABETH CARTER all my estate real and personal during her lifetime. My three daughters: SARAH CARTER, WINIFRED CARTER and MARY CARTER are to live with my said wife and be maintained out of the estate until they marry. When any of the children, sons or daughters, marry or settle themselves my wife may lend them what she wishes. At her decease that part that has been lent any child, is to be returned and then all the estate equally divided between my children: SARAH CARTER, MILLER CARTER, JESSE CARTER, THOMAS CARTER, WINIFRED H. CARTER and MARY CARTER with the exception that my son MILLER CARTER being gone to the Western Country and not having heard from him in a long time and as he left his little daughter with me, the following is provided. Should he not return then to my grand daughter ELIZABETH CARTER (daughter of MILLER CARTER) $300.00. If he returns he is to pay her the $300.00 out of his part.

Appoint my wife executrix.

THOMAS C. CARTER

Wit: SUSANNAH CARTER, NANCY CARTER.

JESSE CARTER, JR., THOMAS CARTER, SALLY CARTER, WINIFRED H. CARTER and JEDUTHUN CARTER security for the executrix.

Court 19 October 1840
As ELIZABETH CARTER has departed this life, JEDUTHUN CARTER is appointed executor with WILLIAM B. ROGERS and THOMAS CARTER his security.

Will Book 1, pages 4-5
20 October 1818
Pr: 18 December 1820

LWT GEORGE MYERS in low state of health but of sound mind and memory.

Lend to my beloved wife MARY MYERS during her natural life or widowhood all my land except what is hereinafter disposed, including the plantation whereon I now live also my negro Viney, stock of horses, cattle, sheep and the household and kitchen furniture.

MYERS will cont'd:

To my three sons: WILLIAM MYERS, STEPHEN MYERS and BENJAMIN MYERS and my daughter SALLY HARDY (wife of MOSES HARDY) in addition to what they have received, $1.00 each. To my son JOHN MYERS, the land where he now lives joins THOMAS CARTER, WILLIAM MYERS, SEN. CLAIBORNE (formerly LEFTWICH), between the meeting house and the river.

To my son ISAAC MYERS all the land I own on the north side of the Pigg River joins WILLIAM TUNSTALL and WILLIAM MYERS. To my son JAMES MYERS after the decease or marriage of my wife, all of the land not heretofore given.

To my daughter POLLEY the negro Viney after the death of my wife. To my sons JACOB MYERS, ISHAM MYERS and JAMES MYERS the balance of the personal estate. Should my daughter POLLEY HARDY die without issue, the negro is to go to my sons JACOB, ISHAM and JAMES MYERS.

Appoint my wife MARY MYERS executrix.

                          GEORGE (X) MYERS

Wit: WILL. TUNSTALL, THOMAS G. TUNSTALL, WESLEY SHELTON.

Will Book 1, page 7
21 July 1820
Pr: 21 May 1821

LWT   HUGH DAILEY in a low state of health though in common sense.

To my wife all the household property to assist in raising the children and all the stock. My wife is desirous to move to her friends hoping she may be more happy with them and in order to satisfy her I give and bequeath the place where I now live, 100 acres more or less, that she may sell it and move to them. The blates(plates?) mold and bason mold which I own in Leesburg, in Loundon County at the home of JESSE DAILEY, I givee to my sons JESSE DAILEY and JOHN DAILEY.

                          HUGH DAILEY

Wit: WILLIAM WARD, JEREMIAH WARD, PEYTON DIXON, WILLIAM DIXON.

                Wills & Accounts Book 1-A

Pages 1-2
15 January 1815
Pr: 26 April 1815

LWT   CHARLES S. HENRY being weak of body but of sound mind and memory.

To my beloved and venerable mother my riding horse and my negro Anna and her four children: Dick, Mary, Umphia and Charlotte. The balance of the negros to be divided between my mother and my brother JAMES HENRY.

To the Rev. JOHN WEATHERFORD 150 acre tract that joins BYRD WOM-ACK and JOHN FITZGERALD. The balance of my land divided between my mother and my brother.

HENRY will cont'd:

To my mother my watch and pencil case, books I own down the country and she may wish my suspender paste buckles. To my brother JAMES HENRY my silver mounted pistols and 50 volumes of his own choice of my books down the country. The balance of my books down the country or here equally divided between WILLIAM EUSTIS, of Staford County and SAMUEL H. HENRY, (son of JOHN HENRY).

The secretary at this place to my Aunt MARTHA HENRY. To my Uncle JOHN HENRY my saddle.

To my friend JAMES CHALMERS my bridle and part of my estate not devised as above. I desire same equal division between my mother and my brother JAMES.

Appoint for my executors down the country: my brother, JAMES H. HENRY and friends ARCHIBALD HARWOOD and THOMAS CLIBURN HOLMS and appoint in Halifax and Pittsylvania my uncle JOHN HENRY and my friend JAMES CHALMERS.

CHARLES S. HENRY

Wit: ALEXANDER BYRD, BYRD WOMACK, NICY WEATHERFORD. JOHN H. HENRY security for JAMES HENRY.

Wills & Accounts Book 1-A

Pages 3-4
2 January 1817
Pr: 30 April 1817

LWT SHADRACK BOAZ low in body but of sound mind and memory.

To my beloved wife ISABEL BOAZ during her natural life my lands whereon I now live, all goods and chattels except as hereinafter given, also my negros Jack and Betty during her natural life or widowhood.

The lands and other property given my sons WILLIAM BOAZ and to THOMAS BOAZ this to be their full part. To my daughter NANCY the negro Ross at the decease of her mother. To my daughter PHEBE 100 acre tract that joins HARVEY and NAPPER on the north to the river and Long Fall Branch. To my daughter ROSEANNAH the negro Dick at the decease of her mother. To my son DAVID BOAZ the land where I now live during his natural life, except what was given PHEBE, but at his death to be sold and the money divided between his if any children.

To five daughters: ELLINOR negro Juday at the decease of my wife; LYDIA negro Silvay; REBECCA negro Jacob at her mother's decease; POLLEY negro Sarah and forty pounds, bed and furniture, horse, saddle, cow and calf; other daughter ROSANNAH. All the money and goods, chattels lent my wife at her death to be divided between my daughters.

Appoint my wife and son DANIEL BOAZ executors.

SHADRACK BOAZ

Wit: JAMES FULTON, ANNA JONES
Proved in Court 24 Sept. 1817: THOMAS J. BOAZ, JAMES STILL(?), THOMAS REYNOLDS, JOHN JONES, STEPHEN SMITH security for WILLIAM BECK.

CALLAWAY, Annah,015, Charles,
203, Chas.Jr.,203, Chas.Sr.,
203, David,148, Hannah,148,
Henry G.,148, Henry J.,133,
James,009,017,091,203,
John M.,148, John,148,
148, Peggy,148, Polly,203,
William,148, Wm.,016
CALLAWAY, Wm.,148, Wm.Jr.,148,
Wm.Sr.,148
CALLIE, Philip,180
CALLOWAY, Henry G.,145
CAMBELL, Samuel,241
CAMMIL, Sarah,174
CAMP, Frances,214,215,
Geo.Sr.,215, George,173,
214, James M.,214, Mary,215,
Nancy C.,214, Nancy,215
CAMPBELL, Abraham,129,
Alex.A.,153, Alexr.,212,
Archibald,081, Betsy,129,
Eliz.,143, Francis,212,
John,241, Nancy,193,194,
Richard,129
CAMPERTON, Jacob,004
CANNIFAX, Benjamin,250,251,
Elizabeth,251
CANNON, Wm.,004
CANNY(?), Benj.Jr.,036
CANTRILL, Joshua,026
CARTER, Amey,133, Charles,072,
081, Christop.,207,208,
Edward,090,186,207,208,
Eliz.,207,208,239, Elizabeth,
256, George,253, Hannah,253,
James,208, Jedithun,167,
Jeduthan,129,207,208,
Jeduthun,084,085,163,164,
238,256, Jeduthure,121
CARTER, Jesse Jr.,256, Jesse,
163,164,216,256, Jesse,207,
208, Joanna,207,208, John,
111,164, Joseph,164,191,
243, Lawson H.,207,208,
Leven,232, Levin,202, Mary,
164,256, Miller,256, Nancy,
256, Rawley W.,208, Rawley,
207,238, Robert,164
CARTER, Rosian,111, Sally,256,
Sarah,164,238,256, Susannah,
256, Taliferie,220, Thomas C.,
164,256, Thomas,164,207,
208,256,257, Winifred H.,
256, Winifred,207,256, Wm.,
201,253
CASEY, Patsey,149, Thomas,149
CASH, Ruth,040, William,040
CEMP, Mary,245
CHADWELL, John,014
CHAFING, Joshua,069
CHALLES, Hugh,004
CHALMERS, James,004
CHAMBERLAIN, ,014
CHANDLER, Allen,192,220,221,
Jesse,012
CHANEY, Abraham,105, Abrum,
129, Charles,105, Ezekiel,
105,183,204, Isaah,105,
Jacob,104,105, James,105,
John,105, Joseph,105,183,
Letty,183, Mary,105, Moses,
105, Nathan,105, Rhoda,183,
Salley,183, Sarah,104,105,
Thomas,183,204,218, Wm.,183
CHAPPELL, James,121
CHARGILL, John,052
CHARLES, Hugh,069
CHATTING, John,058
CHEATHAM, Abia,098,241,
Frances,142, Larkin,142
CHEATHEM, Abia,123
CHEEK, Wm.,254
CHEETHAM, Frances,239, Larkin,
239
CHELTON, John,242, Mark,031,
Thomas,095
CHENSHAW, Wm.,240
CHICK, Anderson,077, Dudley,
077, Hardin,077, Richard,
077, Susannah,077, William,
018,040, Wm.,077
CHILDRUS, Mary,242, Richard,
242
CHIPMAN, John,002
CHISNHALL, John,207
CHURCH, Alice,247, Jonathan Montg.,
247
CISSELL, Thomas,030
CLABROOKS, ,187
CLAIBORNE, Leonard,189, Sen.,
257
CLAIBOURNE, Thos.,012
CLARK, Anna,248, Anney,156,
Joel,085,103, John,181,
Lydda,253, Martha,248,
Mary,001,002,172, Peter H.,
228, Peter,132,133,228,
Priscilla,229, Thos.H.,227,
234, Will.L.,234, Wm.,069,
070,101,125,128,150,179,
193,223,227,234,238,246,248
CLARK, Wm.,249, Wm.L.,221,
227, Wm.S.,193,216
CLARKE, Nancy,181, Thomas,181,
W.,127, Wm.,194
CLARKSON, Constantine,048
CLASS, Leonard,132

CLAY, Amanda A.,182, Green,
022,023, Henry,022,023,
Joseph,181,182, Martha,022,
Mathew,022,023, Matthew,
181,182, Priscilla,022,
Thomas,022,023
CLEMENT, Adam Jr.,160, Adam,
040, Benjamin,039,040,
Charles,160, Daniel,214,
Isaac,040,246, James,040,
John,039,040, Lucreasy,125,
Martha,040, Nathan,214,
Stephen,040,245, Susanna,
039, Vachel,111,151,249
CLEMENTS, Vachel,112,147
CLOPTON, Robert,096
COCK, Thomas,128
COCKERHAM, Chedle,010
COCKRAM, Louvisa,160,161
COCKS, Philip,099
COLEMAN, Anne,157, Chloe,193,
Daniel Jr.,115, Daniel L.,
173, Daniel,086,087,113,
115,157,186,187,245, Polly,
087, Sarah,086, Stephen Jr.,
086, Stephen,045,053,082,
086,087,115,226, Thompson,
087, Wm.,061
COLES, Catherine,170,171,
Isaac,170,171, James T.,
171, John,171, Mary,171,
Robert T.,171, Walter,170,
171,189,212
COLLEY, Charles,141, Wm.,144
COLLIE, Mary,023
COLLIER, Charles,023, Eliz.,
026, Wm.,023
COLLINGS, Wm.,254
COLLINS, Elizabeth,035, Faney,
045, John,045, Joseph,040,
Thomas,044,045, William,
040,044,045, Wm.,018
COLLOM, Robert,064
COLQUET, James,078, Margaret F.,
078
COLQUHOLEN, J.,131
COLQUHOUN, James,115
COLWELL, Seth,042
COMER, Richard,248
CONN, Jo.,055, Joseph,055,
Josephus,187
CONNER, James,235
CONSTABLE, Samuel,030
CONWAY, (Mr.),069, Christop.,
217, Christopher,083,123,
232, Henry,045, James,083
COOK, Abraham,150, Elijah,156,
George,083, Harmon Jr.,150,
Harmon Sr.,149, Harmon,150,
Henry,099, John,016,150,
Ruth,106, Susannah,072
COOLEY, Charles,249
CORBIN, Ambrose,146, Amegi(?),
033, Betsy,146, David,146,
Elizabeth,033, Jincey,146,
Lucy,033, Molly,146,
Randolph,146, Rawley,033,
Sally,146, Susannah,033,
Thomas,033, Wm.,094
CORNWAL, Fushe,239
CORNWELL, Eliz.,142, Stephen,
247
COUCH, George,004, John,004
COUSINS, John,071, Phebe,193
COWPER, Abraham,135
COX, Charity,100, Eliz.,163,
George Jr.,163, George,163,
Isham,163, James,100, John,
004,100,250, Josiah,163,
Patsey,163, Polly,163,
Prudence,100, Sally,163,
173, Thomas,163, Wm.,163
CRADDOCK, Frankey,035,
John Jr.,035, John,035,
Judith,035, Mary,035,079,
Nathaniel,035, Nathl.,137,
Priscilla,035, Richard,035,
036, Sarah,035, William,035,
Wm.,183
CRADOCK, Mary,079
CRAFFORD, Showder,116
CRAG, Thomas,243
CRAWFORD, Arther,146
CREAL, Rhody,050
CREAMER, Christian,132
CREEL, Adam,204, John,019,
048,050,242, Luce,204,
Mathew,242, Micajah,095,242
CRENSHAW, Nathanl.,240,
Polly W.,240, Sally,247,
Sarah W.,240, Susannah,240,
Wm.,240
CREWS, Crescancey,235,
Josiah,196,235,255, Martha,
032, Wm.,201,209
CRITZ, Hamon Jr.,010, Hamon Sr.,
009, Hamon,009
CROCKET, Jeany,015
CROCKETT, Robert,020
CROSS, Mary,107, Wm.,107
CROUCH, John,126, Polley,127,
Susannah,126
CRUTCHER, Sebert,034,035
CULLOM, Elisabeth,063, Robert,
063
CUNDIFF, Elisha,094
CUNNINGHAM, Eleanor,080,
Eliz.,080, Ephraim,080,

Isabel,080, Jenny,080,
Jos.,080, Joseph,001,055,
Patsey M.,236, Patsey,237,
Patsy M.,236, Thomas,001,
043,080, Thos.Jr.,080, Wm.,
080,084
CURRY, Israel,100, James,212,
Nancy,138, Nathan,138,
Peggy,212
DABNEY, Fr.,173, Francis,173,
186,195, George,195,196,
211, Samuel,103,195,196,
211, Wm.,006,191
DADE, Francis,178
DAILEY, Hugh,257, Jesse,257,
John,257
DALTON, Isham,004, John,023,
Lewis,190, Mary,023, Nancy,
023, Robert Sr.,023, Senna,
161, Soloman,023
DANGERFIELD, Alexr.,176, Caty,
176, Dolly P.,176, Eliz.,
176, Ginsey,176, John,150,
176, Leonard,176, William,
176, Willis,176
DANIEL, Kibble,235
DASHT(?), George,171
DAVIDSON, Nancy,108, Rachel,
108
DAVIS, Anna,030, Anne,145,
Benjamin,094,214, Catreen,
142, Effy,142, Elizabeth,
067, Eliz.,145, Elizabeth,
001,115, Frances,142,
Freder..,142, George,086,
122, James,122, John H.,239,
John,006,008,094,122,142,
145, Joseph,094,216,
Lucinda,226
DAVIS, Lucy,094,122,142,149,
199,216, Luscey,149, Martha,
222, Mary,218, Micajah,194,
Nancy,145, Peggy,094,
Phebe,101, Polley,218,
Rosean,142, Sally,142,
Samuel,008, Sarah,008,
Susannah,008, Thomas,094,
145,177,214, William,122,
Wilmoth,008
DAVIS, Wm.,094,095,142,149,
216,218, Wm.Jr.,218
DAWSON, Ann Ivison,063,
John B.,175, Jonathan B.,
063, Jonathan,175
DEADMAN, Ann,046
DEATHERAGE, Philip,006
DEGARNETT, James,175
DEJARNATT, George,234
DENNING, Wm.,193
DEVERETT, Mary,239, Rhoda,239,
Wm.,239
DEVERETT, Mary,239, Rhoda,
239
DEVIN, Eliz.,152, James,107,
Joseph,093,107,108,250,
Robert,065,093,107,108,
109,132,150,200,215,225,
248, Sarah,107, Sucky,152,
Wm.,107,108, Wm.Jr.,093,
107,248, Wm.Sr.,093
DEWS(?), Sarah,079
DEWS, Sarah,175
DICKENSON, Griffith,125,189,
John,209, Patience,053,
Vincent,189
DICKERSON, Crispen,199,
Griffith,038, Susanna,038,
Weir,011
DICKINSON, Griffeth,075,
Griffith,032,173, Noton,
049,052
DILLARD, Ann,137, Elizabeth,
009, James,009, John,009,
Ruth,026,067, Thomas,009,
014,045, Thos.Jr.,009
DILLON, David,016
DIX, Francis,091, Henrietta,
052, James Jr.,075, James Sr.,
075, James,195, Jenney,202,
John D.,202, John M.,100,
197,204,222,225, John P.,
203, John,002,052,075,202,
Kerenhappuch,052,100,
Kerunhappuck,052, Larkin,
052,100,202, Matilda F.,052
DIX, Tandy,075, Thomas,075,
202,239, William,100, Wm.,
052,053,075,202,241, Wm.P.,
202
DIXON, Charles,060, Martha,
023, Peyton,257, Wm.,257
DODSON, Alie(Alice?),096, Amy,
168, David,019,053,105,
Deborah,019, Easley,201,
Edward,224, Elenor,050,
Elisha Jr.,019, Elisha,042,
096, Ellenor,050, Else,050,
Fortan,048, Fortune,019,
116, Franky,201, Geo.Sr.,
144, George,019,030,042,
DODSON, George,050,096,101,
105,138,140,154,201,249,
Jesse,019,050, John,204,
Joseph,049,097,099,219,
Joshua,218, Lasarus,243,
Lazarus,096, Liddie,050,
Lucy,180, Margaret,019,
096,101,140,154,180, Mary,

Joshua,237, Nancy,237,
Sally,237, Samuel,116,
Steven,237, Wm.,237
GRIFFETH, Jonathan,041,042,
Sarrah,042, William,042,
Wm.Jr.,041
GRIFFITH, Rachel,042, William,
041,042, Wm.,028,255
GRIGGORY, John,245
GRIGGS, Axcy,222, George,222,
James,132,222, Jane,132,
John Jr.,222, John Sr.,222,
John,132, Michael,222,
Peter,222, Robert,222
GRUBS, James,192, Sally,192,
Susannah,192
GUILD, Walter,178
GUIN, Geo.Ho.,061
GUNN, Daniel,126, John,102
GUNNEL, Nancy,115
GWIN, John,121, Josiah,113,
Milley,106, Millin,120,
Thomas,113
GWYNE, Edmund,023, John,023,
Richard,024
HADEN, Anthony,191
HAGOOD, Lewis,234
HAGWOOD, Lewis,179
HAILEY, Bryan W.,213, Eliz.,
210, Jas.E.,199, Joseph E.,
211,213, Nancy,211, Pleasant,
213, Polley,212, Richard,
213, Temple,210,213, Wm.W.,
199,211,213, Wyatt,213
HAIN, Obadeah,232
HAIRSTON, George,013
HAIZLIP, Wm.,222
HALEY, Ann,212,213, Joseph E.,
213, Patsey,212, Pleasant,
212,213, Polley,212, Polly,
134,135, Richard,213,
Thomas,213, Wyatt,213
HALL, George,062, Henry,024,
139, James,020, Jean,062,
John Jr.,062, John R.,133,
John,020,062,063, Joseph,
062,063, Mary,020, Mathew,
020, Prisciller,020, Sally,
139, William,233, Wm.,133,
167,169,239
HAM, Thomas,112
HAMBLET, Abner,041, Darcus,
041, Fillithaumy,041,
Hannah,041, James,041,
Morris,041, Rachel,041,
Thomas,041, William,041
HAMILTON, Jane,226, Mary,006
HAMLIN, Alie,006
HAMMACK, Talifaferro,200
HAMMOCK, John,131, Mary,254,
Richard,254
HAMMOND, John Sr.,033,107,
John,063, Sabra,033
HAMPTON, Elizabeth,078,
Hannah,078, Henry,078,
James,078, John,078,079,
Preston,078,079, Sarah,079,
Thomas,078,079
HAMRICK, David,128
HANBY, David,253, John,253,
Jonathan,253, Susanna,253
HANKINS, George,079, Wm.,200
HANKS, Moses,048
HARBOUR, Elijah,254, Elisha,
012
HARDAWAY, Mary,069, Peter,069
HARDEMAN, Thomas,020
HARDEN, Mark,069
HARDEY, George,244, Isham,132,
Joshua,244, Thomas,229
HARDIN, Henry,081, Jimmy,081,
Judith,081, Mark,057,081,
Martin,081,096,137, Wm.,081
HARDWICK, Meskey,111, Micky,
112, Pleasant,111,112
HARDY, ,215, Ann,024, Benjamin,
029, Elizabeth,024, George,
025, Isham,152, John,024,
257, Mary,024, Moses,257,
Polley,257, Sally,257,
Sarah,024, Susanah,024,
Thomas,024,051, Thos.Jr.,
024, William,024
HARDYE, George,214
HARGROVE, James,054
HARMAN, Laban,160
HARMON, John,164, Molly,164,
165, Nancy K.,165, Nicholas,
165, Patsey,165, Polley,165,
Samuel,165, Solomon,164,
165, Thomas,164,165,165
HARN, Thomas,177
HARP, James,173, Mary,174,
Philip,174, Susanna,174
HARPER, Ann,139, Anna,139,
Eliz.,142, George,139,
Jacob,139, Nancy,139,
Nicholas,139, Thomas,139
HARRIS, (Land),070, Achilles,
123, Benjamin,097,099,100,
104,122,123, Betsy,123,
Charles,241, David,008,
054,248, Eliz.,189, Eliza A.,
189, Jean,189, John,008,
242, Joseph,008, Leah,032,
Lucy,123, Mandley,189,
Margreate,189, Mary,098,
Nathaniel,097

HARRIS, Nathaniel,098, Polly,
123, Samuel Jr.,097, Samuel,
028,097,098,189, Susanna,
189, Thomas,085,138, Wm.,
123,239
HARRISON, Andrew Sr.,219,
Andrew,211,212, Ann,027,
Anna,060, Anne,157,
Answorth,177,181, Benj.,
025, Benjamin,024, Betsy,
025, Charles,025,211, Eliz.,
179, Mary,219, Molley,025,
Nathaniel,158, Polley D.,
157, Polly,025, Robert,028,
157
HARRISON, Sarah,025, Sukey,
025, W.,178, Wm.(Mrs),028,
Wm.,025,052,053,060,127,
157,158, Wm.K.,195,196,
Wm.Porter,158
HART, Eliz.,186, James,118,
131,157,192,193
HARVE, Ellender,064, John,063,
Lender,064, Samuel,063,
064, Sarah,064
HARVEY, ,258, Robert,118
HARWOOD, Archibald,258
HASKINS, Frances,090,091
HATCHER, Joseph,141
HATCHETT, Edward,251, Joseph,
146,168
HAWKER, Ambrose,228,229,
Basil,082,083,229, Mary,
083, Philip,156,229, Reubin,
083, Wm.,229
HAWKES, Jinney,156, Polly,106,
Salley,155
HAYMES, Daniel,158, David,158,
Jilicu,158, Joshua,158,
Robert,158,159, Sally,198,
W.,252, Wm.,158,252,
Wm.Jr.,158
HAYNES, Jillica,125
HEADRICK, Caty,146
HEADSPETH, Lemuel,183
HEAL, Solomon,063
HEALE, Susanna,059, Wm.,059
HEARD, George,010, Jesse,010,
Mary,010, Stephen Jr.,010,
Stephen,010
HEDGER, Mary,242
HENDERSON, James,070,156,157,
Mary,090,156,207, Wm.,070,
156
HENDREN, Thomas,064,065
HENDRICK, Caty,145, Elijah,
097, Ezekiel,079, Humphrey,
100, Jane,088, John H.,176,
Margaret,023, Nathaniel,
046,079, Polly,176, Priscilla,
079, Sally,197, Smith H.,176
HENLEY, Jillica,025
HENRY, Charles S.,257,258,
Francis,248, James H.,258,
James,257,258, John,187,
258, Robert,194, Samuel H.,
258
HENSLEY, Benjamin,016
HERNDON, George,130,131,141,
Jane,132, Reuben,132,
Sarah,130,131,223,224
HERRING, Armstead,095,096,
John,095, Langford,095,
Mary,095, Polley West,095,
Washington,095, William,
050, Wm.,095, Wm.Jr.,095
HESTER, Elizabeth,121, Samuel,
121
HICKS(HIX), Miles,012
HICKS, Jinnah,036, Nathaniel,
036
HIGHTOWER, Ann,252, Catherine,
252, Devaurex,218, Deveraux,
162, Deverinx,139, Elizabeth,
252, George,252, John,252,
Polly,252, Stith,252,
Thomas,252, Wm.,252
HILL, Gressell,159, Isaac,100,
Jonathan,063, Joseph,204,
Pheby Booker,100, Thomas,
062,063
HINES, Wm.,138
HINTON, James,069,070,197
HIX, Benjamin,012, Dolly,012,
Elizabeth,012, Frances,012,
Franky,012, James,011,012,
Miles,012, Nancy,012,
Patsy,012
HOBSON, Benjamin,255, Lucey,
255, Polly W.,255, Wm.E.,255
HOCKKER, Polley,106
HODGES, David,049, Edmond,049,
Edmund,048, Elisabeth,045,
James,192,193, Jesse,049,
108,192, Jessey,045, John,
034,049,108,174, Levena,128,
Moses,049,193, Nephany,049,
Polly,192, Thomas,049,052,
Wade,192
HODNETT, Ayres,025,216, Ayrs,
069, Benjamin,025, Daniel,
025, James,025,216, John,
025,243, Mary,216
HOFFMAN, John,150
HOLDER, Benjamin,056, Daniel,
056, Davis Jr.,056, Davis,
056,057, Eliz.,156, Elizabeth,
056, Hannah,056, John,056,

Mary,244, Susanna,056,
Willam,069, Wm.,056
HOLLAND, Joseph,159, Nancy,
158
HOLLAY, Judith,026
HOLLEY, James,230, Joel,230,
Leonard,230, Lewis,230,
Milley,230, Thomas,230,
Wm.,230
HOLMS, Thos.Cliburn,258
HOLT, T.D.,067
HOOD(?), Gatie,211
HOPKINS, Arthur,013, F.,238,
Frances,013, James,013,
145,150,164,238,239,241,
Jean,013, Mary,164,238,
Reuben,238, Samuel,013
HOPPER, Robert,049
HOPSON, Eliz.,195,243,
Elizabeth,103, Mildred,103,
Sa.,060, Samuel,099,103
HOPWOOD, Penelophe,198,
Willis,108, Wm.,101
HOSKINS, Hannah,186, John,186,
Johnson,186, Martha,186,
227, Rebecca,186, Tabitha,
186, Thomas,186
HUBBARD, Davis,034, Edward Jr.,
040, Edward,040, Eliza,174,
Elizabeth,040, Isam,034,
Isham,034, John,033,034,
040,123, Joseph,040,131,
Kezekiah,034, Keziah,057,
123, Kezzia,034, Mary,005,
Moses,150,174,248, Nathaniel,
040, Polly,175, Reuben,040
HUBBARD, Samuel,034,123,
Tabithia,040
HUDSON, Cutbert,096, Cuthbert,
108, Lucy,076,108
HUFFMAN, Nancy T.,176
HUGHES, Archelaus,009,010,
Joseph,124, Pheby,124,
Richard,010, Sally,180,181
HUGHS, Ceziah,107, Micajah,
066
HUMPHRIES, Hannah,018, Wm.,
018
HUNDLEY, Nancy,192, Polley,
205
HUNT, David,078,246, Eustace,
212, John,119,197,234,
Nelly,025
HURT, Absalom E.,113, Absalom,
088, Elizabeth,037,088,
Garland,088,161, James,035,
Joel,045,046, John,018,
Lucy,120, Moses Jr.,088,
Moses,088, Rodey S.,088,
Sally L.,088, West D.,113,
120, West Dandridge,088,
Wm.C.,225
HURTON, ,191
HUTCHERSON, Joseph,123,
Nathan,192,238
HUTCHESON, Mary,213
HUTCHINGS, Aaron,014,137,
Anne,014, Catherine,022,
Charles,014,137, Christop.,
137,152, Christopher,014,
Eliz.,137, Elizabeth,014,
James,077,137, John,014,
137,220, Lemuel,137, Moses,
014,098,137,191, Thomas,014,
022,137, Wm.,214,237
HUTCHINSON, John,090
HUTCHISON, Nancy,117
HUTSON, Abel,224, Drury,224,
Robert,256
INGRAM, Elisabeth,096,
Garland,234, George,234,
Larkin,096,234, Rhody,234,
Tapley,234, William,234
INGRUM, Elizabeth,019,
William,019
INMAN, Edmund,114, Henry,114,
Jesse,114, Nancy,114,
Shadrack,114, Susannah,114,
Wm.,114, Wm.Jr.,114
IRBY, Abraham,245, Amey,214,
215,245, Anne,160, Baster,
169, Baxter,218, Charles,
169, David,245, Eliz.,169,
245, Elizabeth,232, Francis,
067,078,245, Irby,169, Jean,
067, Jencey,078, John,136,
Martha,135, Marthia,245,
Nancy,232, Peter,245
IRBY, Prudence,215, Rebeccah,
245, Samuel,245, William,
233, Wm.(Dr),133, Wm.,163,
169,245, Wm.R.,214, Wm.Sr.,
232, Zachariah,245
IVY, Francis,032
JACKSON, Eliz.(Mrs),087,
Hezekiah P.,254
JAMES, Allen,177, Benjamin,
025, Charity,181, Chrispin,
181, Elizabeth,252, John Jr.,
019, Mathew,177, Nancy,177,
Thomas,156,177, Wm.,177,181
JAMISON, Thomas,012
JARVIS, Winifred,161
JEFFERSON, Alex.,150,241,
Archibald,240, Peter(Col.),
015, Samuel,150
JEFFRES, John,100
JEFFREYS, John,080

JENKINS, Catherine,177,
   Daniel,067, John,035,082,
   093,103,180, Philip,047,
   Tabitha,207, Thos.,086
JENNINGS, Jonathan,253,
   Susannah,253
JOHNS, Daniel,181, Joseph,104
JOHNSON, ,191, Allas,131,
   Arther,048, Daniel,236,
   Elenor,254, Fullington,226,
   227, Geo.W.,227, Geo.Wash.,
   226,227, Isham,035, James F.,
   110,197,226,227, James,006,
   035,110,186,226,227,
   Jane H.,226,227, Jane,226,
   Jeremiah F.,226,227,
   Lean D.,197
JOHNSON, Lettice,197,226,
   Mary P.,197, Moses,048,
   Nancy W.,197, Nancy,226,
   Obediah,048, Philemon,213,
   Richard,033,035,062,064,
   154,159,197,227,251, Salley,
   140, Susannah,213
JOHNSTON, Archibald,066,
   Elisabeth,066, James,066,
   213, Mary,066, Obediah,066,
   Sally,066, Samuel,066, Wm.,
   066
JONES, Anna,258, Barbary,179,
   Buckner,253, Deanitia,252,
   Edward D.,087, Emanuel,063,
   111, Frances,156, George,
   018, Henrietta,252, Henry A.,
   087, Jerusha,159, John,021,
   258, Martha,144,252,
   Mary Jr.,063, Mary,063,
   174, Mosias,252,253,
   Patience,019
JONES, Richard,176,215,216,
   221,233, Robert,243,
   Susannah,252, Thomas B.,
   035,063,159,183,186,208,
   251, Thomas Jr.,063, Thos.B.,
   063,252, Thos.W.,233
JUSTICE, Mary,254
KATES, Archer,063
KEARBY, David,005, Elizabeth,
   008, Francis,005, Henry,005,
   Jesse,005, John,005,008,
   Josiah,005, Sarah,008
KEATES, Charles,063
KEATTS, Archer,249, Charles,
   111,119,249, Curtis,118,
   119, Henry,110,119,148,
   James G.,193, James,119,
   Jas.Gower,110,119, John Jr.,
   110, John,110,111,119,233,
   119, Parskill,110, Richard G.,
   233, Richard,110
KEATTS, Richard,119,193,249,
   Tabitha,119, William,235,
   Wm.,119
KEESE, Milley,031
KEESEE, Arthur,073, Benjamin,
   073, Blackwell,167, Charles,
   167, George,073, Jeremiah,
   073, Jesse S.,073, Jesse,
   173,201, John,073,152,167,
   Mary,166,167, Phebe,073,
   Tabitha,073
KEIN, John,224
KELLY, Elizabeth,096, Hugh Jr.,
   096, Hugh,096, Leah,096,
   Mary,096, Nishe(?),096,
   Patrick,096, Veshe(?),096
KEMP, Lucy,123
KENNON, Charles,025
KENT, Polley R.,203, Stephen,
   204
KERBY, Bolin,096, Elizabeth,
   031, Menry,006, Joana,006,
   Joannah,006, John,005,006,
   247, Lurah,142, Milly,129,
   Moses,247, Nathaniel,247,
   Sarah,142, Susanna,031
KESSEE, Ann,036, Charles,036,
   Jeremiah,036, Jesse,036,
   John,036, Richard,036
KIND, Levinia,003
KING, Cheslay,116, Chesley,
   115, Elijah,003,004,035,
   Grace,116,166,167, James,
   018,045, John,003,004,
   Malachi,004, Nancy,018,
   Peyton,134,162,164, Robert,
   215, Royal,134, Susanah,018,
   Wm.,003,004
KIRBY, Eliz.H.,240,241, Moses,
   239,240,241, Nathan'l.,240,
   241, Sally,239, Sarah,239,
   240,241
KIZZEE, Eliz.,219, Stoball,
   219
LACEY, Tabitha,123, Theop.,
   254
LACKEY, Thomas,056
LACY, Eliz.,206, Theop.,003
LAMB, Caty,090, Walter,090,
   093
LANDAREN, Geo.T.,153
LANDERS, James,177
LANDON, Will,046
LANDSDION, Geo.T.,232
LANDSDOWN, Johnson,176
LANDSFORD, Henry,248

LANIER, David,012,111, James,
   196,223, John H.,238
LANKFORD, Ben,077,079, Benj.,
   014, Benj.Jr.,154, Benjamin,
   040,075,154,254, Hamilton,
   079, Henretta,154, Kitty,
   079, Stephen,079,154
LANSDOWN, Geo.T.,239, J.,166,
   Johnson,166,167, Johnston,
   212
LANSFORD, Cate,018, Catherine,
   018, Elijah,018, Elizabeth,
   085, Henry,018,085,253,
   Isham,018,085,253, Josiah,
   018, Parmanas,222, Susannah,
   018
LAURENCE, Beheath.,145
LAWSON, Clayborn,087, Martha,
   197, Wm.,011
LAY, David,061
LAYNE, Dutton,248
LEAGUE, John,034,128
LEAK, James,015, John,015,
   Joseph,015, Joshua,015,
   Thomas,015
LEAKE, Joshua,015
LEANY, William,034
LEE, Alexander,029, Sarah,029
LEFTWICH, Jesse(& Co.),116,
   Jesse,110,137, Robert,146,
   164, Sen.,257, Thos.,091,
   Will,215, Wm.,221
LEGRAND, Abram,061, Adam Sr.,
   061, Lucy,061,062
LEIGH, Wm.,237
LEV(?), Allend,232
LEWIS, Berry,148, Charles Jr.,
   035,124, Charles,035,099,
   124,125,194,195,211,212,
   242,243,244, Chas.Jr.,032,
   Edward,124, Eliz.,211,
   James,125, Jane,119,243,
   John E.,195, John Jr.,242,
   243, John Sr.,242,243, John,
   103,119,125,148,149,194
LEWIS, John,195,196,235,242,
   243,244, Little B.,199,
   Lucy,211, Merewether,195,
   Nancy S.,195, Nicholas,194,
   211, Rebecka,235, Robert H.,
   195, Robert,103,194,195,
   243, Samuel,074, Sarah,244,
   Winney,031, Wm.,035,119,
   125,235,244, Zach.,117
LEWIS, Zachariah,124, Zas.,
   078
LIDDLE, James,024
LINDSEY, John,199, Wm.,179
LINN, James,117,120,151,
   William,115, Wm.,186,239
LINTHICUM, Sarah,251, Thoma,
   252, Thomas Jr.,251,
   Thomas Sr.,251, Thomas,035
LIPFORD, Anthony,166
LITTLE, Ester,061
LOGAIN, Samuel,131
LOGAN, John,181, Mary,092,
   Wm.,151
LONG, Edward Sr.,132, Edward,
   132, Eliz.,132, Isaac,132,
   James,132, Jane,132, John,
   008,129, Thomas,132, Will,
   132, Wm.,132
LOVE, Robert,159
LOVELACE, James,182,183,
   Nancy,182, Nathanl.,182,
   183, Polley,182, Sally,182,
   Thomas,182,183
LOVELL, John,150, Salley,208,
   Sally,207, Samuel,208
LOVENS, Frances,219
LUCK, Betty,046, Catey Evans,
   046, Francis,046,136,183,
   James A.,183, John,046,
   Joyce,046, Mary,046, Nat.,
   104, Nathaniel,035,046,
   Rhoda,046, Richd.Hubbard,
   046, Sarah,046,136
LUCUS, Wm.,252
LUMKIN, Patsey,142
LUMKINS, Mary,251
LUMKIN, Peyton,194
LUMPKINS, John,202
LYNCH, Abner,134, William,030,
   Wm.,019
LYNN, James,103
LYON, James,253
MABREY, Betsey,183, Mary,183
MABRY, Braxton,069, Rebeccah,
   108
MACK, Robert,080
MADCAFF, James,129
MADDING, Absalom,101, Albert,
   153, Elisha,153,154, Eliz.,
   154, Joel,101, John Jr.,101,
   John,101,176,177, Larkin,
   101, Larking,177, Mary,101,
   Polly,153, Rachel,153,154,
   167, Raleigh,153, Rawley,
   154, Robert,096,153, Sally,
   176, Sarah,101
MADDING, Scarlet,101, Thomas,
   101,153,154, Wilmouth,153,
   Wm.,030
MADING, Champness,042,
   John Sr.,042, John,042,
   249, Mary,042, Rachel,096,
   Robert,042,096, Thomas,042,

   William,042
MADISON, Anne,154
MADKIFF, Agnes,064, Hannah,
   064, John,064, Joseph,064
MAHAN, Alexander,177,178,
   Catherine,178, John,177,
   178, Mary,152, Wm.,177,178
MAIDE(?), William,094
MALICOAH, Lavina,131
MANN, ,187
MAPLES, Edward,132, Wm.,132
MAPPLES, Josiah,056
MARK, John Jr.,082
MARKHAM, John,068
MARLOW, George,073, Rebecca,
   214
MARR, Abbigail,027, Christopher
   026,027, Gideon,020, John,
   020,074,085,116, Joseph,026,
   Richard,020,074, Sarah,020
MARRICK, Elizabeth,086,
   Ellender,086, Henry,086,
   Immalia,086, John,086,
   Rachel,086, Susannah,086,
   Wm.,086
MARSHAL, Daniel,123
MARSHALL, Richard,162
MARTAIN, Sarah(Mulato),058
MARTIN, Abraham,090, Isaac,
   052, James,009, John,090,
   170, Quinn,112, Siller,066
MARTON, John,093, Leanner,093,
   Milly,093, Styth,093
MASSEY, Wilmith,253
MASTIN, Dianer,025
MATHERLEY, Shadrack,134
MATHIS, Betsy,068, Luke,068,
   Nehemiah,068, Thomas,068
MATNEY, James,186, John,155
MATTHIAS, Agatha,249
MATTON, George,190, John,190,
   Polly,190
MAY, John,071,139,253,
   Susannah,084
MAYES, Gardner,129
MAYO, John,243
MAYS, Fleming,228, Gardner,
   097, Letty,234
MCCLANNAHAM, Francis,228,
   John,228
MCCOLLOUGH, Samuel,165
MCCONWAY, John,012,013, Mary,
   012,013, Robert,012,013,
   Sarah,013
MCCOY, Robert,250
MCCUNE, Adam,235
MCDANIEL, ,187,236, Anne S.,
   245, Anne,244,245, Betsey W.,
   163, Chloe,244, Clement,104,
   245, Collen,244, Elizabeth,
   086, Henry,007,255, James S.,
   244, Joel,244,245, Martha,
   163, Nancy,120,244, Polley,
   244, Randolph,179, Rotherick,
   030, Stephen C.,154
MCDANIEL, Winifred,029, Wm.,
   163,185, Wm.C.,244
MCDONALD, Abner,155, Absalom,
   155,245, Absel,155, Clement,
   155, Daniel,155, James,061,
   098,154,155,245, Mary,154,
   Randolph,154,155, Susanah
   154, Wm.,242, Zepora,155,
   Zeriah,155
MCEUZUK(?), Jonathan,017
MCGLASSON, Mathew,031,
   Ubeboth,031
MCGUFFORD, Samuel,079,080
MCHANEY, Betsey,182, Cornel.,
   145, Cornelius,046,079,104,
   174,175, John,174,182,183
MCLANEY, Cornelius,104
MCLAUGHLAN, Charles,160,
   Chas.Sr.,160, Henry,160,
   Patience,160, Polly,160,
   Sarah,160
MCLAUGHLIN, Ales,153
MCLAUGHLOR, Sarah,053
MCMURDY, James,242
MCMURREY, ,249
MCNEALEY, David,176
MCROBERT, Tho.B.,088, Thos.B.,
   087
MEACHUM, Mary,031
MEAD, Molly,051
MEADE, Betsy,200, Edith,200,
   James,199,200,221, Meady,
   200, Meredith,199, Middleton,
   200, Morrison,200, Rosamon,
   200, Talelet,200
MEADOR, Franics,214, James,
   214, Joab,214, Lidia,214,
   Samuel,214, Sarah,214
MEADORS, Joel,214
MEASE, Abraham,145,146, Ana,
   145, Caty,145,146, Christina,
   146, John,145, Philip,145,
   146, Sally,145,146
MECKELBOROUGH, Aldin,142,143,
   Carter,142,143, Eliz.,142,
   Henry,142,143, James,142,
   143, Jane,142,143, Patsey,
   143, Polley,143, Robert,142
MECKELBURROUGH, Jane,142
MEDLOCK, Susan,118
MELTON, William,002
MEREWETHER, Charles,195
MERIWETHER, Thomas,242

MERRYWEATHER, Thos.,011
METTON, James D.,193
MICHEL, Agnes,060
MICKELBOROUGH, Carter,123,
  Elesebath,120, Henry,123
MICKLEBERRY, Robert,121
MICKLEBOROUGH, Carter,153,
  239, Henry,239
MIDKIFF, John Jr.,223,
  John Sr.,223, Lydia,140,
  Mary,223, Thomas,105
MIERS, George Jr.,095, Jacob,
  095, John,077, Wm.,095
MILLER, Isaac,163, Jacob,173
MILLET, Milly,167
MINTER, John Sr.,018
MIRES, George,094
MISE, John,240
MITCHELL, (Widow),150, ,
  045,133, Gideon,115, Helen,
  132, Henry,132, James A.,
  174, James H.,175,183,
  James,024,132,182,183,248,
  John,161,174, Michael,188,
  Samuel,161,174, Sarah,248,
  Susannah,183, Thomas,161,
  Winifred,182, Wm.,132,161
MITCHELL, Wm.,175, Wm.C.,182,
  183
MITCHELL(?), Eliz.,175
MOODEY, Blanks,246, Eliz.Buford,
  246, Elizabeth,246, Judith,
  246, Mary,246, Wm.,246
MOORE, Anna,198, Anne,156,
  199, Azariah,204, James A.,
  199, James,198, Jere,198,
  Jeremiah,199, Levi,198,
  Marriman,199, Mary,199,
  Mathew B.,198, Mathew,198,
  Merriman,198,199, Nancy,
  198,199, Polly,198, Sally,
  198, Terry,198, Thomas,198
MOORE, Thomas,199, Vincent,
  198, Whaley,198, Wm.,156
MOORFIELD, John,071, Nathaniel,
  071
MOREHEAD, Obedience,133
MORGAN, Eliz.L.,246, George,
  046, Haymes,243, Haynes,046,
  180,245,246, John,126,
  Mary T,246, Mary,246,
  Sarah,046
MORGIN, Sarah,114
MORRIS, ,097, Benjamin,242,
  Elijah,230, John,242, Mary,
  242, Polly,114, Samuel,242,
  Wm.,242, Wm.Sr.,230
MORRISON, Rachel,141, Wm.,141
MORTAN(MARTIN), Thos.,093
MORTON, Joseph,053,065,065,
  108,144, Josiah,223,
  Lucy(Lucey),093, Lucy,092,
  William,035, Winney,093
MOSELEY, Samuel,049
MOTLEY, Daniel,116,133,197,
  David,092,133, Eliz.,133,
  166,169, Eliz.D.,210, Henry,
  181, John,133, Joseph M.,
  169, Joseph,133,189,222,
  Patsey,133, Samuel,092,
  116,133
MOXLEY, Daniel,253
MULLER, John,055
MULLINS, Susanna,130
MURPHEY, Cassey,101, James,
  234, Margaret,234, Wm.,223
MURPHY, Ann,122, James,101,
  135, John,122, Lewis,212,
  Richard,003, Rozia,003,
  Sarah,135, Thomas,149, Wm.,
  212
MUSE, Henry S.,241, John T.,
  241, John,240,248
MUSGROVE, Harrison,047
MUSICK(?), Jonathan,017
MUSTAIN, Avery,031,190,
  Jenney,031, Jesse,031,032,
  Mary Ann,031, Mary,031,
  Molly,031, Patsey,214,
  Rebekah,031, Sally,031,
  Thomas,031,032
MUSTIEN, Every,173
MYERS, Benjamin,257, George,
  256, Isaac,257, Isham,257,
  Jacob,257, James,257, Mary,
  256, Polley,257, Stephen,
  257, Wm.,257
NANCE, Betsey,225, Clement,
  085,252, Eliz.,179, Isaac,
  225, Mary,085,253
NANI--, Wm.M.,079
NAPPER, ,258
NASH, Robert,131, W.,192
NEAL, Anna,151, David,189,
  Eliz.Allen,084, Joanna,151,
  Joel,151, John,101,151,
  Mary,151, Samuel,151,
  Simon,151, Stephen Jr.,092,
  151, Stephen Sr.,103,
  Stephen,109,151, Thomas,
  189, Wm.,151
NEALE(NEALEY), Wm.,065
NEIGHBORS, Wm.,036
NELSON, Ambrose,088, Ambrus,
  089, Bazel,089, Eliz.,138,
  159, James,089,124,138,163,
  241, John,080,138, Joshua,
  100, Lydda,138, Milley,163,

Sarah,138, Unity,100, Wm.,
  089,117,138,159,164
NELTON, James,117
NELY, Wm.,065
NEVIL, Sarah,050
NEWBELL, John,157,189
NEWTEN, Thomas,251, Wm.,251
NEWTON, Delila,251, Delilah,
  028, Henry,028
NICHOLS, John,062
NICOLDS, Mishael,151
NIGHT, Polley,204
NOBLES, Leonard,054
NORTEN, Jacob,149
NORTON, Wm.,074
NOWLIN, Anne,152, Bryan W.,
  073,152,176, Bryan W.Jr.,
  152, David,152,176,183,
  James,152,176,241, Lucy,
  152, Mathew,176, Mildred,
  152, Peyton,073,152, Raney,
  176, Richard W.,152, Samuel,
  152,176,188, Sherad,152,
  176,188, Wade,233
NOWLING(NOWLIN), Samuel,254
NOWLING, Bryant W.,137,
  Milley,137
NUCKLES, Lishe,077
NUCKOLDS, Catharine,230,
  Elizabeth,230, John,230,
  Josiah,229, Leve,230,
  Martha,230, Milley,230,
  Morning,230
NUNNELEE, Edward,107,111
NUNNELLE, Edward,200,250
NUNNELLEE, Edward,067,108
O'BRYAN, Wm.,208
O'DONEAL, Ann,174, John,174,
  Stephen,174
O'NEAL, Anne,230
OAKES, Charles,248, Fanny,179,
  Isaac,248, Jane,248,
  Jean(Jane),248, Wm.,248
OLIVER, Drewery,107, Drury,
  045,107, Elizabeth,099,107,
  John J.,102,186, John,045,
  107, Mary,045, Maryan,107,
  Rhoda,133, Thomas,045,
  William,045, Wm.,107
ORGAN, Christop.,238, Dicy,
  238
ORR, William,044
OWEN, Agnes,061,062, David,
  061,062,079,080,156,247,
  Eady,057, Elizabeth,061,
  062, John Jr.,061, John,061,
  062,080,156,244, Mary,156,
  Milley,156, Obediah,061,
  062,080, Peggy,079,080,
  Sally,156, Thomas,014, Wm.,
  057,060,061,080
PACE, Mary,158, Newsom,041,
  Susannah,041,158, W.,041
PAIN, John,080, Sally,147
PALEY(?), Delila,250
PANNILL, Bethenia,116, David,
  034,035,038,104,116, Fanny,
  117, George,116, Jeremiah,
  137, John,034,116, Morton,
  117, Nancy,034,109,110,117,
  Polly,117, Rob.,142,
  Samuel,035,116,117,137,
  175, Sarah Bn.,117
PARHAM, Elizabeth,235,
  Susannah,196, Wm.C.,196
PARISH, Allen,193, Mathew,193,
  Richard,193
PARKER, ,090, David,161, John,
  219, Sally,219
PARKS, John Jr.,014, John,051,
  064,094, Samuel,064
PARR, John,009
PARRIS, John,062
PARRISH, Abraham,090,108,111,
  Abram,033,034,200, Dorcas,
  192, James,217,218, Joanna,
  192, Mary,217, Mathew,150,
  204, Nicholas,200, Rebecah,
  192, Susannah,200, Thomas,
  220,225, Wilson,200, Wm.,150
  John,036,251, Tyre,036
PARSON, John,199, Sarah,051
PARSONS, Anne,042, David,251,
  Eli,140, Freder.,140,
  Gabriel,140, George,064,
  255, Henry,215, Jesse,140,
  John Sr.,140, John,064,
  140, Joseph,042,064,
  Leviney,140, Marget,042,
  Mary,215, Rachel,215,
  Rebecca,215, Richard,064,
  140,215, Sally,140
PARSONS, Samuel,042,064,
  Sarah,140, Wm.,064,140,215
PASS, Hallaway,232, Holloway,
  224, James H.,157, Nathl.W.,
  224
PATERSON, Charles,185, Edward,
  185, Nancy,185
PATHER, Eliz.,156
PATRICK, David J.,136,137,
  Sarah,136
PATTEN, James D.(Dr),123,
  James D.,209,212, Susanner,
  149
PATTERSON, Agatha,252,
  Charles,185, Edmund,185,

Edward,252, Eliz.,006,
  Elizabeth,252, Fanny,252,
  James,121, John,162,252,
  Littleberry,252, Milley,
  252, Nancy,185, Nanney,252,
  Robert,252, Seluda,185,
  Thomas,252, Wm.,252
PATTON, James D.,127,128,153,
  165,172,173,202,217,239
PAYN, John,027, Mary,027
PAYNE, Agnes,028, Anne,028,
  060, Benjamin,233, Catherine,
  113, Charles,027,028,043,
  044, Daniel,008, David,010,
  Edmond,008, Edmund,010,
  George,059, Giles,159,213,
  Hannah,008,010, Jane B.,
  233, John Jr.,043, John L.,
  233, John,007,008,010
PAYNE, John,027,043,044,059,
  075, Josah(?),043, Josiah,
  043, Josias Jr.,059, Josias,
  059, Kiturah,027,060,
  Leanah Lee,127, Leroy,233,
  Mark,008,010, Martha,052,
  Mary,043, Milley,233,
  Rachel,133, Reuben,043,
  255, Reubin,042, Reubon,233,
  Rhoda,043
PAYNE, Robert,023,027,028,
  059,060,075,115,194, Samuel,
  043, Sarah,213, Seanah L.,
  127, Stephen,010, Susanna,
  027,059, Thomas,233, Thos.,
  125, William,098, Wm.,043,
  052,059,060,100,213,232,
  Yanoke,019
PEAK, Jesse,240, Jessy,240
PEARMAN, Nathan,168
PEARSON, Aney,237, Martin,241,
  Wm.S.,241
PEEK, David,250, Jesse Jr.,
  250, Jesse,068, John,250
PEIRSON, Charles,206, Doctor,
  206, Eliz.,206, Mastin,206,
  207, Polley,206, Richmond,
  206, Sherwood,206, Thomas,
  206,207, Wm.,206
PELL, Henry,138
PEMBERTON, Edmund,231, John,
  104, Joseph,104, Wm.,046
PENN, Wm.,182
PERKINS, Agatha,073, Aggatha,
  020, Charles,074, Constant,
  020,073, Elizabeth,074,098,
  George,074, Nicholas,020,
  073,074, Peter,006,011,074,
  Thomas,079
PERMAN, Wm.,015
PERSISE, William,041
PERSIZE, William,041
PESTOLE, John,144
PETERSON, Mary,004, Uniety,
  004
PETTEY, William,042
PETTY, William,042
PHARIS, Pleasant,171
PHILLIPS, George,026
PHILPS, John,068
PICK, Niclas,058
PICKEREL, Solomon,190
PIERCE, John,219,220, Molly,
  219, Zadock,220
PIERSON, Eliz.,206, Wm.,206
PIGG, Ann,058,254,255, Anne,
  057, Clement,192, Clemment,
  058, Clemons,191,192,
  Elisabeth,057, Elizabeth,
  058,192, Hesekiah,192,
  Hezekiah,057,058, James,
  254, John W.,192, John,055,
  057,058,191,192,255, Mary,
  254,255, Pattea,254,255,
  Paul,254
PIGG, Paul,255, Payton,192,
  Polly,192, Rebecah,191,
  Richard,254, Sarah,254,
  255, Wm.,058,192,254
PISTOLE, Abraham,157, Charles,
  143,157, Hannah,157, James,
  157, John,157, Thomas Jr.,
  157, Thomas,157, Thos.Sr.,
  098
PISTOLL, Thomas,011
PITTS, Jesse,188
POLLARD, John,189, Thomas,165
POLLEY, Agness,051
POND, John,040
POOR, (Old),074
POORE, Mary,120
POPEJOY, Nathanl.,136
PORTER, Ambrose,007, Ann,007,
  Arthur,007, Benjamin,007,
  Jane,007, Jemima,007, John,
  007, Joseph,007, Mary,007,
  Milley,007, Susanna,007
POSEY, Jincey,147, Rosey,147,
  Sally,147, Selina,147
POSISE, Betty,108
POTTER, Isaac,178,248
PRESTAGE, John Jr.,028, John,
  028,029, Larkin,028, Letty,
  028, Nancy,028,029
PRESTON, Mary,161, Peggy,161,
  Stephen,161
PREWETT, John,027
PREWITT, Jane,172, Jassheth,
  172

Allen,236, Allet,018,
Alley,236
SLAVE, Alphred,144, Amanday,
224, Ambrose,087,243,
Ambross,117, Amea,012,
Amey,038,052,088,090,151,
206,236,251, Amilia,080,
Amos,174, Amy,182,238,243,
Anderson,141,147,236,
Andrew,012,216, Ann,232,
240, Anna(Mulato),058, Anna,
125,141
SLAVE, Anna,208,257, Annaca,
247, Annaka,027,203,248,
Anne,037, Annekey,091,
Anraca,084, Antenney,232,
Anthony,015,109,164,197,
199,205,236,249, Antony,068,
Arch,074, Archa,120,
Archer,027,088, Armstead,
204,231,238, Aron,174,243,
Arthur,119
SLAVE, August,216, Austin,
Aylee,142, Baccas,075,
Baechus,052, Bailer,003,
Baler,003, Banks,238,
Barnett,236, Bartheny,220,
Bates,236, Beck,126,127,
Becky,170,216, Bell,126,
137, Bells,137, Ben(Mulato),
109, Ben,012,028,080,081
SLAVE, Ben,125,128,137,144,
149,152,170,205,231,236,
Bess,009, Bethey,110,
Bethsheba,141, Betsey,141,
170, Bett,007,027,073,203,
249, Betty,011,027,037,060,
069,076,079,134,162,170,
193,197,198,213,216,217,
230,249,258
SLAVE, Bide,037, Big Bett,058,
Big Dick,236,237, Big Jude,
232, Big Ned,074,231, Bill,
153, Billey,231, Billy,
170,238, Blacksmith,236,
Bob,018,021,044,059,069,
078,082,084,107,109,121,
128,130,141,147,148,205,
207,209,214,230,236, Bobb,
045
SLAVE, Bon,060, Bonaparte,238,
Booker,238, Borwon,092,
Bower,119, Braiston,164,
Brancer,152, Branch,151,
Brandon,087, Branser,176,
Bransley,086, Bratcher,236,
Brister,224, Bristol,151,
Brunswick,109, Buck,027,
127, Burnett,076, Burrill,
236
SLAVE, Burwel,092, Caleb,218,
Calland,171, Cambridge,126,
Cancer,037, Candace,152,
Candice,224, Carine,240,
Carmey,227, Carni,240,
Caroline,170,218, Carson,
238, Carter,152,171, Cas,
121, Casshener,003, Castille,
135, Cate,021,084,148
SLAVE, Cate,149,198,236,249,
Ceala,141, Ceasar,128,158,
Ceaser,119, Celah,218,
Celis,084, Cerus,110,
Chainey,236, Chana,159,
Chaney,192,203,210, Chany,
238, Charity,046,082,092,
137,205,231,235,236,247,
Charles,037,081,127,135,
182,194
SLAVE, Charles,20 ,214,230,
246, Charlotte,012,164,182,
236,257, Cheasy,209, Cherry,
236, Chloe,075,147,236,
Chole,021,068, Christo.,
216, Cindy,110, Cinna,151,
Cintha,207, Cirus,110,
Claiborne,205, Clarburn,
151, Clarey,086, Clarisa,203
SLAVE, Clark,240, Clary,209,
231, Clementina,170, Cloe,
084,086,121,194, Cloey,149,
155, Cob,067, Coleman,171,
Cooling,243, Cooty,226,
Cose,006, Creecy,068,
Critey,088, Crow,055,
Crusie,238, Cuff,120,
Cuffe,055, Cupit,076,
Curtis,236
SLAVE, Custer,236, Cyner,003,
Cyrus,084,092,153,236,
Dafney,094, Daid,247, Dan,
160, Daniel,031,052,078,
088,091,127,144,202,207,
215,230,240,241,243,247,
249, Darcos,120, Darcus,155,
Darkis,205, Darkus,254,
Dave,003,095,205, David,069
SLAVE, David,118,126,174,182,
200,204,214,215,226, Davie,
152, Davy,037,153,188,203,
Deley,127, Delila,174,
Delphia,038,113,124,247,
Delphia,068,125, Delsa,075,
Dicey,037,170, Dick,015,
023,027,078,086,091,110,
126,145,190,193,226,236,238
SLAVE, Dick,240,241,257,258,
Diley,084,127, Dils,197,

Dina,128, Dinah Jr.,076,
Dinah,044,074,076,084,125,
146,156,182,205, Dixon,075,
Doll,015,031,074,151,
Dolla,175, Dolly,153, Dyna,
055, Eady,051, Easter,085,
128,137,145,148,160,206
SLAVE, Easter,210,243,251,
255, Easther,021,058, Eave,
205, Edey,037, Edith,147,
Edmond,141,142, Edmund,203,
236, Edward,170, Edy,231,
236,238,240,241,255, Elias,
236, Elijah,074,203, Eliza,
182, Ellen,182, Ellick,236,
Ellinor,207, Else,164
SLAVE, Else,236, Emanuel,231,
Ennis,183, Ephraim,198,
Esau,209, Eser,147, Essea,
110, Essex,037,124, Ester,
118, Esther,067,126,152,
236, Eve,070,168,226, Ewel,
231, Fan,216, Fann,225,
Fanney,037,084,118,128,
Fanny,003,011,118,127,150
SLAVE, Fanny,183,185,188,190,
193,203,207,231, Febby,205,
Fillis,001,008,059,249,
Filman,236, Finn,044,
Fisher,057, Flora,074,170,
Fluet,061, Fountain,111,
125, Francis,002, Frank,027,
052,120,126,131,151,235,
Frankey,125,209, Frederick,
216
SLAVE, French,198, Gabriel,
126,198,236, Garland,158,
203, George,015,046,059,
070,080,104,118,121,126,
150,151,160,164,168,174,
192,204,205,206,211,226,
236,238,243,247, Gerald,203,
Gerrald,235, Gilbert,121,
Ginney,051,
Gloucester,038
SLAVE, Gloucester,236,
Glouster,194, Goliah,091,
Grace,058,158,236, Gracy,
236, Graybeal,194, Gruff,
038, Gruss,135, Guy,148,
Guye,128, Hager,200, Hall,
069, Hampton,015,037,171,
216, Hannah,060, Hanarn,009,
Handy,243, Hanna,027,
Hannah,012
SLAVE, Hannah,051,074,095,
078,081,084,085,091,117,
121,127,141,142,152,158,
164,218,226,231,251, Hanner,
095, Hannibal,097, Harah,
060, Harris,236, Harrison,
194, Harry(Mulato),058,
Harry,061,073,094,117,
121,144,168,174,205,215,236
SLAVE, Harry,243,247, Hector,
249, Helen,170, Henry,158,
170,171,238,243, Hercules,
086,117, Hester,168,
Hezekiah,194, Holliay,091,
Hollaway,236, Holly,126,
Howard,160, Hui.,y,211,
Isaac(Peet),088, Isaac,038,
120,127,147,152,153,164,168
SLAVE, Isaac,182,190,205,214,
225,240,255, Isaack,069,
Isabell,243, Isam,125,
Isbel,151,210, Isbell,003,
148, Isham,074,174, Iverson,
216, Ivey,003, Jack,015,
057,058,073,084,120,128,
151,170,207,215,236,258,
Jacob,074,075,092,126,163,
168
SLAVE, Jacob,240,258, James,
027,037,051,060,073,077,
104,120,125,127,164,168,
172,193,214, Jane,015,028,
037,052,058,060,075,085,
157,171,247, Janey,002,120,
Janney,086, Jatilda,210,
Jean,251, Jeany,205,
Jefrey,009, Jenney,135,
214, Jenny,003
SLAVE, Jenny,076,097,121,127,
128,172,174,236, Jere,217,
Jerre,158, Jerry,109,240,
Jesse,092,109,128,178,186,
206,210, Jezbel,144, Jim,
102,127,162,204,236,248,
Jimmey,110, Jimmy,109,
Jinney,125,149,151,203,
Jinny,109,194, Jinsey,216
SLAVE, Joannah,205, Joe,015,
027,038,057,058,060,073,
095,117,126,127,149,182,
191,214,218,232,236,243,
251, Joel,158, John,011,
075,117,127,158,199,209,
215,218,231,236,238,
Johnson,151,214, Joice,205,
Jolly,037, Jonathan,207,
Jonney,086
SLAVE, Jord,157, Joseph,142,
210,232,235,240,241,
Jourdon,226, Juda,027,207,
Judah,076, Juday,258, Jude,
018,059,082,131,145,148,
149,182,203, Judey,009,

Judith,021,193, Judy,126,
174,236,237, June,137,
Juney,233, Juno,084,152,
198, Juns,137
SLAVE, Kason,198, Kate,058,
Katy,207, Kear,144, Kese,
155, Keziah,153, Kitt,236,
Kize,083, Kupit,144, Kyer,
095, Lagavina,170, Lain,021,
Landa,171, Landon,170,
Landy,224, Lanksford,224,
Lassy,231, Lavena,109,
Lavinia,236, Lawney,170
SLAVE, Lazenberry,231, Leah,
014, Lee,153,207, Leeve,218,
Leilia,209, Leno,079,151,
Lener,003, Lester,088,
Lethy,236, Lett,236, Lette,
231, Letty,117,153,164,205,
238, Leu,073, Levina,050,
210, Leviney,086, Lewis,037,
075,128,137,151,170
SLAVE, Lewis,171,202,203,205,
236,240,255, Liddia,135,
Liddey,086, Liddia,117,
Lidia,153, Lile,192, Lilly,
074,117, Lindsay,215, Lindy,
214, Linney,203, Lippur,210,
Little Abel,236, Little Bett,
058, Little Bob,147,
Little Cate,021,236,
SLAVE, Little George,226,
Little Jim,193, Little Lucy,
121, Little Ned,231, Liz,
182, Liza,152, Lizza,220,
Locky,231, London,059,
Long Tom,059
SLAVE, Luce,057,091,183,
Lucey,084,118, Lucinda,117,
188,215,216,225,231,
Lucretia,152,170, Lucy,015,
028,031,058,060,068,073,
074,076,084,086,090,110,
118,121,125,135,147,155,
160,174,198,204,207,208,
214,216,218,226,243,251,
251, Luffa,236
SLAVE, Luis,070, Luna,152,
Lunt,141, Luse,134, Lyddy,
236, Lydia,074,092,151,
Madge,170, Major,135,192,
Malindy,223, Mamnuel,120,
Margaret,180, Margary,174,
Maria,190, Marie,206,
Marjory,096, Martha,203,
218, Martin,084, Mary,063,
088
SLAVE, Mary,121,127,131,144,
152,155,193,194,203,230,
257, Matilda,117,164,205,
Matildy,147, Meania,171,
Melinder,003, Micajah,128,
Micka,208, Mickey,238,
Mill,243, Milla,075,
Miller,114,226, Milley,051,
052,060,126,127,152,153,
168,202
SLAVE, Milley,206,216,232,
236,238, Millia,068, Milly,
027,099,151,164,168,182,
194,202,238, Mime,243,
Mingo,149, Minor,088,
Mintay,217, Moll,060,073,
097, Molley,175,207,215,
Moriah,216,235, Moris,226,
Morrice,058, Moses,037,
095,096,114
SLAVE, Moses,131,147,170,216,
Murrier,164, Nan,009,018,
027,060,091,231, Nance,127,
205, Nancy,084,090,110,145,
151,159,166,171,198,201,
204,207,216,226,236, Nat,
074,086,127,215,238,243,
Nathan,174, Natt,174, Ned,
057,059,082,117,164,225
SLAVE, Nel,174, Nell,057,127,
232,243, Nelson,198,236,
Nern(?),037, Nicholas,170,
Nick,194, Old Bob,097,
Old Hannah,230, Old Lucy,
037,110, Old Peter,193,
Old Phillis,037, Old Polly,
236, Old Sarah,126, Oliver,
236, Orange,095,218, Page,
037
SLAVE, Pallace,127, Pallan,
127, Parton,205, Pat,059,
095,152,182,249, Patience,
153, Patrick,037,135,194,
226, Patsey,216, Patt,038,
058,073, Pattey,135, Patty,
118,127,151,174,192,193,
198,235, Paul,075,236,
Pearce,236, Peg,083,095,
Pegg,069
SLAVE, Peggy,126,151, Peter,
012,021,029,051,052,058,
059,068,084,092,107,109,
126,127,142,144,149,151,
152,164,170,193,194,197,
198,202,203,205,206,207,
226,236, Petitha,226,
Peyton,141, Phaney,079,
Pheabe,243, Phebey,232,
Pheby,027,126
SLAVE, Pheby,128, Phil,164,
170, Philada,236, Philas,

251, Philice,067, Philip,
151, Phill,095,162,182,203,
226,236, Phillas,251,
Phillis,002,003,015,059,
068,088,110,120,121,124,
135,141,144,151,152,236,
254, Philly,172, Pindar,226,
Poll,238
SLAVE, Polley,128,171,203,
226,235, Polly,125,236,
Polydare,170, Pompey,097,
127,236, Pompy,003,027,
Pott,144, Price,120,
Primus,037,119, Prisca,236,
Priscilla,038, Priss,232,
Prudence,137, Queen,094,
236, Rachel,038,052,073,
079,110,114
SLAVE, Rachel,117,128,147,
151,168,174,182,184,207,
211,218,228,231,236,238,
247, Rainey,168,190, Ran,
194, Randle,192, Randolph,
038,142,147,150,171,206,
Ranney,163, Ransdom,125,
Ransom,235, Rawley,209,
214,226, Reuben,248, Reubin,
082,236
SLAVE, Rhener,238, Rhoda,037,
109,207,236,243, Rice,059,
Richard,197, Richmon,225,
Richmond,225,231,238,
Ritta,194, Ritter,095,168,
Robbin,151, Robert,170,
Robin,009,076,207, Roda,
074, Rodah,231, Roger,075,
125,251, Rose,015,052,057
SLAVE, Rose,059,090,091,141,
154,155, Ross,258, Ruben,
145,232, Ruth,058, Sabra,
120, Sal,086, Sall,052,109,
123,127, Salle,092, Sally,
037,137,170,193,194,205,
230,236, Sam,037,055,075,
086,117,120,124,125,126,
127,131,153,175,207,216,240
SLAVE, Sam,241,249, Sampson,
120,205, Samuel,155, Sarah,
009,012,037,045,058,071,
074,075,076,091,095,107,
120,141,151,153,158,159,
177,201,231,235,251,258,
Sarry,160, Sary,105,232,
Sauc...,194, Saul,151,
Saunders,236, Scot,217,
Scott,117
SLAVE, Selah,110, Sellar,141,
Selvah,200, Shadrack,226,
243, Sharlot,120, Sherry,
151, Sile,205, Sill,144,
Siller,074,092,117,125,
Silpah,092, Silva,074,
Silvay,258, Silvey,086,
158,205, Silvy Ates,236,
Silvy,236,247, Simon,057,
144,198
SLAVE, Sinda,141, Sindy,192,
Sippier,003, Sirus(Tim),
226, Sirus,214, Smity,236,
Soloman,206, Solomon,174,
Sook,080, Sooky,204,220,
Sophia,087, Sophy,236,
Spencer,184,203, Squar,120,
Squire,037,059,236, Stella,
135, Stephen H.,237,
Stephen,031
SLAVE, Stephen,038,069,079,
091,109,141,145,164,218,
231,236,251, Stepney,121,
182,207,236,237, Stewart,
135, Sucke,074, Suckey,150,
170,190, Sucok,141, Sue,038,
061,078,194,246, Suf,075,
Suffa,237, Sukey,236,
Surry,227, Susey,254,
Sylva,127
SLAVE, Sylva,162, Sylvia,088,
Symie,145, Tabb,158, Tabby,
088,202, Tamer,009,141,188,
Tanday,224, Tassmums,224,
Tazzy,012, Ted,126, Tell,
090, Tempy,191,211, Tena,
199, Tener,198,202,236,
Tenor,037, Terrar,110,
Terry,144, Thomas,114,205
SLAVE, Thompson,238, Tilda,
073, Tildy,231, Tiller,059,
Toby,243, Tom,027,060,068,
084,087,127,128,142,170,
218,238, Tommy,003, Turner,
216, Umphia,257, Ussey,069,
236, Vall,011,015, Velora,
074, Vilet,050, Vilotte,145,
Viney,203,226,256
SLAVE, Viney,257, Violet,182,
193,247, Walter,231,
Warwick,075, Washington,
236,238, Watt,028,121, West,
037,135, Westley,171,
Wheeler,152, Wiatt,230,
Wiley,142, Will,009,038,
055,059,081,092,120,127,
134,141,203, Willey,003,
Wilmouth,210
SLAVE, Wilson,194, Winne,243,
Winney,052,070,076,086,
095,110,118,158,164,
Winston,160, Wise,192, Wm.,

118,127, Woodard,071,
Wynney,127, Yardo,120,
Yellow Cyrus,109, York,069,
097, Yorrick,206, Young Beck
226, Young Lucy,037,096,
Young Pat,037
SLAVE, Young Phillis,037,
Zilpha,058
SLAYDEN, Anna,083, Arter,229,
Benjamin,229, Daniel,083,
180, James,180,229, Joel,
229, John,083,229, Joseph,
229, Lency,229, Lucy,140,
Milley,229, Nancy,180,
Obadiah,229, Peggy,229,
Rachel,229, S.,083,
Shockeley,229, Terry,233,
Thomas,180
SLAYDEN, Tolberd,229, Winston,
229, Wm.,083,180,229
SLAYDON, Daniel,180, Lucy,140,
Nancy,140, Wm.,180
SLAYTON, Arthur P.,049,
Edmund,049, James,049,
John,049, Pattsey,049,
Rachel,049, Susannah,049
SLOAN, Elenor,254, James,254,
John,254, Samuel,059,
Thomas,254, Wm.,254
SMITH, Achillis,016, Allen,
115, Ambrose J.,072, Anna,
055, Augustine,231, Betsey,
225, Booker,015, Bowker,016,
076, Cassander,072, Drury,
055, Edw.Wash.,055, Edward,
044, Elender,072, Elisabeth,
055, Eliz.,208, Elizabeth,
015,016,072,115
SMITH, Frances,144, Geo.K.,
145, George,066,145, Ginna,
055, Guy,016, Hezekiah,086,
Jabez,145,193,205,207,216,
237, James B.,225, James,
115,243, Jane,044, Jesse,
072,243, John Jr.,055,207,
216, John,001,013,015,016,
026,044,055,056,093,132
SMITH, John,141,144,148,161,
170,205,221, Joseph,055,
115,144,223,225, Judith,008,
016, Martha,044,055,056,
071,072, Mary,072, Naomy,
072, Orlando,071,072,162,
Peter,099, Peyton,006,008,
013, Philip,009, Ralph,015,
016,076,148,161,163,205
SMITH, Ralph,216, Randolph,
139, Rhoda,072, Sally,120,
Samuel,015,016,196, Sarah,
044,055, Stephen,016,238,
Thomas,044,055,056,065,
144, Thos.Jr.,044, Whitfield,
072, William,234,235, Wm.,
016,093,121,131,144,156,
157,197,207,208,225
SMITHSON, Francis,181,189,
225, Hezekiah P.,225,232,
Hezekiah,239
SNEED, Dabney Hill,256,
Dabney P.,256, Elizabeth P.,
255, Henry P.,255,256,
Henry,256, John,232,254,
256, Robert,015, Wm.,015,255
SNODDY, Betsey,155, Eliz.,156,
John,155,156, Polley,155,
156, Robert,155, Thomas,155,
William,155, Wm.,156
SNODY, Wm.,172,229
SNOW, Abner,231
SOYARS, James,128,134,137,
217,224,238,239, Wm.,137
SOYEARS, James,117
SPARKES, Edmund,221
SPARKS,,186, Brooks,121,
Edward,027, Elenear,113,
Keziah,113, Mathew,064,
113,121, Matthew,251,
Samuel,064, Thomas,064,
SPILLEA, Wm.,111
SPILLER, Hickman,115
SPRADLING, Jesse,253, Joseph,
253, Levina H.,056, Obediah,
253, Susannah,253
SPRATL(?), George,106
SPRATLEN, George,115,255
SPRATLIN, George,172
SPRATTIN, George,138
SPURLIN, Elisabeth,102
STAMPS, John Jr.,168,211,
John Sr.,168, John,017,
Leah,134, Leanna,168,
Lydda,168, Polley,106,
Thomas,168, Timothy,168,
218, William,106,144, Wm.,
STANDEFER, Israel,010
STANDEFORD, Molley,171
STANDIFER, Susanah,010
STANLEY, Joseph,052
STANLEY, Isaac,071, Joseph Jr.,
071, Joseph,071
STEPHENS, Henry,087
STEPTOE, Wm.,148
STEWART, Martha,133, Nevin,
173, Thomas,15,153,172,173
STILL(?), James,258
STILL, John,144, Wm.,144
STILTS, Patrick,055
STIMPSON, Thomas,229

STIMSON, Erasmus Jr.,197,
Erasmus,017,197, Jeremiah,
017, Loyd,017, Rachel,017
STITH, Drury,055
STOCKTON, John,056,150
STOK, Silvenas,058
STOKES, Allen Sr.,139, Allen,
084,089,098, Christopher,
098, Joel Allen,084, Sarah,
084, Sillv.,089, Silvanus Jr.,
084, Silvanus,071,084,085,
092, Sylvanus,025, Ware,089
STONE, Archer,235, Benj.,145,
196, Benjamin,207,209,235,
Clack,137, Coleman,131,
Dolly,065, Hannah,014,
Henry,014,157, Isaac,220,
James H.,179,235, Jane,117,
157, Jean,113, John Jr.,113,
120,136,148, John,065,113,
118, Joshua Jr.,082,156
STONE, Joshua Sr.,173, Joshua,
064,065,068,070,078,082,
113,131,150,207,246,250,
Leve,127, Mary,046,047,
Nancey A.,234, Prudence,
133, Richard,204, Samuel,
173,193, William,234
STORDE, Eliz.,149
STOTT, Usley,067
STRANGE, Frances,143, James,
143, Jesse,143, John,143,
Mary,143, Smith,143,
Susannah,143
STRATTON, Benjamin,244, Eliz.,
244, Ellender,244, Wm.,070
STREET, Mary,123
STRONG, Samuel,082,253
STU--, John,004
STUART, Thomas,128
STUBLEFIELD, Peter,209, Sally,
209
STULTS, Adam,055
SULLIVALN, Dan.,212
SULLIVAN, Daniel,123,153
SUMATE, Eliz.,143
SUMMERS, Wm.,098
SUTHERLAND, Daniel,225,
Geo.Jr.,098, George,002,
022,027, Nancy,251
SUTHERLIN, Adam,113,194,251,
Adams,120, Fanny J.,165,
Frances,232, Geo.L.,232,
George Jr.,120, George,114,
120,121,155,232, Henry,120,
James M.,165, James,120,
165, John,112,120,121,232,
239,251, Marah,142, Nancy,
232, Patsey,165, Thomas,113
SUTHERLIN, Thomas,120,153,
232, Wm.,112,120
SWANSON, Wm.,241,248, Wm.Jr.,
131,141,144,161
SWENEY, Anne,056, Jas.Semore,
056, Moses,056
SYDNOR, Abram,187
TALBOT, John,016, Nancy,167
TALIAFERRO, Dorcus,071,
Jno.Rich.,014, Richard,007
TALIFERO, Mary,081
TALLOAH, Ann,219, Thomas,219
TANNER, Allen C.,177,189, Asa,
133, Bird L.,149, Creed,141,
149,166,168,169,177, Flaued,
063, Floyd,025,091,092,
Joel,133,182, Joseah,148,
Joseph M.,133, Lucy,148,
149, Mary,149, Mathew,148,
149, Robert,177, Sally,091,
Thomas,092,149
TARRANT, Benj.,023,026,
Benjamin,254, Leonard,013
TAYLOR, Anne,113, Edmund,038,
088,249, James,028, John,
155, Joseph,171,186, Milley,
147, Obediah,159, Shadrack,
104, Zella,155
TERRELL, Julius,218
TERRY, Anne,081,082, Barton Sr.,
166,167, Barton,053,160,
Benj.,004, Benj.Sr.,003,
210, Benjamin,003,025,210,
Champ,168,189, Champness,
039,059,118,167,169,186,
187,253, Charles,093,160,
Christop.,133, Daniel,210,
David,019,029,039,053
TERRY, David,058,059,066,116,
160,166,253, Delilah,133,
Eliz.,166,167, Eliz.Fuqua,
081,082, Elizabeth,003,
Grace,003, Henry Jr.,053,
Henry,053, James,081,
Jeremiah,167,186,187,210,
Jerry,168, Jim,059,066,
082,151, Joseph B.,187,
Joseph Jr.,058
TERRY, Joseph,003,035,058,
059,066,067,082,167,186,
187,254, Lucy G.,210,
Marget,053, Mary,003,
Moses,160, Nathaniel,003,
081,082, Nathanl.,210,
Obediah,182,210, Patsy,180,
Peter,003, Rhoda,081,082,
Robert,003,210
TERRY, Sally C.,210, Sarah,
003,081,082,151, Stephen,